THE

ENGLISH

HERITAGE

VOLUME II: SINCE 1689

THE ENGLISH HERITAGE

VOLUME II: SINCE 1689

Third Edition

FREDERIC A. YOUNGS, JR.
ROGER B. MANNING
HENRY L. SNYDER
E. A. REITAN

HARLAN DAVIDSON, INC.
WHEELING, ILLINOIS 60090–6000

941

Copyright © 1978, 1988
Forum Press, Inc.
Copyright © 1999
Harlan Davidson, Inc.
All rights reserved

Libary of Congress Cataloging-in-Publication Data

Youngs, Frederic A., 1936–
        The English heritage / Frederic A. Youngs, Jr. . . . [et al.].—3rd ed.
            p.   cm.
        Includes bibliographical references and index.
        ISBN 0-88295-980-8 Volume I (alk. paper)
        ISBN0-88295-981-6 Volume II (alk. paper)
        Contents: v. 1. To 1714—v. 2. Since 1689
        1. Great Britain—History. 2. England—Civilization. I. Title.
        DA30.Y68   1999
        941—dc21   99-18849
                                                                CIP

Cover photo: Ruins of Whitby Abbey by Earl A. Reitan
Cover design: DePinto Graphic Design

Manufactured in the United States of America
01 00 99 1 2 3 VP

CONTENTS

Volume I: To 1714
Volume II: Since 1689

PREFACE

 Like its popular predecessors, this third edition of
The English Heritage is intended to introduce students
(and all readers) to a remarkable national heritage
stemming from the four main nations of the United
Kingdom: England, Wales, Scotland, and Northern
Ireland. Many Americans and Canadians are de-
scended from British stock; many others received the
English heritage as immigrants or as the descendants
of immigrants. The fruits of that English heritage have extended throughout
the world, bringing the English language and English concepts of government, law, literature, and religion to former colonies and beyond. No longer
the exclusive property of any nation, race, religion, or culture, the English
heritage today is global in scope and influence.

This book reflects the authors' belief that a concise, introductory text
best serves both the student and the instructor. It quickly grounds the student
in the main aspects of British history and presents the themes that will be
further developed in class. A dependable reference to which the student can
return for clarification, this book also features an excellent collection of illustrations, photographs, and maps that provide visual supplements to the text.
Also, a brief text such as this allows the instructor to incorporate a variety of
supplementary readings and other resources to enrich the course. To this end,
suggestions for further reading (which also may serve as good sources for student papers) conclude each chapter.

The English Heritage, third edition, includes the work of several authors,
though it has been carefully developed as an integrated text. Some of England's
great contributions to the world have been in the form of government, politi-

cal ideas, and law, and a chronological consideration of these provides the main narrative thread. However, considerable attention is also given to economic development, social relationships, and religion. Furthermore, this book includes character sketches, not only of political leaders but of important people in many walks of life. Among the special features in this third edition are periodic overviews of London—including Chaucer's London, Shakespeare's London, the eighteenth-century London of Samuel Johnson, Victorian London, and modern London—one of the great metropolitan centers of the world.

Because the story of the English heritage spans more than a thousand years, the narrative pauses at crucial points to help the reader assess where England stood in its development: at the close of the Middle Ages; in 1783, when King George III presided over a nation of expanding power and high civilization but was badly shaken by defeat in the American Revolution; and in the mid-nineteenth century, the height of the Victorian Age. Finally, the last chapter assesses Britain's position in the world today and its prospects for the future.

For this third edition of *The English Heritage,* the original authors have been joined by Dr. Roger B. Manning of Cleveland State University, who contributed Chapters 5, 6, and 7. Dr. Earl A. Reitan of Illinois State University revised all chapters beginning with Chapter 11 and brought the final chapter through December 1998. Many of the illustrations were provided from a private collection. Special thanks are due to the capable and helpful staff of Harlan Davidson, Inc., for producing a handsome and highly usable book.

Earl A. Reitan, General Editor

CHAPTER NINE

Revolution and Succession
1689–1714

The Revolution of 1688, the "Glorious Revolution," is one of the great landmarks in English history, yet it was no more a revolution than previous accessions except for the manner of James's going. The Revolution was inspired and controlled by the aristocracy and landed gentry to preserve the constitution in its traditional state, so the Revolution settlement itself was conservative and limited in character. There is a European dimension to the Revolution that cannot be disregarded. It could not have occurred without William and his army; William could not afford to let England remain in the French camp. Furthermore, William III (1689–1702) was by any standard the most effective and most active chief executive of any Stuart sovereign. Finally, the legacy that he left in terms of England's new-found prestige and importance in Europe and the commitments he made for continued participation in the coalition against Louis XIV and the succession of the Electress Sophia of Hanover and her heirs all transformed the status and character of England and its dependencies.

THE REVOLUTION OF 1688

Goals of William III

But as important as these considerations are for an explanation of *how* the Revolution occurred, we must not lose sight of the fact that the reasons *why* it occurred were wholly domestic and internal. William's new subjects, preoccupied with domestic matters, were loath to heed the European situation or to accept England's critical role in it. Part of the disillusionment and ultimately the opposition of the Tories to William was the consequence of their realization of William's true motives and interests. The other part of their disillusionment came with the recognition that he was as forceful and domineering as were any of his predecessors. The control that this forbidding, cold foreigner soon obtained over the agencies of English government and the commitments he made of English men and English gold to European causes revived the traditional hostilities of the aristocracy and gentry to autocratic monarchs. This was the fate of William's ambition and reputation.

The Settlement of the Crown

The question of William's promotion to the kingship of England was never much in doubt, but the matter of securing the Revolution and his rule was far less certain. On the collapse of James's government the peers in and about London had met and had taken the government into their hands. Although the country was remarkably quiet, rioting in London and the burning of the chapels and homes of prominent Catholics required speedy action to preserve public order. The lords were soon joined by the surviving members of the Parliaments of Charles II. The assembled leaders requested the prince to assume the civil administration as he had already assumed control over the remnants of the military forces of the crown. A convention summoned by the prince met on January 22, 1689. This body divided essentially on the basis of attitudes toward the succession. Most Tories favored a regency to preserve a semblance of constitutionality and to honor their oaths to James as anointed sovereign. Only the most conservative element favored James's return under carefully controlled limitations. The Whigs were more united in their determination to assert the principles of parliamentary sovereignty by acknowledging a break in the hereditary succession. Most men recognized, albeit reluctantly, that English security was dependent on William's exercise of the executive authority. The question of the legal basis for this exercise was resolved by Mary's refusal to act as queen regnant and by William's equally positive assertion that he would not remain in England unless all executive authority was awarded to him for life. The activities of James II's supporters in the other two kingdoms cut short the discussion of constitutional safeguards in the convention, but before the crown was offered to William and Mary (with all authority vested in William) a Declaration of Rights was passed and was accepted by the new sovereigns; this was subsequently enacted into law to embody the essence of the Revolution.

The Declaration fundamentally changed the character of English kingship. The monarch was subordinated to the common law, the suspending and dispensing powers of the crown were severely restricted, prerogative courts were declared illegal, and the king was prohibited from levying taxes without parliamentary consent. A Whig document, it passed because the Tories supported it to embarrass William and hopefully to create a climate for a regency or rule by Mary alone. The result of their compliance was to enshrine in the constitution what for them was repugnant, a victorious Whig ideology. For the first year and even longer the fate of the Revolution was in doubt. William had only limited financial resources of his own, and they were exhausted by the expedition. Although he requested the same revenues that James II had, he was granted the customs for life but the excise for only four years. These and other revenues were not sufficient to supply the extraordinary requirements of a nation at war.

The Revolution in Scotland and Ireland

Preoccupied with the situations in England and in Ireland, the new king gave Scotland little attention, and consequently that kingdom worked out its own destiny with little interference. The Jacobites, as James's supporters were called, were made up of the Episcopalians in the Scottish Lowlands and the Roman Catholics in the Highlands and were thus more active and stronger in the northern kingdom than in England. William was only able to send part of the Scottish regiments in the Dutch service to Edinburgh to buttress his supporters. Before they arrived, a convention had met, and the crown was offered to William and his consort on April 11. Yet even as the convention sat, Edinburgh castle was in the hands of Jacobites, and forces were raised in behalf of James in Stirling. Fortunately the rebels obtained no reinforcements from abroad. By the end of the summer all the Jacobite troops had capitulated. Because the new government was little beholden to William it was also independent of his influence. The Scots were determined to remove the shackles that James had used to restrain them. The crown-controlled Committee of the Articles that dominated the Scottish Parliament was abolished, and the episcopal government of the church, a useful instrument for insuring royal control, was dismantled.

Ireland was the more immediate problem. Lord Lieutenant Tyrconnel, a Roman Catholic, was one of the most able and determined of James's supporters. He and his coreligionists planned to use this opportunity to secure full control of their own country for themselves. James II came to Ireland in March 1689 planning to use a loyal Ireland as a base for the conquest of England and Scotland. The Irish nationalists refused to submit to his plans, and so James soon found himself in the midst of a war to drive the English and Protestants out of Ireland, a war he pursued with ferocity and determination. With funds provided by the new Parliament, William sailed for Ireland in June 1690. The critical stage of the campaign was soon over. At the River Boyne, William routed

James's forces on the last day of the month. The mopping-up took another year, but William's attention was now directed to the continent.

The Nine Years' War and the Partition Treaties

The Nine Years' War, King William's War, the War of the League of Augsburg—it is known by all three names—had broken out in the fall of 1688 when Louis XIV laid siege to Phillipsburg and the Dutch took possession of towns on the lower Rhine belonging to the archbishop of Cologne. William had wasted no time in bringing his new kingdom into the war. Even before James II had left London for France, William had given orders to the English navy to attack French ships. The Nine Years' War is not one of the great European conflicts if measured in terms of notable battles or of major territorial transfers through the treaty that closed it. For England, the war served as a training session. The most seasoned officers in James's army were the Roman Catholics, and the remaining cadre of English officers and men were mainly raw, unseasoned troops. This fact, coupled with their dubious loyalty, caused William to employ foreign officers—Dutch, Germans, and Huguenots—in the commands. It was this apprenticeship that permitted the army to perform so well in the next war.

William personally commanded his armies in Europe from 1691 to the end of the war. He was not a great general, but he excelled in terms of organization, discipline, and care for his troops. The major sieges, with one exception, were won by the French. In part this was because the king was given inadequate financial support by the Parliament, except in 1690 and 1694. The French were always amazed at William's ability to regroup his forces after a defeat and to return to the field of battle more determined and stronger than ever. It was this war of attrition that eventually persuaded Louis XIV to agree to a peace. By the treaty of Ryswick that brought the war to an end in 1697, the French king was forced to recognize William as king of England, thus recognizing the Protestant succession, a major war aim of the English.

WILLIAM III, KING AND DIPLOMAT

War Finance—The Bank of England

The extraordinary cost of maintaining both a large army overseas and an expanded navy wrought a revolution in English public finance. The changes that took place in William's reign in this sphere are among the most important consequences of the Revolution of 1688. After a year's delay Parliament granted William the customs for only short terms. The king's recurring need for funds during the war required that Parliament be called into session each year. Because of the need for funds to maintain the army and to pay off debts, the

*William III. Miniature by
Sir Godfrey Kneller.
Victoria & Albert Museum.*

regular meeting of Parliament was guaranteed. Determined this time to exercise greater control over royal finances, Parliament now resorted to the expedient of appropriating funds for specific uses, and an accounting was required each year. The vast sums of money required resulted in new taxes, notably the land tax, a temporary expedient that became the basis for governmental income until it was transmuted by Pitt at the end of the eighteenth century. Because of this tax, landowners paid a greater proportion of taxes than at any other time in the eighteenth century. Other taxes were proposed, notably a general excise (a sales tax), but that was found to be intolerable politically, though the excise was extended on specific items.

The most important impact of the war was the new system developed to raise the enormous sums of money required. Formerly the king had to raise loans on the security of his name alone. Now Parliament, assured of its existence through the system of annual appropriations, itself undertook to guarantee the loans that were required to finance the war. With this kind of security the crown was able to secure funds much more readily and at much lower interest rates. The parliamentary guarantee of the king's credit was the basis for the new system of a national debt, a landmark in public finance. A body of trained civil servants was created to continue to carry the system throughout the violent alternation of party administrations that characterized the quarter century that followed the Revolution. The traditional sources of credit used by the crown proved inadequate to the huge demands placed upon them during the war. To compensate for this deficiency the Bank of England was created, a joint-stock, limited liability corporation authorized by act of Parliament in 1694. With seasoned officials at the Treasury—the veteran Lord Godolphin, the Secretary Henry Guy, and the brilliant young chancellor of the exchequer, Charles Montagu—working in collaboration with the predominantly Whig financiers who composed the Bank's board of directors, England was able to produce the funds needed to sustain it and its allies in the struggle with France. The capture of Namur in 1695 can be directly attributed to the success of the new banking establishment.

The Parties and the Cabinet

William's success in securing his three kingdoms, in restoring the strength and credit of the English army and navy, and in fighting Louis XIV to a standstill was not matched in his dealings with the parties and parliament. To begin with, the qualified support for his invasion and succession inclined many politicians to reinsure themselves with the exiled James in case of a Stuart restoration. William's refusal to give his confidence to any of his English ministers and his obvious partiality for his Dutch and other foreign aides created jealousy and resentment. William never really understood or accepted the party structure in England. His first ministries included representatives of all the major party groups as he endeavored to secure broad support for his program while keeping out of the clutches of one particular faction. Initially, he found the Tories most sympathetic to his views on government and the role of monarchy. In the early years of the reign the Whigs' desire to limit the power of the crown was ample reason to keep that party from dominating the ministry. But the setbacks in the land campaign in 1692 convinced the Tories that further expenditures on the army were wasted. William was forced to choose between fighting a war in Flanders with Whig support or pursuing the "blue water policy"—the reliance on the navy and not the army—favored by the Tories. He chose the former. By the end of 1693 the Whigs were in the ascendancy. Their promotion was advocated by Sunderland, who had emerged as the king's political broker or "manager," a practice necessitated by the rise of parties.

One of the most important constitutional innovations of the post-Revolution period was the Cabinet. The Privy Council had declined in authority as the Stuart kings expanded its membership to suit the vanity of the many courtiers who pressed to be included. Its work consequently fell into the hands of standing committees, of which the most important was the committee on foreign affairs. Managed by the senior secretary of state, it had developed into the principal advisory body of the crown. William III preferred the departmental style of government, by which he met separately with each minister. Circumstances dictated otherwise. When he went to Ireland in 1690 he left Mary as regent and instructed her to consult a committee of nine privy councillors who were given the designation of Cabinet Council. Continuing to meet during the king's absences, the Cabinet also met with the king during the winter of 1691–1692, though less frequently. William's attempt to replace it in 1694 with a smaller, less formal body failed. There were regular meetings in the winter of 1694–1695, and the members acted as lords justices for William after Mary's death when he was on the Continent. The continuous history of the Cabinet, an informal body unknown to the law, dates from this time.

The Succession in Spain and England

Throughout his reign William III was preoccupied with the problem of the succession to the throne in Spain. Louis XIV showed his concern for his own reasons. The Treaty of Ryswick was concluded in part so both monarchs could turn their attention to the disposition of the Spanish Empire upon the imminent death of the long-suffering Carlos II. Louis and the Austrian emperor, Leopold I, were each sons and husbands of Spanish princesses. The brides of the French kings in each case were senior but had renounced their claims to the Spanish throne both for themselves and their heirs. The other European powers did not want the crown of Spain to go either to the Bourbons or to the Habsburgs. Louis and William finally agreed that the throne would go to Leopold's grandson by his first wife, the son of the elector of Bavaria. The first partition treaty, concluded in 1699, provided for this settlement, but even as the treaty was being signed the young prince died. Louis and William, both anxious to avoid a major war over Spain, reopened their negotiations. A second partition treaty signed early in 1700 assigned the bulk of the Spanish inheritance to Archduke Charles, Leopold's second son by his third wife.

The death of another young prince, Princess Anne's only surviving child, the duke of Gloucester, meant that the Protestant succession in England was now in jeopardy. William had long favored vesting the succession in the Electress Sophia of Hanover, granddaughter of James I, and Sophia's heirs. But to do so required the assent of Parliament, and a majority of country members had been elected in 1698, many of whom were hostile to the king's continental interests and concerns. The Tory Parliament delivered a series of attacks on the aging king, sending home his Dutch guards and taking back the large grants of Irish land he had made to his favorites. The king seriously considered abdication. But though his health was failing his will remained strong and his ambition constant. These qualities were put to their greatest test at the end of 1700 when Carlos II died. He bequeathed his empire to the younger grandson of Louis XIV, Philip, duke of Anjou, and Louis accepted the inheritance in the name of Philip. A new English Parliament elected in the beginning of 1701 was slightly more Whiggish in composition, and it confirmed the succession of the crown to the Electress Sophia, though the Commons included a number of limitations upon the crown which reflected their dislike of William's foreign advisers.

The Legacy of William III

Though the Dutch were cowed into accepting Philip V's accession in Spain, England was not. The Tories found their public stock falling as a result of their vindictive measures, so to restore confidence and regain the king's favor they passed a resolution asking him to take steps to curb the exorbitant power of France. The king responded promptly, appointing John Churchill, earl of Marlborough, who was the principal adviser to the Princess Anne, as his agent to negotiate a new alliance with the Dutch and the emperor. Fortunately for William, Louis XIV now entered into measures guaranteed to provoke English hostility. He sent French troops into the Spanish Netherlands to shut off English commerce to the continent and sent other contingents into Milan and its dependencies, thus enraging the Austrian emperor, who claimed that territory for his family. Finally, Louis acknowledged the young son of James II as king of England when the old monarch died in exile in September 1701. Armed with a new grand alliance among England, the Dutch Republic, and the Austrian emperor, William returned to England in the fall of 1701, dissolved the Parliament, and began to transfer power once again to the Whigs, the party dedicated to support his continental policies. Though the election returns gave neither faction a real majority, he had the satisfaction of knowing that England would honor its commitments. The king died on March 8, 1702, after a fall from his horse. William died respected but unloved. His adopted country had been well schooled in the arts of war, diplomacy, and government but had not undertaken its tutelage willingly. Now, however, the benefits of William's rule were to be seen, and his successor was able to enjoy the fruits of his labors.

THE EARLY YEARS OF ANNE'S REIGN

The Accession of Queen Anne

The new queen (1702–1714) was hardly a prepossessing figure for the newly emerging power of England. Although Anne was only thirty-five years old, the toll of seventeen pregnancies, chronic ill health, and the gout had already made her old before her time and rendered her a semi-invalid. After the death of her sister, Mary, and her father, James II, she could be accepted as the rightful and legal heir to the throne. A true daughter of the church, her devotion to her people and her country enabled her to draw upon a reserve of affection and loyalty that united at least for a time most of the influential elements in society behind her government.

Anne was a woman who was wholehearted in her loyalties once they were fixed. She immediately turned over her affairs to her most trusted advisers and friends, a triumvirate remarkable in English history. Sarah, Countess of Marlborough, had been Anne's constant companion and closest friend for a score of years. She was given control of the queen's entourage and access to her person by the grant of the offices of Mistress of the Robes, Groom of the Stole, and Keeper of the Privy Purse. Her husband, the duke of Marlborough, was named captain-general of the English army in Flanders and ambassador to the Dutch Republic, with command of the armies of the maritime powers in the Low Countries. The final member of this close-knit circle was another lifelong friend, Sidney, Lord Godolphin. While Marlborough took over the principal direction of foreign affairs and the conduct of the war, Godolphin acted as prime minister at home, with sole responsibility for the Treasury and supervision of the executive. He was also the liaison between the ministry, the queen, and Parliament. If Marlborough as general and diplomat was the architect of England's greatness abroad, it was Godolphin as prime minister who made Marlborough's successes possible by the firm support he provided from home.

Queen Anne. An engraving, c. 1750. Kenneth Spencer Research Library.

The queen's predilection and the long associations with Marlborough and Godolphin meant that the ministry was initially composed almost entirely of Tories. No eighteenth-century ministry ever lost an election, and the new Parliament that was returned in the summer of 1702 followed the traditional pattern by containing a Tory majority. Although possessing the complete backing of the queen, Marlborough and Godolphin had to share power at first with the principal Tory leaders, Nottingham and Rochester, who returned to office respectively as secretary of state and lord lieutenant of Ireland. Both favored the now traditional Tory blue water policy, which ran counter to the Williamite policies adopted by Marlborough.

The War of the Spanish Succession—The First Phase

When England entered the war in 1702, campaigns were conducted by the French on three fronts: in Italy, on the Rhine, and in the Spanish Netherlands against the maritime powers. Spain was dynastically linked to France. The Grand Alliance—England, the Netherlands, and the Habsburg domain, Austria and Hungary—had only a few German princes in league with them initially. In 1703 Bavaria and Cologne joined France while Savoy and Portugal joined the Grand Alliance. As a condition to enter the alliance, Portugal insisted that the maritime powers open another front in Spain and endeavor to place the Habsburg candidate on the throne. Savoy brought some reinforcements to the Austrians in Italy, but the defection of Bavaria and Cologne laid the Rhineland and southern Germany open to French occupation and made an advance on Vienna a practical reality.

Marlborough had already shown superior tactical ability and generalship in the campaign of 1702. Contrary to the prevailing traditions of the time, which favored long and essentially static campaigns devoted mainly to sieges, he preferred to seek out the enemy's army in the field and destroy it, believing thereby that the fortresses would be cut off from resupply and would fall into his hands. The Dutch, whose political representatives at the field headquarters had to give their consent before their troops could be employed, regarded the army as a defensive weapon, as all that stood between them and a French invasion, so they were loath to risk it in battle. Determined not to return to the field in 1704 unless he was given greater authority, Marlborough persuaded the Dutch to let him take part of the troops for a daring march up the Rhine to save the Empire. At the Danube, Marlborough joined the imperial commander, Prince Eugene of Savoy, and deliberately provoked a battle with the Franco-Bavarian army. In one of the decisive battles of European history, they defeated the flower of the French army at the little village of Blenheim on the Danube. The victory saved the Austrian Empire from French control and provided Godolphin with the means to fight off the attacks of the parties at home.

The Church Settlement and Occasional Conformity

After the Revolution of 1688 it was expected that the Dissenters would be rewarded with a relaxation of the laws designed to suppress them as a consequence of their refusal to cooperate with James II against the Anglicans. William III, a Calvinist, was fully committed to religious toleration and was even prepared to go further and remodel the church so that it would be acceptable to Presbyterians if not most of the Dissenters. He was frustrated in his efforts because of the means he used to try to force the Tories to consent. They in turn were opposed to concessions, motivated not only by conscience but also by a desire to protect an Anglican monopoly of political offices. A compromise measure, the Toleration Act, was passed, though its terms were hardly very generous. It was the refusal of the crown to implement the more punitive measures still in force that really gave the Dissenters a measure of peace. Public office, both in the central government and at the local level, was restricted to communicants of the Church of England. Many Dissenters, however, would take communion in the established church once a year to qualify themselves for office and then return to their chapels. The high church party, synonymous with the Tories, was outraged at this behavior. After the dismissal of Rochester in 1703 and Nottingham and his colleagues from the ministry in 1704, the Tories seized upon the issue of occasional conformity to try to break

The Battle of Blenheim, 1704. An engraving, c. 1735. Kenneth Spencer Research Library.

the ministry. Two previous bills designed to eradicate this practice had been defeated in the Lords in 1702 and 1703. Now the Tories in the Commons moved to add the provision to a money bill in late 1704, intending to force its acceptance on both the Lords (who had earlier given up the right to alter money bills) and the queen. The motion to tack the provision onto a bill was defeated but only after a most desperate effort by both sides to garner the necessary votes. The man principally responsible for its defeat was the speaker and new secretary of state, Robert Harley.

Robert Harley versus the Whigs

Robert Harley was one of the most interesting, important, and yet enigmatic statesmen of the early eighteenth century. Born into a Dissenting family, he became the leader of the church party or Tories after starting his political career in Parliament as a country Whig. Elected speaker in 1701 and again in 1702, he proved to be one of the most successful managers of the Commons in English history. Godolphin and Marlborough came to rely on him heavily; by 1704 the three jointly managed affairs. Harley was persuaded to take high office as a secretary of state, though he retained the speakership until the dissolution of the Parliament in 1705. A man of the middle, he was suspicious of the extremists of either party. When Godolphin made an opening to the Whigs in late 1704 to save his majority, Harley was opposed and resisted all efforts to increase the Whig presence in the ministry. In December 1706 the earl of Sunderland, Marlborough's son-in-law and one of the Whig junto or ruling clique of that party, was made secretary of state. Harley was unwilling to accept Sunderland as a colleague and now began to undermine Godolphin. In February 1708 he advised the queen to remove Godolphin and to remodel the ministry. Marlborough refused to support this move and without his prestige Harley could not hope to achieve his aims, so he voluntarily resigned. Just when the Cabinet crisis reached its height, word reached London that the "Old Pretender," Prince James Edward, the son born to James II in 1688, was now on the sea with a French fleet, determined to invade Britain and regain the crown. His landing was thwarted, but the threat and excitement tended to reinforce the Whigs. When parliamentary elections were held later in the spring, the Whigs were returned with a solid majority.

THE LATER YEARS OF QUEEN ANNE'S REIGN

The War of the Spanish Succession—The Second Phase

After an abortive advance along the Moselle, Marlborough returned to the battlefield in Flanders in 1705 for another year of frustration. Only the successful landing of an allied fleet with Archduke Charles in Catalonia and the capture of Barcelona provided any relief from the dismal dispatches from the other theaters. The year 1706 proved to be the annus mirabilis of the war. Marlborough was able to engage the French in battle at Ramillies, south of Brussels, and the resulting victory put most of Flanders into his hands. The English and their allies won a number of important engagements early in the war, but soon the war situation began to deteriorate for the allies. In 1707 the Austrians concluded a truce with the French in Italy, which freed French troops for employment elsewhere. A severe defeat in Spain lost that country for the allies, though the war dragged on there for another four years. Marlborough cleared the rest of the Netherlands, but the Battle of Malplaquet in 1709 was so bloody that it sickened the civilians on both sides. The turn of events at home made Marlborough afraid to risk another major engagement. In spite of two further impressive successes against the French, Marlborough was dismissed from all his offices at the end of 1711, defeated not as a general but as a diplomat and politician.

During the first part of the war Marlborough had practically single-handedly held the Grand Alliance together. For several successive years he set out on exhausting trips around the capitals of Europe after the campaign to persuade the allied princes to contribute troops to the armies in the several theaters. In 1706 when the French first sued for peace, he was firm in his refusal to accept anything less than unconditional terms. When peace negotiations were undertaken in earnest in 1709, however, he insisted on a collaborator, the young Viscount Townshend, and Marlborough left the negotiating to him. It was the same in 1710 when the negotiations were again taken up after Louis XIV's rejection of the preliminaries the previous year. Marlborough's increasing caution and refusal to accept responsibility for anything but his own army was the consequence of political changes at home.

Blenheim Palace. Constructed for the first Duke of Marlborough. Private collection.

The Decline and Fall of the Godolphin Ministry

The duchess of Marlborough is often credited with almost complete control over the queen for the first half of her reign. Yet, in fact, she had lost whatever influence she possessed even before Anne's accession. The duchess, a convert to Whig principles, held views that were unpalatable to the queen. Disagreeing on politics as early as 1702, their relationship became more distant after 1703 when the duchess went into semiseclusion following the death of her only surviving son. Though placed in the queen's bedchamber by her cousin the duchess, the queen's dresser, Abigail Hill, later Mrs. Masham, worked to advance the interests and projects of another relation, Robert Harley. The duchess became increasingly outspoken and strident in forcing her unwanted advice on the queen. The queen turned increasingly to Masham and others, so that by 1710 all communication between the two former friends had ceased. At the end of 1710 the duchess was dismissed from all her offices. This estrangement was an important factor in the fall of Marlborough, Godolphin, and the Whigs.

The Godolphin ministry had fully earned the appreciation of the nation by its impressive accomplishments both at home and abroad. Besides maintaining English naval supremacy, a preeminence dramatized by the scuttling of the French fleet at Toulon in 1707, it had made possible the great victories of Marlborough in Flanders and Germany and had subsidized other allied victories in Italy and Spain. One must add to these accomplishments the taking of Gibraltar in 1704 and Port Mahon in 1708. At home the greatest achievement was the passage of the Act of Union in 1707. Precipitated by the Scottish threat to elect a sovereign other than the one to rule England after Anne's death, the English Parliament in 1705 had moved the queen to appoint commissioners to treat for a union. The Scots were encouraged to participate by the threat of the loss of their privileges in England as subjects of a common sovereign and by the promise of full participation in the lucrative colonial trade. The sixty-two commissioners (thirty-one from each nation) chosen by the queen did their work well. Completing their deliberations in July 1705, they recommended a parliamentary union in which 16 elected Scottish peers would join the House of Lords and 45 Scottish members would be added to the 513 members of the English Commons. After a stormy passage in the Scots Parliament, the recommendations were accepted without qualification, and the union came into being on May 1, 1707.

The increasing and irksome burden of taxation that fell heaviest on the landowners, the jealousy of those excluded from political power, and the growing frustration over the ministry's apparent inability to bring the war to an end, when combined with the estrangement of the queen, eventually brought down Godolphin and his colleagues. The instrument of the change was an unlikely object—an inflammatory, ultraconservative Tory parson. The high church clergy were among the most vociferous and influential opponents of the Godolphin ministry and were a key element in the strength of the Tories. In order to reduce the clergy to subservience, one of the most notorious members, Dr. Henry Sacheverell, a fellow of Magdalen College, Oxford, and a popular preacher in London, was impeached by the Commons before the High Court of Parliament in December 1709. This effort to muzzle the Tory churchman backfired on the Whigs. The martyr cleric became a symbol of Whig oppression and tyranny. All those dissatisfied with ministerial policies of every kind now used the parson to demonstrate their true feelings. Emboldened by the reaction and counseled by Harley, the queen removed her servants one by one, so that by the end of the year Harley and the Tories were in control of the executive. An election held in September returned an overwhelming Tory majority.

The End of Anne's Reign

Ignoring Britain's commitments to its allies, Harley opened secret negotiations with the French. By the winter of 1711–1712 the preliminaries were sufficiently far advanced that Harley, now raised to the peerage as earl of Oxford, felt confident enough to dismiss Marlborough and to make public the negotiations. The abandonment of Britain's allies on the battlefield aroused powerful protest at home and on the continent, but Oxford, now assisted by his principal colleague and rival for authority, Henry St. John (created Viscount Bolingbroke in 1713), proceeded to confirm his arrangements with Louis XIV in the Treaty of Utrecht. In addition to Gibraltar and Minorca, Nova Scotia was ceded to England, marking the beginning of a retreat for the French in North America. The fortifications at Dunkirk were to be razed. Important commercial concessions were granted in Spain and the Spanish Empire, and France recognized the Protestant succession in England. Nonetheless, the success of Oxford in turning out the Whigs and in restoring the Tories to power was ultimately his undoing. He found himself the prisoner of the newly dominant party, unable to play them off against the Whigs and thus retain control; meanwhile the sickly queen began to repent the abandonment of her old friends and advisers. With the queen's health failing, Oxford and Bolingbroke looked to the heir to the crown to shore up their positions. But George, Elector of Hanover, loyal to the imperial cause, could never forgive the ministers who betrayed England's allies in the late war. Oxford and Bolingbroke then sought, independently, to ingratiate themselves with the "Pretender," the son of the late James II. When he refused unequivocally to change his religion for the crown of England they realized his cause was hopeless. Thus when Queen Anne fell mortally ill at the end of July, the Tories were unprepared to manage the succession. The Whigs, on the other hand, were fully prepared to launch a coup if necessary to secure the Protestant succession and had secretly arranged a takeover of the army if this eventuality proved necessary. It was not. When Anne died peacefully on August 1, 1714, George I was proclaimed king without any challenge.

The Press and the Parties

The fall of the Godolphin ministry, the rapprochement with France, and the renewed attack on the Dissenters by the triumphant Tories, which was shown by the passage of the occasional conformity bill in 1711, all inspired political and press battles in England that exceeded even those of the exclusion controversy in their magnitude and ferocity. The party lines had hardened into a clear Whig-Tory split by the beginning of the reign. The successive replacements and then transformation of the ministry had changed its composition from Tory to Whig and back to Tory. The frequent parliamentary elections— 1702, 1705, 1708, 1710, and 1713—were all fought on party lines. Though the parties lacked a formal national organization (that did not emerge until the mid-nineteenth century), the continuity of leadership and principles and the presence of some centralized management, both for elections and control of parliamentary sessions, are clear evidence of the existence of party in Anne's reign. These divisions are particularly well exemplified by the press.

With the lapse of the censorship laws in 1695 a steady increase in publications becomes evident. Newspapers and monthlies began to proliferate, and the first daily newspaper, the *Daily Courant,* made its appearance in 1702. In spite of a parliamentary prohibition, accounts of parliamentary debates appeared in annual histories at the turn of the century. The expanded activity of the press in Anne's reign, culminating in the great battles that dominated the last four years, is one of the most important phenomena of modern English history. By 1714 nearly all the features we have come to expect in modern newspapers—the editorial, the news, the advice to the lovelorn, the periodical essay—had all made their appearance. Newspapers began and ended in startling profusion. Press battles, such as those between Defoe's *Review,* Tutchin's *Observator,* and Leslie's *Rehearsal,* were the order of the day. By 1712 between 50,000 and 60,000 copies of newspapers were sold in London each week, in spite of a stamp tax imposed by Parliament to curb the Whig press. Nearly all the most celebrated writers of the day were drawn into the press wars. Joseph Addison, Jonathan Swift, Richard Steele, and Daniel Defoe were only the best known and the most active. A polemical tract could inspire literally dozens of answers. The most successful and influential tracts, such as Swift's *The Conduct of the Allies* (1711), were sold by the tens of thousands of copies and could swing the opinion of the whole country behind a change in policy. The attacks of Tory writers on Marlborough were sufficient to compromise his reputation for many decades.

The general election of 1710 was fought and won in the press as much as it was on the hustings. Even all the means of a powerful ministry were unable to save the French commerce bill in 1713 thanks to the efforts of the opposition. The electorate represented a surprisingly high proportion of the adult male population, although in many boroughs the right to return representatives was vested in a small number of individuals, often under the influence of a local patron. Nevertheless, recent studies of poll books have suggested the presence of a swing vote, beyond the control of borough-mongers and responsive to changing public opinion. The success of the Revolution of 1688 and the preservation of English liberties are no better illustrated than in the vigor of its press and the strength of its political parties.

GROWTH AND CHANGE

Mercantilism

England's rise to great power status at the end of the wars against Louis XIV was the consequence of English arms backed by English industry and finance. The exploitation of this new eminence was the province of the merchants. The impact of the wars on England and the other European countries has been hotly debated. The depredations of the French privateers on English merchant shipping were tremendous. Yet the English gained as well as lost, and thousands of French ships were taken as prizes during the same period and incorporated into the English fleet. Though the English merchant marine may have been only marginally larger at the end of the period, and little more than it had been a century ago, the contrast with the situation in France and the Dutch Republic was more important and ultimately decisive. Prior to 1688 Dutch ships carried much of the bulk cargo required by England. The Dutch navy also suffered at the hands of the French, and the great burden of war expense took its toll on this small nation: it never recovered from the drain of men, ships, and gold. France, though blessed with far greater resources, both human and material, likewise lost out in the competition with England. England emerged from the war unquestionably the strongest in terms of its fleet.

Some share of this economic success must be attributed to the mercantilist system that was developed in the Commonwealth period and reinforced during the Restoration. Given its classic statement in 1664 in Thomas Mun's *Discourse on England's Treasure by Forraign Trade,* mercantilism stressed the importance of a favorable balance of trade. If England exported more than it imported the consequence would be a steady flow of specie into the country and increased prosperity. The navigation laws, first passed in 1651 and reenacted 1660 to 1663, restricted the colonial trade and imports generally to English bottoms (ships), thus laying the foundation for the growth of the English merchant marine. As the colonies grew in size and the value of their exports increased, English merchants and the king's tax collectors were the beneficiaries. The colonies, restricted to England as a single trading partner, became a principal market for English goods just as they were an essential source of raw materials. The wars were fought to protect old markets as well as create new ones. When Philip V inherited Spain he excluded English and Dutch shipping from trading with the Spanish colonies—a trade regarded as vital to English prosperity. So, too, the Levant and Mediterranean trade was assured by the capture of Minorca and Gibraltar and the scuttling of the French fleet at Toulon in 1707.

The demand in unprecedented quantities for supplies for the services, clothing, sail cloth, armaments, and ships gave a stimulus to industry and larger commercial organizations. The lot of the lower classes, whether urban or rural, was not materially altered. But in general it seems that the trading and mercantile community and landowners benefited as well from the war. The unprecedented demand for money sired the Bank of England, encouraged the union of the old and new East India companies in 1709, created the South Sea Company, and thus established a pattern of large-scale increases in capital formation. The more effective mobilization of resources made England's advance to great power status possible. This was a legacy of William and Anne.

Foreign Immigration

One of the many elements that fired the economic expansion and development that characterized the reigns of William III and Anne was the influx of refugees from the continent. There were two major groups. The second of these was comprised of Germans, largely from the Palatine along the upper Rhine. Driven from their homes by the depredations of the French army during the two wars, they made their way down the Rhine to Amsterdam. From thence many went on to England. William Penn was active in recruiting the Germans for his new colony of Pennsylvania in North America. They were the progenitors of those who came to be called the Pennsylvania Dutch (actually "deutsch" or German). From the sacking of Heidelberg in 1692 down through the first decade of the eighteenth century this migration continued. The severe winter of 1708–1709 increased the flow. The Whigs, then in power in England, welcomed the refugees with an eye to settling them in Ireland to reinforce the Protestant population there. The German immigrants were artisans and merchants for the most part, rather than farmers, and the plantation concept failed. But the "poor Palatines," as they were called, went on to join their predecessors in the New World.

The more important refugee group of this time was the Huguenots. From the time of the revocation of the Edict of Nantes in France by Louis XIV in 1675, there was a steady exodus of Huguenots from that country. Fearful of losing the right to worship as Protestants in their own churches, they fled to the security of more hospitable, Protestant countries, notably the Netherlands and England. They were educated, professional people. Many joined the world of letters or the more prosaic field of journalism and became important middlemen in translating continental literature for the English and in performing a like service for English writings for the continent, where English political theorists were widely read. From their mercantile and banking experiences a network of Huguenots developed around the periphery of France, from Switzerland and Savoy in the south of Europe to England, the Netherlands, and Prussia in the north. They became essential in the rapidly expanding system of public credit and the transmittal of funds, critical to the financing of the French wars on both sides. A number of Huguenots came over with William III—generals like the earl of Galway and journalists like Guillaume de Lamberty and Abel Boyer. Huguenot bankers were instrumental in the establishment of the Bank of England. Others brought new trades and skills such as hatmaking, silversmithing, glassblowing, and silk weaving. Architecture, gardening, and furniture and cabinetmaking also were positively influenced by the newcomers. They were an invigorating and valuable new addition to England's resources, and their loss to France was a grave one.

The Growth of the Professions

The innovation, boldness, and expansiveness that marked the post-Revolution period is exemplified by yet another phenomenon—the rise of a new professional class. To be sure, it was not all new. There already existed lawyers, physicians, clergy, and military and naval officers. But in this period they took on a new kind of importance, increased substantially in number, and improved in expertise and training. Furthermore, they were joined by budding new professions: architects, landscape gardeners, musicians, and, above all, civil servants. The lawyers first came to prominence in the long struggle between crown and parliament that led to the civil wars. The Revolution brought stability and independence to the judiciary. The rise in commercial and political activity, and thus the new prosperity, also meant a rise in litigation. The senior members of the bar, the barristers who alone were permitted to plead before the courts, reaped great profit from their practices. The number of lawyers in the parliament steadily increased after the Revolution, and that meant greater access to places, capped by lucrative and prestigious posts both in the executive and judicial branches of government. The junior members, the attorneys, found increased demand for their services in the creation and management of great landed estates as well as the inevitable preparation and analysis of documents essential to the conduct of business. In all, the emoluments derived from the legal profession accounted for greater accumulations of wealth for this profession than did any other during the period.

The late seventeenth century also saw the emergence of the practice of medicine as a respectable and lucrative profession. The latter character is amply testified to by the sharp rise in the size of fees. In part the improvement in professional status was the consequence of a gradual consolidation of the separate callings of physicians, apothecaries, and surgeons. The first determined the cause of illness and prescribed treatment; the second provided the medicines; the third treated external afflictions. By the mid-eighteenth century the three heretofore distinct classes merged loosely into what were now called "doctors." The loss of control by the College of Physicians over its profession was one factor, as apothecaries and surgeons gained new respectability and the right to prescribe medicine and administer treatment to the sick. Professional training and education was another factor. The graduates of Oxford and Cambridge licensed by the College were augmented by doctors trained in the provinces through apprenticeship and licensed by the bishops. In the late seventeenth century they were augmented by foreign-trained physicians, notably of Leyden. After the turn of the century the Leyden contingent was composed increasingly of Englishmen. In the Georgian period it was the Scottish universities that took the lead, both in the number and quality of doctors produced. The third factor, allied to the second, was the grudging acceptance of the surgeon-barbers into the profession. The two great French wars were the impetus; the surgeons gained substantially in numbers, expertise, and prestige through the heavy demand for their services in the army and navy. After the wars they returned to civilian life and found a ready market for their talents. The surgeons, too, increased the rigor and standards of their training through the development of Surgeons' Hall in London as a training center. Moreover, all branches of the profession of medicine benefited from the proliferation of hospitals in the eighteenth century. These provided training sites and the opportunity to learn and test skills.

The origins of the civil service can be traced back to the clerics who provided the secretariat or scriptorium for the crown from before the Conquest, then to the expanded, more specialized bureaucrats assembled by the early Tudors to administer their new taxes and to manage the secularization of church lands. The next great development came with the assumption by the crown of the collection and management of taxes beginning with tenure of Danby as lord treasurer. It was completed by the great expansion of business generated by the French wars, wars that also greatly expanded the need for a large number of army and naval officers. By the death of Queen Anne one can see the presence of a proficient, indispensable body of civil servants in the treasury, at the court, in the offices of the secretaries of state, and in the army and navy and their support services. Their expertise and experience were so essential to the operation of the government that many civil servants were able to remain in office, secure in their tenure, in spite of the frequent alterations of ministers in the major posts and parties in control of parliament in the two decades after the Revolution. If Samuel Pepys was the Restoration prototype of the civil servant, the later officials who typified the new and enduring model included: the apolitical William Lowndes, employed at the treasury from 1679 and secretary from 1695 to 1724; Josiah Burchett, who commenced his career at the navy office as a clerk to Pepys in 1680 and eventually succeeded to the office of secretary in 1695, a post he held until his death in 1742; and Sir Christopher Wren, who began as a surveyor-general to Charles II's works in 1661, succeeded to the charge of all royal works in 1670, and remained in office until his removal in 1718 (at the age of 86). Nor should one forget that Sir Isaac Newton, in addition to his more celebrated accomplishments, was first warden and then master of the mint from 1696 until his death in 1727.

SUGGESTIONS FOR FURTHER READING

The New Columbia Encyclopedia (4th ed., 1975) is the single most useful reference work for students of history. It is a good place to check names, dates, places, and events. *The Dictionary of National Biography* (1917) provides articles on persons prominent in British history to 1900. *The Concise Dictionary of National Biography* (London, 1961) contains abridgements of every article in the complete *DNB*. Useful guides to important people are *Lives of the Stuart Age, 1603–1714* (1976) and *Lives of the Georgian Age, 1714–1837* (1978). A profusely illustrated overview is *The Oxford Illustrated History of the British Monarchy*, ed. John Cannon (1991). For constitutional development the standard work is D. L. Keir, *The Constitutional History of Modern Britain* (9th ed., 1969). See also Mark Thompson, *The Constitutional History of England, 1642–1801* (1938). Betty Kemp, *King and Commons, 1660–1832* (1957) is a lucid explanation of the shift in political power that began with the Restoration and ended with the Reform Bill of 1832.

For the later Stuarts, good surveys are J. R. Jones, *Country and Court: England, 1658–1714* (1978) and Geoffrey Holmes, *The Making of a Great Power: Late Stuart and Early Georgian England, 1660–1722* (1993). The fullest treatment is to be found in David Ogg, *England in the Reigns of James II and William III* (1955). The Stuart rulers are discussed and illustrated in J. P. Kenyon, *The Stuarts* (1958). For a broad perspective on the long-term consequences of the Revolution settlement see Paul Langford, *Public Life and Propertied Englishmen, 1689–1798* (1991).

Good political histories are Henry Horwitz, *Parliament, Policy and Politics in the Reign of William III* (1977) and Geoffrey Holmes, *British Politics in the Age of Anne* (1987). Political parties are reviewed in Brian Hill, *Early Parties and Politics in Britain, 1688–1832* (1996) and J. P. Kenyon, *Revolution Principles: The Politics of Party, 1689–1720* (1977). Perhaps the most stimulating study of the Revolution era is J. R. Plumb, *The Growth of Political Stability in England, 1675–1725* (1967). The influence of Plumb is seen in *Britain after the Glorious Revolution, 1689–1714* (1969), ed. Geoffrey Holmes.

For court life see R. O. Buchholz, *The Augustan Court: Queen Anne and the Decline of Court Culture* (1992). An important perspective is provided by Gary S. DeKrey in *A Fractured*

Society: The Politics of London in the First Age of Party, 1688–1715 (1985). M. G. Dickson, *The Financial Revolution in England, A Study in the Development of Public Credit, 1688–1756* (1967) is a work of major importance. A broad and detailed appreciation of the period is available in George M. Trevelyan, *England under Queen Anne* (3 vols., 1932–1934).

On foreign policy see Jeremy Black, *'A System of Ambition': British Foreign Policy, 1660–1793* (1992); Paul Langford, *Modern British Foreign Policy: the Eighteenth Century, 1688–1815* (1976), and D. B. Horn, *Great Britain and Europe in the Eighteenth Century* (1967). Earl A. Reitan, *Politics, War, and Empire: The Rise of Britain to a World Power, 1688–1792* (1994) combines foreign policy, military factors, and imperial expansion. A good introduction to the many wars of the seventeenth and eighteenth centuries is M. S. Anderson, *War and Society in Europe of the Old Regime, 1618–1789* (1988). Britain's role in these wars is examined in Jeremy Black, *Britain as a Military Power, 1688–1815* (1998). John Brewer considers *The Sinews of Power: War, Money, and the English State, 1688–1783* (1989). The effects of war are examined by D. W. Jones in *War and the Economy in the Age of William III and Marlborough* (1988) and H. V. Bowen, *War and British Society, 1688–1815* (1997). A good account of the navy is G. J. Marcus, *A Naval History of England, Vol. I: The Formative Centuries* (1961). General surveys of the armed forces are Paul Kennedy, *The Rise and Fall of British Naval Mastery* (1976); James Stokesbury, *Navy and Empire* (1983); Corelli Barnett, *Britain and her Army, 1509–1970* (1970); and *The Oxford Illustrated History of the British Army*, ed. David Chandler and Ian Beckett (1994).

For the Church of England see Norman Sykes, *From Seldon to Secker, 1160–1768* (1959) and E. G. Rupp, *Religion in England, 1688–1791* (1986). People outside the Church are covered by M. R. Watts, *The Dissenters from the Reformation to the French Revolution* (1978) and J. Bossy, *The English Catholic Community, 1570–1850* (1975). G. V. Bennett, *The Tory Crisis in Church and State, 1688–1730* (1975) and Norman Sykes, *Church and State in England in the Eighteenth Century* (1934) are fundamental to an understanding of the relationship of Church and state. See also Geoffrey Holmes, *The Trial of Dr. Sacheverell* (1973).

Charles Wilson reviews economic developments in *England's Apprenticeship, 1603–1763* (2nd ed., 1985), which can be supplemented by Ralph Davis, *English Overseas Trade, 1500–1700* (1973) and D. C. Coleman, *Industry in Tudor and Stuart England* (1975). Histories of London are Roy Porter, *London: A Social History* (1998); Francis Sheppard, *London* (1998); and Stephen Inwood, *A History Of London* (1998). Peter Clark, ed., *The Transformation of English Provincial Towns, 1600–1800* (1984) and Peter Borsay, *The English Urban Renaissance: Culture and Society in the English Provincial Town, 1660–1770* (1989) are good introductions to smaller cities and towns.

Social history is reviewed in J. A. Sharpe, *Early Modern England: A Social History, 1550–1760* (2nd ed., 1997). For the leadership elite see J. V. Beckett, *The Aristocracy in England, 1660–1714* (1986) and Felicity Heal and Clive Holmes, *The Gentry in England and Wales, 1500–1700* (1994). Lawrence Stone, *The Family, Sex, and Marriage in England, 1500–1800* (1977) is interesting and important. See also Anthony Fletcher, *Gender, Sex, and Subordination in England, 1500–1800* (1995). The lives of the poor are examined by Paul Slack in *Poverty and Policy in Tudor and Stuart England* (1988). Standard works on the arts are John Summerson, *Architecture in Britain, 1530–1830* (1953), Ellis Waterhouse, *Painting Britain, 1530–1790* (1953), and Margaret Whinney, *Sculpture in Britain, 1530–1830* (1964).

Geraint H. Jenkins covers *The History of Wales, Vol. 4: The Foundation of Modern Wales, 1642–1780* (1988). Good general histories of Scotland are George S. Pryde, *Scotland from 1603 to the Present Day* (1962); William Ferguson, *Scotland: 1689 to the Present* (1968); and T. C. Smout, *A History of the Scottish People* (1969). The changing relationship is traced in *Scotland and England, 1286–1815*, ed. Roger A. Mason (1986). Brian P. Levack describes *The Formation* of the British State: England, Scotland, and the Union, 1603–1707 (1987). The Act of Union is covered in G. S. Pryde, *The Treaty of Union of Scotland and Ireland* (1950) and K. Brown, *Kingdom or Province? Scotland and the Regnal Union, 1603–1715* (1992). T. C. Smout explores *Scottish Trade on the Eve of the Union* (1963); and P. W. J. Riley examines the implementation of the union in *The English Ministers and Scotland, 1707–1727* (1964).

J. C. Beckett, *The Making of Modern Ireland* (1966) is an excellent starting place. More detail is provided in T. W. Moody, ed., *A New History of Ireland, Vol. IV: Eighteenth-Century Ireland, 1691–1800* (1986). See also Thomas Hachey, *The Irish Experience: A Concise History* (1996). *The Oxford Illustrated History of Ireland* (1991), ed. R. F. Foster is a lavish work. An important study is F. G. James, *Ireland in the Empire, 1688–1770* (1973).

Major biographies include Stephen Baxter, *William III* (1966); Hester Chapman, *Mary, Queen of England* (1953); Edward Gregg, *Queen Anne* (1980); J. P. Kenyon, *Robert Spencer, Earl of Sunderland* (1958); Angus McInnes, *Robert Harley, Puritan Politician* (1970); Winston S. Churchill, *Marlborough, His Life and Times* (1933–1938); Ivor Burton, *The Captain General* (1968); J. R. Jones, *Marlborough* (1993); Frances Harris, *A Passion for Government: The Life of Sarah, Duchess of Marlborough* (1991); Brian W. Hill, *Robert Harley: Speaker, Secretary of State and Premier Minister* (1988); and H. T. Dickinson, *Bolingbroke* (1970).

CHAPTER TEN

Augustan England
1714–1754

The half-century ushered in by the Hanoverian succession has traditionally been regarded as a somnolent one in England. The motto of its most famous politician, Sir Robert Walpole, who dominated the government for virtually half the period, was said to be *quieta no movere*, "let sleeping dogs lie." It has been regarded as a stretch of time singularly devoid of interest and excitement when compared with the reigns of William III and Anne, which preceded it, or the reign of George III, highlighted by the American Revolution, the French Revolution, and the Napoleonic Wars. Its sovereigns, the first two Georges, are regarded as dullards. Yet, as we shall see, it was a far more dynamic and interesting period than the stereotype suggests. Culturally, diplomatically, politically, the gains of the previous quarter century were preserved and extended, and the foundation was laid for the great expansion of England simplistically styled the Industrial Revolution, which embraces the whole of the reign of George III.

THE SETTLING OF THE HANOVERIAN DYNASTY

The New King

George I (1714–1727), a homely, stout, fifty-three-year-old German, was hardly the popular image of a king. Though king of Great Britain, he also remained ruler of Hanover; his continuing interest in the latter and apparent lack of concern for the former upset the British, who habitually resented foreigners and particularly feared their influence on British foreign policy. George was

*George I. An engraving,
c. 1750. Kenneth Spencer
Research Library.*

set in his ways, accustomed to complete mastery over his territories and subjects, and unfamiliar with Parliament and parties. George I dined in public
once or twice a week but initially could discourse only with persons who spoke
German or French. He preferred to spend his days quietly in his chamber,
giving audiences to his ministers. He took his supper with one or both gro-
tesque German ladies in his household: the tall, spindly, middle-aged duchess
of Kendal, George's morganatic wife, and the fat, rouge-cheeked countess of
Darlington, George's half sister, who were respectively but irreverently known
as The Maypole and The Elephant. His entourage also included two German advisers and a Huguenot secretary who managed the king's Hanoverian
concerns. The most popular members of the family were the prince and
princess of Wales who spoke excellent English and were as affable as the
king was reserved.

George I proved to be the most able of the Hanoverian sovereigns of
Great Britain. Trained for the army in his youth, he was an experienced officer
and field commander. He had successfully managed his electorate for more
than a quarter of a century and was an equally shrewd and intelligent governor
of his new domains. Though he may have deferred to his ministers in domestic policy, his knowledge of foreign affairs was unrivaled in England and the
equal to any of his fellow European sovereigns. In following up the Treaty of
Utrecht, in making a rapprochement with France, in negotiating the Qua-

druple Alliance, and in working to end the Great Northern War this proved an invaluable asset to England. Finally, he was a cultured European gentleman, an early patron of Handel. He was eminently worthy to occupy his new throne.

The New Politics

Even before George's arrival in England there was a shuffling of political leaders in readiness for the new order. Bolingbroke was sacked, and the Whigs repossessed all of the great offices of state. The greatest authority was granted to the two secretaries of state—Charles, Viscount Townshend, and James Stanhope. Townshend took the lead in domestic affairs, especially after his brother-in-law, Robert Walpole, succeeded Halifax at the Treasury in 1716; Stanhope was dominant in foreign affairs.

The new ministers sought to consolidate their political gains by calling for the election of a new Parliament. Proclaiming their loyalty to the Protestant succession and denouncing the Treaty of Utrecht, the Whigs triumphed and were returned with a solid majority of 150 seats. When the Whig leaders proceeded to impeach the former ministers, Bolingbroke, who thought his life was in danger, fled to France and entered the service of James Edward Stuart, the Pretender to the British throne. The vindictiveness of the Whigs, the influence of the foreigners in the king's entourage, and the affront offered even to those Tories who had supported the Hanoverian succession, coupled with the fears of the church, turned popular opinion to the Tories. At the height of this reaction the earl of Mar slipped away from court to raise the standard of James Edward Stuart in Scotland on September 6, 1715.

The Jacobite Uprising of 1715

The Jacobite uprising of 1715 was a badly conceived, poorly concerted movement. The Pretender's only hope for success depended on the support of France. The aged French king, Louis XIV, died, however, on September 1, and the duke of Orleans, who became regent for the minor successor, Louis XV, adopted a policy of watchful neutrality—disastrous to the Jacobite cause—because the regent himself was a candidate for the French throne and support from Britain might spell the difference in his ambitions. The Jacobites, nevertheless, pressed on; they had the initial advantage because, as poorly prepared as they were, the government had even fewer forces at its command than they did. The Jacobites' initial successes were short-lived, however. After an indecisive battle at Sheriffmuir, Mar and the Jacobite forces no longer had the means to undertake another engagement. The belated arrival of the Pretender in January, without reinforcements or supplies, was anticlimactic. He returned to France, leaving his unsuccessful supporters to be hunted down in Scotland.

The Diplomacy of Stanhope

The Jacobite rebellion only reinforced Britain's pressing need for allies. James Stanhope moved immediately to rebuild the old alliances. As both envoy and general in Spain in the late war, Stanhope had formed an intimate acquaintance with Archduke Charles, who had succeeded his brother as emperor in 1711. This friendship now became the hinge of Britain's foreign policy. In June 1715 Stanhope made a personal trip to Vienna to persuade Emperor Charles to permit the Dutch to maintain fortresses in the Netherlands as a barrier against French aggression. Following a treaty of alliance with the Dutch in February 1716, Britain signed the Treaty of Westminster in June 1716 by which Austria guaranteed the Protestant succession. Stanhope's most remarkable achievement was an alliance with France, so recently Britain's enemy. The resulting treaty, which provided for a guarantee of the succession of the British and French thrones, was concluded in November and approved by the Dutch in February 1717.

The haste with which the treaty was drafted reflected George I's concern for his Hanoverian dominions. In the Baltic area the Great Northern War (1700–1721), which had begun as a conflict between Sweden and Denmark, had swelled to include Russia, Poland, and Prussia. Though Sweden was the aggressor, its defeat by Russia in 1709 put it permanently on the defensive. Prussia, Denmark, Hanover, and Russia all hoped to secure additions to their territories at Sweden's expense. George I employed the British fleet in the contest, first against Sweden and then later against Russia after the death of Sweden's King Charles XII in 1718. With Stanhope's connivance, British forces were used to secure advantages for Hanover, an action that had adverse political repercussions in England. Finally, Britain regained its favorable commercial position with Spain in a treaty negotiated late in 1715.

The Whig Split and the Triumph of Walpole

The sweep of offices the Whigs enjoyed on George I's accession had still not satisfied all of them. Sunderland was disgruntled as he watched Townshend and Stanhope take charge of offices to which he had pretensions. Townshend and Walpole came to resent the influence of the Hanoverian advisers with whom Stanhope was still influential. This division was exacerbated by the ill feeling that existed between the king and his heir. When George determined to visit Hanover in 1716, Sunderland used the pretext of a visit to Aix for health reasons as an excuse to follow the king to the Continent. There he heightened the suspicions of the king and Stanhope that Townshend and Walpole were in league with the prince of Wales. On his return the king dismissed Townshend and Walpole, and others resigned in sympathy. When the king banished the prince and his wife from his presence soon after, the opposition established itself around the prince.

Because the Septennial Act (1716) extended the maximum life of a Parliament from three to seven years, it would have seemed that the Whig ministers could be assured of lengthy control of government, yet the split in the Whig party made the survival of the ministry tenuous. The dissident Whigs capitalized on popular fears to charge that English interests were subordinated to Hanoverian goals, and after several legislative defeats Stanhope and Sunderland realized they would have to join forces with Townshend, Walpole, and other dissident Whigs. The reunion of all Whig factions was capped by a reconciliation of the king and the prince and a banishment of the Hanoverian advisers in 1720. The consolidation was timely, for the ministry suddenly found itself faced with a grave crisis.

The late wars had saddled England with a substantial public debt. The South Sea Company, organized by Robert Harley in 1711, managed part of the debt in return for the exclusive trading rights in Spain and the Spanish empire, which had been confirmed at the peace table. Offering lower interest rates, the South Sea Company took over the remaining part of the debt not earlier funded by the chartered companies, making a series of stock offerings to finance this undertaking. To create a demand for the stock issues, it paid handsome dividends out of capital—a fraudulent practice—and tendered bribes that may have reached the king himself. The shares rose from £130 to £1,050 in the space of a few months, but as the South Sea bubble burst suddenly, along with other speculative enterprises in the summer of 1720, financial ruin was brought to countless individuals. The crown itself was in danger because the court was deeply implicated, and only the masterly defense by Walpole in the Commons' investigation saved it. Stanhope, who was free from personal guilt, died suddenly during the investigation. As the price of his acquittal, Sunderland had to surrender his office of first lord of the Treasury to Walpole in 1721. Sunderland's unexpected death a year later left the field clear to Walpole.

THE AGE OF WALPOLE

Walpole's Political System

In 1721 Walpole was in a position to assert his political leadership. He had emerged from the South Sea Company crisis without direct taint of corruption, the champion of the investors, a defender of stability. More, however, was needed. He made himself indispensable to the king by shielding George and his friends from the investigation. Sir Robert made himself master of the king's ministers by driving independent or contrary ones out of office. In 1724, for example, he forced Carteret, Stanhope's successor as secretary and

Sunderland's political heir, to resign and then removed him from Westminster by making him lord lieutenant of Ireland. When the exiled Bolingbroke engineered his return by a sizeable gift to the duchess of Kendal, Walpole was able to exclude him from his seat in the House of Lords. In the Commons and in the constituencies, Walpole built up his support by a pacific policy abroad and low taxes at home. Even the death of George I in 1727 did little to shake Walpole's grasp because he could count on the support of Queen Caroline, the brilliant consort of George II (1727–1760). She and Walpole concerted plans for the government, and it was her job to persuade the king to give his assent. Her early death in 1737 was a serious blow to Walpole.

Walpole created a new model for a prime minister. He developed patronage to a fine art. By the judicious use of positions in the gift of the crown, whether in the military services, the church, the civil administration, or the court, he built a stable majority in the Commons. Secret service funds were generously disbursed to control votes in the Parliament and win elections in the constituencies. In the House of Lords the votes of the sixteen representative peers of Scotland, who were chosen from a government-selected list, and of the bishops ensured him a working majority. Walpole's success rested on a combination of royal support, his ability in finance, his skill in forging parliamentary majorities out of the many interests and factions, and, above all, his remaining in the House of Commons and resisting the temptation of a peerage and his consequent removal to the upper house.

Sir Robert Walpole in the House of Commons. An engraving after a painting by Hogarth and Thornhill. Corbis-Bettmann.

George II. An engraving,
c. 1750. Kenneth Spencer
Research Library.

The Opposition and the Excise Crisis

Walpole utilized a solid core of the court's supporters for votes in the Commons, but without the votes of independent, landed members of Parliament, he could not forge majorities. Power was concentrated in the hands of the landed gentry and the aristocracy—great landowners, many of whom controlled one or more seats in Parliament and whose collective interest exceeded that of the government. It was important to the landowners that the taxes remain low, even though taxes levied on land were the most reliable sources from which to raise funds. The other principal sources of government revenue were customs duties and the excise—a tax levied on selected commodities. In 1733, Walpole proposed the introduction of an excise tax on wine and tobacco coupled with a lowering of the land tax to one shilling in the pound (a rate of 5 percent). He expected that it would be warmly welcomed by the landed gentry. For once Walpole misstepped. Dr. Samuel Johnson reflected a widespread attitude when he described the excise as "a hateful tax levied upon commodities, and adjudged not by the common judges of property, but wretches hired by those to whom excise is paid." Initially attacked by the merchants and shopkeepers, who saw that its efficient collection would affect their commerce in contrast to the easily evaded customs, the issue was quickly seized on by the opposition and ballooned all out of proportion. Walpole was forced to abandon his scheme. The power of the press was emphatically illustrated by its role in the uproar.

The main credit for the defeat of the excise went to the resurgent parliamentary opposition. The Tories, discredited and disorganized, had been out of office since 1714, but as early as 1716 they began to join forces with disaffected Whigs. William Pulteney, once considered Walpole's protégé, had not been returned to office in 1720 when the Whig split was healed; soon after he began to cooperate with the Tories. Over the next decade, the weeding out of Sunderland's followers and any other Whig who showed signs of independence gradually swelled the ranks of the opposition. In 1727, under the inspiration of Bolingbroke, the opposition launched *The Craftsman*, which became their principal organ, and developed a program that gave them an aura of respectability. The opposition writers adopted the Roman orator Cato of Utica as their model with which to castigate the ministry. The court Whigs responded in kind, though with less brilliance, settling on Cicero as the one who epitomized their virtues. The basis of the opposition program was the perennial issues of the danger of a standing army and the undue influence of the crown in Parliament by the presence of placemen—political appointees to seats in Parliament—and pensioners. By espousing these sacrosanct themes, the very essence of Whig ideology, Bolingbroke could appeal to the patriotism of the voters. Brilliant writers such as Henry Fielding and Alexander Pope lent their pens. John Gay's *The Beggar's Opera* was only the most successful of numerous stage works sponsored by the opposition. They bore down so heavily upon the embattled Walpole that he introduced censorship for all theatrical productions.

British Diplomacy under Townshend and Walpole

Walpole's policy of stability at home required peace abroad. Townshend, who had returned to the ministry as lord president in 1720, set out to forge a series of alliances that would forward both Britain's and Hanover's interests. By allying Britain with France and Prussia, he sought a coalition designed at once to build a German coalition against Austria and to prevent Russian domination in the Baltic. By providing new security for Hanover, Townshend was in fact following much the same practice as his predecessor. Spain not only rebuffed Townshend's offer of an alliance but also concluded a treaty with Austria, giving more to the Habsburgs than it received. Britain then became more belligerent toward Spain, and British trade with the Spanish colonies deteriorated, reflecting Spain's failure to honor its obligations under the Treaty of Utrecht. Walpole became increasingly concerned for the effect of this hostility on trade and hence revenue. In 1730 Townshend was forced to resign, and Walpole took over the direction of foreign affairs.

Walpole then concluded a treaty with Spain that restored the rights of British merchants to trade in Spanish America, promising in return Britain's support for Spanish dynastic ambitions in Italy. In spite of Walpole's show of

Europe in the Eighteenth Century

goodwill, Spain had never really reconciled its basic hostility to England and its resentment of England's predominance in its colonial trade. The grievances over the loss of Gibraltar, border disputes in America, and the regulation of trading concessions were problem enough. But the real bone of contention was the lucrative and flourishing contraband trade carried on by

English merchants in Spanish America. The Spanish authorities retaliated by seizing British ships and torturing British seamen. The clamor of the public to obtain satisfaction for Spanish atrocities committed against British sailors, the agitation of the merchants for protection, and opposition charges that British honor was at stake finally pushed Walpole into the War of Jenkins' Ear with Spain in 1739.

THE GOVERNMENT OF WALPOLE

Walpole's Economic and Imperial Policies

As first lord of the Treasury, Walpole's main concern was to reform public finance by improving the revenue, cutting expenditures, and reducing the land tax, which was a principal cause of complaint among the country gentlemen in the House of Commons. The long wars with Louis XIV had led to imposition of a hodge-podge of customs duties to fund the huge debts that had been accumulated. Many of these duties were inimical to British trade and manufactures. Walpole cut duties on exports of British manufactured goods and imports of colonial products such as sugar, tobacco, and beaver skins. Lower duties reduced smuggling, which increased the income from the customs. With peace and growing prosperity the revenue of the crown rose and interest rates fell, which enabled Walpole to balance the budget and establish a sinking fund to begin reduction of the national debt.

Walpole's economic policy was popular not only with Whig merchants but with Tory landlords seeking outlets for the products of agriculture and rural industries. Walpole maintained the Navigation Acts and other aspects of mercantilism while seeking to reduce the many ways in which in which these laws interfered unnecessarily with the flow of trade. Parliament legislated restrictions when colonial trade or manufactures created competition with Britain, as in the Hat Act (1732); and the Molasses Act (1733), which attempted to block colonial trade with the French West Indies, was for the benefit of planters in the British West Indies.

Walpole relied on the chartered trading companies to conduct overseas trade, although the monopoly privileges of these companies were challenged by interlopers (unauthorized traders) and smugglers. The Russia Company conducted the valuable trade with Russia, which provided essential naval stores for the navy. The South Sea Company engaged in the legal trade with Spain and the Spanish colonies. The African Company maintained trading posts and forts along the African coast, and gave licenses to private traders to conduct the slave trade. Most important of all was the British East India Company, with its trading posts at Calcutta, Madras, and Bombay. The Company maintained its own army in India to deal with local princes, and built large, well-armed ships to weather the storms and fight off interlopers and pirates on their long voyages around Africa to India. By Walpole's time the main product in the Company's trade was tea, which was obtained from China. The Company began looking for a base that would be more convenient for the East Asian trade.

Walpole was not interested in imperial expansion, since he wished to avoid war and the political and financial complications that it entailed. Nor did he make any efforts to strengthen the colonial governors in their relations with the colonial assemblies. The relationship between the controlling center and subordinate parts remained undeveloped and undefined. As long as the colonies were not a cost to the Exchequer, Walpole was willing to let them manage their own affairs through their assemblies. Despite colonial complaints, in most instances the mercantilist system was beneficial to the colonies as well as to the Mother Country. The colonists had access to the world's greatest trading area under the protection of the world's most powerful navy. The empire prospered under a policy that Edmund Burke later characterized as "salutary neglect."

Scotland

To the north was Scotland, politically and economically incorporated with England by the Act of Union (1707) but culturally a separate nation, with its own history, church, legal system, and traditions. The secretaries of state in London exercised power over Scottish domestic affairs through an official called the lord advocate, who controlled the Scottish legal and administrative structure. The Scottish members of the British Parliament were mainly subservient to the crown and the ministry, for politics to them was primarily a source of patronage and profits.

The Act of Union was at first unpopular in Scotland, but under the Union Scotland began to grow in population and wealth. Lowland Scots found a good market for their cattle in England. The quality of Scottish cattle was improved by the introduction of turnips for winter feed and by better pastures based on clover and grasses. Potatoes, introduced to Scotland via English trade, became a valuable addition to the Scottish diet. Scotland's woolen cloth industry was injured by English competition, but its linen industry grew as domestic and foreign markets expanded.

The most important economic effect of the Union was access to trade with the empire. Glasgow merchants thrived on the growing trade in colonial sugar and tobacco, and a ship-building industry developed to meet the demand. Outgoing vessels needed cargoes, which encouraged the development of Scottish industries. The wealth generated by trade created a demand at home for clothing, furniture, and other personal and domestic items.

Although it had lost its Parliament, Edinburgh continued as the principal city. Though foul and congested, the city remained the social center of Scotland. The most prominent Scottish leaders went to London during the winter for the meetings of Parliament, the courts, and the winter social season. Nevertheless, Edinburgh remained the center of the Scottish administration and courts and the Church of Scotland. Without significant Scottish politics, many ambitious Scots turned to the law and the church to develop careers. Edinburgh was a center of printing and publishing, and its shops and craftsmen made a variety of high-quality consumer goods. Despite the disapproval of the earnest Presbyterians of the Church of Scotland, a theatre was built there in 1746. The University of Edinburgh added to the prestige and cultural life of the city.

Ireland

Ireland was Britain's largest and most important dependency. In the middle of the eighteenth century the population of Ireland (3 million) was almost half that of England and Wales and greater than the combined population of the North American colonies (2 million). Dublin, with a population of 100,000 was the second largest city in the British Isles and one of the largest cities in Europe. Irish trade was roughly equal to that of all thirteen North American colonies. Although the British market was in most respects closed to Irish products, Ireland was a major exporter to Europe of meat, cheese, wool, linen, and hides. Irish provisions became especially important to the British army and navy in time of war.

The political system of eighteenth-century Ireland was designed to maintain British supremacy. The king of England was also king of Ireland, with the right to fill all offices in state and church. The crown exercised its authority through the viceroy [lord lieutenant], usually a prominent English aristocrat, who maintained an elegant court in Dublin Castle. The Irish Parliament was constituted on the British model of Lords and Commons, but legislatively it was subordinate to the British Parliament. The Irish revenue was almost entirely hereditary in the crown, and consequently the Irish Parliament had no significant "power of the purse." The Irish Parliament usually met every two years and sessions were brief, which further reduced its influence.

The people of Ireland were divided politically, socially, and by religion. The Anglo-Irish ruling class was English in language and culture. Their members held the political offices and controlled the Irish Parliament, Church, army, and local government. They were the landlords, merchants, and professional people. The Anglo-Irish kept in close touch with British ideas, books, and fashions; they often felt like outsiders in their homeland and many of the most able and ambitious went to England to pursue careers.

The Church of Ireland was the Irish equivalent of the Church of England. It served the Anglo-Irish, but not well. (A few dedicated and distinguished clergymen, such as Swift, mitigate the severity of this charge.) Most of the bishops and many of the clergy were English. To an English clergymen whose only hope was an Irish post, a move to Ireland was an exile only partially assuaged by the mail, books, and periodic visits to England.

The Scots-Irish were Presbyterian immigrants from Scotland who began settling in Ireland in the reign of James I. They were excluded by religious tests from holding office under the crown or sitting in Parliament, although these restrictions were mitigated by Acts of Indemnity. The Scots-Irish had the right to vote, and the Irish Toleration Act of 1719 gave them the same freedom of worship possessed by the Dissenters in England. Most of the Scots-Irish were farmers or artisans settled principally in Ulster.

The Catholic Irish were approximately 75 percent of the population. Catholic support for James II in the Glorious Revolution brought fierce retribution. Catholic leaders lost their lands and political power while the Protestant Parliament passed laws designed to keep Catholics poor, uneducated, and politically powerless. Catholics could not hold office under the crown, sit in Parliament, hold local office, or vote. The Penal Code declared that Catholics could not possess weapons, enlist in the army or navy, possess a horse worth more than £5, conduct a school or attend a university, practice a profession, engage in business in any incorporated town, buy or inherit land, or be the guardian of a child. Catholic bishops and monks were prohibited; Catholic priests had to register and take an oath of allegiance before they could legally perform their functions. Under these conditions many Catholic Irish left for the continent, where they served in foreign armies or as priests.

While the Irish Protestants used their political power to suppress the Catholics, they also became increasingly resentful of British control of Irish affairs. British politicians used Irish offices and pensions to provide incomes for their friends. Furthermore, Ireland was forced to maintain a large standing army to back up the British army. From time to time the British Parliament used its legislative supremacy to restrict the Irish economy for the benefit of British producers.

By the 1740s, many of the political and social tensions in Ireland had diminished. Despite restrictions, a Catholic middle class of landowners and merchants was beginning to emerge, which had a vested interest in the status quo. Ireland had a shortage of skilled labor, and those Catholic Irish who had developed skills were often permitted to ply their trade. Despite the Protestant ascendancy, the Catholic clergy had learned to manage. Supported by voluntary contributions from the faithful, a network of bishops and priests developed, including rural "mass houses" and even schools. Some Protestants began to think that it was possible to get along with the Catholics without constant suspicion and hostility.

The Fall of Walpole

In 1740 Emperor Charles VI of Austria died, and his daughter and heir, Maria Theresa, succeeded to her father's possessions. Frederick II ("the Great") of Prussia used this opportunity to snatch the province of Silesia from the young queen, thereby launching the War of the Austrian Succession (1740–1748). France, Spain, and Bavaria could not resist the opportunity to join Frederick in his dismemberment of the Habsburg domains, with Bavaria wresting the imperial title away from Maria Theresa's husband. Walpole had no choice but to come to the aid of the beleaguered Austrians. The specter of a hostile Prussia to the east of Hanover and threatening French armies on the southwest only added to Walpole's predicament. When George II, as elector of Hanover, concluded a convention of neutrality to save Hanover (1741) and cast his ballot as elector for the French candidate for emperor, Charles Albert of Bavaria, Walpole's humiliation was complete. The aged (sixty-six-year-old) prime minister was finally forced to retire in 1742 after an embarrassing reversal in the parliamentary elections of 1742 and a series of defeats in the session that followed. By accepting a peerage he escaped the wrath of the opposition in the Commons.

THE PELHAMS

The New Ministry

When Walpole had sacked Carteret in 1724, he had replaced him with the inoffensive but industrious duke of Newcastle, a man who had inherited great wealth and electoral influence. Newcastle's political apprenticeship began when Walpole made him Carteret's successor as secretary of state in 1724. He learned well from Walpole the management of patronage; in time he engrossed control over crown appointments in the church, the colonies, and many other places. Because he and his astute brother but junior colleague, Henry Pelham, had favored the Spanish war and acquiesced in George II's capitulation in Germany, Newcastle did not share his patron's fall. William Pulteney, long Walpole's bête noire and now finally restored to office, was nominally the ministry's leader, but he committed himself to political oblivion by taking a peerage as earl of Bath. Moreover, he allowed the Treasury to go to Spencer Compton, who also took refuge in the Lords, as earl of Wilmington. Carteret, who returned to a secretaryship, proved the one truly vigorous new addition to the cabinet, where his skill in languages and intimate knowledge of European affairs made him a royal favorite.

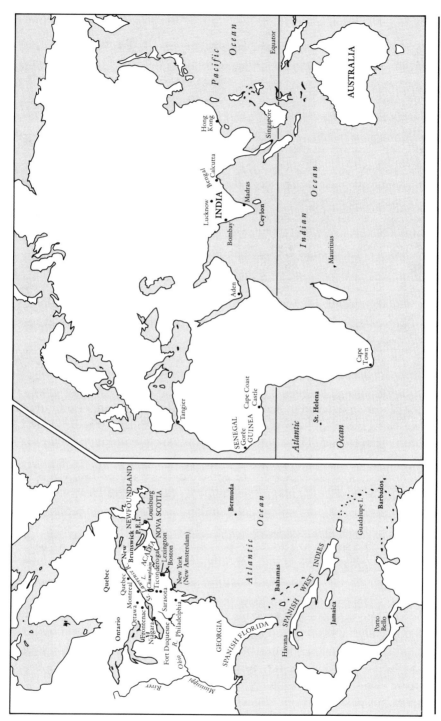

The First British Empire

The War of the Austrian Succession and "Bonnie Prince Charlie"

So far as England was concerned, the middle years of the War of the Austrian Succession were as much a scene of battle at home as they were abroad. Indeed Britain was hardly more successful in Europe than the king was in promoting Carteret. The war largely favored France and its ally, Prussia. England and its allies, especially Austria, which was important for supporting Hanoverian claims, did win a victory at Dettingen in 1743 on which occasion George II personally took command of the troops. Though the French were the opponents, war was not officially opened between the two countries until 1744. The confusion in motives and goals that characterized this conflict is indicated by the several sets of overlapping belligerencies. They included not only the war with Spain but a separate and parallel conflict in the colonies between France and England known as King George's War. Though the real focus of competition lay in the Americas and beyond, the ostensible struggle was in Europe. The critical role of Hanover obscured the real interests of both parties. Carteret, with his preoccupation with European affairs and his disdain for the business of parliamentary management, was forced to give way completely to the Pelhams in 1745, two years after Henry Pelham had been promoted to first lord of the Treasury upon the death of Wilmington.

The newly united ministry faced its most immediate challenge from still another source. Yet another (and final) Jacobite invasion was launched in 1745 by France to neutralize Britain. Led by the Pretender's son, "Bonnie Prince Charlie," the uprising began in Scotland in July, and by September Edinburgh had fallen. But Charles misstepped and pressed into England where his local support soon evaporated. He advanced as far as Derby in December but was then forced by his officers to retreat to Scotland. The king's favorite son, the duke of Cumberland, aggressively pursued him, and the superior resources of the English government soon told. In April Cumberland routed Charles's army, then he mercilessly hunted down the survivors, earning him the epithet "the Butcher."

At about the same time, the king precipitated a crisis in London. In February 1746, the king informed Pelham of his decision to reinstate Carteret, now the earl of Granville, and the earl of Bath, to head the ministry. Pelham responded by resigning, and the entire cabinet resigned en bloc in sympathy. The king was undone because Granville had not heeded Walpole's lesson and had failed to build a base of support in Parliament. Unable to draft a new Cabinet, he and the king were forced to surrender; Pelham and his colleagues returned to office on their own terms. Seeking to pull the teeth of the opposition, Pelham constructed his ministry on a "broad bottom" basis, including as many factions as possible to gain the widest possible support. The only major group left out of the ministry was the faction around the heir to the throne, the prince of Wales.

The Conclusion of the War

Pelham's first responsibility was to bring the war to an end. While England had been putting down an internal revolt, the war had gone badly for the country and its allies on the continent. The French capitalized on early victories and occupied Brussels and the Austrian Netherlands, while Britain's allies, Austria and Sardinia, suffered defeat in southern Europe. Only the death of the Emperor Charles VII (Charles Albert of Bavaria) early in 1745 offered any hope for a negotiated settlement by opening the imperial throne once more to a Habsburg candidate, Maria Theresa's husband, Francis of Lorraine. Indeed English success in arms existed only in one theater, but one prophetically important—North America. The heavy continental military obligations in the wars against Louis XIV and again in the present war had prevented the commitment of substantial forces against Spain in the western hemisphere. Although early disappointments led the British to abandon campaigns in the West Indies, the war went well in the north when, in June 1745, a small expedition of New England colonists supported by British naval forces captured Louisburg, the great French fortress on Cape Breton Island, which was the key to control of the St. Lawrence River, the gateway to French Canada. However, the capture of Louisburg proved more of an embarrassment than a prize; it retarded peace efforts, for the French could not rest until it was retaken. The British public on the other hand was so overjoyed at this victory that its retention became obligatory. In 1747 Pelham suddenly called parliamentary elections to take advantage of his newly found support. The solid majority he won made it possible for him to risk an unpopular peace settlement. French victories in the Low Countries and elsewhere gave little prospect of military success in Europe, though the naval victories of Anson and Hawke in the New World did reassert British supremacy on the seas. France, too, saw reason to negotiate a peace, not least because of a serious famine and a major fiscal crisis in 1747. The peace of Aix-la-Chapelle that followed in 1748 was essentially a recognition of the exhaustion of the belligerents. British ambitions for Canada were temporarily abandoned as Louisburg was returned to France. Both countries recognized that the cessation of hostilities was not permanent.

Pelham and Leicester House

For the remaining years of his ministry, Pelham strove to maintain his political strength in Parliament while restoring stability to the king's finances and prosperity to the economy. His first effort was to reduce taxes. He did so by drastically reducing the size of the fleet and the army. In the political sphere, the coalition of parties Pelham had put together proved effective. The main threat to his regime came from the men who gathered around the king's son, Frederick, the prince of Wales and heir apparent to the throne, who met at the prince's residence, Leicester House. Ever since he had broken with his father, George II, in 1736, the prince of Wales had sought to maintain an independent political base. In spite of financial difficulties, he had built up a formidable circle of advisers in the late years of the Walpole regime. Pelham had weaned most of them back in building his coalition ministry in 1746. But the advancing age of the king (who was sixty-three in 1746) made Frederick's succession inevitable, and Pelham patiently negotiated through intermediaries to prepare himself for this eventuality. The unexpected death of the prince in 1751 dramatically altered the situation. A resumption of Walpolean tranquillity characterized England in the early 1750s until another early death—that of Henry Pelham in March 1754—brought it all to an end. George II was perhaps the most sincere and realistic mourner when he commented, "I shall have no more peace."

HANOVERIAN IDEAS AND SOCIETY

The Age of Reason

At the same time that Britain's stature in European affairs grew, the country participated fully in another European phenomenon, the Enlightenment. As the old religious controversies subsided and the ideological contests abated, a new tone and confident spirit characterized the publications of the major British literary figures. The periodical essay spawned by Joseph Addison and Richard Steele in the *Spectator* (1711) had countless imitators well into the middle of the century when it inspired Samuel Johnson's *Rambler* (1750) and *Idler* (1758). Elegant, devastating satire reached its peak in the mock epics of Alexander Pope. Elegiac pastoral verse glorified the serenity and natural beauty of the countryside, a retreat from the glamour and artificiality of the city.

History as a guide and means of instruction took on new importance as a subject for laborious tomes and learned essays. It reached its peak in the phenomenally popular six-volume *History of England* (1754–1762) by the eminent Scottish philosopher David Hume, who set a standard not to be challenged for a century to come. Hume also epitomized another aspect of the intellectual life of the Age of Reason; his several philosophical treatises deemed all knowledge empirical and struck at the very foundation of religion. Seeking to create a moral philosophy that would accomplish for the world of ideas what Newton had accomplished for the world of science, Hume stands at the intellectual watershed of the eighteenth century.

The refined elegance of Pope and Hume were not the only models for eighteenth-century writers. The savage irony of Jonathan Swift in *Gulliver's*

Travels (1726) attracted a wide audience as did the more conventional but nonetheless compelling imagination of Daniel Defoe in *Robinson Crusoe* (1719). Skill in expression was not limited to one political faction. The dominant Whig propagandists of the Hanoverian period found their match in the powerful Toryism of the most celebrated literary figure of the mid-eighteenth century, Samuel Johnson.

The new quest for knowledge, the growth of a leisured class, and the general increase in prosperity all resulted in a vast and sustained growth in publishing. Whether practical manuals for farmers or justices of the peace, the newly developed novel aimed at readers of both sexes, books catering to hobbies and diversions of the most heterogeneous kind, or essays on topics as varied as economics, raising fish, or guides for the grand tour, the emphasis of the reading material of the new age was on novelty and practicality. The most notable omission from mainstream literature was the focus on religion that had characterized the work of the preceding century.

The Church in the Early Hanoverian Period

Under the new regime, the vehement efforts of the clergy and the high church party to preserve their monopoly of political offices and representation in Parliament, their unrelenting efforts to inhibit and restrict the Dissenters, their churches and schools, their strenuous support of the Tories, and their equivocal attitude to the Revolution and the Protestant succession proved to be liabilities for the church. Only the Whigs' patent weakness in the Parliament and in the country had prevented them from completing the repeal of the Test and Corporation Acts in 1718 and reducing the universities to a place of complete subservience. The opposition of the Anglican archbishop to the proposed statutory repeals condemned him to twenty years of political neglect and isolation. In 1717 Benjamin Hoadly, who had been made a bishop for his services as a political pamphleteer, delivered a famous sermon before the king in which he attacked the very basis of the church's authority by denying its institutional significance and the role of the priest as intermediary between God and worshipper. The furor that resulted both in Convocation and the press gave the crown the excuse to prorogue the Convocation, which was not permitted to meet again until 1855. The hiatus removed the potential vehicle for badly needed church reforms.

The geographical distribution and sizes of the dioceses were woefully uneven, but the income to support the bishops and their offices was even more unequal. In countless parishes the income was insufficient to maintain a clergyman, and the consequence was that many pulpits lay vacant. Not infrequently the incumbents were pluralists, holding several benefices at once. In 1704 Queen

Anne gave back to the church the fee exacted from each cleric as he entered into his benefice, for use by commissioners to raise the income of the poorest positions. This did something to mitigate the most pressing cases, but the essential inequities remained, especially among the bishops, whose annual incomes ranged from a low of £450 at Bristol to a high of £7,000 at Canterbury. Many of the duties of the see fell personally on the bishop who was not authorized to employ deputies or suffragans. The requirement for bishops to attend the House of Lords kept most of them absent from their dioceses for much of the year. Some of the bishops, either because of infirmity or neglect, did not return to their dioceses as often or stay as long as they should have. Furthermore, the uneven size of the dioceses created exceptional burdens for some bishops. Lincoln, the largest diocese, had 1,312 parishes—a marked difference from Carlisle, which had only 100. Edmund Gibson, bishop of London and Walpole's ecclesiastical adviser, proposed a number of plans to correct the worst abuses and to enable the church to carry out its duties, all of which foundered either on the Scylla of ministerial indifference or the Charybdis of lay hostility. Although the civil disabilities of the Dissenters were not removed until 1828 they managed to participate in the political process because a series of indemnity acts relieved them of the statutory penalties. This was the Hanoverian modus vivendi, a compromise that satisfied few but was tolerable to most.

Wesley and the Methodist Revival

The church had fallen into such a state of lassitude that it was unable to meet the spiritual needs of the people. Sermons were cold and formal and did little to evoke enthusiasm and religious fervor. The writings of latitudinarian clergymen such as Benjamin Hoadly, the Deists, and mystical writers such as the nonjuror William Law did little to reinforce a devotion to the established church. To fill this void, Methodism arose within the church. The founder and leader was John Wesley. Ordained in the Church of England and a graduate of Oxford, a member there of a severe, ascetic society, Wesley went with James Oglethorpe, the founder of Georgia, to that colony in 1735. On the voyage he became acquainted with several Moravians, members of a German Protestant sect. On his return to England he was deeply influenced by an eminent member of that sect, Peter Boehler, and embraced the tenets that became the foundation of Methodism: the doctrine of justification by faith, the belief that every man existed in a state of damnation until the moment of conversion, and the recognition that Christ had expiated man's sins. Wesley and the band of followers he attracted from the regular clergy preached the new doctrine with fervor and success. Their objective was to create Methodist societies as churches within the church to rekindle religious enthusiasm and commitment among

Interior of John Wesley's Chapel. Private collection.

Anglicans. Denied a hearing from the pulpits of the established church, the Methodists turned to preaching in fields and any place where they could gain a hearing. In 1739 they created their own chapels, and in 1741 Wesley instituted lay preachers. Those new missionaries were dedicated to saving souls and found an enthusiastic reception among the lower classes, especially in those places where the established church did not reach. In Wales, for example, the great majority of the population joined their chapels.

Though Wesley did his best to keep the societies within the Anglican tradition, he finally broke with the Anglican church in 1783 by appointing a bishop to supervise the Methodists in America. In 1784 he began ordaining clergy for Scotland. The Methodists offered the hope of salvation to those whose lot was most unfortunate and miserable. They were responsible for a general revival of religious feeling in England, both within the Church of England where Anglicans were revitalized and reinvigorated and outside the established church.

A Civilization of Gentlemen

One of the salient features of Georgian Britain was its enormous appetite for knowledge. The great breakthroughs in thought and science had been made in the later seventeenth century. Despite strenuous resistance, as in Swift's *Gulliver's Travels*, the new ideas made rapid headway, disseminated by a flood of books, reference works, and periodicals. The advances of the Georgian age resulted primarily from the efforts of gentleman-scholars using personal observations and simple equipment. The Royal Society, comprised of aristocrats and gentlemen, barristers, physicians, clergymen, merchants, and other dedicated amateurs continued as the center of scholarly activity, holding meetings, reading papers, and publishing the results in the *Philosophical Transactions.* Papers on local history and antiquities, distinctive plants and animals, diseases, travel accounts, sightings of unusual celestial activity, and the like, were published by the Royal Society or in periodicals such as *The Gentleman's Magazine.*

Electricity

One kind of scientific investigation that could be carried out by a gentleman at modest expense was the study of electricity. Electrical experiments first became feasible in the 1740s, when machines were developed to generate static electricity by rubbing a whirling glass globe or tube with one's hand or a pad. The resultant electrical charge was collected and stored in a suspended gun barrel, connected to the rotating globe by a silk cord. In 1745 electrical experimentation was further advanced by the invention of the Leyden Jar, a corked glass container filled with water, which was attached by a wire to the gun barrel. A series of Leyden Jars linked together could emit a powerful electrical discharge. With this simple equipment electricity became a popular subject for scientific study, and electrical demonstrations provided entertainment at social gatherings. People at a party would join hands, laughing and screaming with amazement when the gun barrel was touched by one of the party, causing everyone to leap simultaneously as the shock traveled through them. The King of Prussia made an even more dramatic display, performing the experiment with a regiment of guardsmen, who all rose as one when the electrical connection was made.

Perhaps the age's best-known scientist hailed from England's North American colonies. Benjamin Franklin, a Philadelphia publisher, took electricity out of the realm of party games by demonstrating that lightning was an electrical discharge. Like many inquisitive gentlemen, Franklin had long been interested in weather, tides, winds, and storms. His stroke of genius was to link his interest in weather with the new ideas on electricity. In his *Experiments and Observations* (1751), first published in *The Gentleman's Magazine,* Franklin offered a theory of precipitation based on the assumption that rainfall was caused by changes in the electrical charges of clouds. To demonstrate that clouds were electrified, Franklin made the famous experiment in which he flew a kite into a thunderstorm. The practical bent characteristic of eighteenth-century science was seen when Franklin showed that the damage of lightning— long feared as the thunderbolt of Zeus—could be avoided by the simple device of a lightning rod, fastened to the top of a house or barn or to the mast of a ship.

Despite a few demurrers, Franklin's achievement was accepted almost immediately. It had the simplicity and universality that people of the eighteenth-century admired. Part of Franklin's success was his literary skill: his reports were presented in the form of letters to a friend; his style was warm, frank, and engaging as he revealed the procedures he had followed, the conclusions he had reached, and his missteps along the way. When the Royal Society conferred its Copley Medal on Franklin in 1753 the chairman praised, not only his scientific work but "the public spirit, the modesty, the goodness and benevolence" that he had displayed. Franklin was in every respect an eighteenth-century gentleman, and his scientific achievements were a vindication of the breed.

The Justices of the Peace

The local government structure in England was and is unique in the Western world. Essentially, it was in the hands of the ubiquitous justice of the peace, an unpaid administrator drawn from the local gentry or gentlemen. This office, the origins of which go back to the early Middle Ages, began to take familiar shape in the fifteenth century, and in the Tudor period the office became the center of local government. Until the civil wars it was regulated by the lord chancellor, reviewed and instructed by the Privy Council, and disciplined by Star Chamber. When the prerogative jurisdiction was abolished, the justices of the peace became virtually independent. The Privy Council could still issue directives but did so only in emergencies. The judges in the semiannual assizes had a larger role. They heard criminal cases with which the justices could not or chose not to deal, and they also heard appeals from the justices and rendered decisions on disputes regarding rights to property. In conjunction with the justices the judges issued orders concerning local administration. But any supervisory authority had lapsed by the eighteenth century.

By the Georgian period, the justices singly issued licenses for inns and taverns, heard minor civil cases, and performed other local administrative functions. Acting in twos or more they had much greater authority. Furthermore, all justices were automatically appointed to the commissions for the land and window taxes. It was through these commissions and the petty sessions that they wielded their power. Their administrative authority and their ability to affect taxes gave them substantial political influence. Those over whom they held sway were often empowered to vote in parliamentary elections, hence the justices of the peace had a critical if not deciding voice in elections.

Because of the political influence of the justices, it followed that the political parties, as they evolved, tried to control the appointment of the county justices. Charles II and even more notoriously his brother James II made whole-sale replacements on the bench in an effort to insure the return of members of Parliament favorable to their policies. As Whigs and Tories alternated in con-trol of the government after the Revolution, it had been widely assumed by historians that the same policy prevailed. Strictly speaking, this was not the case, for the power of appointment rested ostensibly and exclusively with the lord chancellor. Nonetheless, recent examination of the records reveals that Lord Somers and Sir Nathan Wright under William III and Wright and Lord Harcourt under Anne did indeed try to pack the bench with their political allies. They did so by adding new members, not by turning out old ones. The result was that they ran out of appropriate candidates, gentlemen who had the income and position to support their appointment, and resorted to appointing men of lesser quality. When Lord Cowper returned to the Lord Chancellor-ship after the Hanoverian succession he realized that the number of justices was unwieldy and began to reduce the size of the county benches, which he did by conveniently rooting out Tories. Cowper's policy was continued by his successor, Lord Macclesfield, so that by the accession of George II most county benches had Whig majorities.

The reason why political control demanded a majority of like-minded justices was that they acted in concert in the quarter sessions. There and at the assizes the bench as a whole had the power to discipline individual justices and overturn their decisions. When Philip Yorke, Lord Hardwicke, began his long (20 years) tenure at the great seal in 1737, he found the Whig domination of the bench virtually complete. However, many Tories had made their peace with the government and for some years in the 1740s actually supported and served in a coalition government. Moreover, it was not deemed proper to dis-enfranchise good Protestant gentry, so that Tories gradually began to appear once more on the lists. Though Hardwicke took nominations from lords lieu-tenants, members of Parliament, and other individuals of importance, the fi-nal decision was his, and the lord chancellor wielded that authority fully. Once appointed, justices were rarely dismissed, except for the period between 1685 and 1725. Secure in their power, and conscious of their responsibility, the jus-tices of the peace generally functioned successfully and well. Whether licens-ing taverns, supervising road and bridge construction and repair, attending to the poor, assessing taxes, hearing cases, or performing a myriad of local ad-ministrative chores, they provided a sound, intelligent, generally knowledge-able, and remarkably vigilant and cooperative local administration for the coun-try. With little supervision by crown or parliament they reached the peak of their power in the 150 years after the Glorious Revolution. The duties they performed they performed because they wanted to do so. Those matters that

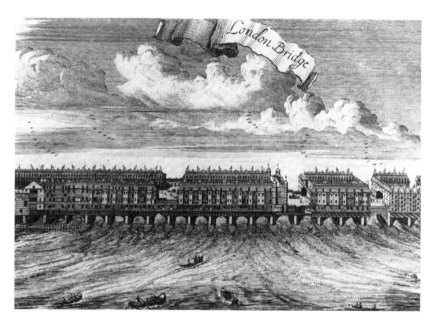

Top: The Tower of London. From an engraving, c. 1720. Bottom: Old London Bridge.
From an engraving, c. 1720. Both, courtesy Kenneth Spencer Research Library.

did not interest them or to which they objected were ignored. Such was the nature of local government in England in the eighteenth century.

TOWN AND COUNTRY IN JOHNSON'S ENGLAND

London and Westminster

The jewel of a revitalized Britain was London. When Samuel Johnson, the great lexicographer, pundit, and famous devotee of London, first saw the great metropolis in 1737 he must have found much to impress him. At this time London comprised more than 500,000 people, ten times more than Bristol, England's second largest city at the time. The eastern-most district was notable for the bustling Pool of London, the inner harbor that served as the main port of commerce. Rising above the Thames stood the Tower of London, imposing in its Norman splendor, a prominent landmark from the river. If Johnson made his way west from the Tower the next object to command his attention was old London Bridge, located opposite the splendid new cathedral of St. Paul's, Wren's masterpiece that dominated the city skyline. The bridge, the only span across the lower Thames until Westminster Bridge was constructed in 1750, had been built over completely. It presented a quaint sight of ramshackle old buildings of varying heights and style, stuck fast together and hanging perilously over the water, with a bustling traffic crowded into the narrow passage remaining between the houses.

Below the bridge, to the east, scores of tenements, warehouses, and wharves crowded the river's edge. Above the bridge there were most impressive structures to behold. The palaces and great houses of the nobility and wealthy on the north bank extended westward to a bend in the Thames where one found Whitehall Palace and the Palace of Westminster. After the bridge, Johnson would have made his way through Stockmarket to St. Paul's churchyard, past the church "already so black with coal-smoke that it has lost half its elegance," then down Ludgate Hill to the Fleet out of the City at Temple Bar. The streets of London were reckoned by a German writer as "the finest in Europe," full of taverns, houses, and shops "where the choicest merchandise from the four quarters of the globe is exposed to the sight of the passers-by [and] a stranger might spend whole days, without ever feeling bored, examining these wonderful goods." This was the part of London that Johnson especially loved, where he lived, worked, and passed his hours in memorable conversation. The bookshops and printers and the attendant writers were so numerous in this district that one short passage called Grub Street gave its name to a whole genre and period of the English press. North of the Strand was an area thick with mansions and highlighted by Covent Garden, the square laid out by Inigo Jones a century earlier and, even in Johnson's time, a market for flowers, fruits, and vegetables.

Passing into Charing Cross Johnson could have seen the Admiralty and the famous Banqueting Hall, which was all that remained of the old Whitehall Palace after it burned in 1698. Ahead lay the Palace of Westminster, seat of the Parliament and law courts—a conglomeration of buildings, chapels, houses, meeting halls, and offices adapted to a multiplicity of uses over many centuries. The most impressive of the structures was Westminster Hall, which dated back to the time of William Rufus, but, hedged in as it was by so many smaller buildings, only its upper portion and roof were exposed to view. Even Westminster Abbey and the parish church of St. Margaret were crowded about, though the lofty towers and the exquisite tracery of Henry VII's chapel were a sight to delight the eye.

Life in London

The appearance of the king's principal London residence, St. James's Palace, was not attractive; a squat, drab structure that dated from the time of Henry VIII, it lies about a quarter of a mile northwest of the Abbey, adjacent to Pall Mall. A series of parks to the south and west furnished an attractive prospect and a popular place for relaxation and recreation for the inhabitants who lived nearby. The most impressive house in the park was that of the duke of Buckingham. To the west, at the end of Hyde Park, lay Kensington Palace, acquired by William III in order to escape the damp and fog of the river. Villages and estates generally occupied the land west and north of Westminster, and these areas remained predominantly rural into the next century. The streets of the town were of all sorts, some "dirty, narrow, and badly built; others again are wide and straight, bordered with fine houses [and] most of the streets are wonderfully well lighted." The parks were not well lit, and the public that thronged them on Sundays tried to be back in the town before dark to avoid becoming a target for the highwaymen who frequented the lanes, one of whom, at least on one occasion, held up the king at pistol point in his own garden.

Beyond the great houses and royal parks, especially in the city, there was squalor, poverty, and filth. Some of those who flocked to London for employment found seasonal work only, serving the needs of the great families when they came into town for the winter season. Much of the year these less fortunate migrants were unemployed and lived by their wits. Robbery and petty thievery were commonplace. Living conditions were wretched; the water was foul taken straight out of the river at the bridge by "a curious machine which turns in either direction, according to the tide, so that it is always in use." The consequence was regular epidemics of cholera and other waterborne diseases until the middle of the nineteenth century. Life expectancy was short. A sur-

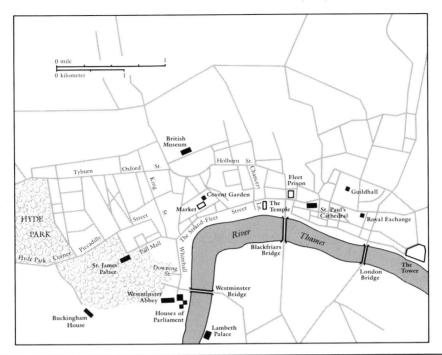

Johnson's London

vey made in 1716 showed that of 1,200 children born in a parish, three-fourths were dead within the year. Parish officials consigned the poor to workhouses where conditions were abominable. In mid-century another survey revealed that of 2,239 children who passed through the workhouse only 168 were alive at the end of five years. The large criminal class and the ever-present press gangs used to provide recruits for the navy and colonists for the Americas made life so dangerous that the young James Watt, who lived in London in 1783, hardly left his house during the entire time of his residence there. Bullbaiting, cockfighting, and public hangings were among the favorite entertainments; beer and gin were the standard beverages. Gin was so cheap and unlicensed dramshops so numerous—by 1736, 6,000 to 7,000 in London alone—that consumption rose to unprecedented heights. The city was in literal danger of extinction as the oppressed lower classes drowned their sorrows and forgot their miseries in alcohol.

Bristol, the Capital of the West

Although no city approached London in size and scope, the increase in population over the century necessarily affected major provincial centers. The city that benefited most from this expansion in the first half of the century was

Bristol. With a population of more than 20,000 people, Bristol displaced Nor-wich as the second largest city in England after the turn of the century, its newfound status the result of overseas trade. As the unofficial capital of the west, Bristol aggrandized at the expense of its neighbors. Its geographical po-sition on the Bristol Channel, dominating the coast, and its function as the gateway to the river and canal network of the Severn and Wye gave Bristol a commanding position. Between 1700 and 1750 the number of ships leaving the city doubled, and it rose again by the 1770s to more than 1,700 ships a year. While Bristol consumed the bulk of the agricultural products produced in its region, it was also a major entrepôt for raw materials, many of which were reshipped to London. Local manufacturers—metalworks, soap, glass, sugar refining—accounted for a considerable portion of the trade. Timber from the Baltic, linen from Germany, agricultural products from such diverse places as the Mediterranean, Africa, the West Indies, and North America all were brought to Bristol. The mining and metal industries of Wales that prospered in the eighteenth century were financed and controlled by Bristol merchants. The heavy commerce in turn generated banks and insurance companies, so much so that Bristol was second only to London in the number of underwriters it supported. By the end of the century, however, Bristol's level of commerce began to decline. The American trade, of primary importance to the city, never regained its strength after the Revolution, and Liverpool and other western ports gradually took over its position. Bristol's heyday, then, coincided with the expansion of the American colonies and passed with their independence.

Country Life

At this time the rest of England was rural. Few towns had more than 10,000 people; most towns were much smaller—in reality mere villages and market-places. The leading families of provincial towns were professional men and merchants whose scale of living was comfortable rather than ostentatious. Rural (landed) wealth was centered in the aristocracy and gentry whose great coun-try houses rose in stark contrast to the humble, often squalid homes of the rural agricultural laborers and the working poor in the towns. The cottagers who found work were fortunate. Often the only support for a family was that of carding and spinning wool, an employment chiefly reserved for women and children. Until the mid-eighteenth century poor families could eke out a liv-ing from the commons, cutting wood, raising geese and perhaps some live-stock, taking odd jobs, and poaching. (The great series of enclosure acts later in the century deprived the poor of these means of subsistence.)

The artisan class flourished in the towns. Cabinetmakers, shoemakers, tailors, butchers, cobblers, smiths, and drapers populated the shops. The resi-dents of the market towns were specially engaged in serving the local landowners and providing for their amusement and comfort. In the west and the northeast of England the wool trade was their main support. Marked by the absence of paved streets, police, and good water and other amenities, the towns were not improved until the second half of the century. In the smaller ones, the parish was often the unit of government, with the church responsible for what little education the lower and middle classes received. As roads and communications improved and the nation increased in wealth and population, the county centers began to take on some of the attributes of the metropolis. Newspapers were founded, theaters opened, booksellers established, and concert assembly rooms erected for the entertainment of local society. But even to the end of the eighteenth century the scale of towns remained small, the diversions they offered limited.

The Country House

London always remained the social center without rival, especially during the social season, coinciding with the meeting of parliament, which extended from late fall to early spring. For the gentry the summer assizes provided the excuse for social interchanges after they had returned to their estates. Apart from London, there remained yet another social center, indeed hundreds of them—the country house of the wealthy. The country house may have reached its apogee in England in the first half of the eighteenth century. That span, the period of the first two Georges, may well contain its finest examples, although fine specimens exist from the times before and after. Hardwicke Hall epitomized the great Elizabethan house, as does Hatfield House the Jacobean. Boughton House, rebuilt and extended by the first duke of Montagu in the 1690s, impresses one by its magnificence and its purity, for it remains essentially unaltered from the time it was completed until the present day. Moreover, its mansard roofs and interior designs evoke Versailles and the French chateaux the duke admired while ambassador to Louis XIV in the 1670s. Boughton House foreshadowed the strong French influence on the English baroque style that emerged after the Revolution. But the increasing prosperity of the country in the century after the Glorious Revolution, and the stability that accompanied it, saw the great country houses flourish; more frequent travel on the Continent, notably the grand tour that was a part of every gentleman's education, provided the models and the inspiration.

In the period leading up to the Hanoverian succession a new distinctive English baroque style of architecture emerged, dominated by the genius and incredible productivity of Sir Christopher Wren. As Master of the King's Works from 1670 to 1718, Wren made extraordinary contributions in state buildings—the west end of Hampton Court, St. Paul's, and the Royal Hospital at Greenwich. He also trained several generations of architects who served under him.

Of these, two stand out—John Vanbrugh and Nicholas Hawksmoor. Vanbrugh was the more creative and flamboyant. Regrettably, few of his houses remain essentially as he designed them, but those that do—Blenheim Palace, Castle Howard, and Seaton Deleval—are masterpieces. Moving from the standard blocklike, rectangular model to the French model typified by Vaux-le-Vicomte outside Paris, the model for Versailles, he built great central halls with dual flanking staircases and then extended quadrant corridors from the center block to wings that projected to form a large forecourt. The monumental nature was his alone. Hawksmoor, working in the shadow of Wren and then Vanbrugh, does not have the individual credits, though the splendors of Queen's College, Oxford, ought to be sufficient for any one.

The heavy ornamentation of the exterior of the baroque houses was outdone by greater magnificence within. Each house had a series of great rooms, apartments of state, reserved for display and the rare, extraordinary royal guest or noble of great distinction. The rooms usually constituted the first floor (English style, above the ground floor reserved for services); the second was used for the family. One finds splendid staircases, entrance walls and ceilings painted with mythological scenes, ornate wood carvings and gilded plaster composing the doors, window frames, and rails, and great tapestries, woven with

Christopher Wren's addition to Hampton Court Palace. Private collection.

Kenwood, by Robert Adam. Private collection.

gold and silver thread, alternating with large oil paintings to adorn the walls. The furniture, covered in needlework or velvet, was massive, in proportion to the house. The formal gardens were equally as splendid.

The Tory glory of the baroque was succeeded after 1714 by the Whig splendor of the Palladian. There was a transitional period, roughly from 1715 to 1730, when a modified Georgian baroque emerged. The grandest house of the period, Cannons, lasted barely thirty years. Worked on by a series of architects, including several baroque authorities, its extravagant scale put it in a class apart. Made possible by the war profiteering of James Brydges, whose wealth won him the noble title of duke of Chandos, its enormous long front gave way to a miniature city whose entertainments and guests included the great Handel. The Whig grandees who dominated the state for the next half century had lofty visions of an England evoking the best attributes of the Greco-Roman world—political, moral, artistic. Reacting against the Tory exponents of the baroque they chose Andrea Palladio of Vicenza as their model and inspiration. His treatise of 1570 was not only a rich source of classical design but also espoused the classic virtues and harmony that the Augustans wished to emulate. The amateur architect and patron Charles, earl of Burlington, not only sponsored an English edition of Palladio's work, but himself designed a model Palladian villa, Chiswick House in Middlesex, modeled on Palladio's Rotunda at Vicenza. In contrast to the projected wings of the baroque house, the great Palladian house used the wings to enlarge the house itself. The professional architects, led by Colen Campbell and William Kent, lacked the glamour of their amateur colleagues or the ostentation of their baroque predecessors. The interiors of Campbell's Houghton Hall, built for Sir Robert Walpole, the prime minister, or Kent's rooms at Hampton Court, built for George I and

George II, hardly match the splendor and color of Wren's royal apartments or Vanbrugh's Blenheim Palace. White-modeled stucco replaced the painted scenes of Verrio and Laguerre or the elegant woodwork of the seventeenth-century house. Sculptures by Rysbrack replaced the woodcarvings of Grinlig Gibbons. Chasteness rather than voluptuousness was now more in favor. The great Whig houses of Wilton (Burlington) and the remodeled Chatsworth, Claremont, Wentworth Woodhouse, and Holkham Hall triumphantly enshrined the classical austerity and virtues of the ancients espoused by the Augustans.

The later Georgian period, completing the eighteenth century, is dominated by neoclassical styles, Greek rather than Roman. Its exemplars are the Adams—John, James, William, and especially Robert—who succeeded their father William in his Scottish practice. Robert moved on to England where he led the family firm to preeminence in their profession. The ubiquitous Robert left his mark on countless houses throughout the United Kingdom, sometimes only a room or two, as in the Anglo-Norman Chirk Castle, but more often not only the house but the furniture, the wall coverings, and even the gardens. Robert Adam, very sensitive to contemporary tastes, incorporated the latest fashions and crazes in his designs. The Pompei room at Osterly Park or the Wedgewood room at Mellerstain are particularly fine examples. But above all one admires the care for detail, the consistency with which he conceived and carried out his ideas. The red room at Osterly Park, with its designs carried out in plaster, in wall coverings, and in upholstery for the furniture and the carpets, is breathtaking in its beauty and symmetry.

The state apartments, music rooms, orangeries, theaters, numerous guestrooms, and large staffs made these homes great public spectacles and social centers. The collections of paintings, sculptures, ancient marbles, glass, and porcelain resulted in a whole series of local museums that were on display for the edification and diversion of gentlefolk throughout England. The increasing size of the estates, the essential importance of the wealth derived from the land, and the need to maintain residence in the county to assert one's political influence meant that these houses were occupied by the owners for the greater part of the year, only empty during the London season, and not always then. As a symbol of power and affluence, as a place of entertainment and education, and as a social and economic center, the country house was one of the period's most distinctive features.

SUGGESTIONS FOR FURTHER READING

Reliable surveys of the period are W. A. Speck, *Stability and Strife: England, 1714–1760* (1977); Dorothy Marshall, *Eighteenth Century England* (2nd ed., 1974); John B. Owen, *The Eighteenth Century* (1973); and Geoffrey Holmes and Daniel Szechi, *The Age of Oligarchy: Preindustrial Britain, 1722–1783* (1993). Basil Williams, *The Whig Supremacy, 1714–1760* (1962) is still a reliable source of factual information. It has been replaced by Paul Langford, *A Polite and Commercial People: England, 1717–1783* (1992).

Politics and political parties have undergone intensive investigation in recent years. J. H. Plumb, *The First Four Georges* (rev. ed., 1974) consists of a chapter on each king. Ragnhild Hatton's *George I: Elector and King* (1978) is a magisterial work. There is no equivalent biography of King George II, but Peter Quennel has written an interesting biography of *Caroline of England: An Augustan Portrait* (1940). *The Prime Ministers*, vol. I, ed. Herbert van Thal (1974), gives biographical essays on the leaders of ministries. A valuable study is Peter D. G. Thomas, *The House of Commons in the Eighteenth Century* (1971). He has also written on *Politics in Eighteenth-Century Wales* (1998).

A good introduction to the age of Walpole is H. T. Dickinson, *Walpole and the Whig Supremacy* (1973). Although incomplete, the definitive study of Walpole is J. H. Plumb's *Sir Robert Walpole* (2 vols., 1956, 1961). A brief biography is Brian Hill, *Sir Robert Walpole: 'Sole and Prime Minister'* (1989). Paul Langford has made a detailed study of *The Excise Crisis* (1975). The opposition to Walpole is covered in Archibald S. Foord, *His Majesty's Opposition, 1714–1830* (1964) and Isaac Kramnick, *Bolingbroke and His Circle* (1968). H. T. Dickinson has written a good biography of *Bolingbroke* (1970). See also Linda Colley, *In Defiance of Oligarchy. The Tory Party, 1714–60* (1982). For political parties see Brian Hill, *Early Parties and Politics in Britain, 1688–1832* (1996).

The party scene after Walpole is described in J. B. Owen, *The Rise of the Pelhams* (1956). An important biography is Reed Browning, *The Duke of Newcastle* (1975), which can be supplemented by John Wilkes, *A Whig in Power: the Political Career of Henry Pelham* (1964). Valuable for both military and political history is W. A. Speck, *The Butcher: The Duke of Cumberland and the Suppression of the '45* (1981). Nicholas Rogers examines *Whigs and Cities: Popular Politics in the Age of Walpole and Pitt* (1990).

The ideas that underlay the contest of politicians and parties are explained in H. T. Dickinson, *Liberty and Property: Political Ideology in Eighteenth-Century Britain* (1977). Dickinson has also edited an interesting anthology entitled *Politics and Literature in the Eighteenth Century* (1974). The press played an important role in politics. See Jeremy Black, *The English Press in the Eighteenth Century* (1987). A cross-section of political and social journalism is available in *The Best of the Gentleman's Magazine, 1731–1754*, ed. Earl A. Reitan (1987).

The standard history of the Church is J. H. Overton and Frederic Relton, *The English Church from the Accession of George I to the end of the Eighteenth Century* (1906). The political problems of the Church are covered by Norman Sykes in *Church and State in England in the Eighteenth Century* (1934). Michael Watts covers *The Dissenters: From the Reformation to the French Revolution* (1986). See also James E. Bradley, *Religion, Revolution, and English Radicalism: Nonconformity in Eighteenth-Century Politics and Society* (1990). John Bossy, *The English Catholic Community, 1570–1850* (1976) is authoritative. Todd M. Endelman covers *The Jews of Georgian England, 1714–1830* (1979). The decline of dogmatic Christianity is examined in G. R. Cragg, *From Puritanism to the Age of Reason* (1966) and Roland M. Stromberg, *Religious Liberalism in Eighteenth-Century England* (1954). For John Wesley and Methodism see Stanley Ayling, *John Wesley* (1979) and Bernard Semmel, *The Methodist Revolution* (1973). R. W. Wearmouth discusses *Methodism and the Common People of England* (1945).

Foreign policy can be followed in Black, Langford, and Horn, cited in Chapter 9. Other relevant books cited in Chapter 9 are Reitan, *Politics, War, and Empire;* Bowen, *War and British Society;* and Black, *Britain as a Military Power, 1688–1815* (1998). Black has also written *British Foreign Policy in the Age of Walpole* (1985). A much misunderstood war is explained by Reed Browning in *The War of the Austrian Succession* (1993).

The navy is covered in books by Kennedy, Stokesbury, and Marcus, cited in Chapter 9. A valuable analysis of the use of seapower is Herbert W. Richmond, *The Navy in the War of 1739–48* (3 vols., 1920). Jeremy Black and Philip Woodfine (eds.) have provided an interesting collection of essays in *The British Navy and the Use of Naval Power in the Eighteenth Century* (1989). N. A. M. Rodger has written *The Wooden World: An Anatomy of the Georgian Navy* (1986). For the British army, see the books cited in Chapter 9.

A good introduction to the economy is John Rule, *The Vital Century: England's Developing Economy, 1714–1815* (1992). Classics in the field are T. S. Ashton, *An Economic History of England: The Eighteenth Century* (1959) and *Economic Fluctuations in England, 1700–1800* (1959). The authoritative work on population growth is E. A. Wrigley and R. S. Schofield, *The Population History of England, 1541–1871* (2nd ed., 1989). The origins of industrial growth are traced in Phyllis Deane and W. A. Cole, *British Economic Growth, 1688–1959* (1969) and Deane, *The First Industrial Revolution* (2nd ed., 1979). For agriculture see Eric Kerridge, *The Agricultural Revolution* (1967) and *The Farmers of Old England* (1973). For the workers, see John Rule, *The Experience of Labour in Eighteenth-Century Industry* (1981).

A broad survey of society is John Rule, *Albion's People: English Society, 1714–1815* (1992). See also Roy Porter, *English Society in the Eighteenth Century* (rev., 1990). Still valuable is Dorothy Marshall, *English People in the Eighteenth Century* (1956). An important new area of research is explored in *The Birth of a Consumer Society: The Commercialization of Eighteenth-Century England,* Neil McKendrick (ed., 1982). An older work with valuable essays on many aspects of English life is A. S. Turberville (ed.), *Johnson's England* (2 vols., 1933). John Cannon covers the aristocracy in *Aristocratic Century: The Peerage of Eighteenth-Century England* (1984). Gordon Mingay is authoritative in *English Landed Society in the Eighteenth Century* (1963) and *The Gentry* (1976). For the rising class of professional people see Wilfred Prest (ed.), *The Professions in Early Modern England* (1987). An interesting perspective is offered by Derek Jarrett in *England in the Age of Hogarth* (1986).

There is a wealth of interesting material on eighteenth-century London in M. Dorothy George, *London Life in the Eighteenth Century* (1951). Other aspects of social history are treated in Borsay, *Provincial Towns* (cited Chapter 9); C. W. Chalklin, *The Provincial Towns of Georgian England* (1974); Penelope J. Corfield, *The Impact of English Towns: 1700–1800* (1982); Marshall, *The English Poor in the Eighteenth Century* (1926); and Mark Girouard, *Life in the English Country House: A Social and Architectural History* (1978). Social unrest is studied in George Rude, *Paris and London in the Eighteenth Century* (1953). Peter Fryer has explored *Black People in the British Empire: An Introduction* (1988).

Fundamental to research in the history of the family are Lawrence Stone, *The Family, Sex and Marriage in England, 1500–1800* (1977) and Rudolph Trumbach, *The Rise of the Egalitarian Family: Aristocratic Kinship and Domestic Relations in Eighteenth-Century England* (1978). *Marriage and Love in England: Modes of Reproduction, 1300–1840* by Alan Macfarlane (1986) is important. See also John R. Gillis, *For Better, For Worse: British Marriages, 1600 to the Present* (1988). A good introduction is Mary Prior, *Women in English Society, 1500–1800* (1985). *The Gentleman's Daughter: Women's Lives in Georgian England* (1998), by Amanda Vickery, explores the lives of genteel women. Bridget Hill has studied *Women, Work, and Sexual Politics in Eighteenth-Century England* (1989).

Intellectual and cultural matters are well covered in *The Cambridge Cultural History of Britain: Vol. V, Eighteenth-Century Britain,* Boris Ford (ed., 1992). Other useful works are Basil Willey, *The Eighteenth Century Background* (1957); Gerald R. Cragg, *Reason and Authority in the Eighteenth Century* (1964); A. R. Humphreys, *The Augustan World: Life and Letters in the Eighteenth Century* (1954); and John Brewer, *The Pleasures of the Imagination: English Culture in the 18th Century* (1997).

P. W. J. Riley has examined the effects of the Act of Union on Scotland in *The Union of England and Scotland: A Study in Anglo-Scottish Politics of the Eighteenth Century* (1979). For "the '45" see Frank McLynn, *Bonnie Prince Charlie: Charles Edward Stuart* (1990). The development of Scotland after the '45 is surveyed in Bruce Lenman, *Integration, Enlightenment, and Industrialization: Scotland, 1746–1832* (1981). R. A. Housman and I. D. White (eds.), explore *Scottish Society, 1500–1800* (1989). The concept of "Britishness" has become a topic of discussion. See Linda Colley, *Britons: Forging the Nation, 1707–1837* (1992) and her article, "Britishness and Otherness: An Argument," *Journal of British Studies*, 31 (Oct. 1992), 309–329.

For Ireland, good introductory books are Beckett and Moody (cited in Chapter 9); Edith Johnston, *Ireland in the Eighteenth Century* (1974); and Francis James, *Ireland in the Empire, 1688–1770* (1973). William E. H. Lecky, *A History of Ireland in the Eighteenth Century* (5 vols., repr. 1972) is a classic, and still a useful chronology of events.

There is a vast literature on the British empire in the eighteenth century. Trevor Lloyd, *The British Empire, 1558–1995* (1996) provides a good introduction. A useful storehouse of information is James A. Williamson, *A Short History of British Expansion, Vol. I: The Old Colonial Empire* (3rd ed., 1959). A comprehensive work is *The Cambridge History of the British Empire* (8 vols., 1929–63), also available in an illustrated edition (1996). It will be challenged by *The Oxford History of the British Empire*, Roger Louis (ed.), a multi-volume work by many authors that is expected to be completed in 1999. A remarkable book is Angus Calder, *Revolutionary Empire: The Rise of the English-Speaking Empires from the Fifteenth Century to the 1780s* (1981).

The concept of an Atlantic world has gained favor: see Peggy Liss, *Atlantic Empires: The Network of Trade and Revolution, 1713–1825* (1983) and *The Atlantic Empire before the American Revolution*, Peter Marshall and Glyn Williams (eds., 1980). Bernard Bailyn examines *Voyagers to the West: A Passage in the Peopling of America on the Eve of the Revolution* (1986). *Bound for America: The Transportation of British Convicts to the Colonies, 1718–1775* (1987) by A. Roger Ekirch covers an important aspect of the empire. See also A. G. L. Shaw in *Convicts and Colonies: A Study of Penal Transportation from Great Britain and Ireland to Australia and Other Parts of the British Empire* (1966). Hugh Thomas summarizes recent research in *The Slave Trade: The History of the Atlantic Slave Trade, 1440–1870* (1998). See also Edward Reynolds, *Stand the Storm: A History of the Atlantic Slave Trade* (1985). The eastern perspective is provided in Holden Furber, *Rival Empires of Trade in the Orient, 1600–1800* (1976).

CHAPTER ELEVEN

Politics and Empire
1754–1783

Throughout the eighteenth century the British people were engaged in one of the most difficult tasks any people can undertake—to build institutions of government that would give strong leadership and maintain order while affording the freedom and opportunity needed for individual achievement and fulfillment. In the reigns of George I and George II the major thrust of politics had been toward stability and unity. By 1754 the forces tending toward authority had accomplished their purpose: the Hanoverian dynasty was secure, crown and Parliament had learned to work together, and the prime minister and cabinet had emerged as the link between them. Political and religious partisanship had declined, the three kingdoms had been brought closer together, and the economy was growing. Strong, secure, and successful, the British nation turned its attention again to the claims of liberty.

The word "liberty" has always had many meanings and great emotional power, but perhaps at no time in history was the word more potent than in the last half of the eighteenth century. When the British spoke of liberty they first meant civil liberties: adherence to legal procedures; religious toleration as provided by law; and freedom of speech, press, and assembly. The concept of liberty also extended to security of private property. Most important of all, liberty included those rights of participation in government without which all other liberties were in jeopardy. The British were proud of their "mixed and balanced" constitution, which divided power among king, Lords, and Commons, with "checks and balances" that prevented any one of the three from dominating the others.

When concern for liberty arose it was usually directed at the ministers of the crown, for their ambivalent position meant that they could be accused of trying to combine the powers of the crown and the Parliament into a monopoly of power that could threaten individual freedom. By the reign of George III Britain had become a great nation, and a great nation needed strong leadership. Yet strong central authority was seen as the principal threat to liberty. The constitutional problems posed by this dilemma contributed to a period of political turmoil at home and in the colonies.

THE SEVEN YEARS WAR

The Duke of Newcastle

The Seven Years War (known in American History as the French and Indian War) began while Britain was in one of the most intense and prolonged political crises of the eighteenth century. Henry Pelham had been a more honest version of Sir Robert Walpole, and from 1748 to his death in 1754 Pelham had presided over an unusual period of political harmony. With the death of Pelham his brother, the Duke of Newcastle, was appointed first lord of the Treasury with the leadership responsibilities that office entailed.

As a Court Whig Newcastle knew the importance of remaining on good terms with the king, and in his foreign policy he normally followed the wishes of George II, especially in respect of the Austrian alliance and the security of Hanover. Newcastle's problem with the monarchy was that King George II was already seventy years of age and could not expect to live much longer. The heir to the throne was George, Prince of Wales, only sixteen, who lived at Leicester House where his mother and his tutor, Lord Bute, dominated him. With some justification, Newcastle was suspicious that Leicester House was seeking to undermine him by currying the favor of ambitious younger men looking to the future.

The House of Commons contained two outstanding leaders. One of them, William Pitt, was a sleeping volcano. Pitt had attached himself to the Pelhams while awaiting the opportunity to fulfill his vaunting ambition. Pitt's rival was Henry Fox, a hard-bitten politician of the Walpole school, who was closely allied with the Duke of Cumberland. When Newcastle chose a nonentity to lead the House of Commons, Pitt and Fox, who heard opportunity knocking, did all they could to make Newcastle's ministry fail. With Fox linked to the Duke of Cumberland, Pitt attached himself to the Prince of Wales at Leicester House.

Outbreak of the War

In the meantime disaster struck. In 1754 the colony of Virginia sent a young man named George Washington with 400 men to threaten the fort that the

French were building at the forks of the Ohio River. Washington was attacked by the French and forced to withdraw. Newcastle was determined to maintain British territorial claims in North America, and the next year he sent Gen. Edward Braddock, a career soldier, with a force of redcoats supported by colonials to drive out the French. Braddock was ambushed in the forests, dying bravely with many of his men, fighting a combined French and Indian force that would not exchange volleys in the open like a European army.

Then, early in 1756, the French gained an easy victory. Sensing that the British fleet in the Mediterranean was unready for war, the French boldly seized Minorca, Britain's key naval base, which was weakly defended by Admiral Byng. Reinforcements sent by Newcastle arrived too late. The British public, which expected the navy to win all its battles, was highly upset. Byng was court-martialled and convicted of failing to do his duty, for which the penalty was death. Since there were extenuating circumstances, the court-martial urged clemency. To show their toughness and appease an angry public, Newcastle and the king refused. The unfortunate Byng was shot on his quarterdeck, as Voltaire remarked wryly, "to encourage the others."

In 1756 a "diplomatic revolution" took place in Europe. The king and Newcastle needed a continental ally to protect Hanover. When the Austrians appeared reluctant to continue the alliance, Newcastle and the king abandoned their past policies and allied with Frederick II, the brilliant and warlike king of Prussia. The Austrians allied with France, allies later joined by Russia. War broke out on the continent in August 1756, when Frederick II made a preemptive strike against Austria. Britain's commitment to Hanover had again involved it in a continental war.

The Pitt-Newcastle Coalition

While Britain was in political crisis, war was breaking out in Europe. It was evident that the elderly Newcastle was not the man to conduct a major war. The House of Commons turned against him and the cry went up for Pitt, who declared boldly: "I am sure I can save this country, and nobody else can." Newcastle resigned and Pitt formed a ministry. George II complained that Pitt "will not do my German business," and the other political leaders withheld their support. Pitt could not muster a majority in the House of Commons: popularity and public opinion might bring a ministry to power but were not enough to keep it there.

In due time reason prevailed and the obvious step was taken: a coalition of Pitt and Newcastle. George II abandoned his opposition to Pitt. Once again he had learned that his right to appoint his own ministers was limited by the House of Commons and, in this instance, public opinion. Newcastle returned to office as first lord of the Treasury, managing the patronage and raising the vast loans needed. Pitt became secretary of state, where his keen strategic sense and choice of energetic commanders gave vigor to Britain's military forces. His dynamic personality and powerful oratory dominated the House of Commons and public opinion. Henry Fox became paymaster of the forces, an office which in time of war had a huge income based on fees. The unhappiest faces were at Leicester House, where the Prince of Wales and Lord Bute, his adviser and tutor, felt themselves betrayed by Pitt.

Years of Victory

When the Pitt-Newcastle ministry took office in June 1757 the war was going badly. Ignoring his earlier pronouncements, Pitt won the favor of George II by appointing a German general, Ferdinand of Brunswick, to command a mixed army of British and Hanoverian troops ordered to defend Hanover. Frederick II of Prussia received a generous subsidy that enabled him to continue fighting despite the heavy losses that he had suffered. Pitt launched amphibious attacks along the French coast to divert French resources from Germany and upset the French court and people. Although the first landings failed, the army and navy gained experience in combined operations, which eventually paid off handsomely.

By 1758 the tide was turning. Ferdinand of Brunswick drove the French out of Hanover and back across the Rhine. When Ferdinand won a brilliant victory at Crefeld in June, Pitt showed his confidence by sending more redcoats. Pitt continued his amphibious raids along the French coast, which compelled the French to devote badly needed resources to coastal garrisons and naval patrols.

Pitt's main objective was to drive the French out of North America. In 1758 he sent one army to attack the French at the forks of the Ohio River (present-day Pittsburgh), another to attack northward from Albany toward Quebec, and an amphibious force to attack the great French fortress of Louisbourg, gateway to the St. Lawrence river. Complex planning was needed for the navy to cross the Atlantic with a fleet of warships laden with 11,000 soldiers and then land them near Louisbourg, but Pitt insisted that it could be done and it was. Under a brilliant young leader, Gen. James Wolfe, the redcoats established a beachhead near the fort and attacked by land while British warships pounded the fort from the sea. When Louisbourg fell, the way to Quebec, the heart of the French settlements in Canada, was open, but it was too late in the season to advance farther. In Britain the news of victories in distant lands aroused great enthusiasm, and Parliament voted unprecedented sums for the campaigns of 1759.

Now Pitt raised his sights. Confident that Canada would fall, he planned campaigns against the French empire in the West Indies, West Africa, and

India while maintaining pressure in Germany and bringing the war home to France with coastal raids. When the French attempted to strike back by attacking Hanover they were decisively defeated by the army of Ferdinand of Brunswick at Minden. The French Mediterranean fleet was defeated at Lagos off the coast of Portugal, and later in the year the navy won a brilliant victory at Quiberon Bay, off the coast of France, when the British ships, driven by a gale, boldly attacked the French amid rocks and shoals. Thereafter the French navy was blockaded in its harbors and the British were free to roam the seas, picking up the remains of the French empire.

In the meantime the British launched an attack on Quebec. Having mastered the difficult art of combined operations, the army and navy reassembled at Louisbourg in the spring. The navy sailed its troop-laden vessels boldly up the St. Lawrence, guided by Capt. James Cook (later the famous explorer) who sounded and mapped the many obstacles that confronted ocean-going warships in the shallow river waters.

The city and fortress of Quebec were located atop a craggy cliff overlooking the river. The French commander, the Marquis de Montcalm, had fortified the only likely landing spot, which was downstream from the city. His second in command, Bougainville (later an explorer), commanded a second force upstream from the city. Wolfe landed his men across the river and attempted to bring Montcalm out of his fortifications by bombarding the city with naval artillery and siege guns. When Montcalm refused to budge, Wolfe launched a direct assault, but his soldiers were repulsed.

Now Wolfe decided it was necessary to attack the city between Montcalm downstream and Bougainville upstream. He found a steep, rocky path up the cliffs to the Plains of Abraham, just outside the city. During the night his infantry overpowered the guards and silently scrambled up the slope, sailors dragging cannon behind them. When dawn broke, Montcalm was informed that the British were arrayed for battle at the gates of the city. Impulsively he left his fortifications, hastily organized his men, and attacked the redcoats, who stood firmly in their ranks, firing the withering volleys that won Canada. As the smoke cleared Wolfe and Montcalm lay dying on the battlefield.

But the troubles of the victors were not yet over. Now the French rallied, trapping the British troops within the fortress, where they held out under great hardships. In 1760 the conquest of Canada was completed with the taking of Montreal, and the besieged garrison at Quebec was relieved. Britain was now the master of North America from the Atlantic coast to the Mississippi.

Pitt had achieved his objectives in North America, and he now prepared for the total destruction of French seapower and empire, the only aspects of French power that threatened Britain. In 1758 the British seized the main French slaving station in West Africa, insuring British control of the lucrative

Atlantic slave trade. In 1759 Guadeloupe, a prosperous French island in the West Indies, surrendered to a British fleet on favorable terms; the other French sugar islands fell later.

The best hope of France was that Prussia would collapse and Hanover with it, which would enable France to trade Hanover for return of parts of her overseas empire. Pitt saw the danger and sent additional aid to Frederick II, which pleased the king and Newcastle. Frederick was able to hold his own and Ferdinand of Brunswick's army pushed the French across the Rhine.

News was slow in arriving from India, where the British East India Company faced a difficult struggle with Suraj-ad-Dullah, the ruler of the great province of Bengal. In 1756 Suraj-ad-Dullah seized the British trading station at Calcutta and threw 146 prisoners into a dungeon, which came to be known as "the Black Hole of Calcutta." Most of the prisoners died from heat or suffocation. Robert Clive, leader of the Company's forces, hurried by sea from Madras with additional forces and captured Calcutta in January 1757. At the battle of Plassey, his outnumbered troops won a decisive victory over Suraj-ad-Dullah. Clive's victory in Bengal changed the character of the British East India Company, which now governed an extensive territory with a large population.

Suddenly Pitt's plans were disrupted by a political change at home. On October 25, 1760, George II drank his morning cup of chocolate and fell over dead. The Prince of Wales was now King George III and his tutor and friend, the Earl of Bute, was the dominant figure at court.

War with Spain

With the accession of George III many considerations led toward peace. In 1761 the French sent out peace feelers, although France was by no means finished; it knew that Spain, fearful of the rise of British imperial power, was willing to come to its aid in the colonial realm. In September Pitt received secret intelligence that Spain was preparing to enter the war; he urged a preemptive strike before the Spanish treasure fleet arrived from America. The cabinet insisted on waiting for Spain to make the first move. Pitt resigned, declaring: "I will be responsible for nothing that I do not direct." Later in the year, after the treasure was safely home, Spain declared war anyway.

Anticipating war with Spain, Pitt had already planned to attack Cuba. In a brilliant amphibious operation Havana was besieged by land, bombarded from the sea, and fell in August 1762 after a two-month siege. The cabinet also approved an attack by the East India Company on Manila, in the Philippines, where the Company wished to establish a base for trade with China and Southeast Asia. The operation was a complete success, but the news got back to England after the peace had been signed and the Philippines were returned to Spain.

The Wiremaster and His Puppets, 1767. The Earl of Bute as the power behind the scenes. Kenneth Spencer Research Library.

The Peace of Paris

In 1762 the main issue was the peace. By that time both France and Spain were ready to give in while they still had something left. The obstacle was Frederick II of Prussia. Early in 1762 Frederick's bitter enemy, the Empress Elizabeth of Russia, died and was succeeded by Peter III, a great admirer of Frederick, who immediately allied himself with Prussia. With France seeking peace, Maria Theresa of Austria had no choice but to make the best settlement she could. Frederick was no longer threatened, but he wished to continue the war for his own territorial gains.

When Frederick II demanded a subsidy for 1762 the new British regime balked. Bute opposed subsidizing Frederick's war in central Europe, which had nothing to do with British interests. Newcastle argued for the subsidy, on the grounds that Britain needed a strong continental ally. When George III, Bute, and the majority of the cabinet insisted that Britain had done all that could be expected for Frederick, Newcastle, after more than forty years in high office, resigned. Bute took over as first lord of the Treasury and George Grenville replaced Newcastle as secretary of state.

The Peace of Paris (1763) gave Britain great colonial gains: France surrendered Canada, the Trans-Appalachian American West, and the slave-trading station of Senegal in West Africa. Britain got Florida (including the Gulf coast) from Spain and Minorca was regained. Cuba was returned to Spain and France transferred Louisiana (including New Orleans) to Spain in compensation for its losses. The news of the East India Company's capture of Manila arrived too late to be included in the treaty, so that potentially valuable base for East Asian trade was returned to Spain. The French empire was virtually wiped out, although France still retained some West Indies islands, a slave-trading station in West Africa, trading stations in India, and the right to fish on the Grand Banks.

When the peace was approved Bute announced that he had accomplished his purpose and resigned. His aloof and retiring personality did not fit into the turmoil of politics, and the theories that he had expounded out of office proved difficult to apply in the real world. His stomach was bad and he did not sleep well; he welcomed a more private life. Reluctantly the young George III accepted the resignation of his tutor and friend, probably realizing that Bute was a weak reed. George III had dropped the pilot and was now on his own.

LIBERTY OF THE CROWN

George III

George III was twenty-two years old in 1760 when he succeeded his grandfather, George II. His father, the ill-fated Frederick, Prince of Wales, bequeathed to him a political doctrine that the young prince adopted: that George II had been "enslaved" by conniving politicians, who used "the influence of the crown" to entrench themselves at court, in the cabinet, and in Parliament. The political ideas of Prince George were shaped by his tutor, Lord Bute, who developed in his pupil a strong sense of purpose: to exercise personally the legal powers of the monarch and to free the crown from dependence upon politicians, political parties, and corruption. His mother, the Princess Augusta, was worried that the pleasures of elite society and the charms of designing women would lead her son astray. George was constantly reminded that he had a higher duty than personal pleasure—his responsibility to his country and his people. In 1762 he married Charlotte of Mecklenburg-Strelitz, a minor German principality. Theirs was a satisfying marriage that produced fifteen children.

The Grenville Ministry

When he resigned, Bute recommended George Grenville as his successor. George III accepted Grenville's ministry as a temporary arrangement, although he disliked Grenville personally and did not give him full confidence. A capable but tactless man, Grenville created a furor when he sought to punish John Wilkes, a charming demagogue, who was linked politically with Pitt. Wilkes was editor of *The North Briton,* an opposition newspaper that had vilified Bute. In issue #45 Wilkes attacked the peace treaty and the policies of the Grenville ministry as stated in the king's speech to Parliament. Agents of the secretary of state ransacked the office where *The North Briton* was published to obtain evidence against Wilkes.

When the case came to trial Wilkes successfully pleaded that he was exempt from arrest as a member of Parliament. The printers were let off on the grounds that their arrest was based on an illegal warrant. The decision was hailed by the Londoners as a defense of civil liberties against an oppressive regime.

The stubborn Grenville next took steps to expel Wilkes from the House of Commons, which ruled that parliamentary immunity did not apply to seditious libel and went on to declare *North Briton* #45 a seditious libel. After being wounded in a duel with a Treasury official, Wilkes fled to France to avoid prosecution and was declared an outlaw. In the House of Commons bitter charges were leveled that the ministry was trying to intimidate members by illegal searches and seizures. The Londoners vented their rage with parades, mass meetings, and riots, shouting "Wilkes and Liberty."

Grenville aroused a similar response in the American colonies. The cost of the war had been enormous and governing Britain's swollen empire brought with it additional expenses. Grenville argued that the colonists were beneficiaries of Britain's victories and should be willing to bear some of the burden. To raise revenue in the colonies he proposed a Stamp Tax, which was passed by a Parliament that little realized the storm this measure would brew in America.

Perhaps Grenville's most serious mistake was his lack of finesse in dealing with the king. Grenville was a competent administrator, but he was also an opinionated bore. "When he has wearied me for two hours," George III said, "he looks at his watch to see if he may not tire me an hour more." The king turned for assistance to his uncle, the Duke of Cumberland, who formed a ministry led by a young nobleman, the Marquis of Rockingham, and supported mainly by the former followers of Newcastle. Grenville was dismissed and George III was called upon to work with the successors of the Whigs who had "enslaved" George II.

The Rockingham Ministry

George III had asserted his personal power in getting rid of Grenville, but he resented becoming dependent on any one political group. He considered the Rockingham ministry a stopgap and found many reasons to complain of its inexperience and ineptitude, qualities which he, incidentally, shared. Efforts were made to bring Pitt into the ministry, which would restore the powerful coalition that had governed Britain during the Seven Years War, but Pitt was unwilling to join any ministry that he did not control. The ministry was further weakened by the death of the Duke of Cumberland in 1766.

The most pressing problem of the Rockingham ministry was to restore order in the North American colonies, which had imposed an embargo on British goods to protest the Stamp Act. The ministry proposed to repeal the Stamp Act, a step reluctantly accepted by the king and vigorously opposed by Grenville and many others who saw it as yielding to intimidation. Pitt supported repeal in a powerful speech denying the right of Parliament to tax the Americans, although Pitt would have Britain maintain imperial control in all other respects.

In an attempt to satisfy everyone, repeal of the Stamp Act was linked with a Declaratory Act, which affirmed the full sovereignty of Parliament over the colonies, including taxation. This muddled solution was passed by Parliament, although many who voted for one bill did not vote for the other. By that time Pitt had finally made known his willingness to lead a ministry, and George III was ready to make another change. The king's clumsy efforts to find a ministry that would be knowledgeable, competent, and willing to follow his lead were unquestionably a contributing factor to the political instability of the early years of his reign.

The Chatham Ministry

The new ministry represented George III's goal of a government with one strong leader who would govern apart from party considerations. In an age of growing partisanship, the idea worked badly. When Pitt took office in 1766 he was raised to the House of Lords as Earl of Chatham, which removed him from his natural forum, the House of Commons. He announced that his would be a nonparty government, which resulted in a ministry without unity and trust, with experienced politicians such as Rockingham and Grenville in opposition. To make matters worse, Chatham's health was bad, and there were long periods where he was unable to conduct business, sunken in a melancholia with both mental and physical effects.

It was necessary to do something about the affairs of the East India Company, which had fallen into chaos and faced bankruptcy. Chatham advocated stronger control of the Company, but the Company saved its independence by a payment to the Exchequer, which further injured its precarious finances. Instead of the strong, capable leader he had anticipated, George III was saddled with a weak ministry that faced serious problems of domestic unrest and imperial policy. Two years later Chatham resigned, and the ministry carried on, led by the Duke of Grafton, an inexperienced young nobleman.

The Grafton Ministry

The political floundering of George III's first decade came to a head under Grafton. Although the American situation was momentarily quiet, the affairs of the East India Company were at a crisis stage, the economy was depressed, the press was unusually contentious, and the politicians were at each other's throats. The pot began to boil when John Wilkes returned from France to run for Parliament in the election of 1768. Wilkes found that he had not lost his ability to arouse the emotions of the metropolitan populace. While he failed to get elected for London, he easily carried the county of Middlesex, which was dominated by metropolitan voters.

When Parliament met, the Grafton ministry was determined to assert its authority and meet Wilkes' demagoguery and rowdy followers head-on. Wilkes was disqualified by the House of Commons, which ordered a new poll for Middlesex. In the meantime Wilkes was sent to prison for his previous offenses, where he lived in high style supported by his enthusiastic followers. Several persons were killed when troops fired on a mob that attacked the prison to free their hero. The result was more riots, as the cry "Wilkes and Liberty" once again rang out.

In the second poll Wilkes was elected without opposition and was again rejected by the House of Commons. A third poll was held in which his boisterous supporters intimidated any prospective opponents. Finally the ministry found a candidate who was willing to stand up against Wilkes and the mob, and a fourth poll was ordered. Although Wilkes again won the vote his opponent, who came in a distant second, was declared the winner. More riots followed until the army was called in to restore order. In 1770 Grafton resigned, to be succeeded by his chancellor of the Exchequer, Frederick, Lord North, who bore an honorary title but was a member of the House of Commons.

The North Ministry

The government of eighteenth-century Britain worked best when king, Lords, and Commons were in harmony, and this desirable state was possible only when there was general agreement on leaders and policies. By 1770 conditions had emerged that made possible a new period of stability and consensus. The king had gained experience, the political oscillations of the 1760s had created a desire for continuity, and the divisive issues presented by Wilkes, America, and India had subsided.

North took office as first lord of the Treasury, and once again—as in the days of Walpole and Henry Pelham—the leader of the ministry was also manager of the finances and a member of the House of Commons. North did not dominate his ministry, as Walpole had done, but he tended personally to the business of the Treasury while giving considerable leeway to the other ministers in their departments. North was a genial person, able in financial matters and an effective speaker in the House of Commons, where he was respected and well liked, even by those who opposed him politically. It was equally important that North was willing to take his cues from the king.

North's parliamentary nucleus of court politicians, placemen, and other dependents of the crown was augmented by some of the former followers of Bute, Grenville, and Grafton—men who had taken office with their leader but who decided to serve the king and the ministers of his choice when their leader left office. North gained additional support from the independent gentlemen in the House of Commons, who approved his good sense, moderation, and sound financial management. The economy revived and North was able to reduce the land tax while finding a modest surplus for debt reduction. North avoided trouble and, for a time, trouble avoided him. By 1770 George III had gained the freedom of action he considered necessary for the monarch to function effectively. He was now an experienced ruler who could not be "enslaved" by politicians, but some charged that the crown had become a threat to the liberty of others.

THE OPPOSITION AND LIBERTY

The Rockingham Party

The political contentions of the first decade of the reign of George III led to the development of a political opposition whose principles, tactics, and persistence harked back to Bolingbroke and the coalition that had overthrown Walpole. The most effective opposition leader was the Marquis of Rockingham, a great aristocrat with extensive estates in Yorkshire and Ireland. The other leaders of his group also were aristocrats. Rockingham believed that his ministry had been undone by an improper use of royal power and that the crown had become a threat to liberty. Despite his high rank and great wealth, Rockingham was a man of modest demeanor who seldom spoke in the House of Lords. He held his following together by virtue of his determination and personal character. The opposition that he led through many years of frustration and discouragement was one of the most remarkable political achievements of his time.

Some of Rockingham's eventual success was due to his secretary, Edmund Burke, an Irish Protestant who came to London to pursue a career as a writer. Rockingham provided Burke with a seat in the House of Commons and used him as his political "man of business." Burke was a hard worker who collected information on a wide range of subjects, corresponded deferentially with Rockingham's aristocratic followers, and provided the philosophical and rhetorical context for the positions adopted by the Rockingham group.

In 1770 Burke published his *Thoughts on the Causes of the Present Discontents*, which became the manifesto of the Rockingham Party. In this pamphlet Burke charged that from the beginning of the reign an attempt had been made to concentrate power in the crown by destroying the power of the aristocracy, led by the Duke of Newcastle, and of the people, led by William Pitt. Without attacking the king directly, Burke argued that an inner ring of politicians had used "the influence of the crown" to manipulate ministries, dominate Parliament, and stifle dissent. He gave special attention to the king's civil list, which he saw as an important source of "corrupt influence" in the House of Commons. Although he deplored factionalism, Burke defended political parties when they were formed to defend fundamental principles. With Rockingham's leadership in mind, Burke called on public-spirited individuals to work together to preserve liberty.

Chatham

Another opposition group gathered around William Pitt, Earl of Chatham, whose health recovered sufficiently for him to return to the political wars in

1770. Chatham was popular in London and other mercantile towns and in the American colonies. Chatham was not a party leader, but he lent his great reputation and powerful oratory to the charge that the ministry had established a corrupt control of Parliament that threatened the rights and liberties of Englishmen. Chatham's most influential follower was the Earl of Shelburne. Shelburne was especially interested in colonial matters and shared his leader's desire to resolve the problems in America in an amicable and generous manner.

LIBERTY AND THE PEOPLE

Radicalism

In the meantime liberty had shown another of her faces in the development of "Radicalism" and the emergence of public opinion as a factor in the political process. The roots of Radicalism were the long-established British fear of a strong executive power in the crown, which was seen as a threat to the role of Parliament as defender of the rights of the people. The career of Wilkes added another dimension to Radicalism: the idea that Parliament itself had been co-opted by the crown and had become a willing participant in the curtailment of liberty. Radicalism was a movement for reform of the House of Commons, including such features as reduction of royal patronage, exclusion of office holders from the House of Commons, measures to reduce corruption in elections, and redistribution of seats to strengthen the more independent and representative elements in the House. A few Radicals went so far as to demand the right to vote for all adult males.

Radical ideas were strongest among middle-class business and professional people, especially in London and Westminster and in the urban sprawl in the counties of Middlesex and Surrey. The popularity of Pitt and Wilkes in London rested upon their appeal to ordinary citizens and their freedom from party affiliations. Radical ideas were also strong in the larger trading and seaport towns, especially where there was a large population of Dissenters. In 1770 Wilkes was elected an alderman of London, and in 1774 he was elected to the House of Commons, taking his seat without controversy.

LIBERTY AND AUTHORITY IN AMERICA

The Imperial Relationship

It was in the American colonies, however, that the struggle for liberty took its most extreme form. The thirteen colonies along the Atlantic seaboard had taken root within the protecting arms of the British Empire. The American colonists considered themselves as Englishmen with all "the rights of Englishmen." They also shared British ideas about liberty, including the characteristic British resistance to strong central authority. The colonists were permitted to manage most of their local affairs and were linked to the Mother Country primarily by the weak authority of colonial governors and the Navigation Acts.

The arrangement was mutually beneficial. Britain gained power and wealth from almost two million energetic colonists in North America. The Americans benefited by participation in the world's largest and most dynamic trading area. They and their ships were protected by the British navy, and they were governed by a Mother Country that was the first in the modern world to combine freedom and order in a manner that worked. In Britain it seemed incredible that the Americans would reject these advantages because they resented their subordinate status. Nevertheless, in 1765 the colonists applauded Patrick Henry when he thundered: "Give me Liberty, or give me Death!"

Grenville and Imperial Consolidation

There can be no doubt that in 1763 the Grenville ministry adopted a policy of imperial consolidation that was intended to strengthen the control of the Mother Country over its territories overseas. The vast accessions of the Seven Years War had transformed the empire. The Grenville ministry was confronted with two related tasks: providing government for newly acquired areas, and giving unity to an empire that had become so large and diverse as to be unwieldy. Grenville had to govern and defend a swollen empire burdened with debt and do so in cooperation with a Parliament that was determined to end wartime levels of taxation.

The British concept of empire remained unchanged: a controlling center with subordinate parts. It was a concept shared by George III, all of his ministries, and the British ruling class as represented in Parliament. What changed in 1763 was the energy and determination with which that concept was enforced. Americans believed that the empire was a community of Englishmen, based on law and mutual respect. That belief was shattered by the Grenville policies: once broken, it could not be restored.

The British empire was primarily an empire of trade. Grenville was determined to strengthen the mercantilist controls that held it together. The Sugar Act of 1764 reduced the duties on molasses to make smuggling less profitable, but it also imposed new duties on important items of trade such as wine. Many items were added to the "enumerated articles," which could be shipped only to Britain. Merchants were required to post bonds guaranteeing that their exports went to legal destinations. American merchants and sea captains saw Grenville's new broom as an unjustified innovation in established patterns of trade.

Grenville also used the armed forces in unaccustomed ways. Customs officials were authorized to use the army and navy to enforce the laws of trade, and a court of admiralty was set up in Nova Scotia to try smugglers. A Quartering Act (1765) required Americans to provide housing for British troops. The Americans held the long-standing British fear of a standing army, and the appearance of redcoats in their midst was seen (not without justification) as an attempt at intimidation. The navy was authorized to impress sailors in American ports. Grenville also enforced earlier laws reserving for the navy large trees suitable for masts.

Faced with heavy expenditures for the costs of the war and the national debt, Grenville was determined that the colonists should pay some of the increased cost of administering and defending the empire of which they were a part. He proposed a stamp tax on legal documents and newspapers. Although the legislation passed with little attention in Britain, where stamp taxes had existed since 1694, Grenville's stamp tax aroused powerful opposition in America. The tax fell heavily upon lawyers and journalists, two of the most articulate and contentious elements of any society. The Americans, whose suspicions of the Grenville ministry had already been aroused, denied the right of Parliament to impose taxation without their consent and declared their determination to adhere to the principle of "no taxation without representation."

The Stamp Act affected all colonies equally, and consequently it gave the Americans a unity in resistance that they had not known before. They invoked in eloquent words their constitutional rights and liberties as Englishmen. Riots broke out in seaports all along the coast, which made it impossible for governors and customs officers to enforce the law. The Stamp Act Congress, called in 1765, brought the colonists together in resistance and established an embargo that injured British merchants at a time when trade was in a depression. Merchants in London and the outports joined with colonial agents in an agitation for repeal.

When the Seven Years War came to an end it was necessary to provide government for the former French territories in North America. As a first step the Grenville ministry issued the Proclamation of 1763 which established the usual governor-assembly form of colonial government for Canada, East and West Florida, and the small ceded islands of the West Indies. The system did not work well in Canada, because it meant that a small group of British merchants controlled the government, since the French-Canadians (as Catholics) could not hold office.

The Proclamation of 1763 also dealt with the Trans-Appalachian West, the area between the Appalachians and the Mississippi, which was reserved for the Indians and the fur trade. Land grants or settlements were prohibited in the region, the boundary of which was established by a Proclamation Line drawn along the crest of the Appalachians. For the immediate future the army was entrusted with preserving order there. Relations with the Indians were left to special agents appointed for that purpose. British restrictions on trade and settlement in the Trans–Appalachian West interfered with the aspirations and future of the American colonists. The Proclamation also aroused the anger of a powerful interest group: land speculators from Pennsylvania and Virginia, with influential supporters in Britain, who had their eyes on lands across the mountains.

In 1763, when Pontiac's Rebellion broke out along the frontier, it seemed even more necessary to strengthen imperial control, and 10,000 soldiers were sent to America. Some detachments were sent to forts scattered throughout the interior, but some soldiers, whom the Americans were required to house, were stationed in the established colonies.

Continuing Conflicts with America

The Grenville ministry had defined the issues that were to continue to poison the relations between Britain and its American colonies. The Rockingham ministry had to deal with the Stamp Act agitation. Rockingham believed that imperial unity had to be preserved, but he viewed the Stamp Act as an imprudent measure not worth the aggravation it caused. As leader of an aristocratic party, he was also eager to win support from the London merchants. Pitt opposed the act on the constitutional grounds that Parliament could not tax the colonists, although it could use customs duties to regulate trade when revenue was not the major consideration.

In 1766 Rockingham proposed that the Stamp Act be repealed. Although many members of Parliament resented colonial agitation, the insistence of the mercantile community led them to accept repeal. Rockingham, like Pitt and virtually all political leaders, was determined to preserve the authority of Britain over its colonies, although he believed that in the case of the Stamp Act it had been unwisely used. He satisfied supporters of the Stamp Act by passage of a Declaratory Act, which declared the sovereignty of Parliament over the colonies "in all cases whatsoever."

Chatham's major concern as prime minister was to settle the American question, which he believed would disappear if the colonists were not taxed. Otherwise he was an ardent imperialist. Repeal of the Stamp Act had produced much grumbling in Parliament and the question of raising a revenue in America came up again. While Chatham was immobilized by illness, Charles Townshend, Chancellor of the Exchequer, who had for some time advocated stronger imperial control over the American colonies, took the lead. To avoid another dispute over direct taxation, Townshend proposed and Parliament passed additional customs duties on colonial imports of tea, glass, paper, paints, and lead.

When Grafton replaced Chatham, his ministry was fully occupied with Wilkes and the Middlesex election. Although Grafton shared Chatham's sympathy with American complaints, most of the support for his ministry came from advocates of firmness toward the colonies. The result was a ministry that sent mixed signals. The establishment of a secretary of state for the colonies showed determination to maintain control from London. The new colonial secretary, the Earl of Hillsborough, ordered colonial governors to crack down on their assemblies and sent two regiments of troops to Boston to support the authorities there. On the other hand, the Grafton ministry decided to repeal the Townshend duties, which had been unproductive anyway, keeping only the duty on tea as a symbol of Parliament's right to tax.

In 1770 a flare-up took place in Boston when British troops fired on a mob that was harassing them. Angry colonists called this event "the Boston Massacre," but cooler heads prevailed in Britain and America and tensions subsided. When Lord North replaced Grafton in 1770 it seemed that the storm in North America had blown over.

Such was not the case. Five years of controversy had left a bitter legacy in the American colonies, and it had also left its mark in Britain. A popular backlash resulted, as violence in America was identified with the riots that Wilkes had aroused at home. Nonetheless, the king and those who supported a strong monarchy feared that any concessions would only encourage disorders at home and in the colonies, leading to a further deterioration of Britain's imperial power.

The king's speech to Parliament in January 1770 spoke of the need to bring the Americans to recognition of "lawful authority." Chatham declared that the Americans must be kept subordinate: "this is the mother country," he intoned, "they are the children; they must obey and we prescribe." Samuel Johnson supported his argument with a powerful pamphlet entitled *Taxation No Tyranny*. Reminding the Americans of their own shortcomings Johnson asked: "How is it that we hear the loudest *yelps* for liberty from the drivers of negroes?"

INDIA AND POINTS EAST

The British East India Company

Although the North American colonies received the most attention, British political leaders faced serious problems of empire in another direction. The British East India Company had been transformed by the conquest of Bengal. Instead of a Company engaging in profitable trade, it became a body with powerful military forces governing territory with a large population and revenue. The leaders of the Company helped themselves to large sums from the Bengal treasury while lesser officials of the Company enriched themselves by engaging in private trade through privileged Indian merchants.

By 1772 the East India Company was on the verge of bankruptcy. By that time the view had gained ground that the Company was a matter of public concern as the institution through which Britain held an indispensable position in India. In 1773 the North ministry led in passage of the Regulating Act, which brought the affairs of the Company under public control. To sweeten the pill, the crown gave the Company a loan of £1,400,000 and the privilege of selling tea through its own agents in the American colonies. Under the new system the Company would be able to undersell competitors: there would be no middleman and the Company would not be required to pay British customs duties, although the modest Townshend duty on tea would still be collected. The provisions concerning the sale of tea brought a reaction in Massachusetts that reopened the slumbering American problem.

THE EMERGING CONFLICT

Rising Tensions in America

Meanwhile tensions were again rising in the North American colonies. The colonists were determined to maintain the independence of their colonial governments and promote their opportunities for trade and territorial expansion. They had also developed a rhetoric to support resistance to imperial authority. They had been reading the attacks of Burke and Wilkes on the growth of royal authority, the intrigues of a faceless cabal behind the scenes, and the corruption of Parliament. They were in touch with British radicals who called into question the legitimacy of long-established privileges in government and religion.

The center of resistance was Boston, where Lord North's India Act of 1773 provided the catalyst. In November 1773, when the first cargoes of East India Company tea arrived in Boston, a violent reaction took place. A group of men disguised as Indians boarded the ships during the night and cast the tea into the harbor. Similar, but less dramatic, resistance appeared in New York, Philadelphia, and Charleston. The American colonies were out of control.

In Britain "the Boston Tea Party" came as a shock. The colonists had challenged the fundamental principle upon which the British empire was based: a controlling center with subordinate parts. It was an article of faith that Britain's power and wealth depended upon its empire. Although North was hesitant, the king, the other ministers, and both houses of Parliament agreed that something had to be done to preserve order in Massachusetts and discourage those in other colonies who might flaunt imperial authority. Ten years of colonial complaints and recalcitrance had worn out sympathizers in Britain, and the

British public generally supported firm policies to assert the authority of the Mother Country.

Realizing that royal authority was insufficient, Lord North turned to Parliament for support. A message from the king requested legislation to secure "the just dependence of the Colonies on the Crown and Parliament of Great Britain." Although Burke urged patience, legislation was passed to strengthen the powers of the governor and military authority. The port of Boston was closed until the colonists reimbursed the Company for the tea. By that time the opponents of royal authority had gained control of most units of local government, and resistance spread from Massachusetts to other colonies.

The North ministry also proposed reform of the government of Canada, where the French-Canadian majority was governed by a small group of British officials and merchants. The Quebec Act of 1774 gave most of the power to the governor, and also recognized the laws and practices of the French-Canadians, including the role of the Catholic Church. To obtain better control of trade with the Indians, the Trans-Appalachian West was attached to Quebec, thus cutting off the westward expansion of the American colonists, who, nonetheless, were already involved in land speculation and settlement in that area.

In April 1775 Gen. Thomas Gage, who had been appointed governor of Massachusetts, was ordered to suppress insurrectionary activities by force. When he sent redcoats to destroy colonial military stores, the minutemen at Lexington and Concord fired "the shot heard round the world." When Gage proclaimed martial law the colonists responded by entrenching themselves on Breed's Hill, overlooking Boston. Two months later some 2,000 redcoats under Sir William Howe attacked the American entrenchments and suffered heavy losses in what came to be known as the Battle of Bunker Hill. The colonists moved closer to outright war when they established an army commanded by George Washington to aid Massachusetts in resisting the British forces there.

As war clouds gathered, American opinion was crystallized by one of the most influential pamphlets ever written: Tom Paine's *Common Sense.* Paine rejected the idea of kingship and called upon the Americans to set an example for the world by establishing a republic based on the will of the people. He saw America as the hope of a world seeking liberty and personal dignity. He foresaw a great future as the new republic expanded, arguing that a nation of continental scope should not be governed by a small island. The pamphlet had enormous influence in persuading Americans that full independence—and nothing less—should be their objective.

In July 1776 the Second Continental Congress took the final step when it adopted the *Declaration of Independence,* which cut the last link with Britain by denying the authority of the crown. In eloquent words the *Declaration* presented to the world the "self-evident truths" which justified the American claim to "the separate and equal station to which the laws of Nature and of Nature's God entitle them." King George III was condemned as the source of "repeated injuries and usurpations, all having in direct object the establishment of an absolute Tyranny over these States." The Declaration was an appeal to world opinion, to public opinion in Britain, and to Americans, who were called upon to commit to the task "our lives, our fortunes, and our sacred honor."

Whether George III deserved the harsh condemnation of the *Declaration of Independence* was by that time immaterial. The American colonists were prepared to fight for independence and American representatives went to France seeking French aid. Powerful British forces were assembling to assert the supreme authority of crown and Parliament and maintain the unity of the empire. Several thousand German mercenaries were hired to strengthen the undermanned British army. In the dockyards warships were being refitted while

George III
at the time of his coronation.
By Sir Joshua Reynolds.
Royal Academy of Arts.

the press gangs roamed the streets and taverns of seaport towns to find the sailors needed to man them.

George III, most of the cabinet, and the overwhelming majority of the Parliament and the British public agreed that it was time to settle the matter for once and for all. Lord North, the minister of moderation, economy, and consensus, found himself the leader of a ministry at war.

CIVIL WAR WITHIN THE EMPIRE

War Begins

The outbreak of hostilities came as a surprise to the ministry and the British public, but there was a sense of relief that the die had been cast. British strategy was to occupy and hold the major cities, taking advantage of Britain's supremacy at sea, its well-disciplined army, and its ample financial resources. Gen. William Howe, who had succeeded Gage, abandoned Boston and occupied New York City, where Loyalist sentiment was strong. Though Howe drove Washington off Long Island, he did not succeed in destroying Washington's army. In this campaign Howe received naval support from his brother, Adm. Richard Howe, who commanded British naval forces in North American waters. Washington retreated into New Jersey, whence he retaliated on Christmas Eve, 1776, when he crossed the Delaware River at night and captured a contingent of Hessian mercenaries at Trenton.

By 1777 the British realized that they had a major colonial war on their hands and that peaceful reconciliation would not be possible without a decisive victory. They now planned a two-pronged attack, which would separate New England from the rest of the colonies and establish British forces in the Middle Colonies, where military occupation and naval blockade would be most effective.

The main thrust was an attack from Canada to gain control of the Hudson River valley and isolate New England. The Canadian operation was commanded by "Gentleman Johnny" Burgoyne, a political general eager to make his mark. Burgoyne would be supported by Gen. William Howe, who would first occupy Philadelphia and then move his forces northward through the Hudson Valley until the two prongs met. Burgoyne led his troops down from Canada toward the Hudson Valley, where he expected to be joined by Howe coming up from New York City. It was a case of the right hand not knowing what the left hand was doing. Howe achieved his first objective, but he was not able come to the aid of Burgoyne, who was left to make his way by himself.

By September Burgoyne was in deep trouble in the woods of upstate New York. His transportation bogged down because he did not have enough Canadian men and wagons. He had burdened himself with a heavy train of artillery, which was difficult to move by land. Thousands of New England militiamen were gathering to trap him. In October 1777 Burgoyne was surrounded at Saratoga and compelled to surrender.

The Battle of Saratoga was a turning point in the war. The French now were convinced that the Americans had a chance, and the American representatives in France, led by Benjamin Franklin, took advantage of the opportunity. In February 1778 France signed an alliance making French soldiers, seapower, and money available to the Americans. The French had no intention of regaining their empire in North America; their purpose was to weaken Britain and open up trade with the former British colonies. The French disavowed any intention of reconquering Canada, and both sides agreed not to make a separate peace.

By 1778 the British realized that they faced a different kind of war. While the British needed victory, Washington needed to avoid defeat. If Washington could keep his Continental Army in the field long enough, the Americans would win. Washington's army lived from hand to mouth, but somehow funds were always found to keep the army together. The militia supported itself, appearing to fight and then disappearing into the towns, farms, and forests of a vast land. The Americans commonly owned weapons and were accustomed to using them. Although Washington's army was small, several hundreds of thousands of men fought against the British at one time or another. The American Revolution really was a "people's war."

THE WORLD WAR

Reassessment in Britain

The defeat at Saratoga and the entry of France into the war led to important political developments in Britain. The war with France shifted attention from the American colonies to the West Indies, which were exposed while Britain was tied down in North America. The defeat at Saratoga led the North ministry to adopt a new strategy. British ground forces could not cope with a rebellion that could be suppressed at one place only to pop up again at dozen others. Therefore, the new strategy was to defeat the Americans with seapower by cutting off French aid and American trade until the rebel cause faltered. The New England campaign was abandoned and the war in America was reduced to a holding action in New York, Philadelphia, and other seaports. The major British effort in North America was to hold the southern colonies, for they were the most valuable in terms of mercantilist doctrines.

When France entered the war there was some hope in Britain that Spanish involvement could be avoided. Despite the blandishments of the French, Spain had no desire to encourage colonies to revolt against their Mother Country. In response to British overtures, Spain replied that its price for neutrality was Gibraltar, a price that Britain was unwilling to pay. When the British showed that they were determined to hold what they had, Spain declared war in 1779. Spain's main objective was to gain strategic bases that it could use to protect its empire from British threats, especially Gibraltar, Minorca, Florida, and Jamaica. The Spanish, however, did not make an alliance with the Americans. Thereafter Britain's efforts were concentrated on the maritime war against France and Spain. This was the kind of war that the British were accustomed to waging, and winning. In Parliament and in the country generally there was a sense of relief that Britain could now turn its guns against its traditional enemies. By 1780 it was clear that the war had become one of attrition, in which Britain had the advantage. "This war like the last," George III wrote, "will prove one of credit."

In 1781 France and Spain concentrated their efforts in the Caribbean, with unexpectedly favorable results. The French admiral, the Comte de Grasse, with a fine fleet, captured Tobago and other small British islands while the Spanish took Pensacola, the key to West Florida. The French also landed ground forces of almost 5,000 in Rhode Island, under the command of the Comte de Rochambeau. Rochambeau planned to cooperate with Washington in an attack on New York City, when unexpectedly favorable circumstances arose farther south.

In the southern colonies Gen. Charles Cornwallis had been carrying out the "southern policy" of his government. In a series of battles, Cornwallis suffered heavy losses, and in August 1781 he retreated to the coast, where he dug in at Yorktown and waited to be relieved. At that very moment Adm. de Grasse, with a splendid fleet, came northward from the Caribbean. Sensing their opportunity, Washington and Rochambeau moved their forces southward in forced marches. Too late the British realized that Washington was not attacking New York, but had already passed Philadelphia on his way south to trap Cornwallis. Washington, his Continental Army and militia supported by French gold and guns and seven thousand French troops, reached Yorktown in September. Cornwallis, outnumbered two to one, was besieged by land while de Grasse had him trapped by sea. In October 1781 Cornwallis surrendered and the war in America was finished.

When Lord North received the news of Yorktown he paced the room and cried: "Oh God! It is all over." Britain still had ample resources for war, but North realized that the defeat at Yorktown would destroy the political will to continue fighting. Parliament met in November 1781 in a spirit of gloom. The independent country gentlemen, who held the balance of power in a closely divided House of Commons, turned against the war. Like Robert Walpole forty years earlier, Lord North knew that he must yield to the wishes of the House of Commons, despite the support of the king. And the resignation of North very likely meant that Britain would throw in the towel.

POLITICAL CRISIS AT HOME

The Movement for Political Reform

The fall of the North ministry was directly attributable to defeat in the American War, but the news of Yorktown was only the final blow. For the previous two years the North ministry had been under political attack which had undermined confidence. Rumblings of discontent first appeared among the gentry of Yorkshire in December 1779. Christopher Wyvill, a Yorkshire clergyman, led a county meeting that called for reform of wasteful expenditures that contributed to "the influence of the crown." The "County Movement," as it was called, spread like wildfire through England in the winter of 1779-1780. The county meetings prepared petitions that were presented to the House of Commons. The petitions did not oppose the war; mainly they dealt with grievances such as heavy taxation, wasteful expenditures, and the use of public money to establish a corrupt influence over members of the House of Commons.

When Parliament met in February 1780, Lord Rockingham and Burke were ready. Burke proposed a plan of "economical reform," which included a wide variety of reforms in the management of the public money, but his main concern was to eliminate or reduce those expenditures of government that contributed directly to the political support of the ministry. Burke's plan of reform gave primary attention to the civil list, which he charged was loaded with patronage and pensions that were used to establish "corrupt influence" in Parliament. The Rockingham group was bolstered by Charles James Fox, previously a follower of North, who was a brilliant debater and an intense opponent of the king and the war.

Then the followers of Lord Shelburne stepped in, led by John Dunning, an astute lawyer. Abandoning the specifics of Burke's bill, Dunning offered the general proposition that "the influence of the crown has increased, is increasing, and ought to be diminished." After hours of excitement and intense oratory Dunning's resolution passed. Dunning followed with a motion declaring the right of Parliament to regulate the civil list, which was passed without audible dissent. Lord North was ready to resign then and there, but the king persuaded him to remain.

At this point the reform movement took a new direction. Wyvill became convinced that economical reform could not work as long as the House of Commons itself was unreformed. He proposed "parliamentary reform," including triennial elections and an increase in the number of county members.

Rockingham was strongly opposed to parliamentary reform, for he controlled a number of small boroughs himself. Lord Shelburne, who had been cool to Burke's plan of economical reform, came out in favor of parliamentary reform. Rockingham and Shelburne had always been rivals rather than colleagues, and their difference over parliamentary reform meant that the two opposition groups were more divided than ever.

The Fall of North's Ministry

The news of Yorktown, which arrived in November 1781, marked the beginning of the end for the North ministry. In circumstances reminiscent of Sir Robert Walpole in 1742, North wrote to King George III:

> "The torrent is too strong to be resisted; Your Majesty is well apprized that, in this country, the Prince on the throne, cannot with prudence, oppose the deliberate resolution of the House of Commons; Your Royal Predecessors (particularly King William the Third and his late Majesty) were obliged to yield to it much against their wish in more instances than one: They consented to changes in their Ministry which they disapproved because they found it necessary to sacrifice their private wishes, and even their opinions to the preservation of public order, and the prevention of those terrible mischiefs, which are the natural consequence of the clashing of two branches of the Sovereign Power in the State."

George III refused to accept North's definition of the constitution. He felt that North had abandoned him in time of need. The king was determined not to accept Rockingham as prime minister, for that would mean he had lost his freedom of action in the appointment of ministries. Rockingham was committed to peace with France and Spain, American independence, and Burke's bill for "economical reform," all of which George III resolutely opposed. After protracted negotiations, George III found he had no choice but to accept Rockingham's terms. A ministry was formed headed by Rockingham, with Fox and Shelburne as secretaries of state. Negotiations began for American indpendence, and Burke's "economical reform" bill was passed, much to the king's dismay.

THE CROWN, THE COMMONS, AND THE PEACE

The Shelburne Ministry

The political scene was suddenly changed in July 1782, when Rockingham died and the king turned to Lord Shelburne as his successor. Shelburne's per-

Rowlandson's cartoon of Fox and North as "The Right Honourable Catch Singers," 1783.
Personal collection of Henry L. Snyder.

sonal following was small, but he hoped that the support of the king and a broad policy of reform would win support for a nonparty ministry.

Charles James Fox, Burke, and other followers of Rockingham were outraged, for they felt that one of their group should have been chosen. They disliked Shelburne intensely and felt that he had sold out to the king to advance his own political ambitions. Led by Fox, this group resigned and went into opposition. Lord North and his followers waited their opportunity, since both groups now courted them. A year earlier Shelburne's small contingent in the House of Commons had been strengthened by the arrival of William Pitt, younger son of Lord Chatham, who took his seat in the House of Commons and immediately distinguished himself by his intellect, poise, and oratory.

The End Game

While Britain was torn by political turmoil, the war was turning in its favor. The Battle of Yorktown marked the end of the war on the North American mainland, but every effort was made to hold Canada, Nova Scotia and the Grand Banks, Florida, the British West Indies, Gibraltar, the West African slaving posts, and the territories of the East India Company. George III knew he would need bargaining chips at the peace table. He intended to hold the major American seaports until a treaty was made that guaranteed the rights of the Loyalists.

By 1782 the war at sea had changed. The British navy had finally achieved its full potential, and France and Spain were nearing the end of their resources. The French and Spanish fleets in the West Indies planned a combined attack on Jamaica. In April, Admiral Rodney intercepted the French fleet at the tiny islands called The Saintes. Rodney won a decisive victory, capturing de Grasse and destroying the French fleet. In 1782 the navy scored another dramatic victory by relieving the besieged garrison of Gibraltar, one of Spain's major objectives. Shelburne insisted that a major effort be made to hold the Rock, and Adm. Richard Howe, who had returned to service with the fall of the North ministry, led a powerful armada for this purpose. Howe's fleet broke through to resupply the garrison and Gibraltar was held. Previously Minorca had been lost after a heroic siege, its garrison hopelessly weakened by scurvy.

Seapower also made it possible for France to challenge the British in Eastern waters. The French were active in India, stirring up the Indian princes against the East India Company with promises of aid. Warren Hastings, the warlike governor, fought desperately to preserve the East India Company's position. In 1782–1738 a French fleet appeared on the coasts of India and was fought to a standstill by an inferior British fleet in five close-run battles. The end of the war in 1783 left the British in control of their territories. Piers Mackesy has commented: "The struggle had opened in a gray dawn at Lexington; its last shot was fired eight years later on the other side of the world outside a dusty town in southern India."

The Peace of Paris

By 1782 France was financially ruined and desperately needed peace. Spain was the main obstacle to peace, but when the British held Gibraltar the Spanish were ready to give in. As the war wound down Shelburne offered generous peace terms to the Americans, who jumped at the chance, leaving their French ally in the lurch. When the American negotiators proposed a separate peace on the basis of independence, Shelburne accepted the inevitable and agreed. The Americans were granted the Trans-Appalachian West, but their demand for Canada was rejected. They promised repayment of pre-Revolutionary debts and compensation for the American Loyalists. Neither of these promises was fulfilled.

Although the peace treaty guaranteed fair treatment to the American Loyalists, large numbers of them fled to Nova Scotia and Canada, where they faced a hard life, for they were mainly business and professional people, ill-prepared for a frontier existence. Therefore the British government gave them some assistance in getting settled. To deal with the large influx of people, Nova Scotia was reconstituted into three units: Nova Scotia, New Brunswick, and Prince Edward Island. The Loyalists who fled to Canada did not wish to live among the French inhabitants of Quebec, so they were given land along the upper St. Lawrence and the shores of the Great Lakes, where they laid the foundations of the province of Ontario.

In the meantime, peace negotiations with France and Spain were also proceeding. Shelburne's long-range goals included good diplomatic and commercial relations with the French. By January 1783 the draft treaty was ready for presentation to Parliament. Britain's losses were moderate. France was conceded fishing rights on the Grand Banks, the West Indian islands of St. Lucia and Tobago, Senegal, and Goree in West Africa, which gave access to the Atlantic slave trade, and its trading posts in India were returned. As to Spain, the outcome of the negotiations had been determined on the battlefield. Spain kept Minorca and Florida, which it had already captured, but the stubborn defense of Gibraltar had made the Rock a symbol of national pride and Shelburne refused to give it up.

When Shelburne's peace proposals came before the House of Commons there was an outcry that they were too generous. It was obvious that the followers of Fox and North had come together to overthrow the ministry. Shelburne saw the handwriting on the wall and resigned, despite the urging of the king to put up a fight. The king had to accept a coalition ministry led by Fox and North. Once again King George III had been compelled to yield on his most important principle: the right of the king to choose his own ministers. It was evident that the Fox-North Coalition Ministry would not last long if George III had any choice in the matter.

The Fox-North Coalition

The main concern of Fox and the Coalition Ministry was the continuing problems of the British East India Company. Lord North's Regulating Act of 1773 had not worked well, for the governor and council established by the act had quarreled constantly, the crown had no authority over them, and the Company could not remove or control them. A rash of complaints were made about abuses of power by Warren Hastings, and a series of parliamentary investigations created a consensus that something had to be done. The Company was bankrupt and in no position to resist. In 1782 the directors of the Company were pressured into recalling Hastings to face charges.

In 1783 Fox presented the Coalition's East India Bill, prepared primarily by Edmund Burke, who had been actively engaged in the parliamentary investigation of Hastings. The problem faced by the Coalition was to establish effective public authority over the affairs of the Company without giving the crown control of the patronage and power exercised by the Company. To solve this problem Fox proposed to bring the Company under an independent body of seven commissioners, appointed for four-year terms, to be named in the act. A howl went up when it was revealed that the commissioners to be named in the bill were all friends of Fox or North. There would be another nine commissioners named by the directors to manage the trade of India.

From the time the Coalition had taken office the king had been searching for a credible replacement. He approached Pitt and his cousins, the Grenvilles, who were willing if the king would use all his powers to provide them with parliamentary support, including calling an election. John Robinson, the king's expert manager of elections, took discreet soundings among borough-mongers and found that he could deliver a majority. The East India Company and other mercantile groups in London provided money and support.

The Triumph of the King

In December 1783 George III dismissed the Fox-North Coalition and imposed a ministry of his own choice led by the young William Pitt. The leaders of the Coalition passed one resolution after another against Pitt, who simply ignored them. In March 1784 the Pitt ministry won a crucial measure by one vote, and then Pitt lowered the boom. George III, scenting victory, dissolved the Parliament and called the promised election.

The election of 1784 was one of the most decisive in the eighteenth century. The ministers of the crown normally could control the outcome of elections, but the election of 1784 was unusual in the extent to which appeals to public opinion were part of the electoral process. The election was also unusual in its decisiveness, for more than one hundred of Fox's followers lost their seats and Fox himself faced a strong challenge in his constituency of Westminster, where he had always been popular. George III was actively involved in electoral details and contributed as much as he could of his personal funds to defeat the Coalition. When the dust settled the king had won a notable victory, and he could rejoice in the thought that "he who laughs last, laughs best."

THE PROBLEM OF IRELAND

The Rise of Irish Nationalism

"Britain's necessity is Ireland's opportunity." The truth of this saying was proven dramatically during the American Revolution, for the Irish followed the American example to gain more independence for themselves. The Irish shared many of the grievances felt by the Americans, and Irish patriots adopted much of the American political rhetoric and argumentation.

Nevertheless, Ireland differed from the American colonies in many ways. The main difference was that Ireland was a lot closer to Britain. For strategic reasons, Ireland could not be allowed enough independence to make it possible for Britain's enemies to use the island for intrigues or military operations. The patronage of the Irish government and Church was important to British politicians and churchmen. The Irish army was an important supplement to the British army. Many British aristocrats owned landed estates in Ireland that might be threatened by Irish independence.

The movement for Irish independence was led by the Protestants: the Anglo-Irish who controlled government and the Church, and the tough-minded, hard-working Presbyterians who were settled mainly in Ulster. In the early eighteenth century the Protestant Irish accepted British domination—although not without complaint—because they were economically prostrate and needed support from Britain to maintain their ascendancy over the Catholic majority.

By the second half of the century Ireland was prospering and religious conflict had diminished. The penal acts, especially those prohibiting Catholics from owning businesses or lands, were laxly enforced, if at all. Catholics were permitted to educate their children and a small Catholic middle class began to appear. As religious dissensions declined, the Protestant Irish felt new confidence and were prepared to take their political affairs into their own hands.

Ireland and the American Revolution

When the American War broke out public opinion in Ireland favored the Americans. The Anglo-Irish elite was concerned that the claim of the British Parliament to legislate for the colonies, including taxation, could also be applied to Ireland. Irish landlords, farmers, manufacturers, and merchants resented restrictions on Irish trade for the benefit of special interests in Britain. A large number of Scotch-Irish Presbyterians had emigrated to the American colonies, where they were strong supporters of independence. Their ideas radiated back to their relatives in Ireland. The press was strongly pro-American, as were the Presbyterian clergy. Public dissatisfaction was strengthened by economic depression, which was made worse by the interruption of trade caused by the war.

In 1779 a combined French-Spanish fleet cruised the Channel and an invasion was expected. The year before, John Paul Jones had sailed boldly into Belfast harbor and captured a British ship. Since most of the Irish army was deployed elsewhere, the Irish Protestants formed themselves into a militia known as the Volunteers, comprised of middle-class Protestants who could afford to provide their own weapons and uniforms. The Volunteers became important as a center of political agitation.

By 1780 political demands took priority over economic or military concerns. The struggle passed to the Irish House of Commons, where Henry Grattan, a powerful orator, took the lead. He demanded freedom for the Irish Parliament to pass legislation for its own internal affairs (legislative independence) while remaining joined to Britain for foreign policy, defense, and trade. Back in London the Rockingham party, led by Edmund Burke—himself an Irishman—supported the Volunteers, using the uprising in Ireland as another issue on which to attack Lord North. A convention of the Volunteers at Dungannon in February 1782 virtually set itself up as an alternative government.

Legislative Independence

When the Rockingham ministry took office in 1782 it was obvious that something had to be done about Ireland. The new viceroy was the Duke of Portland, a wealthy nobleman who held extensive estates in Ireland. Shortly after he arrived in Dublin, Portland reported that the authority of the crown had vanished. When Grattan presented a resolution in the Irish Parliament declaring legislative independence, no one dared oppose him. The Rockingham Ministry quickly conceded what it could no longer hold. The laws that gave the British crown and Parliament authority over Ireland were repealed. Appeals to British courts were ended. Politically Ireland dangled, connected to Britain only by the power of the crown and strong economic and cultural ties.

Despite the dramatic events of 1782, much of the old system remained. The viceroy continued as an independent executive acting for the British crown, conducting the executive functions of government and controlling an extensive patronage. As a member of the British cabinet, the appointment of the viceroy was determined by British politics, not Irish. The Irish House of Commons remained unrepresentative, even of the Irish Protestants, and many Irish patriots saw parliamentary reform as the next step. Irish Catholics had gained little from the movement, which they had generally supported; they began to organize to claim political rights for themselves and an easing of the restrictions under which they lived.

REASON AND RELIGION

Edward Gibbon

The eighteenth century is often called "the Age of Reason," for philosophy and science seemed to replace the revealed truth of the Bible and the wisdom of the ancient Greeks and Romans. Edward Gibbon used history to expound a rationalist analysis of institutions and society that had disturbing implications for those who were complacent about Britain and its empire. The first volume of Gibbon's *The History of the Decline and Fall of the Roman Empire* appeared in 1776 and was immediately recognized as a masterpiece. Gibbon was provided with a parliamentary seat by the North ministry, writing his account of the breakdown of the Roman empire when the empire of his own country seemed to be coming apart at the seams.

Gibbon's purpose was to contrast the freedom and rationality of the early Roman Empire with the corruption, violence, and fanaticism that followed. He depicted the Roman Empire in its first century almost as a Utopia, where reason, public spirit, and tolerance prevailed. In his view the Roman decline began with the growth of comfort and self-satisfaction among the upper and middle classes, who left government and security to the emperor and the legions. Eventually this power became corrupted and abused, and the decline of the empire had begun.

A second factor was the spread of Christianity among the common people, who sought in religion the satisfaction denied them in their everyday lives. Gibbon's account of the rise of the Christian Church, which he attributed to human factors, not the will and purposes of God, and his scornful treatment of many Christian beliefs and practices, brought down upon him the wrath of those who were devoted to the Church and its teachings. He was masterful in depicting the energy and devotion of the Christians while detailing the bitterness of their interminable theological disputes and the savagery with which they attacked their enemies, including fellow Christians with whom they disagreed. Weakened by corruption, militarism, civil strife, and the stubborn separateness of the Christians, who were loyal to their Church and heavenly king, the Roman Empire fell victim to the German invaders, who further debased the level of government and society. As one of the reasons for the fall of the Roman Empire and Roman civilization Gibbon listed "the domestic quarrels of the Romans," an idea relevant to those who observed the political contentions that led to and followed the fall of Lord North's ministry.

Gibbon was not just an Englishman seeking to draw lessons suitable for his countrymen. His perspective was cosmopolitan. He urged respect for the high civilization achieved in his own time and defense of this civilization against those who would destroy what they could not understand. Gibbon ended his account of decline on an optimistic note. He was confident that a collapse into barbarism would not recur and that the civilization of his own time would increase "the real wealth, the happiness, the knowledge, and perhaps the virtue, of the human race."

Samuel Johnson

The outlook of the Age of Reason was challenged by Samuel Johnson, whose powerful intellect, wide knowledge, eloquence, and sound judgment raised him from the ranks of hack writers to the leading literary figure of Georgian Britain. His father operated a bookstore, which enabled him to read widely in his boyhood, and his family was able to provide one year at Oxford, but beyond that he had to make his way in the world as a writer. He arrived in London in 1737 when an expanding middle class provided new markets for published materials, and a great number of publishers, booksellers, and writers sought to capitalize on the opportunity.

Johnson had the good fortune to obtain employment with Edward Cave, who in 1731 had founded the *Gentleman's Magazine,* a monthly that provided a cross-section of articles from newspapers and other periodicals. Johnson became Cave's editorial assistant, writing special articles as well as accounts of foreign news and the parliamentary debates. Johnson wrote the debates out of his head, using only rough notes of the speakers and topics but giving the gist of the argument in his own splendid prose. He felt guilty about passing off his own creations as authentic speeches, but the debates were enormously popular and the speakers were flattered to have their ideas presented in such an eloquent style. Johnson's career on the *Gentleman's Magazine* gave him a wide acquaintance with politics, journalism, and the literary world, and after his direct connection ceased he continued the friendships established during his years at the magazine.

In 1747 Johnson published a plan to prepare his *Dictionary of the English Language,* and with the support of a group of publishers he spent the next seven years completing this great work. Johnson's dictionary was built on historical principles. He went through important works of English writing, noting words in their context and having his copyists copy passages on slips of paper. From these slips he prepared definitions based on usage. Johnson's *Dictionary* gave not only the definition (or definitions) of each word, but included the citations upon which the definition was based, thus providing a history of the language and a stockpile of apt quotations.

Some of Johnson's best writing appeared in two essay journals, the *Rambler* (1750–1752) and the *Idler* (1758–1760), in which he dealt with moral questions as they related to everyday life. Johnson rooted his ethics in an honest assessment of human experience, avoiding both optimism and fatalism. He gave special attention to the illusions and self-deceptions by which people give a false meaning and purpose to their lives, while conceding good-naturedly that these are often necessary to make life tolerable. Johnson developed a sonorous, dignified style, calculated to communicate a sense of authority while convincing the reader with well-chosen examples that hit home.

In politics Johnson is often called a "Tory," but that term had lost much of its meaning by mid-century. His view of politics was that of the honest, independent citizen prepared to cock a skeptical eye at politicians and their minions. Johnson looked to the king to rise above party politics and popular demagogues and give the nation leadership based on concern for the general welfare. For this reason he supported King George III, with whom he once had a long conversation that he regarded as one of the great experiences of his life.

Johnson was conservative in his desire to preserve an ordered society, which he regarded as best for most of the population. He suspected that calls for "Liberty" grew out of personal ambition or unreasonable expectations, neither of which was likely to contribute to the public good. In *The False Alarm* (1770) Johnson attacked the famous rabble-rouser John Wilkes, whom he later discovered to be a fine fellow, despite his politics. Johnson wrote several pamphlets supporting the policies of the crown against the American colonists who, in his view, were stiff-necked malcontents resisting an imperial system that was beneficial to all concerned. With his shrewd realism and practical good sense, Johnson opposed political or religious movements that depended upon shallow rhetoric and emotional arguments. He found Wilkes and the American colonists both deficient in that respect.

Samuel Johnson was a deeply religious man, committed to historic Christianity in an age when the rising trend of thought was toward rational skepticism. For Samuel Johnson religion stepped in where morality failed: it was a source of divine strength when one could not make it on his own; it was a source of divine wisdom where one could not understand for himself; it was a source of forgiveness for those shortcomings that one could not overcome. Johnson suffered acutely from depression—an affliction known in the eigh-

The Royal Crescent, Bath. Private collection.

teenth century as melancholia or the spleen. For support in dealing with this problem he turned to religion, especially the beautiful language of the *Book of Common Prayer.* Johnson clung to his Christian faith because he needed it.

One of Johnson's friends, a Scottish lawyer named James Boswell, collected anecdotes and reminiscences about Samuel Johnson. In 1791 Boswell's *Life of Johnson* was published and instantly recognized as a masterpiece. Boswell had a marvelous ability to use detail to build up a picture of an individual—warts and all. Boswell's *Life of Johnson* is a recognized classic, and still the source to which we go to find the Samuel Johnson who, through his works and conversation, influenced one of the most important generations in British political and cultural history.

SUGGESTIONS FOR FURTHER READING

In addition to the general works noted in the preceding chapter, a good introduction to the period is J. Steven Watson, *The Reign of George III* (1960), which has been replaced in part by Paul Langford, *A Polite and Commercial People: England, 1727–1783* (1992). Ian Christie, *Wars and Revolutions: Britain, 1760–1815* (1982) is a competent survey. Two good biographies of King George III are by John Brooke (1972) and Stanley Ayling (1972). For historical assessments of the king see Earl A. Reitan, *George III: Tyrant or Constitutional Monarch* (1964).

The most influential of twentieth-century historians was Sir Lewis Namier. His *Structure of Politics at the Accession of George III* (2nd edition, 1957) should be supplemented with his essays reprinted in *Crossroads of Power* (1962). Namier began a survey of the period from 1760 to 1782. He only completed the first volume, *England in the Age of the American Revolution* (2nd edition, 1961), which bears the subtitle *Government and Parliament under the Duke of Newcastle.* Additional works in the series were by his students: John Brooke, *The Chatham Administration* (1956); Bernard Donoughue, *British Politics and the American Revolution: The Path to War, 1773–75* (1964); and Ian Christie, *The End of North's Ministry* (1958). For an evaluation and appreciation of Sir Lewis Namier see Linda Colley, *Namier* (1989).

Other valuable works on politics are Richard Pares, *King George III and the Politicians* (1953); Brian Hill, *Early Parties and Politics* (cited in previous chapters); Frank O'Gorman, *The Emergence of the British Two-Party System* (1982); Christie, *Wilkes, Wyvill and Reform* (1962); George Rude, *Wilkes and Liberty* (1962); Peter D. G. Thomas, *John Wilkes: A Friend to Liberty* (1996); Herbert Butterfield, *George III, Lord North and the People, 1779–1780* (1949); John Cannon, *The Fox-North Coalition: Crisis of the Constitution* (1969); and Lucy Sutherland, *The East India Company in Eighteenth Century Politics* (1952). The role of the Church in politics is examined in James E. Bradley, "The Anglican Pulpit, the Social Order, and the Resurgence of Toryism during the American Revolution," *Albion* 21, (Fall, 1989), 361–388. Bradley has also traced the influence of Dissenters in *Religion, Revolution, and English Radicalism: Nonconformity in Eighteenth-Century Politics and Society* (1990).

The Prime Ministers: Vol. I, Sir Robert Walpole to Sir Robert Peel, ed. Herbert M. Van Thal (1974), is a convenient introduction to the series of prime ministers who held office during the king's first decade. Important biographies are Peter D. G. Thomas, *Lord North* (1976); Ross J. S. Hoffman, *The Marquis: A Study of Lord Rockingham, 1730–1782* (1973); and John Norris, *Shelburne and Reform* (1963). The best study of Edmund Burke's political views is Frank

O'Gorman, *Edmund Burke His Political Philosophy* (1973). A valuable appreciation of Burke can be found in *The Relevance of Edmund Burke,* ed. Peter Stanlis (1964).

For foreign policy, see books by Langford and Horn cited in Chapter 9. Books on foreign policy and war by Reitan and Black (cited in earlier chapters) are also relevant. H. M. Scott, *British Foreign Policy in the Age of the American Revolution* (1990) is essential. Richard Middleton covers *The Bells of Victory: The Pitt-Newcastle Ministry and the Conduct of the Seven Years War, 1757–1762* (1985). See also the collection of essays in *England's Rise to Greatness, 1660–1763* (1983), ed. Stephen Baxter, especially Baxter's essay entitled "The Conduct of the Seven Years War." Good biographies of Pitt are by J. H. Plumb (1953), Stanley Ayling (1976), and Marie Peters (1998). Kathleen Wilson, *The Sense of the People: Politics, Culture and Imperialism in England, 1715–1785* (1998) shows the broad public support for overseas expansion.

A useful book on the American Revolution from the perspective of a British scholar is Ian Christie, *Crisis of Empire* (1966). Charles Ritcheson examines *British Politics and the American Revolution* (1954). Piers Mackesy, *The War for America* (1965) is a masterful work that puts the American problem in the broader context of a major war and an imperial crisis. For the navy see Nicholas Tracy, *Navies, Deterrence, and American Independence: Britain and Seapower in the 1760s and 1770s* (1988) and John A. Tilley, *The British Navy and the American Revolution* (1987). For the army, see Sylvia Frey, *The British Soldier in America* (1981) and Christopher Hibbert, *Redcoats and Rebels* (1990).

Two relevant books on Canada are Gustave Lanctot, *Canada and the American Revolution, 1774–1783* (1967) and Philip Lawson, *The Imperial Challenge: Quebec and Britain in the Age of the American Revolution* (1989). The Irish dimension of the crisis is examined in R. B. McDowell, *Ireland in the Age of Imperialism and Revolution, 1760–1801* (1979). For India see Michal Edwards, *The Battle of Plassey and the Conquest of Bengal* (1963) and Penderel Moon, *Warren Hastings and British India* (1947). James A. Williamson provides an interesting account of Capt. Cook's explorations in *Cook and the Opening of the Pacific* (1948).

For Edward Gibbon see Roy Porter, *Gibbon: Making History* (1989). Among the mass of scholarship and literary criticism on Samuel Johnson, the best place to begin is Boswell's *Life;* followed by Thomas Kaminski, *The Early Career of Samuel Johnson* (1987); and John Cannon, *Samuel Johnson and the Politics of Hanoverian England* (1995).

CHAPTER TWELVE

The Revolutionary Age
1783–1815

In the year 1783 George III had been king for twenty-three years. He was a conscientious, hard-working ruler who had learned from bitter experience how to use the powers vested in him. His efforts to strengthen the personal role of the monarch he regarded as restoring the practices of the past. In 1782 George III suffered a severe political blow when Parliament turned against the American War and compelled him to accept a ministry headed by his political enemies and pledged to American independence. In December 1783 George III reasserted his royal powers by dismissing the Fox-North coalition and appointing as prime minister the twenty-four-year old William Pitt, son of the elder William Pitt, Earl of Chatham. The king completed the discomfiture of his political opponents in the spring of 1784 when he used the power of the crown to call an election, in which the Pitt ministry won a decisive victory. The king, who had been humiliated in 1782 had, it appeared, restored the power of the king to govern through ministers of his own choosing.

GEORGE III AND WILLIAM PITT

George III

George III demonstrated in 1783–1784 the decisive role that a determined monarch could play in eighteenth-century politics, but those exciting events marked the high point of the personal power of the king. George III had placed Pitt in office, but he was also dependent on Pitt, who was the only alternative

to the king's political opponents. Furthermore, Pitt was enormously competent, and the king was willing to allow him to deal with the economic and
administrative problems that dominated the postwar period. In 1787–1788
George III suffered an attack of mental illness that lasted about four months.
Thereafter he was concerned about his health and reduced his involvement in
public business.

When war broke out with France in 1793, the king gained stature as a
symbol of national unity, but the needs of war thrust more responsibility upon
Pitt and his cabinet. In 1801 a political crisis in which Pitt resigned was followed by another of the king's mental breakdowns. Although the king recovered, he was now advanced in years and his political involvement had to be
further curtailed. By 1811 his sanity was permanently lost, and when he died
in 1820 he was little more than a memory. The long reign of the king who had
taken the throne determined to restore the royal power proved to be a reign in
which the British monarchy was irretrievably set in the direction of the figure-
head monarchy of today.

William Pitt and Charles James Fox

Throughout the eighteenth century, British government worked best when
the king had the services of a strong, capable prime minister who could lead
the cabinet, supervise finance and administration, and win parliamentary support for his policies. William Pitt was such a man. From the beginning of his
ministry he showed himself to be a masterful person, despite his youth, and he
never ceased to be the dominant figure in his ministry, even as he drew other
powerful leaders to his side. He was a superb administrator, using his post as
first lord of the Treasury to extend Treasury supervision into many facets of
government. In the House of Commons, where oratory could have a powerful
effect, Pitt was inferior to none. He was responsive to new ideas, quick to see
how they could be applied to the improvement of government, and also sensitive to humanitarian concerns such as prison reform and the abolition of the
slave trade. His ministry, however, depended on a conservative king and a body
of supporters in Parliament who were content to leave well enough alone. Thus
his achievements fell short of his aspirations.

One of the important features of eighteenth-century politics was the
development of a "loyal opposition." The opposition led by Lord Rockingham
had eventually brought about the downfall of North's ministry and the end of
the American Revolution. When Rockingham died in 1782, Charles James Fox
took his place. It was Fox who was dismissed by George III in December 1783
when young William Pitt was installed in power. For the remainder of their
lives, Pitt and Fox were political rivals. Like Pitt, Fox was a superb orator and
debater, and in his few brief periods in office he showed himself to be a capable administrator. Detested by the king, Fox looked to George, Prince of

William Pitt the Younger.
By John Hoppner, 1805.
By courtesy of
The National Gallery, London.

Wales, who had just turned twenty-one and was ready to play a role in politics, mainly by efforts to get more money to support his extravagant lifestyle. When the king lost his mind in 1787–1788, it looked as if Fox's gamble would pay off. When the king recovered and learned that Fox and the Prince of Wales were already preparing to assume power, his dislike for his renegade son and his political friends became implacable.

Fox became the leader of those who called themselves Whigs. Fox's key principle was his concern for the independence of Parliament and the rights of individuals, which he believed were threatened by the tendency of the crown to draw power to itself. He supported parliamentary reform, the reduction of royal patronage, freedom of the press, religious toleration, and the abolition of the slave trade. By taking his stand in opposition to royal power, Fox condemned himself to political frustration, but he won a place in the hearts of his contemporaries as a powerful defender of liberty.

Pitt and Reform

It was Pitt's task to restore confidence and unity to a nation torn by partisan strife and shaken by defeat in the American Revolution. Britain had emerged from the war in desperate financial straits, and Pitt, as first lord of the Treasury, had primary responsibility for restoring the finances of the government.

It was in this area that Pitt's rationality, efficiency, and openness to new ideas were most effectively displayed. He improved financial management by refinancing the national debt, consolidating and simplifying the revenues, reducing smuggling and other evasions of taxes, and improving the management and audit of public money. Another important concern was to improve the revenue by encouraging trade through a series of trade treaties with other countries. Pitt's goal was a surplus of revenue over expenditure, which could be used to begin reduction of the national debt. When the necessary surplus was achieved in 1786, he created a sinking fund to be earmarked for debt reduction. Although Pitt's surplus was soon to be consumed by new wars, Pitt's sinking fund had an important psychological effect, for it demonstrated that Britain was again financially strong.

Pitt also took the lead in the reform of Parliament. In the previous decade, complaints had frequently been made that the House of Commons was dominated by the crown and failed to represent the views of the people. The influence of the crown was thought to be derived from small boroughs controlled by local magnates, while the growing electorates of the shires and populous towns were underrepresented. In 1785 Pitt proposed a moderate measure of reform that would disfranchise thirty-six small boroughs (with compensation) and distribute the seats to London and the larger counties. George III disapproved of tinkering with the ancient constitution, and many of Pitt's supporters were reluctant to support any proposal to change the distribution of seats, no matter how moderate or justifiable. The measure was soundly defeated—and with it, Pitt's attempt at parliamentary reform. Fox and his friends raised the issue in 1793 and again in 1797, but without success. Rejection of parliamentary reform in small installments meant that a great crisis was likely to take place eventually. For the moment, however, the political class was content to leave things as they were.

Another problem was Ireland, which had received legislative independence in 1782. Pitt tried to counteract the weakening of British political control by strengthening the economic ties that bound Britain and Ireland. In 1785 he presented his Irish Commercial Resolutions, in which he proposed to institute free trade between Britain and Ireland in exchange for an Irish contribution to the cost of maintaining the navy. Again a statesman-like policy failed. British economic interests that feared Irish competition mounted a powerful lobby against Pitt's proposals, and the Irish resented Pitt's insistence on support for the navy.

Pitt and the Empire

When Pitt came to power in December 1783, the British empire had, as we have seen, been rocked by the loss of the American colonies. One of his major concerns was to restore British trade, shipping, and seapower, which were thought to depend on the empire. The immediate problem facing the young minister was the restoration of commercial relations between Britain and its former American colonies. Pitt favored a generous arrangement, but strong opposition developed in Parliament and the nation, based on the contention that the Americans, having chosen to leave the empire, should no longer enjoy its advantages. Under the Fox-North Coalition, Orders in Council had been issued that declared that American ships would be considered as foreign ships and thus subject to the restrictions of the Navigation Acts. Overtures were made to establish diplomatic relations with the new American states, and in 1785 John Adams was received as the first American ambassador to the court of St. James's.

Relations with the American states had an important bearing on the British West Indies, for the American states were an important market for West Indian products and supplied the West Indies with grain, fish, barrel staves, and other necessities. The new trade regulations meant that this trade could not legally be conducted in American ships. The West Indies interest in London protested this policy vigorously, but to no effect. The British government expected that Canadian colonies could supply food and timber products, and that imperial trade would benefit if West Indian products went directly to Britain. Despite their cries of alarm, the British West Indies continued to be profitable. When war broke out with France in 1793, Britain saw the need to restore trade relations between the West Indies and the United States. In 1795 Jay's Treaty gave American ships increased access to the West Indian market.

Pitt faced serious problems in dealing with the Canadian colonies, which had been profoundly affected by the American Revolution. Prior to the war, Canada consisted principally of the French settlements along the St. Lawrence River. As mentioned above, the American Revolution led to a large influx of Loyalists into Canada. They demanded a representative assembly and English law, but the French inhabitants preferred to preserve their traditional laws and customs. Pitt's solution was the Canada Act of 1791, which divided Canada into two parts. Quebec (Lower Canada), which was primarily French, preserved French law, land tenure, and the rights of the Roman Catholic church. Ontario (Upper Canada) had English land tenure and law. Both colonies had assemblies, but there was one royal governor whose power over both provinces was dominant. Nova Scotia, New Brunswick, and Prince Edward Island were already separate colonies. Thus the Pitt ministry provided a system of government for the Canadian colonies that proved workable for the next half century.

Pitt's major imperial problem was to establish control over the powers of the British East India Company in India, a bone of contention in Britain for the previous two decades. In the Seven Years' War the East India Company had acquired authority over the great province of Bengal and had become involved in government and war, while its commercial activities fell upon evil days. Two other problems also emerged: the influence exercised by the East India Company upon British domestic politics, and notorious abuses of power by the Company in dealing with the native inhabitants of India. When Pitt took office the demand in Britain for legislation regulating the Company was overwhelming; the only question was the form that it would take.

Pitt's India Act of 1784 (amended in 1786) provided a compromise solution. The Company continued to govern its territories in India, but a Board of Control in London and a strong governor-general in India established public authority over the Company. The first governor-general was Lord Cornwallis, who atoned for his defeat at Yorktown by introducing a new standard of rectitude and efficiency into the government of the Company's territories in India.

The Pitt ministry extended the Empire into a new area when it began British settlement in Australia. Up until this time, one of the common sentences passed upon convicted felons was transportation, ordinarily to America. With American independence, however, Britain lacked a place to send such convicts, and for several years the government could only confine them to derelict ships (hulks) anchored in the Thames. The Pitt ministry proposed to relieve the situation by settling the convicts in Australia, which had been discovered by Captain Cook in 1770. The first shipload of convicts arrived in Australia in 1788, and Sydney was established as a penal colony governed by a military commander and a garrison. After considerable hardship, discharged soldiers and freed convicts began to settle the region, and the new colony took root.

THE BEGINNINGS OF INDUSTRIALISM

Economic Growth

The eighteenth century was a period of remarkable economic growth in Britain. These economic changes were so far-reaching in their effects that historians have called them "The Industrial Revolution." There are many reasons why Britain became the first industrial nation. The government of Britain combined political stability, individual freedom, and security of property in a mix conducive to enterprise and investment. Britain's institutions of banking and credit were well developed, and its far-flung trade and Empire provided capital, raw materials, and markets for industry. Strong domestic demand, fueled by wealth derived from trade and agriculture, stimulated new methods for increased production of goods. The availability of coal, iron, and waterpower was an important factor. A growing population provided labor for factories and mines; a prosperous agriculture produced the food and fiber needed

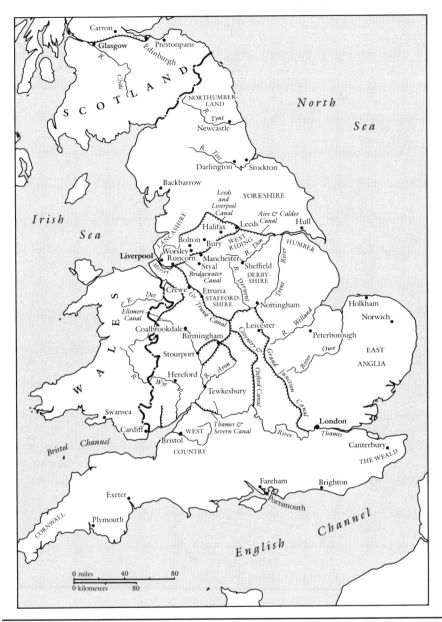

The Industrial Revolution

to sustain an industrial economy. Thus in the later half of the eighteenth century a unique set of circumstances, brought together by a generation of unusual inventiveness and enterprise, made Britain the leader in a movement that transformed the world—the Industrial Revolution.

Iron, Steam, and Coal

One important feature of the early industrial age was the manufacture of cheaper and more abundant iron. Prior to the eighteenth century, iron was smelted with charcoal, which made it necessary to locate most iron works in forests (to obtain fuel). In the eighteenth century the Darbys, a family of iron makers located in the Severn Valley, developed a method of smelting iron with coal by first converting the coal to coke. The most striking of the new industrial ironmasters of Britain was John Wilkinson, who built an ironworks across the river from the Darbys. His cannon boring machine greatly improved the range and accuracy of his cannon and could also be adapted to make cylinders for steam engines. He promoted iron products in a variety of ways: he built iron barges, installed an iron pulpit in the local church, and was buried in an iron coffin. Wilkinson was a strong-willed, hard-driving person who could take advantage of new processes and transform iron making from a small family enterprise into a large-scale industry. As a result of these new processes, iron production in Britain more than doubled from 1760 to 1788, and quadrupled again in the next seventeen years.

Another feature of industrialism was the development of a vital new source of power—the steam engine. Engines powered by steam had been in use since the late seventeenth century, but they were highly inefficient and were used mainly to pump water out of coal mines. In the 1760s a Scottish instrument maker, James Watt, began developing a more efficient type of steam engine. He also invented a device to convert steam power to a rotary motion. In 1774 Watt went into partnership with Matthew Boulton, a Birmingham businessman, to manufacture steam engines. Watt's engines were first used for coal mines, smelting, and forges and were later adapted to textile manufactures, rail transport, and ships.

Iron smelting and the steam engine made necessary a larger supply of coal. Coal had been an important product since Tudor times, and Britain possessed an abundant supply of it, much of it near the surface. Until the industrial age, coal was used principally for home heating. By the eighteenth century the coal trade from Newcastle to London was extensive and an important source of revenue for the crown. When steam engines provided a means to pump water out of coal mines, miners could work farther underground. By 1800, coal mines were being opened up in Scotland, Wales, and the west of England. In the 1830s the railroad created another new demand for coal and also lowered the cost of bringing it to markets, thus making coal more practical as a source of energy for industry.

Textiles

In some respects the textile industry was the spearhead of British industrial growth. Textile manufacture was long established in England; ever since the

Early steam engine designed by James Watt. By courtesy of The Science Museum, London.

later Middle Ages woolen textiles had been one of England's most important products. For centuries woolen cloth manufacture had been a cottage industry—artisans and their families working in their own homes scattered throughout the towns, villages, and countryside. In the later eighteenth century a revolution took place in the manufacture of textiles, as machines were developed that were too large and expensive to be owned and operated by the workers in their homes. This revolution first took place in the process of spinning yarn, where Richard Arkwright became the leader in development of the factory system.

Arkwright got his start in textile manufacture by developing a spinning machine driven by waterpower. Although his role as an inventor is dubious, there can be no question of his ability as an organizer of production. He built his first factory along an isolated river in Derbyshire and brought in pauper children to tend his machines, housing them in a dormitory near the factory. Arkwright was one of the first textile manufacturers to use steam power, thus freeing himself from the need to locate his mills in labor-short areas where waterpower was available. Like Wilkinson, he may be seen as typical of the new industrialists whose imagination and determination were transforming the production of goods in Britain.

Arkwright was engaged in spinning cotton, and it was in the cotton textile industry that the new methods were most rapidly developed. Eli Whitney's invention of the cotton gin greatly increased the supply of raw cotton. The

Iron bridge, Coalbrookdale. Private collection.

introduction of the power loom after 1815 brought the factory system to the weaving of cloth, but with disastrous effects upon the hand weavers, who had increased in numbers due to the abundance of cheap yarn. Although figures for productivity in the industry are sketchy, it is estimated that the value of manufactured cotton cloth increased from £4,000,000 in 1783 to £15,000,000 twenty years later. The value of cotton manufactures doubled again in the next twenty years, by which time cotton manufacture had passed the woolen textile industry, which was slower to change.

Pottery

Another old industry that was transformed by new industrial processes was the manufacture of pottery. Josiah Wedgwood, a Staffordshire potter, introduced the factory system in the manufacture of earthenware, not only to increase productivity but also to improve the quality and uniformity of his products. Wedgwood's superior product was due to excellent design, carefully controlled processes, and workers with specialized skills resulting from the division of labor. The middle class could afford his basic patterns, which, when decorated by his superb artists, were fit for the crowned heads and aristocracy of Europe. He built a model town near the factory to house his employees, although not all of them appreciated the discipline and efforts at self-improvement that went with it. Since he needed reliable transportation to bring in clay and coal and to take out his products, he was an active investor in canals. When Pitt's Irish Commercial Resolutions (1785) threatened his industry with cheaper Irish products, he actively opposed them. A man of cultivated tastes and generous impulses, Wedgwood was a pioneer who generally presented the more attractive face of industrialism.

Transportation

Changes in the production of goods would have had limited effect without improvements in transportation. By the mid-eighteenth century turnpike roads (toll roads) had greatly improved the movement of people and goods by coach or wagon, and the growing size, speed, and reliability of ships contributed to the growth of trade. With its many rivers, England had made important use of water transportation from the earliest times. In the later eighteenth century, canal building greatly improved water transportation, especially in the new industrial areas of the north and west of England.

A remarkable nobleman, the duke of Bridgewater, led the building of canals. Bridgewater wanted to exploit the coal on his estates near Manchester; his answer was to build a canal to carry the coal to the Mersey River. In this task he benefited from the services of a talented engineer, James Brindley, who designed a complex canal that included tunnels, aqueducts, and levees to bring coal barges to their destination. In 1776 he finished his second canal, which gave access to the River Mersey and Liverpool. Bridgewater's canals were successful and encouraged a canal building boom that provided cheap transportation for coal, clay, bricks, farm products, and other bulky items necessary in an industrial society.

Agriculture

The Industrial Revolution would not have been possible without an increased supply of food made possible by new agricultural methods adopted by far-sighted landlords and farmers. Fodder crops such as clover and turnips made it possible to raise more animals, keep them fit during the winter, and provide meat and milk throughout the year. Selective breeding improved the size and productivity of cattle and sheep. The manure produced by the animals provided essential fertilizer for the fields. New crop rotations and agricultural implements improved productivity and made it possible to bring more land under cultivation. The diffusion of these agricultural innovations was hastened by a marked upswing in the prices of food, wool, and hides, especially during the long wars against revolutionary and Napoleonic France.

By the later eighteenth century, the new methods of agriculture led to an extensive movement for enclosure of the open fields. In 1760 probably half the arable land was still farmed in the large open fields divided into strips, a social convention going back to medieval times. The new methods, however, could not be introduced under the old communal system, and progressive landlords sought to enclose the open fields into smaller individual plots divided by fences or hedges. Enclosure usually required an act of Parliament and the agreement of the holders of three-fourths of the land. Commissioners were appointed to determine individual rights to the land and to divide the land into equitable shares. The principal benefits of enclosures went to those with the largest amount of land. Those with small landholdings found it difficult to survive without the perpetuation of the communal life of the former system. Villagers who did not have rights to land, but who had rights in the common pastures and woodlands, also found themselves at a disadvantage. While enclosure generally increased the productivity of agriculture and provided a necessary base for industrial growth, it was a harsh blow to many of the rural poor.

Industrialism and Society

All elements of British society shared, to some extent, in the process of industrialization. Government provided internal stability, security of property, and enforcement of contracts. The cost of government was high, especially during the long wars with France, and contributed significantly to distortions in the economy, but despite these burdens the British economy continued to grow. The aristocracy and gentry were the dominant class politically, and they took a substantial share of the national wealth for themselves. Much of this wealth they spent on stately homes and comfortable living, but they did contribute to economic growth. As landlords they played an important part in agricultural improvement, and their investments in trade, manufacturing, mining, canals, and turnpike roads were significant. The farmers, including many small freeholders, were directly responsible for the pace of agricultural advance, for they were the people who actually implemented the new agricultural methods in the fields.

Professional men, such as lawyers, physicians, and the clergy, were increasing in numbers and prosperity, and they were often found organizing banks and canal companies, as well as providing capital for industry as silent partners. Wealthy merchants also invested in industry, although they were more likely to follow the traditional pattern and invest in land for the social prestige that land ownership could bring. Despite the contributions of the leaders of preindustrial Britain, much of the capital for industry seems to have been derived from the profits of industry itself. The new industrialists were hardworking men who lived modestly. They saved their money and put it back into the business. Their sons or grandsons might join the leisured class, but the early industrialists pulled themselves up by their own efforts, and their success

The London Match Makers. Women and children shown working in an East End factory.
Corbis-Bettmann.

or failure depended primarily upon their own abilities and resources, occasionally aided by a bit of good luck.

Finally, one must look at the contribution of the working class, whose quick hands and strong backs were the basis of the Industrial Revolution. In the preindustrial age, many workers had combined agriculture and handicraft industries. The factory system, however, drew workers from the land into new industrial towns at the same time that enclosures were depriving workers of rights that they had formerly possessed in the common lands of the agricultural villages. Those workers who remained in agriculture became a distinct social class, the agricultural laborers. Now dependent on land-holding farmers for their wages, the agricultural laborers suffered further from the effects of industrialization, which largely ruined the market for the handicrafts that had for centuries supplemented their meager incomes. Lacking prospects for employment in the villages, others left the land for the factory towns, where they swelled the already growing population. A rapidly growing population seeking employment in industry was an essential factor in the Industrial Revolution, and it created a new social class, the industrial working class, which became increasingly conscious of its particular needs and grievances.

The standard of living of the urban working class in the early industrial age poses one of those questions that evokes conflicting opinions. Although historians disagree on this point, there can be no doubt of the sense of injury felt by industrial workers, and especially by craftsmen in long-established industries. The competition of factory-made goods destroyed the value of the craftsmen's skills, and machines that could be tended by children took away the dignity formerly possessed by skilled labor. The Luddite riots of 1811 and 1812 were an early example of the tensions emerging in the new industrial age. The Luddites were framework knitters who made the long knitted stockings used by gentlemen in the eighteenth century. They found their position seriously eroded for a variety of reasons: extreme fluctuations in costs and markets due to wartime conditions; changing styles that reduced the demand for their product; and new machinery that produced cheaper stockings. They identified themselves as followers of a mythical "King Lud" and protested by issuing manifestos and breaking the new machines for making stockings.

The Luddites were not a depressed industrial proletariat; they were from the aristocracy of labor, proud of their status and skill. Their expressions of outrage were not purely economic. They were a response to the loss of personal dignity and security which their craft and parliamentary regulation had

Eighteenth-century shops, Woburn Walk, London. Private collection.

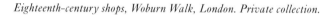

formerly guaranteed. It was among such persons that protest against the new industrial system was most likely to be found.

Lurking over all was the sense of insecurity found in the depersonalized wage relationship of the new industrial system. The working people of England had always labored long and hard, but in turn they expected to be protected by their employers against short-term fluctuations in prices, wages, and employment and to be provided for by the parish if afflicted by long-term hardship arising from unemployment, disability, or old age. Many factory owners in the new industries, however, felt little responsibility for their workers. The concentration of industrial growth in certain areas and the distress resulting from war, inflation, poor crops, and economic fluctuations contributed to a breakdown of the old system of poor relief.

The propertied classes who paid the rates (local taxes) for poor relief complained of an excessive burden, and the poor complained that they were not provided for as required by law. Sometimes the poor reacted with riots and destructiveness; sometimes they read Tom Paine and agitated for political power; sometimes they formed labor unions, in defiance of the Combination Acts. Much of the time they suffered in silence, but they grew increasingly conscious of their grievances. The revolution in production that had created the new industries had also produced a new social force—the industrial working class—that was thereafter an important factor in British life.

It would be unfair, however, to characterize all these changes as detrimental to the new urban working class. Indeed one of the positive features that accompanied the Industrial Revolution was a general improvement in what one historian has described as the "standards of comfort" in this period. Wheat had replaced coarser grains as the basic ingredient of bread for all classes. The basic diet included a larger portion of fresh meat. The dramatic increase in the production of coal and the improved transportation that made it available to more areas of the country meant warmer homes and better-cooked food.

Tea became the national beverage, displacing beer and harder spirits. Since it was prepared by boiling water, tea was beneficial to public health, considering the lack of sanitary water supplies. The consumption of soap and candles rose sharply in the 1790s to a rate double that during the beginning of the century. Cheap cotton cloth replaced leather, wool, and linen and permitted even the lower classes to have changes of clothing and laundering, which impacted positively on health. Even the unattractive housing of the cities had virtues. Construction with brick and stone and the increasing use of glass windows was a considerable improvement over windowless cottages, often constructed of wood and dried mud, with dirt floors and thatched roofs, however quaint and attractive they may appear to us now.

Britain and the French Revolution

The French Revolution

In 1789 the French crown was bankrupt. In desperation, King Louis XVI called the ancient parliament of France, the Estates-General, for the first time since 1614. The impecunious king looked to the estates of the realm—the clergy (First Estate), the nobility (Second Estate), and the people (Third Estate)—to come to his aid. When the Estates-General met, the gentlemen and lawyers who came forward as leaders of the Third Estate, joined by some of the nobility and clergy, demanded that the Estates-General be transformed into a National Assembly, which would draw up a new constitution for France. The king yielded, and great excitement spread through France. The French Revolution had begun.

At first the aspirations of the National Assembly were well received in Britain. British political ideas had been widely disseminated in France through the works of Locke and by French writers such as Voltaire and Montesquieu. The British felt a sense of pride that the haughty French had seen fit to follow their example. When Fox heard that the people of Paris had seized the Bastille, the hated symbol of arbitrary power, he declared: "How much the greatest event that has happened in the world and how much the best." Pitt was less enthusiastic about the new political currents in France but was relieved to think that internal difficulties would make France less of a problem for British foreign policy. British reformers were encouraged by the ferment in France. The Revolution Society, formed to celebrate the centennial of the Glorious Revolution of 1688, praised the French for following the same course and looked for a revival of the reforming spirit at home.

The initial reaction in Britain soon turned to horror as the moderate leaders of the National Assembly were supplanted by radicals determined to overthrow the monarchy and the other forms of privilege in France and to establish a democratic republic. The domestic upheaval in France was complicated by foreign intervention as Austria and Prussia came to the aid of the French king. In 1793 the radical revolutionaries seized power, executed the king and queen, introduced mass conscription, and suppressed dissent with the guillotine. The revolutionary armies repulsed the Austrians and Prussians and then burst into the Netherlands, the Rhineland, and northern Italy. Soon, deposed princes, nobles, and churchmen were arriving in Britain as refugees, telling tales of atrocities and bewailing their loss of property and status.

George III, the Pitt ministry, the aristocracy and gentry, the church, and most of the propertied middle class were shocked at the wreckage and were disturbed by the thought that British radicals might attempt a similar upheaval. British dislike of France as the national enemy was heightened by the view of France as the center of a revolution that, given an opportunity, would also destroy the balance of social relationships in Britain.

Conservatives and Radicals

The war with revolutionary France was, in one sense, a return to the long-standing conflict between Britain and France in Europe and overseas, but it had a new dimension—a conflict of ideologies. Revolutionary France was dedicated to the triumph of reason over tradition, secularism over religion, equality over privilege, and patriotic fervor over the cosmopolitan culture of eighteenth-century Europe. The dominant effect of the French Revolution in Britain was a strong reaction not only against French power but against French ideals and, by extension, against most forms of domestic discontent.

The chief spokesman of the reaction against French ideology was Edmund Burke, whose *Reflections on the Revolution in France* (1790) first sounded the alarm. Burke had spent most of his political career in opposition, as a parliamentary spokesman for the marquis of Rockingham and an opponent of "the influence of the crown." When the crisis with the American colonies arose, Burke was a critic of the North ministry's attempt to subdue the Americans by force. In the political crisis of 1780–1784, he appeared as a reformer. After Rockingham's death in 1782 he became a follower of Fox.

In 1790, however, Burke came forward as a defender of the status quo, arguing that the developments in France were not simply an attack on abuses but a revolution that would destroy the fundamental basis of society, leading eventually to conflict, chaos, and despotism. When Fox expressed sympathy with the French, Burke broke openly with his colleague and gave his support to Pitt. Burke's writings against the French Revolution became a classic exposition of a conservative philosophy.

Replies to Burke were not long in coming. Tom Paine, whose *Common Sense* (1776) had encouraged the American colonists to seek independence, responded with *The Rights of Man* (1791). Paine's ideas were the conventional radicalism of the eighteenth century, but he possessed the gift of stating his views in a direct, pungent manner, which struck home to the ordinary person. He ridiculed Burke's high-flown reverence for institutions based on the injustices of the past, and urged that they be replaced by institutions that would protect the rights and dignity of all men. Paine's works provided the intellectual foundation for a revival of middle-class and working-class radicalism.

The ideals of the French Revolution were expounded in more moderate form by William Godwin. Godwin was a doctrinaire rationalist, whose *Political Justice* (1793) held forth the prospect of human progress to perfection as a result of the triumph of reason over tradition and ignorance. Godwin was not a revolutionary who sought to destroy the past by force, but the results he anticipated from the march of reason were every bit as revolutionary as those urged by Paine. In 1792 Mary Wollstonecraft, a remarkable young woman who later married Godwin, penned her own reply to Burke, *A Vindication of the Rights of Woman*. She urged equality for women, especially in education and careers, which would enable them to develop their full potential as people.

Britain at War

The political and ideological conflict engendered by the French Revolution was intensified by war. In 1793 France, already at war with Austria and Prussia, declared war on Britain, Spain, and the Dutch. By this time the British had come to believe that war was inevitable and necessary, and Pitt changed from the minister of peace and moderate reform to the leader of a European coalition against French power and French revolutionary ideals. Pitt was not a great war minister. Moreover, his stubborn belief that the war would be short because of an imminent French collapse proved to be mistaken. Pitt's strategy was to rely principally on British sea power, using it in areas such as the Baltic, the Mediterranean, and the Caribbean that he regarded as vital to British trade. He preferred to leave the land war to allies subsidized by British gold.

In 1797 a brilliant young French officer, Napoleon Bonaparte, won a startling victory over the Austrians in northern Italy. In 1798 he invaded Egypt. At this point British sea power struck a heavy blow as a bold naval officer, Horatio Nelson, destroyed the French fleet at the Battle of the Nile and trapped the French army in Egypt. Napoleon escaped and returned to France, where in 1799 he seized power with the title of first consul.

By 1800 both sides were ready for peace. Napoleon had defeated a coalition of European powers and was consolidating his control of France. Britain still ruled the seas but was desperate for relief from the costs and strains of war. High food prices and economic dislocations caused widespread distress. In 1797 mutinies broke out in the navy, and in 1798 revolt flared in Ireland. The Peace of Amiens (1802) was an uneasy truce, but nonetheless welcome to both Britain and France.

Political Consolidation

In the meantime, the need for resistance to France led to a consolidation of political forces behind the Pitt ministry. Most of Pitt's parliamentary supporters were conservative in outlook and hostile to proposals for change. George III gained new popularity as the symbol of national unity against France, and he became firmer than ever in his defense of traditional institutions. In 1793 and 1794 the largest part of the Whigs, led by the duke of Portland, gave their support to Pitt, although they maintained their own identity and commitment to Whig issues such as parliamentary reform and equal rights for Catholics (Catholic emancipation).

Fox was left the ineffectual leader of a small band of opposition Whigs, who were no longer a threat to the ministry or taken seriously by the public. In 1797 Fox's friend, Charles Grey, moved proposals for parliamentary reform. Pitt had never been more than lukewarm in his support of parliamentary reform, and he used the war and radical agitation as an excuse to insure that the proposals were overwhelmingly defeated. The Pitt ministry possessed what appeared to be unshakable control of the government.

The triumph of conservatism in government was matched by public opinion. In general, Burke's point of view triumphed: the French Revolution was seen as a destructive force that must be contained in Europe, lest it infect Britain. Criticism of existing institutions was stigmatized as unpatriotic. Although Pitt was more moderate than many of his followers, political pressures led the Pitt ministry to take strong measures to suppress radical agitation. In 1794 the Habeas Corpus Act was suspended to permit imprisonment without trial of persons suspected of political agitation. In 1795 the Treasonable Practices Act defined treason to include words as well as actions. The Seditious Meetings Act, passed the same year, prohibited meetings of more than fifty persons without license from the local magistrates. Food riots and naval mutinies led to further repressive measures in 1799: radical societies were dissolved, and the Combination Acts prohibited the formation of unions by workingmen to bargain with employers. The unity of the nation in the face of revolutionary France was primarily a matter of national feeling, but it was strongly reinforced by the use of the powers of the government to suppress criticism and organized expressions of dissent.

One should not, however, overstress the extent of such repression. The machinery for this purpose was already in existence and little changed. The number of actual prosecutions was well below those that followed the 1715 and the 1745 rebellions. Despite repressive legislation, there was widespread public sensitivity to the claims of liberty, a result of the radical movements that began with Wilkes and were given continued prominence by Fox and well-educated middle-class radicals. If Pitt sometimes violated these concepts he was also aware that, in safer circumstances, they deserved to be preserved.

Ireland

The problem of political control was most marked in Ireland, where French agitators and the prospect of French assistance inflamed indigenous discontent. Although the Irish were divided by deep social and religious differences, they shared a common resentment of British rule. The Patriot movement of the early 1780s, coming at a time when England was preoccupied with the

American Revolution, had resulted in an unaccustomed degree of autonomy for the governing class. With Britain struggling to cope with French power, in 1791 Irish radicals formed an organization called The United Irishmen to fight for independence. Originally the United Irishmen included both Protestants and Catholics and were committed to moderate reform, but eventually they became predominantly Catholic and advocated a radical republic.

In 1798 the United Irishmen rose in a desperate insurrection. The uprising was doomed from the start: most of the leaders were seized before it began, and poorly armed artisans and peasants were no match for the Irish militia. Their leader, Theobald Wolfe Tone, arrived from France with French aid too late to be of use. At this point Pitt decided that stronger control of Ireland was essential. He sent Lord Cornwallis, his favorite troubleshooter, to pacify Ireland and unify the British Isles.

Cornwallis proposed an Act of Union, similar to that which had successfully joined England and Scotland in 1707. The Irish Parliament would be abolished, and the Irish would send members to the British Parliament at Westminster—a group of elected peers and bishops and one hundred members of the British House of Commons. The formation of the United Kingdom would, of course, give the Irish free trade with Britain and the Empire, a policy that Pitt had long advocated. The Anglo-Irish leadership class was totally dependent on British power in the face of French intrigues and domestic insurrection. With the further inducement of generous promises and bribes, they were persuaded to agree to the Act of Union, and the new Parliament of the United Kingdom first met in 1801.

An important corollary to Pitt's Act of Union was his proposal for Catholic emancipation—the admission of Catholics to Parliament and political offices. Pitt recognized that the United Kingdom could not succeed without the support of the Irish Catholic population, but he did not fully realize the resistance that such a proposal would encounter in Britain. King George III, in between bouts of mental illness, declared his unalterable opposition to the idea, which he saw as fatal to the position of the Church of England and its Irish counterpart, the Church of Ireland. Pitt faced strong opposition in his Cabinet, in the House of Lords, and among many of his followers in the House of Commons. Realizing that he had overreached himself, he abandoned Catholic emancipation and resigned, being replaced by Henry Addington in 1801.

BRITAIN AND NAPOLEON

Land Power Verus Sea Power

Pitt's resignation, and the Peace of Amiens that followed in 1802, marked a brief breathing space in the long struggle between Britain and revolutionary

France. Napoleon needed time to consolidate his power, which he had accomplished by 1804, when he assumed the title of emperor. After the Peace of Amiens he began building up an army and fleet, ostensibly for an invasion of Britain, and in 1803 the Addington ministry, upset by Napoleon's restless inability to adhere to the agreements he had made, again declared war.

In 1804 Pitt, who returned to office to form one more coalition against Napoleon, replaced Addington. Pitt was in ill health and had lost some of his former supporters, but his name and ability could still rally the nation. In 1806 Pitt died, to be followed by a coalition ministry ("Ministry of All Talents") in which Fox played an important part until his death a few months later. Once again Britain was at war with France, but this time without the two leaders who had held the center of the political stage for almost twenty-five years.

The dominant fact of British history from 1804 to 1814 was the long struggle against Napoleonic France. When Pitt returned to power in 1804 he persuaded Austria and Russia to join with Britain in another coalition that would be supported by British money and sea power. Abandoning his plans for an invasion of Britain (or perhaps they were a ruse), Napoleon marched quickly against the Austrians and Russians, whom he defeated at Ulm and Austerlitz in 1805. The next year he defeated the Prussians at Jena, and in

Illustration of the Battle of Trafalgar. After a painting by J. M. Turner. Corbis-Bettmann.

1807 he made a favorable peace with the tsar of Russia. In 1808 he occupied Spain. Napoleon had defeated the major powers of Europe and was busy reorganizing the smaller states of Germany and Italy. As it would in 1940 when Hitler's armies dominated Europe, Britain stood alone.

Napoleon's dominance on the continent was offset by Britain's growing trade and industry, and by its command of the seas. In 1805 a British fleet under Nelson defeated a combined French-Spanish fleet off the coast of Spain near Cape Trafalgar. Thereafter France could not threaten Britain by sea, and British sea power could be used to destroy French shipping, blockade the Napoleonic Empire, support allies, encourage local insurrections, and capture colonies.

Since the conflict between British sea power and French land power had created a stand off, the two antagonists turned to economic warfare. Napoleon scornfully dismissed the British as "a nation of shopkeepers" and tried to destroy the British economy by depriving Britain of its European market. His "Continental System" was an attempt to close the Napoleonic Empire to British goods. The British, in turn, reacted with the Orders in Council, which established a blockade of Napoleonic Europe. The British blockade affected neutral nations especially, and, along with impressment, contributed to the outbreak of the War of 1812 between Britain and the United States.

The Napoleonic Wars

Neither policy was entirely successful, although each nation imposed considerable hardship on the other. Britain found new markets for its manufactured goods overseas and maintained some of its European customers through smuggling. Even Napoleon's France needed some British goods, a measure of which was permitted entry through a system of licenses. Though the economic warfare had some effect, the eventual decision was to be made back on the field of battle.

Seeking an opportunity to engage Napoleon on land, the British turned to Portugal and Spain, where French occupation had encountered strong national resistance. In 1808 Arthur Wellesley, later the duke of Wellington, was sent to Portugal to expel the French and begin the process of driving them out of the Iberian Peninsula. Wellington was thoroughly patrician, a firm, dignified, and stern disciplinarian, and a master of careful, systematic warfare. Faced by a hostile local population and Wellington's methodical progress, the French slowly gave way. Wellington's Peninsular War was a secondary factor in the eventual defeat of Napoleon, but it gave the British the sense that they had found a way to get at "Boney" and a commander who could make the most of it.

Tory Control of Britain

In the meantime, the deaths of Pitt and Fox and the long struggle against Napoleon led to the emergence of new political leaders and a new party alignment in Britain. The name "Tories" was revived for the conservatives who had previously followed Pitt. The Tories were strong supporters of the monarchy, the Church, and the status quo in social relationships. They adopted as their watchword Burke's veneration for traditional institutions, but without his keen eye for the abuses to which any long-established ruling class is liable.

Pitt had also been supported by a strong contingent of Whigs led by the duke of Portland. The Portland Whigs continued their cooperation with the Tory government, but they still maintained some of the old Whig tradition of resistance to royal power and support for religious toleration. The opposition Whigs, formerly followers of Fox, were now led by Charles Grey. They continued in their belief that parliamentary government, religious toleration, and individual liberties were threatened by the power and influence of the crown, swollen by the needs of war. In the House of Commons there was a small group of radicals who continued to press for familiar radical goals, such as a more representative House of Commons and the reduction of political corruption. A large number of independent members who usually supported the Tories were also to be found in the House of Commons.

In 1812 Lord Liverpool became leader of a reorganized Tory ministry, holding that position until incapacitated by a stroke in 1827. Liverpool was a poised, confident, capable aristocrat whose father had risen from humble beginnings to a position of great influence under Pitt. Addington (now Lord Sidmouth) became home secretary, thus assuring the Tories that domestic agitators and dissidents would be dealt with firmly. In 1811 George III was declared permanently insane, and George, Prince of Wales, now middle-aged, fat, and grumpy, took his place as Prince Regent. The Regent, who had once flourished in the company of Fox and other Whigs, continued the policies of his father, including support for the Tory ministry.

Liverpool was able to attract and utilize young men of talent who came forward as Tories because the Tories offered the only opportunity to hold office. One of Lord Liverpool's younger ministers was Lord Castlereagh, a handsome, intense Irish nobleman who refused an English peerage so he could continue to sit in the House of Commons representing his Irish constituency. Castlereagh became foreign secretary under Liverpool, serving with distinction in that post until his death in 1822. Another brilliant young Tory was George Canning, whose intellect and oratorical ability made him a powerful force in the House of Commons. Liverpool admired Canning and wished to use him in his ministry, but Castlereagh and Canning were bitter personal enemies, and this fact made it impossible to bring Canning into office.

The third of the capable young Tories, with a long career of public service before him, was Robert Peel, the son of a prosperous Lancashire textile manufacturer. Peel made his mark as a protégé of Liverpool, first in the War Office and then, when Liverpool became prime minister, as chief secretary in Ireland. The ability of Liverpool and the talented younger Tories, combined with the conservatism of the country, gave the Tories a grip on power that postponed parliamentary reform, Catholic emancipation, and other controversial issues indefinitely.

Victory and Peace

As the Liverpool ministry settled into place, the tide of battle began to turn in Europe. Napoleon overreached himself in 1812 when he sent a powerful force against Russia. He defeated the Russians in battle and occupied Moscow, but he could not obtain a formal surrender from the tsar. Defeated later by the Russian army, as well as by the onslaught of a terrible Russian winter, Napoleon's soldiers were left to struggle back to France while their commander desperately tried to recruit another army. The Russians, Austrians, and Prussians all joined the war—the first time that all three powers had been included in one coalition. Britain served as paymaster to the coalition, and British gold flowed as never before. Nationalist uprisings against the French took place in Germany and Italy, and in Spain, Wellington, buoyed by Spanish hatred of the French, continued his methodical advance. In 1813 Napoleon was decisively defeated at Leipzig, in eastern Germany, while Wellington crossed the Pyrenees

Mountains and entered the south of France. In 1814 Napoleon surrendered and was exiled to the little Mediterranean island of Elba.

As the victorious allies advanced, they began to think of the peace settlement. Castlereagh, the British foreign secretary, was determined that the allies should act together in the peace negotiations and in the postwar period. He was also concerned that France should be brought back into the community of nations, and thus he advocated a peace that would stabilize the French government, check French expansion, and be acceptable to most French citizens.

The settlement made with France was along the lines advocated by Castlereagh: a Bourbon monarchy under Louis XVIII and a constitution; Britain restored most of the captured French colonies; the allies abandoned claims for indemnities; and France, at British urging, agreed to abolish its slave trade. Considering the turmoil that France had brought to Europe in the previous twenty-five years, the peace with France was an enlightened one. And Castlereagh's role in the settlement had given Britain a role in European diplomacy that it had not previously had or desired.

The peace with France went easily in comparison with the problems and great power rivalries that complicated a settlement of Germany, Italy, and eastern Europe. Thus the decision was made to call a general conference at Vienna, which met in September 1814. The Austrian emperor provided lavish entertainment for a brilliant assemblage, but representatives of the four major powers, led by the Austrian chancellor, Metternich, made the important decisions. When disputes arose concerning Poland and Saxony, Talleyrand, the astute representative of France, was able to obtain an important voice for his country.

The conference was interrupted in March 1815 when Napoleon escaped from Elba, landed in France, and rallied his veterans to his standard. The duke of Wellington was put in command of a mixed army of British, Dutch, and German soldiers, which defeated Napoleon at the Battle of Waterloo (June 1815). Napoleon was then sent off to the island of St. Helena, an obscure British possession in the South Atlantic, where he spent his remaining years under British guardianship. The great struggle that had dominated Europe for more than twenty years had finally ended.

Shortly before the defeat of Napoleon at Waterloo, the Congress of Vienna completed a settlement for the territories that had been conquered by France. Each of the major powers had its own dynastic or territorial ambitions, but in general they were determined to restore the European balance of power and to prevent a renewal of revolutionary outbreaks. A strong buffer was placed to the north of France by the union of Holland and the Austrian Netherlands (Belgium) to form the Kingdom of the Netherlands. Austria was made dominant in northern Italy by control of Lombardy and Venetia.

The Bourbon monarchy was restored in Spain, but the Spanish colonists in the New World continued the struggle for independence that had begun during the Napoleonic period. Germany and Italy continued to be divided among small or medium-sized states, although no attempt was made to restore all the petty states of the prerevolutionary period.

Britain was rewarded with colonies and naval bases. The retention of Gibraltar, the acquisition of Malta, and a protectorate over the Greek islands confirmed British power in the Mediterranean. The Cape Colony in South Africa, Mauritius in the Indian Ocean, and Ceylon provided bases on the route to India. Britain also strengthened its possessions in the West Indies and Central America. Britain's policies regarding search and seizure on the high seas were left unchallenged, although these had been a cause of great complaint among neutral nations and had been a major factor in the War of 1812 with the United States. In short, the Vienna settlement confirmed the naval and imperial supremacy that Britain had gained during the Napoleonic Wars.

The dynastic and territorial provisions of the Vienna settlement appeared to be a return to the balance of power diplomacy of prerevolutionary Europe. But Castlereagh took Britain a step further by committing the United Kingdom to cooperation with the major European states for the purpose of preserving peace. In the eighteenth century Britain had been involved in European alliances for specific purposes: to maintain the balance of power; to protect the Netherlands or Hanover; and to have a continental ally in the struggle with France and Spain for colonies and sea power. Many of these reasons still applied. But in the glow of the joint effort by which Napoleon had been destroyed, Castlereagh advocated a British commitment to Europe in a Quadruple Alliance with Austria, Prussia, and Russia, expanded to include France in 1818, which was designed to keep the major powers in harmony.

"The Concert of Europe," as it was called, meant different things to Metternich than it did to Castlereagh. Metternich looked for cooperation among the crowned heads of Europe to put down revolutionary movements. Such a policy was less acceptable in Britain. The British already possessed constitutional government, representative institutions, civil liberties, religious toleration, and national unity. They could not, in good conscience, set themselves against movements on the Continent that advocated those same ideals. This was the dilemma that destroyed Castlereagh's foreign policy and, indeed, Castlereagh himself.

B R I T I S H   S O C I E T Y   I N   A   R E V O L U T I O N A R Y   A G E

Stability and Change

The remarkable feature of British society in this age of political, economic, and intellectual change was its stability. To some extent social stability was artificial—a defensive posture adopted by a ruling class using the powers of government to bolster its position. But for the most part, the stability of British society was genuine. The traditional institutions and social relationships of Britain were accepted by the bulk of its population as good, to be defended against French ideologues or domestic radicals. A long period of war imposed new social stresses but also contributed to the sense of national unity that saw Britain through to victory.

But in this age of conservatism, new ideas were taking root in Britain that were, in their own way, as revolutionary as the political and diplomatic upheavals taking place abroad. In France, dissatisfaction with existing institutions had created an ideology of revolution; in Britain, where existing institutions were more satisfactory, the goal was not revolution but reform.

One approach to institutional change was philosophical or analytical, examining institutions rationally in terms of their function. The principal exponent of this approach was Jeremy Bentham, whose *Introduction to the Principles of Morals and Legislation* was published in 1789. Bentham believed that institutions should be judged by their utility—by their contribution to human happiness. He ridiculed Burke's mystical appeal to the accumulated wisdom of the past as nonsense designed to perpetuate privileges for which there was no reasonable justification. Bentham was especially interested in law and prisons, both of which were admirably designed to inflict vengeance but which had little effect on the incidence of crime. In his view, the Poor Laws ran counter to human nature and thus were not a rational method to deal with poverty. By 1809, when he wrote his *Plan for Parliamentary Reform* (published in 1817), Bentham was convinced that other necessary reforms would not take place until Parliament was itself reformed to remove the unrepresentative franchises and distribution of seats that made the House of Commons unresponsive to the nation. Bentham was not a politician and did not sit in Parliament; his great contribution was to present an intellectual defense of reform, based upon reason and utility.

The rationalistic approach to reform advocated by Bentham and his followers was matched by reform movements based upon religious and humanitarian considerations. In 1777 John Howard, a man of independent means dedicated to prison reform, published a landmark work, *The State of Prisons in England and Wales.* At that time prisons were rarely used as places to serve sentences. Instead, they were used to hold accused persons until their trial, or for debtors who were imprisoned until their debts were paid. The prisons were a source of income to the jailers, who charged excessive fees while keeping their prisoners in the most wretched conditions. Sometimes debtors would pay their debts but be held indefinitely because they could not afford to pay the jailers' fees. Conditions were even more intolerable on the congested, disease-ridden hulks in which prisoners sentenced to transportation were confined. Howard campaigned ceaselessly for the improvement of prisons and obtained some legislation that was largely ineffective.

In 1807 Sir Samuel Romilly, then solicitor-general, succeeded in obtaining passage of a Bankruptcy Act that provided a legal process by which debtors could settle their debts and be freed. The next year Romilly began a crusade to reduce the number of offenses that required capital punishments—for even such a minor crime as shoplifting by a child was punishable by death. Romilly was opposed by the full majesty of judges and lawyers, who thought in terms of punishments and fees; but Romilly's lifetime of dedicated labor began to bear fruit after his death.

Religion

The Church of England was part of the established apparatus of power and privilege and as such felt threatened by the secularism of the French Revolution and the scoffing of Tom Paine. Archbishops and bishops were appointed and promoted by the crown and sat in the House of Lords, thus they had to be politicians as well as spiritual leaders. The church regarded the Test and Corporation Acts, which limited political offices to Anglicans, as the essential basis for its established position. The churchmen were strongly supported in this view by the king, the Tories, and most of the political class. The efforts of Dissenters (non-Anglican Protestants) to obtain repeal of these laws failed repeatedly, although annual Acts of Indemnity relieved much of the burden. The controversy concerning political rights for Catholics (Catholic emancipation) brought the downfall of Pitt and continued to be one of the most divisive issues in politics.

While the church was struggling to preserve its political and legal privileges, it was being criticized from within for its lack of spiritual vitality. A group known as "Evangelicals" worked to bring about a revival of traditional Christian concepts of personal salvation and holiness and to imbue churchmen with a more dedicated approach to their calling. The most prominent of the Evangelicals was William Wilberforce, member of Parliament for Yorkshire and a personal friend of Pitt and other political leaders. As a young man Wilberforce experienced a "conversion" that made his Christian faith the center of his life. He joined with other Evangelicals in the encouragement of Bible reading, prayer, and good works. Wilberforce looked to the political and social leaders of the nation to support his cause. In his book, *A Practical View of the Prevailing Religious System of Professed Christians in the Higher and Middle Classes* (1797), he criticized nominal Christianity and urged a revival of religious and moral commitment.

Wilberforce and the Evangelicals devoted themselves to many good causes, but the most important one was the abolition of the slave trade, in which they were supported by many humanitarians who did not share their religious convictions. Wilberforce agreed to take the lead in Parliament, and in 1788 a parliamentary committee was formed to take evidence. In 1792 Wilberforce, drawing upon evidence from the committee report, moved for abolition of the slave trade.

Both Pitt and Fox supported his motion, but neither wished to divide his supporters on the issue; Wilberforce's motion failed. Wilberforce continued to make an annual motion against the slave trade, but the measure was not passed until Fox put the government behind it in the "Talents" ministry of 1806–1807. The efforts of Wilberforce and others also bore fruit in an antislave trade clause in the Treaty of Vienna (1815) and eventually in the abolition of slavery itself.

Poverty

Public attention to the problem of poverty focused on the Poor Laws, for the local authorities were confronted with an extent of poverty that the existing law had never been intended to handle. The Elizabethan Poor Laws were based on the assumption of a stable society where people spent their lives in one locality, prices and wages varied little from year to year, and the community (i.e., the parish) was responsible for providing a minimum subsistence for all its members. Such assumptions were invalidated by violent fluctuations of prices, wages, and employment in this revolutionary age.

The problem was not just a matter of providing for the unemployed, although fluctuations in employment frequently placed large numbers of able-bodied workers into this category. Even employed workers were compelled to seek poor relief; as prices rose, wages based on traditional wage rates were often inadequate to support the workers and their families. The employers who dominated the process by which wages were set strongly resisted increases in wages. Workers could not leave their parishes in search of better-paying work elsewhere, for to do so would forfeit their rightful claim to poor relief. The Poor Law authorities attempted to meet their responsibilities by supplementing wages with relief payments (the Speenhamland system).

As a result, employers were enabled to keep wages low, for the rate payers (local taxpayers) subsidized their workers, while employed workers became dependent upon poor relief. The public was confused by the arguments among those who viewed poverty as the result of personal faults, those who advocated a free market in labor that would require both employers and workers to respond to economic fluctuations, and those who felt a sense of community responsibility for the poor. From any of these perspectives, the Poor Laws were inadequate.

One observer of the problem, an Anglican clergyman named Thomas Malthus, believed that there was nothing that public policy could do about poverty. In 1798 Malthus published *An Essay on the Principle of Population* (revised in 1803), in which he argued that population would always increase faster than food supply, and thus poverty, famine, war, and vice were inevitable. Malthus's main concern was to refute the views of William Godwin, who anticipated the steady advance of mankind to perfection, but the main influence of his book was in discussions of poverty and the Poor Laws. In Malthus's view, humanitarians and the Poor Laws only made the population problem worse, for they permitted the poor to have more children than they could provide for. The "dismal science" of Malthus appalled philanthropists and humanitarians, but its "tough-minded" realism had a powerful influence upon the social thought of the age.

A more typical reaction to these problems was presented by a journalist of genius, William Cobbett. A tough, John Bull patriot, Cobbett was angered by the fiscal demands of government and the luxury of the upper classes at a time when an inflated currency and rising prices were destroying the livings and self-respect of the British working class. Cobbett deplored the effects of industrialism in destroying the simple life and cottage industries of the old England he knew and loved. He excoriated the politicians, aristocrats, bankers, and government contractors who profited from public expenditures while the cost fell on those who toiled in fields and factories. He was a patriot who looked back, regretfully, to an England that would be no more, and who expressed, in angry but powerful words, the sense of loss felt by humble people.

*S*UGGESTIONS *FOR* *F*URTHER *R*EADING

General surveys include J. Steven Watson, *The Reign of George III, 1760–1815* (1960); Asa Briggs, *The Age of Improvement, 1783–1867* (1959); and Ian Christie, *Wars and Revolutions: Britain, 1760–1815* (1982). Christie's *Stress and Stability in Late Eighteenth-Century Britain: Reflections on the British Avoidance of Revolution* (1984) summarizes the results of a lifetime of study.

Books on politics that continue to be useful are Richard Pares, *King George III and the Politicians* (1953); Brian Hill, *Early Parties and Politics* (cited in previous chapters); and Frank O'Gorman, *The Emergence of the British Two-Party System* (1982). *The Prime Ministers, Vol. I: Sir Robert Walpole to Sir Robert Peel*, ed. Herbert Van Thal (1974), has been cited earlier. Accounts of domestic radicalism are Albert Goodwin, *The Friends of Liberty: The English Democratic Movement in the Age of the French Revolution* (1979) and D. G. Wright, *Popular Radicalism: The Working Class Experience, 1780–1880* (1988). The conservative reaction to the challenge of revolutionary France can be followed in James Sack, *From Jacobite to Conservative: Reaction and Orthodoxy in Britain, c. 1760–1821* (1993).

On foreign policy, *The Cambridge History of British Foreign Policy, 1783–1919*, ed. G. P. Gooch and Adolphus W. Ward (3 vols., 1922–1923) is a good place to begin. A more modern survey is Muriel E. Chamberlain, *"Pax Britannica": British Foreign Policy, 1789–1913* (1988). Studies on the fringes of British foreign policy are M. S. Anderson, *The Eastern Question, 1774–1923* (1966) and H. C. Allen, *The Anglo-American Relationship since 1783* (1959).

A good introduction to the long wars with France is Arthur Bryant, *The Years of Endurance, 1793–1802* (1942) and *The Years of Victory* (1944), written to strengthen British morale during World War II. H. V. Bowen, *War and British Society, 1688–1815* (1998) explores the effects of the French wars on the British people. In addition to previously cited books by Kennedy and Stokesbury, the naval war can be followed in G. J. Marcus, *A Naval History of England: Vol. II, The Age of Nelson* (1971) and Oliver Warner, *The British Navy: A Concise History* (1975) and *Trafalgar* (1959). C. S. Forester provides interesting reading in *The Age of Fighting Sail* (1956). For the army see Richard Glover, *Peninsular Preparation: The Reform of the British Army, 1795–1809* (1963) and *Britain at Bay: Defence Against Bonaparte, 1803–1814* (1973). The negotiations that led to the peace settlement in 1814–1815 can be followed in J. G. Lockhart, *The Peacemakers, 1814–15* (1968) and Charles K. Webster, *The Foreign Policy of Castlereagh, 1812–1815* (1963, first pub. 1931).

Many interesting political biographies are available, among them John Brooke, *King George III* (1972); Stanley Ayling, *George the Third* (1972); and Roger Fulford, *George the Fourth* (1949). John Ehrman has written a definitive three-volume biography of William Pitt the Younger which is also a detailed history of his times; Derek Jarrett, *Pitt the Younger* (1974) is a briefer work. Other important biographies are John W. Derry, *Charles James Fox* (1972); G. M. Trevelyan, *Lord Grey of the Reform Bill* (1920); Amanda Foreman, *Georgiana, Duchess of Devonshire* (1998); Howard Fast, *Citizen Tom Paine* (1943); Jerome D. Wilson, *Thomas Paine* (1989); Eleanor Flexner, *Mary Wollstonecraft: A Biography* (1972); Philip Ziegler, *Addington: A Life of Henry Addington, First Viscount Sidmouth* (1965); C. J. Bartlett, *Castlereagh* (1966); Derry, *Castlereagh* (1976); P. J. V. Rolo, *George Canning: Three Biographical Studies* (1965); Elizabeth Longford, *Wellington* (2 vols., 1969, 1972); and Christopher Hibbert, *Wellington: A Personal History* (1997).

The Industrial Revolution has produced a voluminous literature, but perhaps the best works for the beginning student are T. S. Ashton, *The Industrial Revolution, 1760–1830* (1948); Phyllis Deane, *The First Industrial Revolution* (1965); M. W. Flinn, *The Origins of the Industrial Revolution* (1966); and Peter Mathias, *The First Industrial Nation* (2nd ed., 1983). John Rule, *The Vital Century: England's Developing Economy, 1714–1815* (1992) has chapters on the various sectors of the economy.

For manufacturing see M. Berg, *The Age of Manufactures, 1700–1820* (1985); M. W. Flinn, *The History of the British Coal Industry, Vol. II, 1700–1830* (1984); J. R. Harris, *The British Iron Industry, 1700–1850* (1988); and S. D. Chapman, *The Cotton Industry in the Industrial Revolution* (1972). The agricultural changes that were an important factor in economic change are discussed in Gordon Mingay and J. D. Chambers, *The Agricultural Revolution, 1750–1880* (1966). Canal building is treated in Hugh Malet, *Bridgewater, the Canal Duke, 1736–1803* (1977). Population growth is covered in E. A. Wrigley and R. S. Schofield, *The Population History of England, 1541–1871* (2nd ed., 1989) and *The British Population: Patterns, Trends, and Processes* (1992) by David Coleman and John Salt.

For a broad interpretation of the social changes of this period see *The Cambridge Social History of Britain, 1750–1950*, ed. F. M. L. Thompson (3 vols., 1990). A stimulating work is Harold Perkin, *The Origins of Modern English Society, 1780–1880* (1969). See also John Rule, *Albion's People: English Society, 1714–1815* (1992). The impact of the Napoleonic Wars is treated in Clive Emsley, *British Society and the French Wars, 1793–1815* (1979). Family life is described by Geoffrey Alderman in *Modern England, 1700–1980: A Domestic History* (1986). Histories of London cited earlier are Roy Porter, *London: A Social History* (1998); Francis Sheppard, *London* (1998); and Stephen Inwood, *A History of London* (1998). James Ayres, *Building the Georgian City* (1998) is a study of urban life and architecture.

Edward R. Norman examines the *Church and Society in England, 1770–1970: A Historical Study* (1976). See also A. D. Gilbert, *Religion and Society in Industrial England: Church, Chapel, and Social Change, 1740–1914* (1976). The Evangelical movement in the Church is discussed in E. M. Howse, *Saints in Politics* (1952) and Ford K. Brown, *Fathers of the Victorians: The Age of Wilberforce* (1961). See also biographies of Wilberforce by Robin Furneaux (1974) and John Pollock (1977). Important aspects of the revival of religious commitment are discussed in T. W. Laqueur, *Religion and Respectability: Sunday Schools and Working Class Culture, 1780–1850* (1976) and Roger Anstey, *The Atlantic Slave Trade and British Abolition, 1760–1810* (1975). Bernard Semmel explores *The Methodist Revolution* (1973). John Bossy examines *The English Catholic Community, 1750–1850* (1975). Lee Grugel looks at *Society and Religion during the Age of Industrialization* (1979).

J. V. Becketts surveys *The Aristocracy in England, 1660–1914* (1986); L. Davidoff and C. Hall look at *Family Fortune: Men and Women of the English Middle Class, 1780–1850* (1987). The working class is covered by G. D. H. Cole and Raymond Postgate in *The British Common People, 1746–1946* (1947) and in an enormously learned and stimulating book by E. P. Thompson, *The Making of the English Working Class* (1964). An important dimension of working class movements is examined in D. Vincent, *Literacy and Popular Culture: England, 1750–1914* (1989). Robert K. Webb identifies *The British Working Class Reader, 1790–1848* (1955). Arthur. J. Taylor attempts to answer a difficult question in *The Standard of Living in Britain in the Industrial Revolution* (1975).

Many books on overseas trade and empire have been cited in previous chapters. Good introductions are *The Cambridge History of the British Empire, Vol. II: The Growth of the New Empire, 1783–1870* (1961) and James A. Williamson, *A Short History of British Expansion, Vol. II: The Modern Empire and Commonwealth* (3rd ed., 1959). A brilliant work is Vincent T. Harlow, *The Founding of the Second British Empire, 1763–1793, Vol. II, New Continents and Changing Values* (1964). An important area of expansion is discussed in C. Northcote Parkinson (author of "Parkinson's Laws"), *Trade in the Eastern Seas, 1793–1815* (1937) and *War on the Eastern Seas* (1954).

CHAPTER THIRTEEN

Conservatism and Reform
1815–1850

In 1815 Britain was compelled to face the challenges of peacetime in a world that had been profoundly changed by a quarter century of revolution and war. Britain's involvement in the wars of the French Revolution and Napoleon had led to a commitment to share in the task of preserving peace. Its political institutions had held the nation together until victory was won, but now Britain's leaders were required to deal with important constituencies who were determined that peacetime would bring fuller participation in the political process. The growth of population and the emergence of industrialism in key industries had enlarged the British economy, but had also brought into being powerful economic interests that posed new challenges to the existing order.

Having devoted twenty-two years to the struggle against revolutionary France, the British people rejected revolutionary solutions at home. Their instinctive reaction was to cling to that which was time-tested and familiar. Yet new problems could not be dealt with without new ideas, and by 1815 a variety of new ideas had become available. The result was a period of intense political, economic, and social stress leading to a series of reforms that, by 1850, had shaped an institutional framework for the first industrial and urban nation.

POST-WAR BRITAIN

Government

The British political system had withstood the ambitions of Napoleon, but it was ill-equipped to deal with the problems of peace. King George III was aged and insane, living out his last years (he died in 1820) in Windsor Castle. His son and heir, George, the regent for his father, who had once been a bright, lively, charming man-about-town, had now become a fat, peevish, middle-aged voluptuary. His youthful attachment to Charles James Fox and the Whigs was forgotten, and as regent he continued the Tories in office. The regency possessed none of the dignity or mystique of monarchy, and the Regent petulantly surrendered to his ministers those remnants of royal power his father had struggled to preserve. He was separated from his wife, Princess Caroline, a coarse, eccentric woman who lived in Italy accompanied by a disreputable entourage. Their daughter Charlotte, heir to the throne, died in 1817, leaving the succession to the Regent's brother. As he had all his life, George spent freely on himself, his palaces, and the entertainment of his friends. In a period when difficult economic adjustments had to be made, he was not the kind of person who would strengthen public attachment to the principle of monarchy.

The Tory ministry of Lord Liverpool, which had seen Britain through to victory, was ill-prepared to grapple with the adjustment to peace. Liverpool was a capable, fair-minded man, but cautious in action. As foreign secretary, Lord Castlereagh was hard-working and willing to take decisions that would involve Britain in peacetime commitments to Europe. Lord Sidmouth (Henry Addington) was home secretary, a man frightened by dissidents and determined to hold the line against those who threatened the existing order of things. The cabinet was overwhelmingly aristocratic and quite unsuited to cope with the political and economic discontents that were unleashed when the war ended.

The Tory Party, which was the backbone of the ministry's support in Parliament, was conservative in outlook, dominated by landed aristocrats and gentlemen, and opposed to reforms of Parliament or the Church that would threaten its grip on power. The Whig opposition was led nominally by Lord Grey, once the protégé of Fox, who in 1797 had proposed reform of the House of Commons. Long exclusion from power had reduced the Whig numbers and weakened their morale. Whig commitments to parliamentary reform and abolition of religious privileges had little support in Parliament and the country. To some extent Whig hopes for the future rested upon able, aggressive middle-class Whigs such as the energetic lawyer and publicist, Henry Brougham. These middle-class Whigs were active advocates of administrative, legal, and parliamentary reform.

British Society

In 1815, the Industrial Revolution had just begun to transform British society. Most of the population of thirteen million lived in rural villages or hamlets, engaged in agriculture or handicraft industries. By 1851 Britain had become the first urban nation: the population had increased to 21 million and slightly more than half the population lived in urban communities.

The London metropolitan area continued its sprawling growth, but much of Britain's population increase was in new industrial towns such as Birmingham, Manchester, Leeds, and Sheffield. These towns were characterized by ugliness, grime, congestion, poorly built housing, lack of sanitary facilities and pure water, and an absence of civic amenities such as parks, playgrounds, schools, and libraries. Despite the long hours, low wages, and insecurity of employment characteristic of early industrialism, the towns continued to attract workers from the growing population of the countryside.

Although Romantic poets found much to praise in rural England, the working people of this leafy realm found that industrialization was changing their lives, in many instances not for the better. The long wars with France had brought prosperity to agriculture: more land had been brought under the plow than at any time before or since. To take advantage of high wartime prices, the new crops and methods of agriculture that had developed in the previous century were rapidly introduced. The new agriculture required extensive investment in buildings, hedges, drainage, and fertilizer, a process that required substantial capital and a continuing extension of enclosure. Villagers who lost lands or customary rights without adequate compensation, either found employment in the rising industrial towns or were employed by farmers at low wages which at times were supplemented by poor relief.

During the war, high prices and rents had enabled the landed aristocracy and gentry to live comfortably and build splendid country homes that were elegantly furnished. With the end of the war this artificial prosperity came crashing down, with disastrous effects on all levels of rural society. Furthermore, rural England had depended for much of its livelihood on handicraft industries, now threatened by industrialism and, after 1815, foreign competition. For some, rural England still provided an attractive and secure place to live. But many of its young people were compelled to leave for the industrial towns, and those who remained were often reduced to a poverty made no less distressing by quaint surroundings.

It is a common mistake to underestimate the importance of the established Church in the life of early nineteenth-century England. The Church was part of the power structure, a position guaranteed by the Test and Corporation Acts of the late seventeenth century. Only Anglicans could hold public office or sit in the House of Commons. Other Protestants could vote, and exceptions were made to enable them to hold local offices. But Catholics were excluded from a political role. The Church also had important powers in local government. The Tory party was determined to maintain the political privileges of the Church, and the movement to give Catholics equal political rights (Catholic Emancipation) was stoutly resisted.

Methodism, which had begun as an effort to renew the spiritual vitality of the Church, had now become a separate denomination with an important influence in the lower middle class and working class of the towns. Presbyterians, Congregationalists, and Baptists continued to hold an influential body of earnest, hard-working people. In whatever form, religion was still an important part of English life.

As Britain grew into an industrial and urban society, education was one of its weaknesses. The Scots, with their local schools and fine universities, were the best educated, an asset that was an important advantage as many of them sought employment in England or the empire. In England the so-called "public schools" (Eton, Westminster, and others) had not gained the eminence that they later obtained. The upper and middle classes were educated at home by tutors or in the local grammar schools. The Church of England maintained a variety of schools, and the academies of the other Protestant denominations offered schooling in useful skills such as book-keeping, navigation, surveying, and the like. A variety of privately operated schools, many with only one or two teachers, offered primary education for those who could pay modest fees. Sunday schools were operated by religious bodies to provide the rudiments of literacy to the children of the poor.

Oxford and Cambridge boasted magnificent buildings, libraries, and endowments, and their curricula retained the humanistic and clerical emphasis of the past. The two universities boasted some fine scholars and some students got an excellent education, but instructional standards were slack, and they were often seen as finishing schools for gentlemen rather than institutions of higher learning. This situation led Jeremy Bentham and other reformers to establish University College, which became the core of the University of London.

Scotland, Ireland

The United Kingdom of Great Britain and Ireland was far from being as united as its name implied. The political union of England and Scotland in 1707 had been successful, but the Scots preserved their separate administrative system, judicial system, educational institutions, and church. Edinburgh was the intellectual and social center of Scotland, and the development of the "New Town" was transforming Edinburgh into the attractive city it is today. Glasgow was a major center of trade with Ireland, North America, and the West Indies. A cluster of brilliant eighteenth-century thinkers and scholars, among them David Hume and Adam Smith, had led "the Scottish renaissance" that continued into the nineteenth century. The Scottish universities at Edinburgh,

Glasgow, St. Andrews, and Aberdeen maintained high standards. The novels of Sir Walter Scott gave Scots new pride in their national history and character. The visit of King George IV to Scotland in 1822 was seen as symbolic of the acceptance of Scotland as a distinctive and respected part of the United Kingdom.

The Act of Union with Ireland (1801) was less successful. Ireland continued to be governed by a viceroy and a secretary sent from England. The Anglo-Irish ruling class, many of whom were absentee landlords, controlled the Irish government and judicial system and the 100 Irish seats in the British House of Commons. Dublin, like Edinburgh, had become an attractive provincial capital, dominated socially by the Anglo-Irish. The Scots-Irish, who lived mainly in the north of Ireland (Ulster), were Presbyterian in religion and determined to uphold the Protestant ascendancy. They had the right to vote, although otherwise their political role was modest.

The Irish Catholic majority had received the vote in 1793, but they were excluded from political office or election to Parliament. Although there were some Catholic middle-class and professional people, the Catholics were overwhelmingly tenant farmers, increasingly dependent on the potato and growing rapidly in number. The potato, supplemented by milk and vegetables, could support a family on a small plot of land, and as the population increased the land was subdivided into ever smaller plots. The response of the Catholic Irish to economic deprivation and abuse by landlords was periodic violence, a tactic that the Protestant authorities met with force. Encouraged by French ideas and their own second-class status, the Catholic Irish were ripe for revolt whenever the opportunity arose.

TORY CONSERVATISM, 1815–1822

Foreign Policy

More than twenty years of war had convinced the Tories that stability at home required peace abroad. For this reason the Liverpool ministry, led by Lord Castlereagh, the foreign secretary, was willing to make an unprecedented commitment to European peace. In 1814, Britain had joined with Austria, Prussia, and Russia in an alliance to complete the defeat of Napoleon and keep the major powers working together in the peace settlement. At the Congress of Vienna in 1815 the Austrian Chancellor, Metternich, advocated great power cooperation to preserve peace and stability ("the Concert of Europe"), a concept that Castlereagh strongly supported. The entrance of France into the alliance in 1818 was welcomed by Castlereagh as a further stabilizing force.

The principal problem that the Concert of Europe offered to Britain was Metternich's determination to use the alliance to preserve the the existing political and social order against liberal demands for constitutional and representative government. In 1820 revolutions broke out in Spain and several Italian states. Metternich reacted by calling a congress of the allied powers, which agreed to Austrian intervention in Italy to suppress the revolts. In 1822 another congress met to consider the revolution in Spain, and in 1823 the French sent an army to restore the despotic King of Spain to his throne. Intimations were raised that something might be done to restore Spanish control over the former Spanish colonies in Latin America.

Castlereagh protested strenuously against these actions, especially the French intervention in Spain. He held that the Concert of Europe had been formed to prevent general war and not to intervene in the internal affairs of the European states. The revolutionaries were demanding constitutional government, representative institutions, and civil liberties—rights that the British people already possessed and could not justifiably deny to others. Furthermore, any attempt to restore Spanish control over the former colonies would threaten Britain's access to trade in Latin America. By 1822, when he committed suicide, Castlereagh had come to the painful realization that Britain's domestic institutions and overseas interests made it impossible to cooperate in any meaningful way with autocratic states such as Austria, Prussia, and Russia.

Castlereagh was succeeded at the Foreign Office by George Canning, a brilliant, individualistic, and highly nationalistic man whose boldness and independence stood in contrast to Castlereagh's painstaking diplomacy and search for cooperation among the European powers. Canning could not stop French intervention in Spain, but British sea power could and did block any attempt to restore Spanish authority over the former Spanish colonies in Latin America. The young United States, acting independently, took a similar position in the Monroe Doctrine. In 1826 Canning successfully supported constitutional monarchy in Portugal, where Britain had long had a close relationship and British sea power could be a determining factor.

In 1821 Canning faced a difficult situation when a revolution broke out in Greece, as the Greeks sought independence from the Ottoman Empire of the Turks. Metternich viewed the Greek revolt as another popular uprising that should be suppressed in the interests of stability. The Russians, however, prepared to aid the Greeks, because they saw an opportunity to gain territory and influence in the Balkans and both Russians and Greeks were Eastern Orthodox Christians. The cruelty with which the Turks attempted to subdue the Greeks offended European opinion. The Greeks, fighting for freedom against an oppressive regime, evoked in the British public memories of ancient Greek democracy. The colorful romantic poet, Lord Byron, dramatized the Greek cause in 1824, when he died in Greece trying to aid the rebels.

Canning was faced with a dilemma: he wished to support the Ottoman Empire as an obstacle to Russian expansion into the Mediterranean, but he could not in good conscience support the Moslem Turks against the Christian Greeks. He endeavoured to bring about Greek independence without contributing to an extension of Russian influence in the area. He decided that his goal could be achieved only by direct British involvement. When the Turks received assistance from the ruler of Egypt, British, French, and Russian warships destroyed the combined Turkish-Egyptian fleet at the Battle of Navarino (1827). The next year the Russians invaded the Balkans, and in 1829 the Turks were compelled to sign a peace agreeing to Greek independence. By that time Canning was dead, a political crisis has blown up in England, and Metternich's concept of a Concert of Europe had broken down badly. Britain's commitment to a continuing role in the European balance of power had come to a close.

Domestic Dissension

In 1815 the Liverpool ministry found that victory abroad had unleashed pent-up demands at home. In the later years of the war a spirit of restlessness and dissatisfaction had been evident in many sectors of the public. One problem had nothing to do with the war; it was a series of bad crops, always a major factor in preindustrial economies. With the end of wartime demand, farm prices fell precipitously, and farmers were confronted with inflated wartime rents at a time when there was a sharp fall in agricultural incomes. Trade and industry also suffered, as European competitors entered into markets formerly cut off by war, selling their goods at desperation prices. The demobilization of large numbers of soldiers and sailors, accompanied by shutdowns of wartime industries, resulted in high unemployment. Assistance to the unemployed was left to the justices of the peace and the parishes, as required by the Poor Laws, and the system broke down completely under this unusual strain.

When the war ended, the first objective of the Liverpool ministry was to deal with the problems of agriculture. The Tory Party was above all the party of the landed interest. Faced with acute agricultural distress, the ministry responded with a Corn Law intended to keep the price of wheat high by imposing a tariff on imports. This action satisfied landlords and farmers but aroused a torrent of protest from industrialists and urban workers who complained that the policy kept food prices high at their expense. The duties on imported wool were also increased, a benefit to agriculture at the expense of the woolen cloth industry.

The money supply was an important factor in the adjustment to peace. During the war the Bank of England had suspended payments in gold; thereafter the money supply was based on paper currency, but money inflation had not become serious until the last years of the war. With the return of peace financiers, merchants, and economists advocated a return to money backed by gold, and this step was taken by the Liverpool ministry in the Bank Act of 1819. The immediate result was sharply deflationary, accentuating the postwar depression, although probably beneficial in the long run. Those who suffered from business setbacks and unemployment accused the government of being more responsive to the wishes of financiers than to the needs of the nation.

Economic problems were made even more volatile by a giant backlog of working-class discontent. The old system that had regulated quality and wages had broken down during the war, and had been swept away by a Parliament dominated by landowners. Hard-pressed employers cut wages and often went bankrupt, leaving their workers to fend for themselves. Some of the most serious distress was found in declining industries, such as the hand-loom weavers, who could not compete with the new power looms. The workers expressed their grievances in the only way they could: through mass meetings, violence and threats of violence, and attacks on the factories and machines that took bread out of their mouths. The effect was to strike fear into the ruling class of the nation, who saw in this turmoil a threat to constitutional government, social stability, and private property.

The postwar depression contributed to a revival of Radicalism, a movement for political reform that found support in both the middle class and the working class. Although Radicalism included a wide variety of goals, the key issues were those that affected the distribution of political power—the privileges of the crown, the aristocracy, and the Church, and the structure of the House of Commons. In Parliament, the aristocratic Whig leaders favored reduction of the political influence of the king and his ministers, but they were dubious about changes in parliamentary representation and the right to vote.

The Whig Party, however, attracted a number of middle-class reformers who had no such inhibitions. The most articulate of these was Henry Brougham, a talented Scot. Brougham's brilliant intellect and restless energy were devoted to a variety of causes: reform of the law and prisons, free trade, abolition of slavery, public education, the Poor Laws, and parliamentary reform. In Ireland, Catholic Emancipation, which would destroy the dominance of the Protestant ruling class, became a major issue. The disputes that had been shelved during the long period of war could be deferred no longer.

The agenda of reform was partially shaped by systematic thinkers through books, pamphlets, and periodicals. The ideas of Jeremy Bentham were expounded by "Philosophic Radicals" such as James Mill, who wrote extensively on politics, economics, education, the Poor Laws, prisons, colonial policy, and the history of India. Mill took a leading role in founding the University of

London as a Benthamite counterweight to the genteel, clerical traditions of Oxford and Cambridge. The main contribution of Philosophic Radicalism was to develop the habit of rational analysis of political and social institutions in terms of their costs and benefits to society. Seen in this light, the ancient institutions that Burke had idealized as the product of some mysterious collective wisdom began to appear as unwarranted sources of power and income for a privileged minority.

Closely related to the rational analysis of the Benthamites was the economics of a group known collectively as "the Classical Economists," who derived their ideas principally from Adam Smith's *The Wealth of Nations*. The outstanding figure among the classical economists was David Ricardo, the offspring of a Dutch-Jewish speculator who had settled in London. Learning from his father, Ricardo took advantage of wartime finance to make a fortune. He also married an English woman and was converted to the Church of England. In his *Principles of Political Economy and Taxation* (1817) Ricardo argued that political attempts to control the economy could only impede economic activity and reduce the level of national investment and wealth.

In 1819 Ricardo became a member of Parliament, where he was regarded as an authority on economic questions. His ideas were influential in the return to the gold standard, and he was an effective critic of the Corn Law, a pillar of the Tory creed, which he viewed as an unwarranted benefit to landlords at the expense of the productive part of the nation. He also opposed the Poor Laws, where he adopted a Malthusian approach, arguing that population would always fluctuate in proportion to productivity, with the result that wages for a substantial part of the population would inevitably hover around the subsistence level.

The economics of Smith and Ricardo placed economic policy in an entirely new light. Gone was the concept of a stable community in which each element of society had its proper status and proper reward. In its place was "the invisible hand" of the market, governing rents, profits, wages, and interest rates, and shaping the lives of individuals and nations. By destroying the older economic views, the classical economists left the field open to aggressive middle-class bankers, merchants, and industrialists who were confident that they could succeed in a free market and were prepared to work themselves and their employees hard to do so.

Radicalism also found support among the growing working class of the towns, who were increasingly conscious of the effects of political decisions upon their lives. Newspapers and periodicals, taking advantage of the rapid growth of literacy, spread the new ideas to middle class and working class readers. Henry Hunt, the most powerful political orator of his time, promoted the cause of political reform in large mass meetings. Francis Place, a London tailor, was a master at organizing the artisans and shopkeepers of London and Westminster. In 1793 Place gained prominence as leader of the London breeches-makers in a strike. He became a friend of Bentham and Mill and established a library which became a gathering place for Radicals. Place's views were those of the skilled artisans and small shopkeepers. He was himself an employer and was not an advocate of mass democracy, but he believed that the well-established working man was entitled to a voice in the political process.

A similar movement developed in Birmingham, where the metal trades were organized in many small units and relations between masters and men were close. In Manchester, however, working class discontent took a different direction, for Manchester was the center of the textile industry, where the factory system had created strong antagonism between employers and factory workers. Yorkshire was different again, for there the emergence of the industrial system had left pockets of poverty as handicraft workers fought a losing battle against machines.

Despite these variations, three common complaints can be seen running through working class protest: the dignity of work was debased by the new industrial system; the wealth produced by labor was unfairly distributed; and the structure of authority was weighted against those who worked. The workers, feeling ignored by the aristocracy and gentry and oppressed by middle class employers, developed a sense of alienation that continued unabated for more than a century, and has never fully disappeared.

Repression of Dissent

The reaction of the Liverpool ministry to Radicalism was repression. Drawn from a long-established political and social elite, it was difficult for the ministry, members of Parliament, and local magistrates to accept a challenge to their authority from persons whom they saw as far beneath them in the social scale. The rise of radical agitation in 1815 and 1816 led the government in 1817 to strengthen the powers of the local magistrates. In 1818 public expressions of discontent diminished, but in 1819 another economic slump provoked a new round of protests and mass meetings. Henry Hunt and other agitators traversed the nation, demanding redistribution of parliamentary seats and a broadening of the franchise.

The most striking confrontation took place in Manchester, where a great crowd assembled peacefully in St. Peter's Fields to listen to Hunt and other radical speakers. The Manchester magistrates, fearful of a riot, panicked and sent in the militia, assisted by soldiers, to arrest the speakers and disperse the crowd. In the melee which followed, eleven people were killed and over 400 wounded. The government was disturbed by the reaction of the magistrates, but felt compelled to support their actions. The dissidents, in mocking reference to the Battle of Waterloo, referred to this "victory" of saber-wielding soldiers over unarmed citizens as "Peterloo".

When Hunt was brought to London for trial he was hailed as a hero. The government responded with the "Six Acts", which further restricted public meetings and the dissemination of inflammatory literature, and placed heavier duties on newspapers. It appeared that more confrontations were imminent.

At this point an extraneous event attracted public attention and served as an outlet for popular discontent. In 1820 King George III died, and his son, the Regent, succeeded him as King George IV (1820–1830). To the dismay of George IV and the Liverpool ministry, the new king's estranged wife, Caroline, decided to return to Britain and claim her place as queen. George IV was determined not to accept her and demanded that his ministers obtain a divorce by act of Parliament. The public, however, supported Queen Caroline as a means of showing their detestation for the king and his ministers. The Whigs and radicals, seeing a good popular issue, came to the defense of the Queen.

The result was a parliamentary and public hubbub that thoroughly embarrassed the ministry and gave popular discontent an outlet. Conveniently for George IV and the ministry, Queen Caroline died the next year. By that time the worst problems of the postwar period had begun to ease. But the affair of Queen Caroline revealed the resentments and sense of alienation that existed in many sectors of the British people.

TORY LIBERALISM, 1822–1829

Economic and Social Reform

By 1822 the worst of the post-war adjustment was over, the economy was improving, political tensions were declining, and the Liverpool ministry was ready to take a more liberal direction in its policies. The death of Castlereagh in 1822 made necessary a reorganization of the ministry, which enabled Lord Liverpool to bring forward Tories who were more progressive in their views. George Canning replaced Castlereagh as foreign secretary, Robert Peel became home secretary, and William Huskisson entered the cabinet as president of the Board of Trade.

It was agreed that the Tory ministry would continue to stand fast against parliamentary reform and Catholic Emancipation. On matters of foreign policy, economic policy, and social reform the ministry took new directions that have been labelled "Tory Liberalism." Although conservative where the distribution of political power was concerned, the Tories showed themselves willing to respond to new economic and social needs. The Tories were heirs to a long tradition of upper-class responsibility for the welfare of the lower orders of society. As a party identified with the landed interest, they were not unwilling to use the power of government to interfere with urban or industrial elites.

The key figure in giving the Tory Party a concern for social reform was the home secretary, Sir Robert Peel. Son of a Lancashire cotton manufacturer, Peel had been prepared at Harrow and Oxford for a political career. He was a man of great personal integrity and strength of character: he was conservative, in that he did not act hastily; he was liberal in that he was willing to respond to needs that were clearly demonstrated. Peel became the recognized leader of those Tories who recognized that an elite could hold power only if that power was used for the welfare of all. Thus he helped define a conservative philosophy rooted in the works of a devoted Whig, Edmund Burke.

At the Home Office Peel was primarily concerned with police, law, and prisons, problems that had become acute as a result of industrialization and urbanization. He took the lead in a broad reform of the criminal law, including legislation that greatly reduced the number of crimes that carried the death penalty. He also responded to the work of prison reformers and legislation was passed to improve the conditions of prisons.

In 1829, facing a political crisis and public disorders, Peel established the London metropolitan police. The government needed trained policemen to control riots, for calling in the army often made matters worse. Members of Parliament and visitors to London, as well as inhabitants, favored a police force, for they were victimized by London's huge criminal class. Headquartered at Scotland Yard in Westminster, the "bobbies" soon gained respect and provided a model for other towns.

The Tories also took steps toward a more liberal commercial policy, signalled by the appointment of William Huskisson to the Board of Trade. Picking up the legacy of Pitt, Huskisson led in a broad reduction and simplification of the customs duties, thereby improving the revenue and removing obstacles to the flow of trade. The Navigation Acts, which protected British ships at the expense of trade, were modified to allow a freer flow of shipping between the colonies and Europe.

Huskisson also took a liberal attitude toward another major economic issue, the Corn Law, but this was a subject that was sacrosanct to the Tories, and he made only modest progress. The Tories were prepared to be liberal with the economic privileges of others, but not with the tariff protection given the landed interest. As the party of agriculture, the Tories had little reason to be sympathetic to factory owners. Repeal of the Combination Acts in 1824 permitted workers to form trade unions, although legislation the next year deprived the unions of the right to strike.

The Breakdown of Tory Unity

In 1827 Lord Liverpool suffered a severe stroke, and it became necessary to reconstitute the ministry. The Tory Party by this time had become deeply divided: the Duke of Wellington spoke for conservative Tories, while George Canning was the recognized leader of those committed to "Tory liberalism." King George IV, recognizing Canning's ability, experience, and wide popularity, called upon him to form a ministry. Wellington and Peel, uneasy with Canning's long-stated support for Catholic Emancipation, refused to join, but some of the Whigs gave Canning their support. Later in the year Canning died, worn out by strain and overwork.

After further dissensions Wellington, with Peel as his spokesman in the House of Commons, formed a ministry controlled by the conservative Tories; many of the Canningites refused to support Wellington. Thus the Tory Party, which had controlled British governments since the days of William Pitt, began to fall apart. It appeared that a new political alignment was emerging, which was likely to bring into the open those constitutional issues that Lord Liverpool had avoided—parliamentary reform and the privileges of the Church of England.

Wellington and Peel were immediately faced with the Church question. The Test and Corporation Acts were regarded by the Church as essential to its privileged position, for in principle they permitted only Anglicans to hold public office. The application of the acts to other Protestants was riddled with exceptions, but the exclusion of Catholics was of some importance in Britain and was regarded as vital in Ireland. In 1828 Wellington and Peel were confronted with a demand from Protestant Dissenters for relief from the Test and Corporation Acts. Needing their support in the struggle against Catholic Emancipation, they yielded, and the acts were repealed insofar as they applied to Protestants.

In the meantime, a storm blew up in Ireland. Daniel O'Connell, a powerful orator and agitator, had organized the Catholic Association to work for Catholic Emancipation, which would dramatically change Irish politics, including the election of the 100 Irish members of the House of Commons. In 1828, O'Connell came forward as candidate for Parliament in an Irish by-election and won with a strong majority, although, as a Catholic, he was legally ineligible to sit in Parliament. Wellington and Peel faced the possibility of civil war in Ireland. Again they felt they had no choice but to give way, and in 1829 they declared themselves in favor of Catholic Emancipation.

George IV raged; the Church of England was aghast; the Tory Party split wide open; and the country squires, so long supporters of the Tories, felt betrayed. The Catholic Emancipation Bill was passed by a combination of ministers, officeholders, liberal Tories, Whigs, and Radicals. At that critical moment King George IV further complicated matters by dying, which made a new election necessary at a time of political ferment. A great crisis was at hand.

The Reform Bill Crisis, 1830–1832

The Background of Reform

The movement for parliamentary reform that had begun in the 1780s had been halted by the French Revolution and the conservative reaction, but complaints concerning the unrepresentative character of the House of Commons had not ceased. By 1830 the desire for change was in the air, and the House of Commons was seen as the principal obstacle to essential reforms. The indictment of the House was varied: the dominance of the House by ministers, placemen, and other beneficiaries of "the influence of the crown"; the small boroughs controlled by aristocratic patrons or men of great wealth; the decayed towns that still sent two members to Parliament while new industrial towns were unrepresented; the manipulation of elections by interest groups; the disorder which accompanied voting in many constituencies.

Despite these complaints the House of Commons had been accepted as broadly representative of, and responsive to, the national interest. By 1830 this sense of confidence had broken down. Conservative Tories had seen Tory ministers use their influence in Parliament to pass Catholic Emancipation. Industrial leaders resented the control of the House of Commons by the landed interest, who used their disproportionate weight to maintain the Corn Law. The working class had come to think of the House of Commons as a bastion of privilege that protected the interests of landlords or mill owners while leaving workers at the mercy of economic forces. Radicals saw parliamentary reform as the first step toward reforms of money, trade, the law, local government, and the Poor Laws. Humanitarians saw the House of Commons as the defender of atrocious criminal punishments and slavery. Whig politicians seemed to be excluded indefinitely from the sweets of office. Rather suddenly the election of 1830 brought these various forces together, and parliamentary reform became the overriding issue of the day.

The new king and his ministers little suspected the storm that was brewing. King William IV (1830–1837) was a bluff, straightforward man, without strong political opinions apart from his desire to preserve what was left of monarchical power and the general dislike of change characteristic of the Hanoverians. Wellington and Peel continued in office: stung by Tory charges that they had betrayed the Church, they were more determined than ever to hold the line. In the election of 1830 the aristocratic Whig leaders bided their time, and the cause of parliamentary reform was put forward by middle-class advocates. William Cobbett, the journalist, attacked the reign of privilege; Francis Place stirred up popular demonstrations in London; Thomas Attwood, a Birmingham banker, organized the Birmingham Political Union to agitate for parliamentary reform. In Yorkshire Henry Brougham, the Whig reformer, campaigned brilliantly on the issue.

A revolution in France in July, which expelled a reactionary king, offered a lesson that William IV did not overlook, but it does not seem to have affected the election. In the south of England agricultural laborers rioted, burning hay-stacks and destroying threshing machines; although their concerns were eco-nomic, their actions added to the sense of emergency.

When the new Parliament met in November, 1830, Wellington made clear his determination to oppose any kind of parliamentary reform. The first im-portant vote of the session was on the civil list, the financial provision for the king, royal family and household, and many civil government offices. The civil list was a matter of great personal interest to the new king and to the ministers, who controlled the civil list patronage. For more than a century the civil list had been attacked as a center of "corrupt influence." Members with griev-ances against the crown seized the opportunity, and the ministry was defeated by a combination of Whigs, liberal Tories, Radicals, and disgruntled country gentlemen. Wellington and Peel resigned, and King William IV asked Earl Grey, leader of the Whigs, to form a government. The door to reform was ajar.

The Great Reform Bill

Earl Grey was sixty-six years old in 1830—a poised, confident aristocrat who had entered the House of Commons in 1786 as a follower of Charles James Fox. In 1797 he had presented an unsuccessful proposal for parliamentary re-form; when he took office in 1830 his commitment to parliamentary reform was clear but unspecified. The leading spokesman for the ministry in the House of Commons was Lord John Russell, a younger son of the Duke of Bedford, who had been an advocate of parliamentary reform for more than a decade. It was Russell who led in drawing up the Reform Bill and piloting it through the House of Commons.

The bill that Russell presented in March 1831 was more drastic than had been expected. The bill preserved the principle of separate county and bor-ough constituencies, but it extended the franchise to those persons whose prop-erty was thought sufficient to guarantee a responsible use of the vote. The county franchise for freeholders remained the same (property with a rental value of 40 shillings per year). Tenants with secure or long-term tenancies worth £10 per year or more would receive the right to vote, as would tenants with short-term leases (amended to include tenants-at-will) worth £50 per

Earl Grey Column and Statue,
Newcastle-upon-Tyne.
Private collection.

year. These provisions would greatly increase the number of county voters, but the landlord-tenant relationship was such that the new franchise would strengthen the influence of the aristocracy and gentry in the counties.

In the boroughs the bill made two important changes: a redistribution of seats and the establishment of a uniform borough franchise. In its final form, the bill disfranchised fifty-six small boroughs and took one seat from thirty others, making available 143 seats for redistribution to populous counties and large towns such as Manchester, Birmingham, and Leeds. The borough franchise, which had varied widely, was made uniform: the owner or tenant of property with an annual rental value of £10 per year and who met other qualifications—such as payment of rates (local property taxes)—received the vote. In most boroughs the bill extended the franchise, but in some democratic boroughs it actually reduced the number of voters. The ministry rejected a proposal for the secret ballot, and open voting continued in the counties and boroughs, thus maintaining the influence of landlords and employers. Similar bills for Scotland and Ireland accompanied the main bill.

Passage of the Reform Bill was a great national struggle. Although historians may dispute the intentions of the reformers and the effects of the bill, there can be no doubt that those who lived through the events of 1831–1832 felt that decisions of fundamental importance to Britain were being made. In March 1831 the bill was approved by the House of Commons by one vote, but when it appeared that it might be whittled away by amendments Grey persuaded the reluctant William IV to call an election.

The election of 1831 was a national referendum on the bill, supporters demanding "the bill, the whole bill, and nothing but the bill." Well-organized pressure groups held parades and mass meetings in London, Birmingham, and other major towns. In the election, the advocates of reform won a clear victory, and in the new House of Commons the bill passed, 367–231. In October the House of Lords rejected the bill, setting off a new round of mass meetings, protests, and riots. The Whig ministry took strong measures to put down disorders, and called the Duke of Wellington back to duty to mobilize the troops if necessary.

Russell introduced the bill again in December. It passed the Commons without difficulty, but in April 1832 the bill was blocked in the House of Lords by an amendment that the ministry refused to accept. Grey asked William IV to create enough new peers favorable to the bill to pass it. When the king refused, the Whig ministry resigned. Wellington tried to form a government, but this time public opinion had gained such irresistible force that he was forced to withdraw.

Grey and the Whigs returned to power, fortified by the king's promise to create peers if needed to pass the bill. Faced with defeat, Wellington and other Tory peers agreed not to vote against the bill, and it was passed in the House of Lords on June 4, 1832. Three days later the royal approval was given, although William IV refused to perform the ceremony personally, sending commissioners instead.

Passage of the Reform Bill of 1832 was a triumph of public opinion and the House of Commons over the king and the House of Lords. Throughout the crisis, King William IV had shown his distaste for the bill, but when faced with what appeared to be a dangerous situation he twice yielded to political and popular pressure: first by calling an election to strengthen support for the bill in the House of Commons, and then by agreeing to create peers to get the bill through the House of Lords.

The aristocracy were also forced to yield. After the election of 1831 Wellington and the Tories were helpless in the House of Commons; they made the House of Lords the last defense against a bill that they saw as a serious blow to aristocratic power. Faced with the king's promise to create new peers, backed up by a majority in the House of Commons and a determined public opinion, the Lords had no choice but to give way.

Throughout the two-year crisis Grey and the Whig ministers remained remarkably cool, balancing strong determination to preserve order with the need to gain the maximum political advantage from legitimate political agitation. One must not forget that it was the unreformed House of Commons that passed the bill and the unreformed electorate that produced the majority needed to do so. It was the aristocratic Earl Grey who provided the essential leadership, aided in the House of Commons by a younger son of one of Britain's wealthiest aristocrats. The old system had responded to the demands of a new age.

The British people were the real heroes of the Reform Bill crisis. Middle-class and working-class leaders shared in a masterful organization and manipulation of public feeling. The political issues involved were thoroughly aired in books, periodicals, pamphlets, and other publications. The amount of violence was minimal but enough to have a salutary effect. The public remained united in its determination to have the bill despite strong differences of opinion concerning many of its features. By their determination and steadiness during a two-year crisis, the British people demonstrated that constitutional change could be achieved peaceably, and that they were ready for a broadening of the political base.

ECONOMIC EXPANSION
AND HARD TIMES, 1830–1850

Economic Growth

By the time of the Great Reform Bill, industrialization in Britain had proceeded from the initial stage in which a few industries were involved to the stage of broadly based development. In 1830 the factory system was well established in the cotton textile industry, and by 1850 the new industrial system dominated textile manufacture in both cottons and woolens. The factory system was also being extended to iron and pottery, and steam engines were providing power for factories, mines, trains and ships. Foreign trade grew rapidly, as did British shipping, making Britain the premier commercial and maritime nation. The British navy patrolled the shipping lanes, making them safer for ships of all nations. Agriculture and associated village industries continued to be the basis of the economy. Enclosure of the open fields and common lands proceeded rapidly, making possible increased productivity through the use of the new agricultural methods.

Perhaps Britain's most important industrial advance from 1830–1850 was in engineering and the production of machinery. British engineers and skilled workmen led the world in designing and building steam engines, locomotives,

Stephenson's Locomotion Number One. Private collection.

steamships, factories, roads, bridges, docks, and cranes. The British were without rivals in using machine tools to make industrial parts manufactured to close tolerances. Many of these engineers, inventors, and machinists were men from humble families who found opportunities in an expanding economy that needed their talents.

The most characteristic feature of industrial expansion from 1830–1850 was the building of railways. For more than two decades inventors had been working to develop a steam locomotive, and rails had long been in use for coal carts. It was George Stephenson, son of a Northumberland coal mine engineer, who first put the two together successfully. His greatest triumph was the Liverpool and Manchester Railway, opened in 1830, where he demonstrated the superiority of his steam locomotive over stationary steam engines. Stephenson directed construction of the thirty-one mile railway, using cuts, bridges, and viaducts to produce a roadbed with gentle grades. Stephenson and his son, Robert, also a railway engineer, became leaders in a railway boom which by 1850 provided Britain with 6,000 miles of track and greatly stimulated related industries, such as coal, iron, and engineering.

Although the railway companies had expected that their principal business would be carrying freight, initially most of their revenues came from passenger traffic, which also required building stations, waiting rooms, and buffets. Suddenly people were freed from their towns and villages and able to travel easily to other places to do business, visit relatives, or see the sights. By 1850 the railroads had carried 72 million passengers. The economic effects of railway building are obvious; the social and psychological effects of fast, cheap travel can only be conjectured.

In the public eye the chief rival of the two Stephensons was Isambard K. Brunel, also a son of an engineer. Brunel distinguished himself in the building of the Thames tunnel, the Great Western Railway, and many remarkable bridges and docks, in which he made imaginative use of structural iron. His most notable efforts, however, were devoted to the application of steam power to ocean-going vessels. In 1838 his wooden paddle steamer, the *Great Western*, crossed the Atlantic under steam. Brunel used an iron hull and a screw propeller for his second ocean-going steamship, the *Great Britain*, which made several trans-Atlantic crossings before it ran aground off Ireland in 1846.

Brunel's most ambitious project was the *Great Eastern*, designed to be large enough to go all the way to India without re-coaling. With a huge iron hull, ten boilers, eight engines, and propelled by paddle wheels and a screw propeller, the *Great Eastern* was one of the engineering marvels of the age and was the largest ship built until 1901. The *Great Eastern* lost money for its owners every year until it was broken up for scrap, but it served a useful purpose in laying the trans-Atlantic cable in the 1860s.

Brunel's suspension bridge, Bristol. Private collection.

Steamships were already being used on inland waters, where refueling was simple, but the quantity of coal needed by early steamships made them inefficient for ocean travel, and the bulk of the world's ocean traffic was carried by wooden sailing ships until 1870. By that time the powerful steamships pioneered by Brunel were replacing the graceful clipper ships with their billowing clouds of sail. Beauty's loss was efficiency's gain.

Economic Distress

The progress of British industry was much affected by periodic fluctuations, and the business cycle began to appear as the bane of modern capitalism. An early speculative boom took place in 1825, followed by a business recession complicated by poor harvests. By 1835 an upswing was taking place that was aborted by the panic of 1837. By 1840 a full-scale depression was in being which reached its low point in 1842. From 1844–1846 the railway boom stimulated the economy, followed by another breakdown in 1846. By 1850 strong economic growth had begun which continued with few setbacks until 1873.

These economic fluctuations should not be attributed entirely to industry. The banking system, based on gold, could not adjust money and credit to needs. Most industrial firms were owned by families or partnerships and lacked capital or reserves to withstand a momentary downturn. The domestic market was small and inelastic, and for that reason British industry depended on the vagaries of foreign trade and foreign exchange. Industrialism presented Britain with a new set of problems, but it also generated the growing wealth by which these problems could be resolved.

One of the results of economic fluctuations was unemployment and distress among the industrial working class. The classical economists, who followed the principles of Smith and Ricardo, held that economic fluctuations were the unavoidable consequences of economic laws and served a useful purpose in redirecting economic activity into the most profitable channels. This philosophy of economic individualism was strongly criticized by Thomas Carlyle, product of a stern Scottish upbringing, who insisted in powerful, angry words that the new industrial world must adopt a faith more powerful than submission to economic laws—a faith that called for leadership and hard work to improve the moral and material well-being of the community.

Despite the influence of laissez-faire ideas, humanitarianism and a sense of social responsibility led Parliament and the public to consider regulation of employment in factories. In 1832 Michael Sadler, a Tory gentleman from Yorkshire, led a parliamentary committee that investigated child labor in the factories and issued a remarkable report. Although Sadler lost his seat in Parliament in 1833, the Factory Act of that year responded to the abuses revealed in his report by prohibiting employment of children under nine and limiting the hours of work of children from ages nine to eighteen.

Sadler's place as the conscience of Britain was taken by Lord Ashley, later Earl of Shaftesbury, whose investigations into the labor of women and children in the coal mines shocked the nation and led to the Mines Act of 1842. For many years Shaftesbury worked for legislation to limit the employment of children to ten hours per day, which would also have the practical effect of a ten-hour day for adult workers in the same factory. Finally in 1847 legislation was passed limiting the working day of women and children to ten hours. Although Parliament was willing to regulate the labor of women and children, there was strong reluctance to interfere with the labor of adult males, who were considered to be free agents, responsible for making their own contracts with employers.

POLITICS AND REFORM, 1833–1841

Whig Reform

The Great Reform Bill was justified by its supporters, not as an end in itself, but as the means to other reforms. The Parliament that met in 1833, the first elected under the new system, was, however, not much different in its leadership and membership from former parliaments. The Whig leaders, Earl Grey and Lord John Russell, had won a great political and popular triumph and were not eager to assume new challenges. Because they had suffered a defeat, the Tories realized that unity was essential to block a flood of unwelcome legislation. For leadership they continued to look to Robert Peel, whose staunch opposition to the Reform Bill had restored some of the confidence he had lost by giving way on Catholic Emancipation.

Earl Grey, who had earned his niche in history, retired from office in 1834. After several months of Whig floundering, King William IV called upon Peel to form a government. An election in 1835 strengthened the Tories, but an alliance of Whigs, Radicals, and Irish members made it necessary for Peel to resign a few months later. Once again a British monarch had learned that his right to appoint his own ministers and provide them with a majority through an election was limited by political realities.

The Radicals were enormously heartened by their achievement in the Reform Bill crisis. Their energy and conviction enabled them to push through Parliament some important legislation before the reform spirit evaporated. In 1833 slavery was abolished within the British Empire, legislation that affected primarily the British West Indies and the Cape Colony on the southern tip of Africa. The Municipal Corporations Act (1835) applied to incorporated towns the general principles of the Reform Bill. A uniform structure of municipal government was established, consisting of mayor, aldermen, and councillors, with the franchise extended to all resident householders who paid rates (the property tax). Perhaps the most important feature of the act was authorization to impose rates for public purposes. As a result municipal corporations began making improvements in streets, sanitation, police, and other local facilities, although major advances of this kind did not come until the 1870s and after.

A similar reform was the Poor Law of 1834, which was aimed at economy and improved administration. The new law established central control of poor relief under a Poor Law Commission with extensive powers to reorganize administrative units, inspect local poor law practices, and prescribe standards for poor relief. The poor were encouraged to fend for themselves by making poor relief less attractive than the worst-paid employment, and by requiring indigent people to live in poor houses. These houses were called "bastilles," and in many places opposition to the new poor law was intense. In actuality, local administration of the Poor Law was often more flexible than the terms of the law required. But the Poor Law of 1834 did introduce a degree of uniformity and rigor that had been lacking under the old system, without abandoning the principle of public responsibility for maintenance of the poor.

In 1835, frustrated by the resignation of Peel, King William IV turned again to the Whigs. Lord Melbourne, a genial, easy-going aristocrat, became the leader of a ministry supported by Whigs, Radicals, and Irish members that lasted until 1841. In 1837 King William IV died, to be succeeded by his niece, Queen Victoria (1837–1901), a sprightly eighteen-year-old-girl. Victoria looked to Melbourne for advice, and he became her friendly father-confessor and adviser. In 1839, when Melbourne felt it necessary to resign, the young Queen stubbornly showed her displeasure with Peel by refusing to add Tory ladies to her bedchamber. Peel, as always respectful toward monarchy, refused to take office, and Melbourne returned for another two years.

In 1840 an important new influence entered Victoria's life when she married Albert of Saxe-Coburg-Gotha, a handsome, dignified, capable German whose serious purpose made him the most "Victorian" of her subjects. For Albert a new role was devised, that of Prince Consort. Victoria was intensely in love with Albert, and the two worked closely together, but the exclusive responsibility of the Queen to exercise the royal power was never questioned. Under Queen Victoria the monarchy regained some of the respect it had lost under her two predecessors.

Political Pressure Groups

By 1837 the reforming spirit of the ministry, never very strong, had subsided, as Lord Melbourne presided urbanely over the quarreling coalition that sup-

*Queen Victoria
and Albert, Prince Consort.
Corbis.*

ported his government. In the meantime new political issues had arisen, stimulated by the severe depression which began in 1837 and reached its depth in 1842.

One of these issues was political democracy, frustrated in the Great Reform Bill and now brought into prominence by a working-class movement called Chartism. The goals of the Chartists were stated in *The People's Charter*: universal manhood suffrage, equal electoral districts, annual elections for Parliament, vote by secret ballot, abolition of property qualifications for Parliament, and the payment of salaries for members of Parliament. The last two would make it possible for working men to sit in Parliament, and the first four would create a House of Commons that was democratically elected and subject to annual review. Advocates claimed that the Charter bore a million signatures.

The Chartists relied upon agitation through speeches, newspapers, pamphlets, mass meetings, and torch-light parades to create the kind of working-class support that had been so important in the passage of the Reform Bill. The Charter was presented to the House of Commons in 1839 and 1842, each time supported by public demonstrations. The House of Commons refused to consider a document that would transfer political power from gentlemen and substantial property owners to "the great unwashed." Encouraged by a revolution in France, the last great Chartist effort took place in 1848, but the mass demonstration held in London fizzled in the rain.

Chartism was too narrowly based to succeed. Support for the movement was found almost exclusively among the urban working class. The movement lacked capable leaders and was torn between those who advocated violence and those who preferred orderly agitation through normal political channels. As the economy improved, the appeal of the movement waned, and working men found they could promote their interests more effectively through trade unions. Eventually, however, all but one of the Chartist goals (annual Parliaments) were achieved.

The depression also aggravated the growing conflict between the rising forces of industrialism and the established position of agriculture. The issue was the Corn Law, which industrialists challenged with appeals to the new economic doctrines of laissez-faire and free trade. The landed interests defended the Corn Law, not only as vital to their prosperity and the national food supply, but also as a bulwark of the established institutions and values of Britain.

In 1839 the Anti-Corn Law League was formed, led by Richard Cobden and John Bright and supported primarily by middle-class businessmen. For the next seven years the League carried on a highly effective campaign of agitation and propaganda. To employers the League offered the prospect of lower food prices as a means of keeping wages low. Although suspicious of an organization dominated by factory owners, many workers were attracted by the promise of "cheap food." The agitation was strengthened by the strong sense of injustice produced by economic distress. Chartism and the Anti-Corn Law League expressed the view of important segments of the British public that the reformed Parliament was still insufficiently responsive to their needs.

THE MINISTRY OF SIR ROBERT PEEL, 1841–1846

Political Parties

During these years of economic fluctuations, political controversy, and social discontent, the dominant political figure, in office or out, was Sir Robert Peel. During his brief tenure of office in 1834–1835 Peel had found that the shattered fragments of the Tory Party were insufficient to support a Tory ministry, despite gains in the election of 1835.

Peel then set to work to build a broader base of support, relying on his Tory nucleus but seeking to attract others who believed reform had gone far enough. Peel proclaimed a political philosophy that was both conservative and constructive: preservation of existing institutions and values by timely reform where needed, and redress of grievances where a strong case had been made. He addressed his appeal to "that class which is much less interested in the contentions of party, than in the maintenance of order and the cause of good government."

In contrast to Peel's commitment to principles, the Whig ministry of Lord Melbourne was a loose coalition of disparate groups, without coherent goals. By 1841 Melbourne had lost his parliamentary support and called an election. Peel and his party, who had adopted the name "Conservatives," won a clear majority and organized a Conservative government.

Peel and Reform

As prime minister from 1841–1846, Peel brought to the office a degree of integrity and competence that marked him as one of the major political figures of the nineteenth century. He was a master of public finance. In his budgets he restored the income tax and removed many of the customs and excise duties that hampered industrial growth and the flow of trade. By 1846 the only important tariff remaining was the Corn Law, which was sacrosanct to the Tories.

The Railway Act of 1844 introduced some regulation of this important new industry. Other important legislation of Peel's ministry strengthened the role of the Bank of England in controlling the money supply and simplified the process of forming business corporations. In short, the Peel ministry was conservative in constitutional matters but responsive to the needs of a rapidly expanding industrial nation.

Despite his masterful leadership and unquestioned competence, Peel met his downfall when the two issues least susceptible to rational solution converged in a single crisis: Ireland and the Corn Law. In 1845 a potato blight struck Ireland, and that unhappy land, almost totally dependent upon the potato for subsistence, was devastated. Neither the British government nor private charities were able to cope with the situation. Irish poor-law institutions utterly collapsed, as landlords failed (or were unable) to accept their responsibilities in a disaster of such magnitude. In the next several years a million Irish emigrated, primarily to Britain or America, and another million died.

Under the circumstances, Peel could no longer support the tax on food embodied in the Corn Law, especially when faced with mass agitation by the Anti-Corn Law League. Furthermore, he was personally convinced by the arguments of the free trade advocates. Despite his election pledge to preserve the Corn Law, and the insistence of the landed interest that the Corn Law was vital to British agriculture, Peel bowed to what he considered pressing necessity.

In 1846 Peel introduced proposals for sweeping tariff reform, including repeal of the Corn Law. In so doing he split his party. With the protectionist

Tories (led by the young Benjamin Disraeli) voting against him, the Corn Law was repealed with the support of Whigs and Radicals. Peel was forced to resign and never held office again.

The resignation of Peel, and his death in 1850, removed from British politics its most thoughtful and competent leader. But the time was passing when Britain needed leaders of the stature of Liverpool, Castlereagh, Canning, Grey, and Peel. The postwar adjustment had been made and the worst problems of the early industrial age had been dealt with. Britain had met these challenges in a helter-skelter, confused manner, but the decisions dictated by logic had been made and accepted.

Britain was now entering a period of political calm, when the energies of the nation could be permitted to follow their own courses. Waiting in the wings were Peel's most talented pupil, William Gladstone, and his most ambitious rival, Benjamin Disraeli. Eventually their time would come.

SUGGESTIONS FOR FURTHER READING

The standard history of the development of British government is David L. Keir, *The Constitutional History of Modern Britain, 1485–1951* (9th ed., 1969). The role of the monarch in the past two centuries, with special attention to the twentieth century, is examined in Vernon Bogdanor, *The Monarchy and the Constitution* (1995). For a broad survey and analysis see Michael Bentley, *Politics without Democracy, 1814–1914* (1996). Politics in the early part of this chapter are covered in William R. Brock, *Lord Liverpool and Liberal Toryism, 1820–1827* (1967). Eric Evans covers *The Great Reform Act of 1832* (1994), and E. A. Smith deals with the key figure, *Lord Grey, 1764–1845* (1990). Among recent studies of post-Reform politics are Peter Mandler, *Aristocratic Government in the Age of Reform: Whigs and Liberals, 1830–1852* (1990); Robert Stewart, *Party and Politics, 1830–1852* (1989); and Ian Newbould, *Whiggery and Reform, 1830–41: The Politics of Government* (1990).

Foreign policy was a major concern of the Victorians. *The Cambridge History of British Foreign Policy, 1783–1919*, G. P. Gooch and Adolphus W. Ward (eds.) (3 vols., 1922–1923) is a good place to begin. More modern surveys are Muriel E. Chamberlain, *"Pax Britannica": British Foreign Policy, 1789–1913* (1988) and Kenneth Bourne, *The Foreign Policy of Victorian England, 1830–1902* (1970). Respected older studies by C. K. Webster in many editions are *The Congress of Vienna, The Foreign Policy of Castlereagh,* and *The Foreign Policy of Palmerston, 1830–1841.* Important specialized studies are M. S. Anderson, *The Eastern Question, 1774–1923* (1966) and H. C. Allen, *The Anglo-American Relationship since 1783* (1959).

For Britain's navy see Oliver Warner, *The British Navy: A Concise History* (1975); James Stokesbury, *Navy and Empire* (1983); and Paul M. Kennedy, *The Rise and Fall of British Naval Mastery* (1986). For the army see Correlli Barnett, *Britain and Her Army, 1509–1970* (1970).

Good surveys of Victorian economic development are Phyllis Deane, *The First Industrial Revolution* (1981); J. D. Chambers, *The Workshop of the World: British Economic History from 1820–1880* (1961); S. G. Checkland, *The Rise of Industrial Society in England, 1815–1885* (1964); and Peter Mathias, *The First Industrial Nation: An Economic History of Britain, 1700–1914* (1983). Trevor May, *An Economic and Social History of Britain, 1760–1970* (1987) is a well-written British textbook. Eric J. Evans fuses political and economic history in a useful textbook, *The Forging of the Modern State: Early Industrial Britain, 1783–1870* (1996). A vigorous left-wing presentation is E. J. Hobsbawn, *Industry and Empire: An Economic History of Britain since 1750* (1990).

There are many studies of working class movements in the early industrial age. A good starting point is Edward H. Hunt, *British Labour History, 1815–1914* (1981). See also D. G. Wright, *Popular Radicalism: The Working Class Experience, 1780–1880* (1988) and Asa Briggs, *Chartist Studies* (1959). The standard of living of the industrial working class is reviewed in A. J. Taylor (ed.), *The Standard of Living in Britain in the Industrial Revolution* (1975).

Victorian studies are rich in social history. A broad survey is Asa Briggs, *A Social History of England: From the Ice Age to the Channel Tunnel* (1994). F. M. L. Thompson, *The Rise of Respectable Society: A Social History of Victorian Britain, 1830–1900* (1988) is a basic work, as is *The Cambridge Social History of Britain, 1750–1950*, F. M. L. Thompson (ed.), (3 vols., 1990). G. M. Young, *Portrait of an Age: Victorian England* (1977), is a classic account. A stimulating work by Harold Perkin is *Origins of Modern English Society* (1991). An interesting set of case studies is offered in Asa Briggs, *Victorian People* (1970). J. F. C. Harrison traces the history of *The Common People* (1984). Family life is described by Geoffrey Alderman in *Modern England, 1700–1980: A Domestic History* (1986). For urban growth see Roy Porter, *London: A Social History* (1998), and Asa Briggs, *Victorian Cities* (1964).

A good general introduction to social policy is Keith Laybourn, *The Evolution of British Social Policy and the Welfare State, c. 1800–1993* (1995). *Crime and Punishment in England: An Introductory History* (1996) by John Briggs, Christopher Harrison, Angus McInnes, and David Vincent is a good place to begin study of that subject. Students interested in police can begin with Charles Reith, *The Police Idea* (1938) and *A History of Police in England and Wales* (1978) by Thomas Critchley. Derek Howard tells the story of *The English Prisons: Their Past and Future* (1960).

Recommended general histories of British education are by John Lawson and Harold Silver (1973) and by Keith Evans (1985). Robert K. Webb identifies *The British Working Class Reader, 1790–1848* (1955). Good introductory books are Doreen Yarwood, *The Architecture of Britain* (1973), Percy M. Young, *A History of British Music* (1967), and Eric D. Mackerness, *A Social History of English Music* (1964).

Much has been done in recent years on the lives of Victorian women. Barbara Kanner's *The Women of England: From Anglo-Saxon Times to the Present* (1979) and *Women in English Social History, 1800–1914* (3 vols., 1987) are guides to further reading. Pat Jalland and John Hooper have edited documents dealing with *Women from Birth to Death: The Female Life Cycle in Britain, 1830–1914* (1986). The emerging political role of women is presented in *Equal or Different: Women's Politics, 1800–1914*, Jane Rendall (ed.) (1987). Gertrude Himmelfarb examines *Marriage and Morals among the Victorians* (1986). A valuable comparative study is Sheila Rowbotham, *A Century of Women: The History of Women in Britain and the United States* (1997). Barbara Caine has written a history of *English Feminism, 1780–1980* (1997).

Religion was an important part of Victorian life. Standard works are Josef Altholz, *The Churches in the Nineteenth Century* (1967) and Owen Chadwick, *The Victorian Church* (2 vols., 1979). The social influence of religion is examined in Edward R. Norman, *Church and Society in England, 1770–1970: A Historical Study* (1976). Non-Anglican Protestants were especially influential in the Victorian period, as shown by Stephen Koss in *Nonconformity in Modern British Politics* (1975). Bernard Semmel examines *The Methodist Revolution* (1973). For Catholicism see E. R. Norman, *The English Catholic Church in the Nineteenth Century* (1985). Lee Grugel has produced *Society and Religion during the Age of Industrialization* (1979) and a collection of documents entitled *Religion in Victorian Society* (1985).

Books dealing with the rich intellectual life of Victorian Britain are Josef Altholz, *The Mind and Art of Victorian England* (1976); Richard Altick, *Victorian People and Ideas* (1973); and Walter Houghton, *The Victorian Frame of Mind* (1957).

A good survey of Scottish history is William Ferguson, *Scotland: 1689 to the Present* (1968). See also I. G. C. Hutchison, *A Political History of Scotland, 1832–1924* (1986) and T. C. Smout, *A Century of the Scottish People, 1830–1950* (1986). Good books on Ireland are J. C. Beckett, *The Making of Modern Ireland, 1603–1923* (1969); Lawrence McCaffrey, *Ireland: From Colony to Nation State* (1979) and *The Irish Question: Two Centuries of Conflict* (1995); and Thomas Hachey, *The Irish Experience: A Concise History* (1996). *The Oxford Illustrated History of Ireland* (1991), R. F. Foster (ed.), is a lavish work. Cecil Woodham-Smith tells the story of a turning point in Irish history in *The Great Hunger* (1962).

The empire was an important element in Victorian Britain's sense of power and confidence. A brief, incisive survey of the British empire is Trevor Lloyd, *The British Empire, 1558–1995* (1996). Another good textbook is Denis Judd, *Empire: The British Imperial Experience from 1765 to the Present* (1996). A comprehensive work is *The Cambridge History of the British Empire* (8 vols., 1929–1963), also available in an illustrated edition (1996). It will be challenged by *The Oxford History of the British Empire*, ed. Roger Louis, a multivolume work by many authors that is expected to be completed in 1999. Good books on India are Penderel Moon, *The British Conquest and Dominion of India* (1989) and Muriel Chamberlain, *Britain and India* (1974).

A representative selection of biographies for this chapter includes the following: Christopher Hibbert, *George IV: Regent and King, 1811–1830* (1973); Philip Ziegler, *King William IV* (1971); Cecil Woodham-Smith, *Queen Victoria, 1819–1861* (1972); Elizabeth Longford, *Queen Victoria: Born to Succeed* (1974) and *Wellington: Pillar of State* (1975); Stanley Weintraub, *Victoria: An Intimate Biography* (1987); Daphne Bennett, *King Without a Crown: Albert, Prince Consort of England, 1819–1861* (1977); Christopher Hibbert, *Wellington: A Personal History* (1997); Norman Gash, *Lord Liverpool* (1984); John Derry, *Castlereagh* (1976); Peter Dixon, *George Canning: Politician and Statesman* (1976); John Derry, *Earl Grey: Aristocratic Reformer* (1992); David Cecil, *Melbourne* (1954); L. G. Mitchell, *Lord Melbourne, 1779–1848* (1997); Ellis A. Wasson, *Whig Renaissance: Lord Althorp and the Whig Party, 1782–1845* (1987); Norman Gash, *Mr. Secretary Peel* (1985) and *Peel* (1976); John Prest, *Lord John Russell* (1972); Oliver MacDonagh, *The Emancipist: Daniel O'Connell, 1830–1847* (1989); Jasper Ridley, *Lord Palmerston* (1971); Donald Southgate, *"The Most English Minister": The Policies and Politics of Palmerston* (1966); Jeffrey Finlayson, *The Seventh Earl of Shaftesbury* (1981); Wendy Hinde, *Richard Cobden: A Victorian Outsider* (1987); Keith Robbins, *John Bright* (1979); and Donald Read, *Cobden and Bright: A Victorian Partnership* (1968). There are many specialized studies of Victorian industrialists and engineers. Among the best are L. T. C. Rolt, *The Railway Revolution: George and Robert Stephenson* (1962) and *Isambard Kingdom Brunel* (1973). J. B. Priestley, *Charles Dickens: A Pictorial Biography* (1962) is a delight.

CHAPTER FOURTEEN

Mid-Victorian Britain
1850–1886

By 1850 Britain had reached a remarkable degree of political stability, economic prosperity, and social harmony. The wrenching changes of the early industrial age were finished and the British people could enjoy the benefits of the increased productivity that industrialism brought. The political system rested on a broad base of public acceptance, in contrast to the continent, where the revolutions of 1848–1849 brought turmoil and disappointment with no real resolution of the problems that had led to them. Overseas the British saw a strong and growing foreign trade, unchallenged by European competitors and unthreatened by local disorders. The middle years of the century were a period of steady development, as the new urban-industrial Britain became an increasingly important partner of the long-established financial, commercial and agricultural interests. For the fortunate generation that came of age in 1850 the future was indeed promising.

POLITICS, FOREIGN POLICY, AND THE EMPIRE

Government and Politics

In 1867 Walter Bagehot, a perceptive journalist, described the British constitution as combining "a simple, efficient part" and "historical, complex, august, theatrical parts." The monarchy was the most important of the "theatrical" parts of the British government. In 1867 Queen Victoria was in semiseclusion, mourning the Prince Consort, Albert, who had died in 1861.

Victoria still met with her ministers and read the dispatches, exercising the accepted functions of the monarch: "the right to be consulted, the right to encourage and the right to warn," as Bagehot put it.

Earlier, with Albert at her side, Queen Victoria had carried out the role of monarch in a manner which had won the approval and allegiance of her people. The high point of the royal family was reached in 1851, when Victoria and Albert presided proudly over the Great Exhibition, housed in the glittering Crystal Palace and displaying the industrial, technological, and cultural achievements of Britain and other countries. When Albert died Victoria entered a prolonged period of mourning until encouraged to return to public view by a shrewd Conservative Prime Minister, Benjamin Disraeli, who realized the magic of monarchy as identified by Bagehot.

Bagehot's "simple, efficient part" of the British constitution was the Cabinet, comprised of political leaders who were compatible enough to work together with some degree of harmony. Unlike the United States, which has separation of powers between the executive and legislative branches, Cabinet members also sat in Parliament. Cabinet ministers served in the government as holders of major offices, but their power rested ultimately upon the support of a majority of the House of Commons. The members of the House of Commons (MPs), were chosen by the voters in elections under the system established by the Reform Bill of 1832. Elections were required to take place within seven years of the previous election, but an election could be called sooner by the Queen if requested by her ministers.

At first glance a two-party system seemed to function in the ebb and flow of Cabinets, as Cabinets that were predominantly Whig, led by Lord John Russell, Lord Aberdeen, or Lord Palmerston, alternated with Tory Cabinets led by Lord Derby and Benjamin Disraeli. In reality, however, the political process was a good deal more complex. With a weak party system, Cabinets were loose coalitions of political leaders, using committed partisans as the core of their parliamentary followings but needing additional support from other members whose party affiliations were less firm.

Lord John Russell and other Whig leaders depended on the support of the Radicals, Irish, and other advocates of change. They were pushed in the direction of reform, but they were uncomfortable in the role of reformers. The Tories had lost the followers of Sir Robert Peel, who, like their leader, were reformers with a Tory point of view. In time a loose coalition called "Liberals" began to emerge, combining progressive Whigs, Peelites, and Radicals. Those Tories who had rejected Peel in 1846 were led by Lord Derby and the brilliant young politician, novelist, and dandy—Benjamin Disraeli.

In this confused party situation, a major role was played by Lord Palmerston, a man of strong character and personal independence, who was enormously popular in Parliament and the country. Palmerston was not a party man, and as Prime Minister from 1855–1858 and 1859–1865 he presided over a coalition of Whigs, Peelites, and Radicals who accepted his vigorous foreign policy in exchange for modest installments of institutional reform. As Chancellor of the Exchequer, William E. Gladstone, a Peelite, cut taxes and expenditures, completed the movement to free trade, and eventually accepted parliamentary reform.

The Foreign Policy of Palmerston

In foreign policy the dominant figure was Lord Palmerston, who served as Foreign Secretary or Prime Minister for twenty-four of the thirty-five years from 1830 until his death in 1865. Jaunty, confident, ebullient, Palmerston communicated the John Bull patriotism of Britain—"a political, a commercial, and a constitutional country," as Palmerston described it, that had reconciled individual freedom, representative government, and the rule of law.

Ever since Canning, Britain had avoided close commitments to Europe, yet it was very much to Britain's interest to preserve the balance of power in Europe and to encourage cooperation among the major states to preserve peace and avoid new revolutionary outbursts. At the same time, Palmerston and the British public sympathized with liberal and national movements on the continent, which could become destabilizing factors. Although France had moved in the direction of constitutional government, France was still the traditional rival. In 1830, when a revolution broke out in the Netherlands, Palmerston worked with the other powers to bring about an independent Belgium free of French influence.

The bête noire of Victorian Britain was Russia, that vast, autocratic, militaristic, expanding state that lurked on the verges of what the Victorians called the civilized world. Russia threatened Britain's interests in the Baltic, the eastern Mediterranean, the Middle East, India, and the Far East. Britain was most likely to be stung into action when Russia brought pressure against the Ottoman Empire, the decaying bulwark against Russian expansion into the Mediterranean and the Middle East.

Palmerston's approach to foreign policy was seen in 1848–1849, when a series of revolutions rocked Europe. His major concern was to preserve peace. A revolution in France established a democratic republic, but it also threatened a new period of war. Louis Napoleon, nephew of the great Bonaparte, was elected president, and in 1852 he proclaimed himself Napoleon III, ruler of the Second Empire. Palmerston saw the new regime as a stabilizing force and extended British diplomatic recognition. He also gave British support to a revolution that liberalized the north Italian state of Sardinia. The other revolutions collapsed or had only modest success. Palmerston had intervened where he could, and he had not shed British blood or spent a significant amount of British money.

Palmerston's nationalistic bravado was demonstrated in 1850 in a petty incident, the Don Pacifico affair. Don Pacifico was a Portuguese Jew who claimed British citizenship on the grounds that he had been born in Gibraltar, a British possession. His house in Athens had been attacked by a mob, and Don Pacifico called upon the British government to help him collect damages. Palmerston came vigorously to the aid of Don Pacifico, acting in such an independent manner that he humiliated the Greeks and thoroughly offended France and Russia who were also concerned, as well as Queen Victoria, who was furious.

When his political enemies attacked his conduct of foreign policy, Palmerston replied with a resounding speech in which he boldly proclaimed the British government's support of its citizens, anywhere in the world: "As the Roman, in days of old," Palmerston concluded, "held himself free from indignity, when he could say *Civis Romanus sum* [I am a Roman citizen]; so also a British subject, in whatever land he may be, shall feel confident that the watchful eye and strong arm of England, will protect him against injustice and wrong." The House of Commons and the British public loved it; the Queen, the politicians, and the diplomats had no choice but to give way.

The less successful side of mid-Victorian foreign policy was seen in the Crimean War (1854–1856). In 1853 Russia and the Ottoman Empire entered into one of their periodic conflicts resulting from Russian ambitions in the Balkan peninsula and the Black Sea area. Although the Prime Minister, Lord Aberdeen, wanted to avoid war, hostility toward Russia in the press and public sentiment forced the government to come to the aid of the Ottoman Empire. The British were joined by France, whose Emperor Napoleon III was eager to play an important role in European affairs, and by the north Italian state of Sardinia.

The war was fought in the Crimea, a peninsula on the north shore of the Black Sea, and consisted primarily of a costly siege of the Russian fortress of Sevastopol. The allied generals managed the war with gross ineptitude, which was reported in full detail by war correspondents who accompanied the troops. The British public, which had initially supported the war, was appalled and infuriated by reports of needless deaths and hardships. The redeeming feature of the war was the dedicated work of Florence Nightingale, resourceful daughter of a duke, who brought a group of women to the Crimea to care for the wounded and thus helped establish nursing as a profession for women.

To still the public outcry, Palmerston was made Prime Minister in 1855, and some prestige was salvaged when Sevastopol fell. The death of the Russian Tsar also contributed to peace, which was made in 1856. The result was that Russian expansion in the area was checked, although the problem remained to fester for another two decades.

Palmerston and the British public generally sympathized with continental aspirations for national unity, even though these threatened the stability of Europe. In 1859 the King of Sardinia, aided by Napoleon III, provoked a war with the Austrians, who ruled northern Italy. The war soon led to nationalist uprisings in other parts of Italy. Palmerston and Lord John Russell, the Foreign Secretary, openly displayed their sympathy with the Italians. British support contributed to the Sardinian victory which, by 1861, had led to the proclamation of the Kingdom of Italy under the Sardinian crown. The Austrians managed to hold their territories, and Napoleon III intervened to preserve the Pope's governance of Rome.

The issue was less clear for Britain in the American Civil War. The initial British view was that the Confederate states, like the Italians, had a right to independence if they wanted it; furthermore, the southern states were major suppliers of cotton to British industry. Palmerston's government at first took a firm tone with the Lincoln administration, especially when the Northern blockade of the Confederacy brought up the issue of freedom of the seas. When the Civil War became a war against slavery, however, a more compelling moral issue replaced that of Confederate independence. Despite hardships in Britain due to the Union blockade of southern cotton, Confederate hopes for a British declaration of war were disappointed.

The Move Toward Democracy

The travail of the American republic was of considerable interest in Britain because the United States, for good or ill, was seen as the principal example of popular democracy, a topic that had become important in British politics. The idea of democracy had not died with Chartism. John Stuart Mill in his *Considerations on Representative Government* (1861) argued that democracy was the best form of government because it fostered creative and productive individuals and built a broad base of loyalty to the state. Through the democratic process, he contended, the general interest would be served since particular interests would cancel each other out. Mill would exclude illiterates, nontaxpayers, bankrupts, and welfare recipients from voting, since they could not be regarded as capable of exercising the franchise responsibly. He saw merit in giving more than one vote to persons whose education or profession marked them as better qualified than most for the responsibilities of citizenship. He even went so far as propose the vote for eligible women.

The most influential opponent of an extension of the franchise was Lord Palmerston, the Prime Minister, whose death in 1865 removed the principal obstacle to reopening the question in Parliament. The conversion of William

E. Gladstone, Palmerston's capable and energetic chancellor of the Exchequer, gave the advocates of democracy a powerful new voice to plead their cause.

In 1867, the year of Bagehot's *The English Constitution*, the casual, un-structured character of mid-Victorian politics began to change as the death of Palmerston opened the door to new leaders and issues. Palmerston's successor was the Whig leader, Lord John Russell, now in the twilight of his long and distinguished career. The most vigorous member of the Cabinet was Gladstone, who came forward as the leader of the political coalition known as the Liberals.

In 1866 Russell and Gladstone proposed a bill for reform of the House of Commons which called for a moderate extension of the franchise. Parliamentary reform, which had been in abeyance since the Reform Bill of 1832, suddenly gained enormous public popularity, and the politicians discovered that they had aroused a sleeping giant.

The result was a series of debates of great intensity and bitterness as old political alignments were shattered. Russell and Gladstone, abandoned by the more conservative Whigs, resigned, and were replaced by a Tory ministry led by Lord Derby and Benjamin Disraeli. Popular support for reform, as demonstrated in mass meetings and public demonstrations, persuaded Derby and Disraeli to bring forward their own bill, hoping to win support for their party from the newly enfranchised voters. In the ensuing debates Gladstone, Bright and others succeeded in amending Disraeli's bill to make it more generous.

The Reform Bill of 1867, as eventually passed, extended the franchise to urban workingmen, with a modest redistribution of seats to industrial areas. The electorate was almost doubled, although many adult males were still excluded from the vote (as were all women). The issue—clearly seen and debated—was establishment of a democratically chosen House of Commons as opposed to a political system that gave power to persons of property, education, and established social position. The hazards as well as the advantages of democracy were thoroughly aired, and when the bill was passed Lord Derby admitted that Britain had taken "a leap in the dark."

The British Overseas

Britain's overseas interests continued to be of the greatest importance, although the value of political control of colonies was diminished by the policy of free trade. British bankers and merchants pursued their business throughout the world and the British merchant marine and whalers plied the seven seas. The principal value of British trade was in the sale of manufactured goods and the importation of basic commodities such as cotton, wool, tea, foodstuffs, fertilizers, jute, whale oil, palm oil, and tropical woods. In some respects people were Britain's most important export, as thousands of enterprising emigrants left the British Isles every year to seek new homes and opportunities in the

United States, Canada, the Australian colonies, New Zealand, and the Cape Colony and Natal in southern Africa.

In the age of free trade the British government had little to do with the activities of its nationals abroad. The British navy patrolled the seas from its bases at Nova Scotia, Bermuda, Gibraltar, Malta, the Falkland Islands, the Cape Colony, Mauritius, Aden, Ceylon, Bombay, Singapore, and Hong Kong. The consular service offered some help to British businessmen and travellers and the Post Office extended its overseas services. Otherwise the British government preferred to let well enough alone, except in instances such as the Opium War with China (1839–1842) which opened that great empire to trade with Western nations.

The trend in those colonies where the British had settled in large numbers was toward greater self government. In 1837 uprisings in Quebec (Lower Canada) and Ontario (Upper Canada) led the Melbourne government to send Lord Durham, a radical Whig nobleman, to visit the Canadian colonies and make recommendations. *The Durham Report* (1839) proposed unification of the two Canadas with "responsible government," i.e., vesting the executive powers in a cabinet with the support of the majority of the assembly. The first of Durham's recommendations was adopted in 1840, although responsible government was not granted until 1847.

In the next few years responsible government was extended to the Australian colonies (1855) and New Zealand (1856). In southern Africa the Cape Colony and Natal offered special problems, both in the relations of the two white peoples—the British settlers and the long-established Dutch inhabitants (the Boers)—and between the white peoples and the native black populations. After the abolition of slavery in 1833, many of the Boers migrated into the interior and established two frontier republics, the Orange Free State and the Transvaal. British claims in this area led to friction between the Cape Colony and the Boer republics, but in 1852–1854 the independence of the Boer republics was confirmed. In 1872 the Cape Colony and Natal received responsible government.

The most striking example of the extension of self-government within the empire was the British North America Act (1867), which joined Canada (Ontario, Quebec) and the maritime provinces (Nova Scotia, New Brunswick, Prince Edward Island) to form a united Canada. The office of governor-general maintained the link with Britain, and the imperial relationship continued in such matters as foreign policy and defense. The federal government, located in Ottawa, followed the cabinet model, with ministers responsible to Parliament. The federal government possessed power in all matters not specifically delegated to the provinces. Provincial governments were constituted on a similar pattern and provision was made for the addition of new provinces as settlement proceeded westward. Thus the principles of self-government developed in the Mother Country were extended to its offshoots in various parts of the world.

India, with its complex political structure, its ancient and diverse cultures and religions, its hereditary animosities, and its great value, was a special case. Much of the British cotton textile industry depended on the Indian market. Pitt's India Act of 1784 had entrusted the government of the British territories in India to the British East India Company, under the supervision of a governor-general in India and a Board of Control in London. In 1833 the Company ceased to engage in trade and became exclusively a governing body. The Company developed its own civil service and an army with British officers and Indian soldiers called sepoys. From time to time wars broke out with Indian princes which led to extensions of the Company's territories, but the Company never ruled more than two-thirds of India with the rest continuing under native princes dominated in varying degrees by the British. The Company also established a base at Singapore to serve the growing trade with China and the East Indies.

British rule brought many modern advantages to India: effective central government, a professional civil service (open to Indians in the lower ranks), railroads, postal and telegraph systems, a vast free trade area that stimulated economic development, peace between the Hindus and Moslems, famine control, and the English language—the only language common to all of India. On the other hand, the British rulers remained aloof from the Indian population, British manufactured goods destroyed native handicraft industries, and British rule interfered with many traditional customs and practices.

In 1857 a great crisis broke out in India when the sepoys in some regiments mutinied. For a time it appeared that the authority of the small cadre of British officials and military officers might collapse. After hard fighting, which included the dramatic rescue of a British garrison in Lucknow, the Sepoy Mutiny was suppressed by the British authorities using other Indian regiments. The result of the Mutiny, however, was the dissolution of the East India Company and the establishment of direct British rule of India through a Secretary of State for India. The civil service and army were continued as before and British investment in railroads and industry was encouraged. The new regime, while showing greater respect for Indian customs and beliefs, also contributed to a growing gulf between the British authorities and the Indian population.

A major item in the trade of the East India Company was tea, most of which came from China. The rulers of that ancient empire were suspicious of foreigners and made the trade difficult by confining it to the port of Canton. The port authorities were corrupt, and there were few items that the Chinese would accept in trade other than gold and silver. Exasperated by Chinese trade barriers, Britain decided to open trade with China by force, using as justification Chinese imprisonment of British opium smugglers. The "Opium War" (1839–1842) opened China to foreign merchants, and gave Britain a base on the offshore island of Hong Kong.

A STOCKTAKING: MID-VICTORIAN SOCIETY

The Idea of Progress

By 1850 Britain had entered a period of political stability, economic growth, and social harmony. The British were proud of their achievements and compared their lives favorably with the despotisms, revolutions, and wars of Europe. Despite great problems of poverty, ignorance, and crime, the general attitude of the mid-Victorians was optimistic. The key concept of the age was "Progress"—belief that the present was better than the past and confidence that the future would be better than the present.

To some extent the Victorian concept of Progress was materialistic, supported by statistics showing the increase of population, trade, industrial and agricultural production, and national wealth. But it was also idealistic, for the Victorians took pride in the advancement of scholarship, science, and technology; the material achievements of the age were valued as contributing to the spiritual and moral improvement of the nation.

One example of the Victorian belief in Progress was Thomas Babington Macaulay's *History of England,* which began appearing in 1848. Macaulay's work dealt primarily with the Glorious Revolution of 1688–1689 and its consequences, but he took the opportunity to remark upon the advances—intellectual, material, spiritual—that had been made since that time. Macaulay was a staunch Whig and proud of the principles that he associated with Whiggism—constitutional and parliamentary government, economic individualism, intellectual and religious freedom, and national pride.

Another notable symbol of Progress was the Great Exhibition of 1851, presented in the Crystal Palace, an astonishing prefabricated structure of iron and glass. Prince Albert was the guiding spirit of the Exhibition: its purpose was to display the industrial, technological, scientific, and artistic achievements of the age. Although the Great Exhibition drew displays from all over the world, most of the exhibitors were British and it served as a showcase for Britain's industrial leadership. Cheap railway excursions brought thousands of visitors from all over Britain to observe and take pride in the achievements of their country.

The pride of the mid-Victorians in their economic progress was not unwarranted. From 1831–1851 the population of Great Britain increased from 24 million to 27 million, and from 1851–1871 it increased to 31.5 million. The

Victoria and Albert opening the Great Exhibition at the Crystal Palace, 1851.
Painting by Henri Selous. Corbis.

factory system was by this time fully established in the textile industry, and production of textiles increased from £60 million in 1845 to £84.5 million in 1870. In 1856 Henry Bessemer patented a process for converting molten pig iron into steel, thus introducing the age of cheap, abundant steel.

An important feature of the British economy was the technological industries, such as engineering and the manufacture of machine tools, where Britain led the world. The revolution in transportation and communications continued with the building of railroads, development of the steamship, improvement of domestic and overseas postal services, and the opening of the trans-Atlantic cable in 1866. Jules Verne's novel, *Around the World in Eighty Days* (1873) was science fiction verging on the possible. And it is not surprising that this French author chose a resourceful English gentleman as his hero.

The Landed Class

Considering the cries of alarm raised by the repeal of the Corn Law, it is ironic to find that the years from 1850–1870 were the golden age of British agriculture. New methods increased productivity, a growing home market sustained prices, and the effects of foreign competition had not yet been felt. In addition to the profits of agriculture, landowners also benefited from the growing value of mineral rights and urban properties.

Great aristocrats, such as the Duke of Bedford, collected enormous incomes, lightly taxed, from both urban and agricultural land. Aristocrats dominated the royal court and the glittering social functions related to it. They entertained lavishly in their London townhouses or at their splendid country estates, provided with every comfort by swarms of domestic servants.

Members of noble families were liberally sprinkled throughout cabinets, the diplomatic service, and the army. The House of Lords was the special preserve of the aristocracy, including the bishops. Although most decisions of importance were made in the House of Commons, the House of Lords could delay, alter, or reject controversial legislation. The Lords also exercised power as the supreme court of law.

The country gentry prospered and maintained their domination of the government and society of the shires. The life of the landed gentleman continued to exert its fascination, and the aristocracy and gentry were strengthened by the influx of men successful in government, business, and the professions, or by marriages of heirs to their daughters. The legal arrangements that guaranteed the transmission of the estate to one heir (usually the eldest son) continued; younger sons were provided for by careers in the law, the Church, the army, or the empire. Long-established traditions of deference, and the continuing opportunity for successful business and professional men to enter the ranks of the gentry, meant that the landed class remained powerful and influential.

Urbanization

The most notable feature of mid-Victorian society was the transformation of Britain into an urban nation. The census of 1851 showed that, for the first time, the number of urban inhabitants exceeded those living in rural areas, and the proportion of the population living in an urban setting continued to grow.

The greatest urban center of all was London, the name commonly applied to the metropolitan area that included the City of London, Westminster, and the urban sprawl into the counties of Middlesex and Surrey. London grew because it served a variety of functions, all of which were growing. London was the capital of a dynamic nation and the heart of the world's greatest empire; London was one of the world's busiest seaports; it was the hub of international finance, insurance, and commodity trading; it was an important manufacturing city, principally conducted in small factories and shops; it was a center of communication, publication, fashion, entertainment, and polite society.

As a result of this rapid growth the older parts of London were changing: the City became increasingly a business district, losing population, and the centers of population, shopping, entertainment, and fashionable residence moved westward. The distinctively Victorian growth of London was seen in

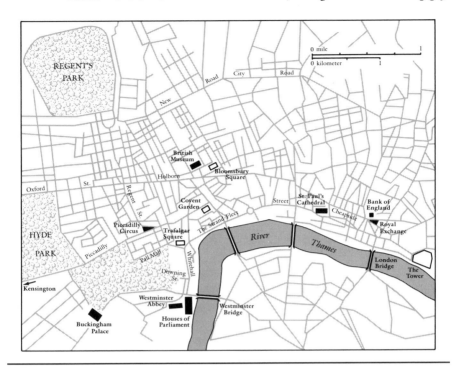

Victorian London

its residential areas and suburbs, made possible by the Underground and the commuter train.

To the north the area called Bloomsbury, developed principally on land owned by the Duke of Bedford, maintained the classical dignity of the early nineteenth century in its stately squares and tree-lined streets. The presence of the British Museum, the University of London, and various charitable and religious foundations gave it a somewhat intellectual tone. Kensington, to the west, displayed a Victorian air, with its tall rows of flats, often ornately decorated, and imitation Gothic churches. A cluster of museums, built on the site of the Great Exhibition of 1851, contributed to the dignity of Kensington.

The true Victorian suburbia was found farther out, at places such as Wimbledon and Bethnal Green, where rows of brick houses with bay windows and tiny gardens, well supplied with schools, churches, and shops, provided homes for the growing white-collar class as well as the "respectable" working class. The suburbs were a new element in the British social structure and exerted great influence upon Victorian politics, morality, family life, literature, domestic arts, and religion.

Even more dramatic than the growth of London was the rise of provincial towns, whose rapid growth was a counterbalance to the dominance of London. Although London was the largest seaport, other ports attracted an in-

St. Pancras Station, London.
Private collection.

creasing trade. Bristol, for centuries the principal western port, continued to be important, although it was eclipsed by the rise of Liverpool and Glasgow, both of which served major industrial areas. On the east coast Newcastle and Hull flourished as ports, with special interest in shipbuilding and fisheries respectively. Old, well-established towns such as Norwich and Nottingham, which for centuries had served as market towns with domestic industries, added new industries while preserving much of their preindustrial character.

The most notable provincial towns, however, were those that were the result of the Industrial Revolution. Manchester, center of the cotton textile industry, was dominated by an elite of landlords, bankers, and businessmen. Birmingham was famous for the metal trades, conducted in small shops by skilled craftsmen, who had a strong sense of civic responsibility. In Yorkshire, Leeds was the center of an important industrial complex, and another cluster of industries grew up in Scotland in the valley of the Clyde, with Glasgow as its principal city.

The pride of the industrial towns was most notably displayed in magnificent town halls and civic centers. Great Victorian railroad stations, accompanied by grandiose hotels, proclaimed by their size, opulence, and location the central importance of the railroad in Victorian life. Banks and insurance

Industrial Halifax.
Private collection.

companies tried to match the dignity of the public buildings with ornate structures which exemplified in granite and marble their (presumed) financial solidity.

Factories and working class housing were still located near the center of the city, but commuter trains and improved roads made it possible for the middle class to leave the grime and noise of the central city for residential areas of brick houses with churches, schools, and parks nearby. The provincial towns tried to emulate London as cultural centers too, with "red-brick universities" and civic libraries, museums, and art galleries, but in this respect London stood unchallenged.

Politically the provincial towns had become a powerful new force. They were dominated by prominent business and professional men, and the churches were influential. Well-off middle-class women were active in civic and charitable institutions. A literate working class that read newspapers and formed trade unions and "friendly societies" became an important factor in local and national politics. These towns were less influenced by the traditions of the past and were more inclined to seek rational justifications for political institutions or public policy. The political leader who could gain the allegiance of the provincial towns would unlock a powerful new force, especially after the Reform Bill of 1867.

THOUGHT AND SOCIETY

The Problem of Poverty

When the Victorians spoke of Progress they meant not only the improvement of political institutions and material well being, but the "March of Mind"—the increasing ability of people to understand their world, control it for their benefit, and govern their personal and corporate conduct according to reasoned principles.

The most intractable problem faced by Victorian thinkers was the problem of poverty, for the remarkable achievements of the time had also created vast areas of privation, ignorance, immorality, vice, and crime. Although a bewildering variety of answers was available, the crucial issue was well-stated by Disraeli: how could "two nations," the comfortable and the deprived, be reconciled and eventually brought together in a community of mutual well being?

In the mid-Victorian period the rigorous doctrines of Utilitarianism and the classical economists were softened by a growing sense of community. The developing ideas of John Stuart Mill demonstrated the changes that were taking place in social thought. A child prodigy, Mill was educated by his father, James Mill, in rigid Utilitarian doctrines. In young manhood he found his emotions touched by Romantic poetry. He lived up to his father's expectations, writing extensively on political and economic questions, but he also recognized that strict logic must be bent to allow for human considerations. In his later years Mill continued to support the economics of laissez-faire as applied to production, while conceding that some interference with economic laws was needed to secure a more equitable distribution of the wealth produced by industrial society.

In his famous *Autobiography*, published in the last year of his life (1873), he wrote:

> The social problem of the future we considered to be, how to unite the greatest individual liberty of action, with a common ownership of the globe, and an equal participation of all in the benefits of combined labor.

In short, Mill had become what he and his contemporaries called a "socialist."

The most common mid-Victorian answer to the problem of poverty was to trust in people's ability to master their destiny through the translation of knowledge into practical uses. The Victorians made popular heroes of great engineers, who had demonstrated their ability to understand nature and utilize natural forces to serve human needs. Samuel Smiles, a prolific writer, gained popularity with his *Life of George Stephenson* (1857) and his *Lives of the Engineers* (1861–1862). In Smiles's view, the successes of the engineers grew out of their knowledge, determination, and resourcefulness, qualities that he extolled in *Self Help* (1859) and other works praising moral character, self-reliance, and hard work. Smiles's confidence that moral and technological advances could build a better world was shared by many, although his cheery optimism seemed scarcely warranted in view of the problems of the time.

Literature and the theater were also concerned with the problem of poverty in the midst of plenty. Charles Dickens, the foremost novelist of the age, had known poverty as a child, and he never lost his respect for the dignity of humble people. His novels dealt primarily with the middle class but he portrayed vividly the lives of the common people, lovingly cataloging their simple virtues and their patience under circumstances over which they had no control. Dickens offered no political or economic nostrums: his response to the problem of poverty was reliance upon one's own intelligence and resourcefulness, a dose of good luck, and mutual helpfulness in adversity.

The leading Victorian poet, Alfred, Lord Tennyson, shared some of the Victorian confidence in Progress and technology, but he was acutely sensitive to the losses, as well as gains, that came with change. In *Locksley Hall* (1842) Tennyson foresaw savage war, as well as peaceful commerce, and he anticipated revolutionary changes of global scope. Nevertheless, he was optimistic. He was proud to be part of his dynamic new world. He looked forward to a time when "the war drums throbbed no longer, and the battle flags were furled, / In the Parliament of man, the Federation of the World."

The Victorian theater dealt with similar themes. As the middle class began to provide the bulk of the theater audience, the classic plays of the Elizabethan playwrights or the Restoration comedy lost popularity, to be replaced by the melodrama. The melodrama featured colorful spectacle, often drawing upon subjects that were in the news. But its primary appeal lay in a clearcut struggle between right and wrong, often with a noble hero, an evil villain, and a sweet young girl the pawn in their struggle. Financial distress frequently was the central factor in the plot. Action was constant as one crisis followed another, leading to the inevitable happy ending.

Dion Boucicault, a talented Irishman who won and lost several fortunes as a playwright and impresario, was the master of this genre. His plays dealt with themes with which his audiences could identify: fear of mysterious danger (*The Vampire*), revolution (*The Reign of Terror*), current events (*The Relief of Lucknow*), slavery (*The Octoroon*), labor problems (*The Long Strike*), urban poverty (*The Streets of London*), and crime (*After Dark*). The naïveté of the Victorian melodrama is ridiculed today, but its simple idealism was that of a people to whom right and wrong were quite clear. The crises of the melodrama were real to middle class audiences who knew how quickly they could pass from comfort to misery; and its happy ending reflected their faith in a just world where virtue and prudence flourished and wickedness and improvidence led inevitably to disaster.

The Impact of Science

In 1859 this generation of hopefulness and generous feelings received a severe blow. For several decades philosophers and scientists had been considering the effects of natural processes over time. Charles Lyell's *Principles of Geology* (1833) explained the surface of the earth as the result of gradual changes taking place over millenia, as mountains were thrust up and worn down or as rivers cut valleys and built deltas. Lyell's account left little for the hand of God who, according to the Victorian understanding of the Scriptures, had created the land and seas, mountains and valleys in the year 4004 B.C.

The idea of evolution was already in the air when Charles Darwin applied it to living things in his *On the Origin of Species by Natural Selection* (1859). The key to Darwin's book was his doctrine of natural selection, which held that the world of nature was a struggle for existence in which life forms with small advantages were able to survive and pass those advantages on to their offspring, while other life forms, less well endowed, fell by the wayside. In *The Descent of Man* (1871) Darwin applied his evolutionary doctrine to human origins.

Darwin's concept changed God from a beneficent Providence to a creator who left his universe to struggle for survival; nature was found to be "red in tooth and claw." Human beings were seen to be a product of struggle, rising gradually to supremacy over the prostrate bodies of their rivals. The mild-mannered biologist with the bold thoughts had introduced a jarring note into the optimism and good feeling of mid-Victorian Britain.

The concept of evolution gave a new turn to discussions of the social problems of the age. The churches supported the traditional Scriptural doctrines of God as creator, governor, and sustainer of all things—a loving God who provided the means of redemption and fulfillment for all his children, in this world and in the world to come. Advocates of science such as the brilliant biologist and controversialist, Thomas Henry Huxley, rejected traditional religious explanations, contending that human intelligence had liberated humankind from supernatural explanations and hopes. In Huxley's view, the doctrine of evolution was invigorating, for while it left people to make themselves through their own efforts, their previous achievements gave them reason to believe that they could make further progress up the evolutionary ladder.

Herbert Spencer, a philosopher more popular in the United States than in Britain, formulated a philosophy of "Social Darwinism." Spencer held that human societies evolved in a manner similar to biological evolution, moving from simpler to more complex forms through the principle of natural selection. In his view, social evolution was to the advantage of humankind and should not be checked or distorted by legislation or ill-considered humanitarianism. The "tender-minded" sympathies of Mill, Dickens, and Tennyson were challenged by a new "tough-minded" realism which accepted conflict as a necessary part of all existence and essential to Progress. Thus "the March of Mind" continued, but in directions little contemplated by an earlier generation.

GLADSTONE AND DISRAELI

Gladstone and the Liberal Party

Bagehot's analysis of the British constitution was published in 1867, the year that brought a new element into British politics—the beginnings of political democracy. Like the Reform Bill of 1832, the long-range implications of the Reform bill of 1867 were more important than the immediate changes. Cabinets and Parliaments continued to be comprised of the same kinds of people, and the two most prominent political leaders, Gladstone and Disraeli, had been in politics for a long time. Yet both of these leaders forged to the front because they were able to understand, accept, and take advantage of changed political circumstances. The new political scene was that of emerging democracy: leaders, parties, and platforms with national appeal and national constituencies.

Although Disraeli had proposed the legislation that became the Reform Bill of 1867, the expanded electorate turned in 1868 to Gladstone and the Liberals. Gladstone was a man of great intellect, energy, administrative ability, and moral fervor. Throughout his long political career, he exhibited a remarkable ability for personal and political growth. He had begun his political career as a Tory opposed to the Reform Bill of 1832; he had adopted the reforming conservatism of Sir Robert Peel; and eventually he had accepted the justice and inevitability of political democracy. Gladstone dominated his ministry in administration, Parliament, and public debate. He gave to the office of Prime Minister a degree of national leadership that looked forward to the twentieth-century concept of that office.

Gladstone advocated caution in foreign policy, avoiding involvement in the swift Prussian victories over Austria (1866–1867) and in the Franco-Prussian War(1870–1871), which completed the unification of Germany and of Italy. At considerable cost to his personal popularity, Gladstone made a statesmanlike settlement of American claims for damages done by the *Alabama*, a Confederate warship built in Britain. Thus Gladstone minimized external involvements to concentrate on domestic reform.

Gladstone's major concern was to obtain economy and efficiency in government by removing privilege and waste. Adoption of the secret ballot (1872) was a major contribution to purity in elections and a blow to the influence of landlords and employers. Open competitive examinations were introduced for the civil service and the army was extensively reformed, including the abolition of the purchase of commissions. Similar reforms were made in the navy and the royal dockyards. Another major undertaking was revision of the tangled jurisdictions of the ancient courts of common law.

The Forster Education Act (1870) sought to provide elementary education for every child. The government increased its grants to existing schools, which were primarily operated by religious denominations. Local school boards were established to provide schools maintained by the rates (local taxes) where existing schools were insufficient. Gladstone was also concerned to reduce the grievances of Ireland. In his first ministry, he carried through the disestablishment of the Protestant Church of Ireland, which was supported by taxes although most of the Irish people were Catholic.

Gladstone was also important in the emergence of the Liberal party, a new kind of political party that supported its parliamentary contingent with party organizations in the constituencies. Although many of the leaders of the Liberal Party had worked together for some time, the Reform Bill crisis of 1866–1867, the election of 1868, and the reforms of Gladstone's first ministry welded them together. On the local level, Liberal associations and clubs organized the voters and fought elections.

The Liberal Party appealed to business and professional men, clerks, shopkeepers, and skilled workmen, with a strong leavening of earnest Protestants from the Church of England and other denominations. The goals of the Liberal Party were defined by Gladstone's first ministry: a conciliatory foreign policy, reduction of imperial commitments, economy in government, institutional reform, free trade, individual responsibility, and removal of Irish grievances.

By 1874 those policies had created opponents and brought rankling discontents. The public had become tired of change and was upset by other aspects of Liberalism, such as the temperance movement, which worked to limit access to liquor through licensing pubs. In the election of 1874 Disraeli and the Conservative Party won a decisive victory on a platform of saving the country from Gladstone's weak foreign policy and his restless urge to reform.

Disraeli and the Conservative Party

The Conservative Party was, to some extent, the successor of the Tories, as the Liberal Party was of the Whigs, but both of these parties were different in important respects from their predecessors. As leader of the Conservative Party Disraeli's achievement was to develop a party that capitalized on the British desire for continuity and tradition, while giving the party a mildly progressive program.

The Conservatives also developed a network of local party organizations linked together by the Conservative Central Office. The Conservative Party was still dominated by the aristocracy and gentry, but Disraeli succeeded in winning a broad base of support among businessmen, urban workers, and people in small towns and villages. Like Gladstone, Disraeli was a superb publicist. The age of democratic leaders and parties was emerging.

Disraeli's ministry (1874–1880) avoided political and administrative reform of the Gladstonian type, and pursued policies of "Tory Democracy" to deal with the social problems of the newly franchised urban working class. Another Factory Act (1878) codified and extended earlier legislation dealing with working conditions in factories, and the Public Health Act (1875) established a sanitary code. The Artisans' Dwelling Act (1875) was the first important attempt by government to improve the wretched housing of the poor. The Merchant Shipping Act (1878) was passed to improve the safety and health of British seamen. Trade unions, which had been legalized under Gladstone, were given the right to picket. A national prison system replaced the vile local jails.

As a Conservative, Disraeli sought to preserve the institutions of the past by making them serve national purposes. He persuaded Queen Victoria to abandon her seclusion, and in 1876 she was given the grandiloquent title, Empress of India. He also showed deference to the House of Lords and the Church of England, and made clear his determination to preserve British authority in Ireland.

Disraeli's Foreign and Imperial Policy

Disraeli gained attention for himself and flattered national patriotism by activity abroad. The unification of Germany and Italy changed the European balance of power and introduced a period of great power rivalries that eventually became threatening to Britain. Disraeli could do little to affect the European balance of power, but he could strengthen Britain's role in the world by attention to its overseas interests. In 1875 he scored a major success when he purchased 44 percent of the stock of the Suez Canal Company, thus gaining for Britain a voice in the management of that vital waterway to the East.

In 1877 a revolt in the Balkans led to another war between Russia and the moribund Ottoman Empire. The Russians came to the aid of their "Slavic brothers." When they made extensive territorial gains, Disraeli intervened to support the Turks and check Russian expansion. The Turks suddenly made peace, giving the Russians almost everything they wanted, and Disraeli was left out on a limb. At that point the German Chancellor, Otto von Bismarck, called a conference in Berlin to involve all the major powers in a settlement of the Balkan problem. The Congress was a great success for Disraeli, who succeeded in obtaining modifications of Russia's Balkan gains. He also received the island of Cyprus as a British base to guard the Eastern Mediterranean and the Suez Canal. Austria-Hungary was given control of the province of Bosnia-Herzegovina.

Another aspect of Disraeli's policy was to promote the empire as essential to national greatness. The jewel of the empire was India, and in 1876 Disraeli dramatized his imperialism with a magnificent ceremony in which Queen Victoria was crowned Empress of India. Russia was seen as the principal threat to British power in India, and in 1878 British fear of Russian expansion led to an ill-advised expedition into Afghanistan which was still causing trouble when Disraeli left office.

Disraeli also tried to resolve the problems of southern Africa. Conflict was endemic on the borders separating the British colonies from the two Boer republics of the interior. In the 1870s these problems were aggravated by the discovery of diamonds in disputed territory. In 1877 Disraeli's government, seeking to unify the area, annexed the Orange Free State and the Transvaal. Two years later, with the Boers still smouldering as a result of this action, war broke out with the fierce Zulus. Disraeli left the problem of Boer resistance and the Zulu War to his successor. By the end of his ministry, Disraeli had found that the flowers of empire came with dangerous thorns.

Gladstone Again

In the meantime Gladstone had taken his attack on Disraeli's policies to the people. As Liberal candidate for Parliament from the Scottish county of Midlothian, he delivered a series of powerful speeches which were reported throughout the nation. Gladstone attacked Disraeli's opportunism and manipulation, holding before the British public the ideal of a foreign policy based on moral principles and international law.

His words fell on responsive ears, for by that time Disraeli's showy foreign policy, dangerous imperial ventures, and lackluster domestic reforms had begun to pall. The election of 1880 gave a new mandate to Gladstone and the Liberals. Much to the dismay of Queen Victoria, who disliked his appeals to public opinion, Gladstone returned to office as leader of a Liberal ministry.

Gladstone soon found that the problems of the new decade did not lend themselves to clear solutions, especially those growing out of the imperial rivalries of the great powers. He had severely criticized Disraeli's involvements in Afghanistan and the Boer republics, and he was able to pull out of Afghanistan while maintaining appearances. The Boer republics offered a more difficult problem, for influential elements in the Liberal Party were reluctant to bring British control to an end. While Gladstone temporized, the Boers of the Transvaal, led by Paul Kruger, rose in revolt and defeated a British detachment at Majuba Hill (1881). Faced with a difficult and costly war, Gladstone agreed to independence for the Transvaal but under circumstances that appeared to be an acceptance of defeat.

Gladstone also found that the rising tide of imperialism drew him into unwanted involvements in Egypt and the Sudan. In 1882 disorders broke out in Egypt and foreign involvement appeared inevitable. Since Egypt was important to the safety of the Suez Canal, Gladstone proposed joint intervention with France. When the French refused, Gladstone sent a British force to restore order. Gladstone was left with a protectorate he did not want, but at that point he saw no alternative but to bring solvency and good government to Egypt through British rule.

The problem was further complicated by an uprising in the Sudan led by a religious fanatic known as the Mahdi. Gladstone had no desire to become involved in the Sudan, but he did agree to send a British detachment under General Charles Gordon to evacuate the Egyptian garrisons there. Gordon, a strong-willed individualist with his own opinions of what should be done, tried to form a counterforce to check the Mahdi and found himself trapped in Khartoum. After considerable discussion and delay Gladstone sent an expedi-

Benjamin Disraeli, Earl of Beaconsfield. By Sir John Everett Millais, 1881. By courtesy of The National Portrait Gallery, London.

tion to rescue Gordon which arrived too late—Gordon and his men had been massacred two days earlier by the forces of the Mahdi. The entire episode was seen as a national humiliation and cast a cloud over Gladstone's second ministry.

Gladstone's major domestic problem was Ireland, where economic grievances joined with Irish nationalism to make the island ungovernable. Gladstone's policy was to reconcile Ireland to the Union by redress of economic grievances, but he found that the Irish, led by Charles Stewart Parnell, a Protestant, wanted both land reform and self-government (Home Rule). Parnell's methods were to encourage violence in Ireland and to use the Irish members of the House of Commons to disrupt the proceedings of Parliament.

Gladstone offered a carrot and a stick. The stick was a Coercion Bill, which gave the authorities sweeping powers to seize and detain persons suspected of violence. The carrot was an Irish Land Act (1881) that gave the Irish peasants the three F's: fair rent, fixed tenure, free sale. Parnell would settle for nothing less than Home Rule and violence continued, although the murder of the new British secretary in a Dublin park shocked both the British and Irish into some restraint. The growing power of Parnell, both in Ireland and as leader of the Irish Nationalists in the House of Commons, made some resolution of the Irish problem essential.

Faced with stalemate in his domestic reforms, dissension in his cabinet, and open resistance in Ireland, Gladstone's solution to the problem of governing the British Isles was another installment of democracy. In 1884 and 1885 he pushed through Parliament a two-part electoral reform. The Reform Bill of 1884 removed the last important exception to universal manhood suffrage by enfranchising the agricultural workers. A companion measure in 1885 ended the ancient electoral system based on shires and boroughs and established single-member districts.

Gladstone's electoral reforms further alienated some supporters, and his problems were complicated by public dismay aroused by the debacle of Gordon at Khartoum. With his parliamentary support in doubt, Gladstone resigned, and the Conservatives, now led by Lord Salisbury, formed a caretaker government until an election could be held.

In the election of 1885 Gladstone and the Liberals lost ground but were still the largest party in the House of Commons; the Irish Nationalists, now firmly in the grip of Parnell, held the balance. Gladstone stood quietly by, hoping that Salisbury and the Conservatives would take the plunge for Home Rule, as Disraeli had done for parliamentary reform in 1867. Gladstone's cunning was unmasked when his support for Home Rule was revealed by his son.

Parnell then gave his support to Gladstone, and when Salisbury resigned early in 1886 Gladstone organized a ministry committed to Home Rule.

Gladstone's Home Rule Bill would have continued the supreme authority of the United Kingdom in matters of foreign policy and defense while establishing in Ireland a separate Irish executive and parliament to deal with domestic matters.

Gladstone's bill shattered the Liberal Party, for an influential group of Liberals, led by Joseph Chamberlain, opposed Home Rule. In June 1886, the Home Rule Bill was defeated in the House of Commons. When Gladstone appealed to the nation by calling another election the Liberal Party suffered a stinging rebuff. Gladstone resigned, and Salisbury formed a Conservative government which, with the exception of one Liberal interlude, governed Britain until 1905. Gladstone had gambled and lost, and the Liberal Party which he led was no longer the dominant force in British politics.

By 1886 a new set of challenges had emerged. The long-established leadership of an elite of birth and wealth was giving way to the uncertain prospects of political democracy. Prime ministers and cabinets held office because they were able, through political parties, to win public support. The diplomatic position of Britain had been changed by the unification of Germany and Italy and the growth of imperial rivalries. The British economy faced unaccustomed competition from new industrial nations, and British agriculture was depressed by food-stuffs brought from abroad by railroads and steamships.

The optimism and confidence of the mid-Victorian period were slipping. An emphasis on comfort and pleasure replaced the striving of the mid-Victorians as the glories of the Victorian noontide passed into the glow of the late-Victorian afternoon.

SUGGESTIONS FOR FURTHER READING

Many books cited in chapter 13 are useful for this chapter and are not repeated here. Useful general surveys are Brian H. Harrison, *The Transformation of British Politics, 1860–1995* (1996); Malcolm Pearce, *British Political History, 1867–1995: Democracy and Decline* (1996); and T. A. Jenkins, *The Liberal Ascendancy, 1830–1886* (1994). The relevant volume in *The New Oxford History of England* is K. Theodore Hoppen, *The Mid-Victorian Generation, 1846–1886* (1998). Two important interpretive works by George Kitson Clark are *The Making of Victorian England* (1962) and *An Expanding Society: Britain, 1830–1900* (1967). Interesting studies of the mid-Victorian period are William. L. Burn, *The Age of Equipoise: A Study of the Mid-Victorian Generation* (1964) and Geoffrey Best, *Mid-Victorian Britain, 1851–1875* (1971).

For constitutional and legal development, Keir, *Constitutional History* (cited chapter 13) gives a general overview, which can be supplemented by Oliver MacDonagh, *Early Victorian Government, 1830–1870* (1977) and T. A. Jenkins, *Parliament, Party and Politics in Victorian Britain* (1996). The role of Queen Victoria and her successors is assessed in Frank Hardie, *The Political Influence of the British Monarchy, 1868–1952* (1970). The leap to democracy is covered by Maurice Cowling in *1867: Disraeli, Gladstone, and Revolution: The Passage of the Second Reform Bill* (1967). See also J. P. Parry, *The Rise and Fall of Liberal Government in Victorian Britain*

(1993); Angus Hawkins, *British Party Politics, 1852–1886* (1998); Eugenio Biagini, *Liberty, Retrenchment, and Reform: Popular Liberalism in the Age of Gladstone, 1860–1880* (1992); and John Belchem, *Popular Radicalism in Nineteenth-Century Britain* (1996). Robert Blake, *The Conservative Party from Peel to Thatcher* (1985) takes up the origins of the Conservative Party. Stephen Koss, *The Rise and Fall of the Political Press in Britain: The Nineteenth Century* (1981) takes up that important actor in the political process. See also Aled Jones, *Power of the Press: Newspapers, Power, and the Public in Nineteenth-Century England* (1996).

Many books on foreign policy cited in chapter 13 continue to be useful. A magisterial work is Charles K. Webster, *The Foreign Policy of Palmerston, 1833–1870* (1951). See also Paul W. Schroeder, *Austria, Great Britain, and the Crimean War* (1972). Cecil Woodham-Smith explains *The Reason Why* (1954). In addition to military books cited in chapter 13, British use of military force can be seen in *Queen Victoria's Little Wars* (1972) by Byron Farwell.

Books on economic development by Deane and Cole, Mathias, Chambers, Checkland, and Hobsbawn (cited ch. 13) continue to be useful for the Mid-Victorian period. Robert Gray examines *The Factory Question and Industrial England, 1830–1860* (1996). The development of working-class organization is traced in Henry Pelling, *A History of British Trade Unionism* (1992), E. H. Hunt, *British Labour History, 1815–1914* (1981), and Trygve Tholfsen, *Working Class Radicalism in Mid-Victorian England* (1977).

On Victorian society, many books cited in chapter 13 also apply to this chapter. Rural society is well served by F. M. L. Thompson, *English Landed Society in the 19th Century* (1963) and Gordon Mingay, *Land and Society in England, 1750–1980* (1994). *The Victorian City: Images and Realities*, H. J. Dyos and Michael Wolff (eds.) (1973) is magnificently illustrated. Gordon Mingay's *The Victorian Countryside* (1981) is the rural equivalent of Dyos and Wolff. Fascinating books by Mark Girouard are *Life in the English Country House: A Social and Architectural History* (1978), *The Victorian Country House* (rev. ed., 1979), and *The Return to Camelot: Chivalry and the English Gentleman* (1981). Sally Mitchell describes *Daily Life in Victorian England* (1996).

On social policy see Eric Midwinter, *Victorian Social Reform* (1968), Eric Evans, *Social Policy, 1830–1914* (1978) and David Roberts, *Victorian Origins of the British Welfare State* (1960). See also Peter Marsh, *The Conscience of the Victorian State* (1979) and Paul Smith, *Disraelian Conservatism and Social Reform* (1967).

In addition to books on women cited in chapter 13, see Jane Purvis's collection of essays entitled *Women's History: Britain, 1850–1945* (1995). Gender roles are examined by Jean Bethke Eshtain in *Public Man, Private Woman: Women in Social and Political Thought* (1993). A wide-ranging analysis is provided by M. Jeanne Peterson in *Family, Love, and Work in the Lives of Victorian Gentlewomen* (1989). Martha Vicinus edited a collection of essays entitled *A Widening Sphere: Changing Roles of Victorian Women* (1977). An ancient profession that flourished in the Victorian period is examined by Judith Walkowitz in *Prostitution and Victorian Society: Women, Class and the State* (1980).

For the influence of Darwinism see William Irvine, *Apes, Angels, and Victorians* (1955); Gertrude Himmelfarb, *Darwin and the Darwinian Revolution* (1959), and Michael Ruse, *The Darwinian Revolution* (1979). An important synthesis of Victorian thought is T. [Thomas] William Heyck, *The Transformation of Intellectual Life in Victorian England* (1982). Two books that deal with important countertrends are Benjamin E. Lippincott, *Victorian Critics of Democracy* (1974) and Richard Jay, *Critics of Capitalism: Victorian Criticism of "Political Economy"* (1986).

The religious conflicts that were so important are examined by Bernard M. G. Reardon in *Religious Thought in the Victorian Age* (1995). The social ideas of the Church are examined in George S. R. Kitson Clark, *Churchmen and the Condition of England, 1832–1885* (1973) and Kenneth S. Inglis, *Churches and the Working Classes in Victorian England* (1963). For Victorian Catholicism see J. Derek Holmes, *More Roman than Rome: English Catholicism in the Nineteenth Century* (1978).

Education continued to be a controversial subject. In addition to books cited in chapter 13, consult Eric Midwinter, *Schools in Society: The Evolution of English Education* (1980) and John S. Hurt, *Education in Evolution: Church, State, Society and Popular Education, 1800–1870* (1971). An interesting collection of essays is provided in *Religion and Irreligion in Victorian Society,* Richard J. Helmstadter and R. W. Davis (eds.) (1992).

General histories of Scotland, Ireland, and the empire cited in chapter 13 continue to be useful for this period. Additional works are K. Theodore Hoppen, *Ireland since 1800* (1989) and Oliver MacDonagh, *State of Mind: A Study of Anglo-Irish Conflict, 1780–1980* (1983). For "the crown jewel" of the empire see *India Britannica* (1983) by Geoffrey Moorhouse; and Christopher Hibbert, *The Great Mutiny of India, 1857* (1978).

In addition to some of the biographies cited in chapter 13, important political biographies are Peter Stansky, *Gladstone: A Progress in Politics* (1979); H. C. G. Matthew, *Gladstone, 1809–1898* (1997); Robert Blake, *Disraeli* (1967); T. A. Jenkins, *Disraeli and Victorian Conservatism* (1996); F. S. L. Lyons, *Charles Stewart Parnell* (1977); Maurice Cranston, *John Stuart Mill* (1958); and Joseph Hamburger, *Intellectuals in Politics: John Stuart Mill and the Philosophic Radicals* (1965). Other books about Mill are Bernard Semmel, *John Stuart Mill and the Pursuit of Virtue* (1984) and Maurice Cowley, *Mill and Liberalism* (1990). Biographies of prominent figures in other aspects of Victorian life are Peter Brent, *Charles Darwin: A Man of Enlarged Curiosity* (1981); Sheridan Gilley, *Newman and his Age* (1990); Robert K. Webb, *Harriet Martineau: A Radical Victorian* (1960); Cecil Woodham-Smith, *Florence Nightingale, 1820–1910* (1983); and John H. Waller, *Gordon of Khartoum: The Saga of a Victorian Hero* (1988). The *Autobiography* (1873) of John Stuart Mill is in a class by itself.

CHAPTER FIFTEEN

Democracy and Imperialism
1886–1914

In 1886 an observer of the British scene would have expected a tranquil future. The institutions and achievements of the previous seventy years seemed unthreatened. The prestige of the monarchy was secure; cabinet government and the two-party system were well established; a democratic electorate was a source of strength to traditional institutions; British industry still led all competitors; Britain was the world center of finance and trade; the pound sterling was the acceptable medium of exchange around the globe; the sun never set on the British empire; and Britannia ruled the waves. Yet there were many changes in the wind which, from our perspective, can be seen as anticipations of modern Britain.

POLITICAL LEADERS AND PARTIES

Lord Salisbury and the Conservative Party

If Queen Victoria was the symbolic grandmother to the age, Lord Salisbury was its father figure. Salisbury was a strong and thoughtful aristocrat whose goal was to maintain stability and resolve the tensions generated by the previous twenty years of political conflict and institutional change. With the exception of a three-year period of Liberal Rule (1892–1895), Salisbury served as Prime Minister from 1886–1902. He concentrated his attention on foreign and imperial affairs. On domestic matters he relied heavily on his nephew, Arthur Balfour, a cool, polished intellectual who had abandoned philosophy for a career in politics.

Under Salisbury the Conservative Party took on a new character, preserving its base in the aristocracy, the landed gentry, and the Church, but adding an increasing number of wealthy business and professional men. The Conservative Party became the champion of the rights of all kinds of property, whether of commerce, industry, or land. It claimed to be the patriotic party, which defended British interests in foreign and imperial affairs with unique vigor. It also attracted an important minority of working men, who disliked moralistic Liberal reforms such as restricting the sale of strong drink.

Salisbury was firmly opposed to Home Rule for Ireland, which gained him the support of Joseph Chamberlain and the Liberal Unionists, who had broken with Gladstone over Home Rule. Conservative policy toward Ireland was embodied in the Ashbourne Act (1885) which sought to reduce Irish discontent by assisting tenants to purchase their land ("killing Home Rule with kindness"). Kindness was accompanied by coercion, and tough measures were introduced to preserve order and protect property.

The ministry continued Disraeli's policy of concern for social problems in an effort to win working class support. As political boss of Birmingham, Joseph Chamberlain had been a leader in promoting civic projects loosely called "municipal socialism." Consequently, the Liberal Unionists gave the government a thrust toward social legislation that was lacking in Salisbury's more conservative followers. Legislation passed under Salisbury did not break new ground, but included another factory act (1891), the abolition of fees for elementary education (1891), and workmen's compensation for injuries suffered on the job (1897). Encouraged by the Liberal Unionists, the Salisbury ministry sponsored the Local Government Act of 1888, which established elected councils for county government and a similar form of government for sixty-one urban centers (county boroughs) and the London Metropolitan area (the London County Council).

The Liberal Party

In the meantime the Liberal Party, split by Gladstone's commitment to Home Rule and consigned to opposition, also began to develop a new character. The departure of Chamberlain and the Liberal Unionists gave an opportunity to younger Liberals who advocated a new thrust. The established Liberal goals—political democracy, institutional reform, civil liberties—had been largely achieved. The new Liberals were concerned with economic and social problems that could not be regarded solely as matters of individual responsibility. They looked to government to intervene in the life of the nation to provide what was called "the ladder and the net"—opportunity for individual advancement with minimal standards guaranteed for everyone. Liberalism kept its strong sense of moral crusade against privilege, wasteful public expenditure, and abuse of power.

In 1891 the aged Gladstone, still displaying remarkable intellectual and physical vitality, accepted the need to satisfy the advocates of new directions in the Liberal Party. He adopted as party policy the Newcastle Program which had originated as resolutions passed by the National Liberal Federation, an organization of constituency activists. The Newcastle Program included disestablishment of the Church of Scotland and, in Wales, the Church of England. Other proposals were free elementary education, and empowering local governments to prohibit the sale of alcoholic drink. Irish Home Rule continued to head the Liberal Party program.

In 1892 Gladstone and the Liberals won a slim plurality (273–269) over the Conservatives. The Liberal Unionists (46) and the Irish Nationalists (81), held the balance. Supported by the Irish members, Gladstone and the Liberals returned to power. In his last ministry Gladstone attempted to achieve some of the social goals of the Liberal Party but Parliament, and probably the majority of the nation, was unreceptive.

Ireland was again Gladstone's major concern, and Ireland again proved to be his downfall. In 1893 Gladstone succeeded in getting a Home Rule Bill through the House of Commons, only to have it defeated in the House of Lords. Shortly thereafter he suffered a severe stroke and resigned, to be succeeded by Lord Rosebery, a genial peer who was spokesman for the moderate wing of the Liberal Party. In 1895 Rosebery resigned and an election returned power to Salisbury and the Conservatives, supported by Chamberlain and the Liberal Unionists. Home Rule for Ireland languished for another fifteen years.

The retirement of Gladstone marked the end of an era. Throughout his long political career Gladstone had given to British politics intellectual power, moral fervor, and a rare ability to recognize and respond to new needs. He had raised the public's expectations of what good government was and what government could do. In this way, he prepared the way for the expansion of the role of government in the twentieth century.

THE CONDITION OF THE PEOPLE

Agriculture and the Landed Interest

Late Victorian Britain was a wealthy land, enjoying the fruits of Britain's financial, commercial, and industrial leadership. Yet contemporaries worried about what they called "the Great Depression," which historians normally date as extending from 1873–1896. This "Great Depression" was not a dramatic economic collapse, like that which began with the stock market crash of

1929 and lasted until World War II. Rather, it was a general decline of prices, profits, and interest rates, with effects that varied from one industry to another.

Agriculture was hardest hit, for a dramatic fall in farm prices resulted from opening up new agricultural areas in the American Middle West, the prairie provinces of Canada, Australia, and the pampas of Argentina. Development of the railroad, steamship, and refrigerator ship made it possible to bring these products to market in the industrial centers of the world. With the repeal of the Corn Laws, British agriculture was left without tariff protection. To some extent, agriculture was able to adjust by turning away from wheat and wool to producing fresh dairy products, meat, fruits, and vegetables for urban markets, but such changes required changes in agricultural skills, farm equipment, land use, and landlord-tenant relations.

Despite the decline of agricultural rents, laments for the landed aristocracy and gentry would be premature. By the late Victorian period much of the wealth of the aristocracy had been invested in gilt-edged securities or well-established industries, and with the fall of prices the purchasing power of fixed-income investments was increasing. The growth of population and towns meant that the value of urban properties or land suitable for urban development increased.

By the long established process of social osmosis, successful businessmen and professional men, or their heirs and daughters, were drawn into the upper class, bringing with them their wealth. Lord Randolph Churchill, for example, younger son of the Duke of Marlborough, found that marriage to an American heiress could freshen the family coffers. Declining wages and living costs made it possible for the upper class to continue to maintain large numbers of domestic servants. On the periphery of this upper class lived a great many younger sons, maiden aunts, dowered widows, and other dependents with high social status although modest incomes. These were the comfortable people, parodied by Oscar Wilde and gleefully dissected by George Bernard Shaw.

Industry

British industry was not affected to the same degree as agriculture, but clearly it was not keeping pace with industrial growth in rising industrial nations such as Germany and the United States. In 1900, for example, both the United States and Germany passed Britain in the production of steel. Other industries where Britain had formerly held unchallenged supremacy, such as textiles, shipbuilding, and engineering, were also meeting stiff competition, as was the coal industry. Although Britain developed new industries producing consumer goods, the basic industries upon which its industrial leadership had been based were losing ground to newer and more progressive producers elsewhere.

Why this decline in industrial competitiveness? Many reasons can be cited: Britain's factories and machines were old and British industry did not keep pace with technological developments; the growing power of trade unions inhibited change; the export of capital abroad in search of higher profits drained Britain of resources needed to remain competitive; Britain's free trade policy injured the economy when its major competitors were protecting their home markets with protective tariffs. In too many instances, when a British businessman was successful, he (or his heir) lost interest in the business and turned to the life of a gentleman.

In 1896 Ernest E. Williams published a book, *Made in Germany*, which was widely read. Williams argued that the German economy was gaining on the British because the Germans had a domestic market protected by tariffs, because they were more aggressive in selling their products abroad, and because they had excellent technical education. In 1902 a similar book by Fred McKenzie, *The American Invaders: Their Plans, Tactics, and Progress* urged British businessmen to develop new products and methods of manufacture and to sell their products aggressively. The message seemed clear: British businessmen were complacent and unprogressive and were already paying for it in lost profits and reduced domestic investment.

The Middle Class

The maturing of the economy was generally favorable to the growth of the middle class. Employment was increasing in government, the law and other professions, large-scale business and financial institutions, the press and publishing, and similar occupations. Declining prices made it possible to maintain a middle class lifestyle with modest income.

Although the term "middle class" is difficult to define, Englishmen in the late Victorian period had a reasonably clear idea of what it meant. To some extent the term middle class referred to income: below a certain income it would be difficult to maintain a middle-class style of life; above a certain income the life of the gentleman beckoned, with its powerful attraction to the Englishman.

The middle class can also be defined in terms of work: the middle-class man applied himself to a business or a profession, and he ordinarily wore a hat, suit, and white shirt to his place of employment. As public transport developed, he commuted to work from his home in a large residential area or a suburb, while the working class remained in the central city where their jobs were.

Top: Victorian middle-class housing. Newcastle-upon-Tyne. Bottom: Working-class housing. Newcastle-upon-Tyne. Private collection.

But the Victorian middle class was also identified by lifestyle: the husband went regularly to work; the wife stayed home to manage the house; and there was some domestic help. The family was the center of middle-class life. Parents gave careful attention to the nurture, education, discipline, and manners of the children. Reading and music were everyday activities, centered on the novel and the piano. Family activities such as church-going, visits to relatives, parlor games, and seaside holidays were part of the middle-class lifestyle.

Although the middle class advocated economy in government, they were civic minded and willing to support local improvements, such as town halls, libraries, museums, and hospitals. They were aroused by social issues, such as education, poor relief, and the evils of drink and prostitution, and were willing to make charitable contributions to alleviate these problems. They did not expect much from government, saved for a rainy day, and took care of their own.

Questioning of Values

The opulence of the aristocracy and the comfort of the middle class were accompanied by nagging anxieties about matters formerly considered to be certain. Most fundamental of these was the conflict between science and religion. Already weakened by the ideas of Darwin and Huxley, the authority of traditional Christianity was further eroded by Biblical criticism, which undermined faith in the divine inspiration of the Bible. The elegant and poetic *Life of Jesus* by the French theologian Ernst Renan was translated into English in 1888 and became a great success. Renan depicted Jesus, not as the Son of God, but as a man—generous, sensitive, dedicated, at one with nature and all humankind—but nevertheless a man. The naturalistic view of religion was strengthened by James Frazer's *The Golden Bough* (1890 ff.), a study of primitive religion, which showed the extent to which Christianity shared motifs common to ancient paganism.

As religion waned it was replaced by a new value system that looked to society, instead of God, to fulfill people's lives. In an age of growing secularism the Victorian conscience remained, stung by the disparity between the lives of the comfortable classes and the poverty of a large portion of the population. John Ruskin, an art historian turned social commentator, strenuously denied that most of the population should be condemned to privation in the interests of economic growth. He appealed to the sense of community and fair play so deeply ingrained in the British public.

William Morris—poet, artist, craftsman, radical politician—called his countrymen back to the virtues, skills, and human satisfactions of the preindustrial age. Morris detested machine-manufactured products and gave particular attention to "the lesser arts" such as pottery, weaving, furniture, and wallpaper, which formed taste and gave beauty to everyday life. In short, the characteristic Victorian beliefs in Progress, competitive capitalism, economic growth, and laissez-faire were being challenged by some of the most thoughtful and persuasive writers of the time.

Flowergirls working in London, c. 1900. Corbis–Bettmann.

The Status of Women

Another aspect of the questioning of traditional values was the changing status of middle-class women. The Victorians idealized women as creatures of delicacy and tender feelings who must not be exposed to the rough and tumble of everyday life. At the same time women were expected to assume a wide range of responsibilities in the home and bear up under a host of personal and physical privations.

The middle-class woman did not work outside the home and was expected to devote herself to the role of wife, mother, and manager of the household. At her best, the Victorian middle-class woman was a powerful influence in shaping the values of the nation, and in the age before modern household appliances she performed or directed an enormous amount of useful and necessary work. At worst these women lived empty, dependent lives as elegant decorations, symbolic of the material success of the head of the household, and filling their time with visits, light reading, shopping, or feeling "under the weather."

Women's fashions contributed to limiting the lives of women of the comfortable classes, for they were remarkably impractical. Extravagant of material, they were characterized by numerous petticoats, huge bustles, and trailing skirts. A still more disabling fashion was tightly laced corsets, which reduced many women to suffocation in pursuit of a twenty-inch waist. There was great reticence to discuss the body and its functions and sexuality was not supposed to cross a woman's mind, although society accepted it as a preoccupation of men. Nevertheless the size of middle-class families declined as knowledge of birth control spread, thus freeing women from the servitude and dangers of frequent pregnancies and childbearing.

Despite traditional notions, increasing numbers of middle-class women found it possible to free themselves from the trammels of conventional views. To attain independence women needed decently paid jobs in comfortable surroundings, which could not be obtained without education and a change in the attitude of employers. Improvements in secondary education and the establishment of women's colleges opened up new opportunities for women. Teaching and nursing were the most common careers; in 1891 there were more than 53,000 women nurses and over 146,000 women teachers. Middle-class young women obtained employment in offices as secretaries and "typewriters" (stenographers). The telegraph and telephone provided many jobs for women, since before direct-dialing it was necessary to call a central office to be manually connected through a switchboard. By the end of the century 40 percent of those employed in the telegraph and telephone services were women.

Women of the upper and lower classes also began to seek political and legal rights. In this respect, as in so many others, John Stuart Mill was in the vanguard of his time. In *The Subjection of Women* (1869) Mill argued that "the legal subordination of one sex to the other—is wrong in itself, and now one of the chief hindrances to human improvement; and that it ought to be replaced by a principle of perfect equality." He emphasized especially the almost total authority of the husband over his wife, with the potential for abuse which that entailed.

Despite ridicule and angry denunciation, progress was made. In 1891, in the Jackson decision, the courts ruled that a husband could not coercively confine his wife to his home. In 1883 Parliament gave wives the right to sell or dispose of their property as they wished, and in 1893 a wife's property or contracts became her own legal responsibility. Women became eligible to hold office and vote in local government, and be employed in the civil service. In 1897 a women's suffrage bill to obtain the vote for parliamentary elections made some progress. In the same year a number of women's suffrage organizations joined in the National Union of Women's Suffrage Societies. The very conventional woman who reigned over the kingdom, Queen Victoria, vehemently opposed the notion of equal rights for women with no sense of the paradox of her position.

The Working Class

One of the puzzles of "the Great Depression" is its effect upon the British working class. In general, it appears that the industrial worker with steady employment was better off: his wages did not fall as much as prices, and thus his purchasing power was increased. Factory acts improved the conditions and safety of industrial employment. The working week was still long, but a half-day on Saturday and Sunday off were almost universal. Better housing was available; municipal governments energetically improved civic services such as streets, water, sewers, parks, and libraries; elementary education was provided and in some towns additional technical education for adults.

These advances were seen in the extent to which the "respectable" working class adopted middle-class values. Men in the upper levels of the working class, such as shop foremen or skilled machinists, were able to keep their wives at home, enjoy a neat house and hot meals, relax with friends and neighbors in the evenings or on Sundays, attend Church or chapel, and read a daily newspaper. For the working class the most dreaded hazard of all was the poorhouse, usually as a result of old age, sickness, disability, or unemployment, for they had little to live upon except their weekly wage.

For those workers who were unskilled or whose employment was insecure, poverty of the most extreme kind was the normal existence. The sweated workers—those who were paid piece wages—were especially vulnerable, for they lacked even those modest supports that factory workers had gained from the factory acts or their trade unions. Then there was the great mass of wretched people, especially in large cities, who had no steady means of support and lived a hand-to-mouth existence based primarily upon crime, vice, begging, or casual labor.

In 1890 William Booth, founder of the Salvation Army, published a book with wide impact, *In Darkest England and the Way Out*, which told of the lives of these people. Charles Booth (no relation to William Booth) published eighteen volumes entitled *The Life and Labour of the People of London*, supporting with copious detail his conclusion that approximately one-third of the population of London lived in degrading poverty, insecurity, and ugliness. In York Seebohm Rowntree, member of a wealthy family of chocolate manufacturers, found similar conditions. The Victorian conscience was shocked and no longer willing to accept the premise of earlier generations that such conditions were an inevitable concomitant of an advanced economy.

Working-Class Movements

One important factor in changing the conditions of working class life was the growth of trade unions. The organization of skilled workers had proceeded steadily in the 1850s and 1860s, and in 1873 trade union membership numbered about 700,000. In the 1880s the focus of unionism turned to the "operatives"—workers with some skill, such as railway workers and miners, but who were not trained through the apprenticeship system, as in the craft unions. By the end of the decade "the new unionism" was organizing unskilled workers, including some with irregular or piece-work employment.

The plight of unskilled workers was dramatized by a series of spectacular strikes: the women matchworkers of London (1888), the London gasworkers (1888), and the London dock strike (1889). Earlier a group of craft unions had formed the Trades Union Congress to bring about cooperation between unions in political activities and in collective bargaining. By 1900 the trade union movement had grown to almost 2,000,000 members. Women workers remained largely unorganized, as did most piece workers.

Hostility to trade unions was strong among employers, who attributed some of their competitive problems to union demands and restrictions. The middle class in general disapproved of the conflict which erupted sporadically during organizing efforts and strikes. In 1901 there was widespread satisfaction when the courts, in a celebrated decision, held the unions responsible for damages resulting from a strike at the Taff Vale railway in Wales. Nevertheless, when Queen Victoria died trade unions had become an important part of British life.

The working class was also able to make its influence felt through political action. Political democracy meant that the two major parties had to compete for the working class vote, and both parties supported the process by which government accepted increasing responsibility for public health, safety, and poor relief.

In the 1880s the socialist ideas of Karl Marx began to have some influence in Britain, and in 1884 H. M. Hyndman organized the Social Democratic Federation, a Marxist political party appealing to the workers. The Fabian Society, also founded in 1884, was a small body of middle-class intellectuals dedicated to democratic socialism. Leaders of the group were Sidney Webb, Beatrice Potter (later Mrs. Webb), and the playwright, George Bernard Shaw. Their goal was to replace private ownership of major industries with public ownership. They advocated the use of democratic processes to achieve their purpose and relied upon books and pamphlets to spread their ideas.

Keir Hardie, a Scottish coal miner, was a leader in founding the Independent Labour Party, which in the 1890s succeeded in electing a handful of members of Parliament on a vaguely socialistic platform. He was elected to the House of Commons in 1892, and created a sensation when he entered that gentleman's club wearing a workingman's cloth cap.

In 1900 a Labour Representation Committee met to consider forming a political organization for the election of labor candidates to Parliament. This group soon turned to association with the Liberal Party as the most practical means of exerting political influence. Through trade unions and political action the British working class began to make its presence felt. But British workers were not revolutionary; they preferred to work through existing institutions.

FOREIGN POLICY AND EMPIRE

The Foreign Policy of Salisbury

While gradual changes were taking place in Victorian society, a disturbing change had taken place in Britain's external relationships. Salisbury was already an experienced diplomat when he became Prime Minister. During his ministries, foreign and imperial affairs remained his major concern. While keeping a close eye on the rise of international tensions, militarism, and alliances, he attempted to follow a policy that some called "splendid isolation."

The unification of Germany in 1871 had created in central Europe a powerful new state with a strong military tradition. The German chancellor, Bismarck, was primarily concerned to consolidate his gains, but while doing so he faced the enmity of France, smarting from its defeat in the Franco-Prussian War of 1870–1871. In 1881 Bismarck attempted to stabilize relationships in eastern Europe and check the intrigues of France by forming an alliance among Germany, Austria, and Russia, but this goal was frustrated by the rivalry between Austria and Russia for influence in the Balkans. Forced to choose between the two, Germany strengthened its ties with Austria. France and Russia responded by making an alliance in 1894 which aroused German fears of "encirclement." Thus the major powers of Europe divided into two camps, each heavily armed and each suspicious of the other.

Salisbury wanted to avoid involvement in continental conflicts, but he did not wish to be without friends in such a menacing situation. His major efforts in Europe consisted of a series of overtures to Germany which he hoped would reduce German anxieties and permit a relaxation of European tensions, but these overtures were unsuccessful. Salisbury took special pains to eliminate causes of friction with the United States, which was becoming recognized as a potential great power. Steps were also taken to reduce imperial rivalry with France.

In 1902 the Salisbury government stunned public opinion by making an alliance with Japan, the rising power in East Asia. Directed against Russia, the Anglo-Japanese alliance was a clear recognition that, in that part of the world, Britain could no longer maintain its interests alone.

Imperial Rivalries

Britain also faced new challenges in the imperial world, as the major powers sought to improve their diplomatic leverage, military potential, and economic competitiveness by acquiring colonies overseas. France tried to balance the

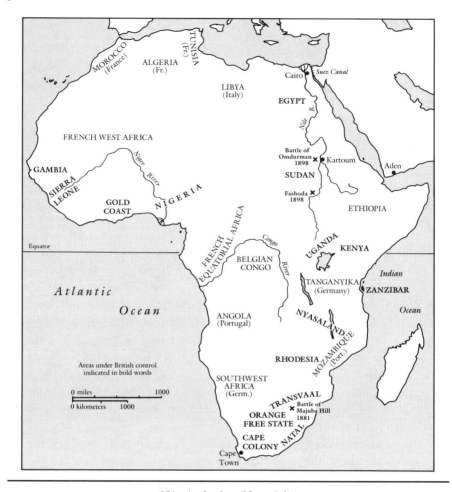

Africa in the Age of Imperialism

power of Germany by developing new sources of labor and wealth in North Africa, West Africa, and Southeast Asia. Germany began building a navy and picking up whatever bits of colonial territory were still available. As a result of the Spanish-American War, the United States acquired the Philippines and Puerto Rico. In 1895 Japan entered upon a career of imperialism by defeating the moribund Chinese empire and acquiring Formosa (Taiwan).

Suddenly Britain's imperial supremacy, unchallenged since the Congress of Vienna, was seriously threatened. Britain's industrial economy was predicated upon easy access to overseas food, raw materials, and markets. In an age of protective tariffs, each new acquisition by an industrial competitor cut off British access to an existing or potential area for trade. Another major factor in imperial expansion was the search for secure places for long-term investment, since the return on capital at home was declining. Capitalists were unwilling to invest money in long-term projects such as mines, plantations, railroads, and port facilities unless they were assured of political stability and a sympathetic government.

The ambitions of politicians, soldiers, and local leaders contributed to the pressures for expansion. Newspaper editors, now appealing to a mass market, needed stories and crises to generate sales, while the books and lectures of travellers and the determination of churches and missionaries to Christianize and civilize the heathen added to imperialist fervor. "God, Gold, and Glory" led the industrial nations of Europe into imperial rivalries with costs that were far out of proportion to the benefits to be derived from colonies.

In the 1880s imperialism was at its height. After occupying Egypt in 1882 Britain consolidated its control of the Egyptian government and economy. In 1898 Britain occupied the Sudan, which was regarded as vital to the security of Egypt. At the battle of Omdurman a British force with modern rifles and artillery defeated the poorly armed forces of the religious leader called the Mahdi. The battle concluded with a dashing cavalry charge in which young Winston Churchill participated.

In East Africa the British navy had a base at the island of Zanzibar that was used for patrolling the Indian Ocean, but Britain had not shown interest in establishing colonies on the mainland. In 1885, however, the Germans claimed the East African territory of Tanganyika (now part of Tanzania). Salisbury reacted by asserting British control of Kenya. In 1888 the British East Africa Company was chartered to begin the development of Kenya, and in 1890 internal disorder in Uganda led the Company to establish its authority there. A year later conflicts with Arab slave traders persuaded the British to occupy Nyasaland (now Malawi).

In West Africa France was the principal imperial rival. The British had maintained trading stations in West Africa since the later seventeenth century, but the abolition of the slave trade had made these stations of little value and at times proposals had been made to abandon them. By the 1880s, however, West African territories had become valuable for palm oil and rubber, and intense economic competition began between the British and French for position in the region. In 1886 the Salisbury ministry gave a charter to the Royal Niger Company to develop trade in the area of the Niger River. The Company extended its influence vigorously until 1900, when the British government took control of Nigeria.

By that time the French were seeking British support against Germany in Europe and were eager to settle disputes with Britain concerning West African possessions. A momentary crisis arose in the Sudan, where the British force sent to deal with the Mahdi encountered at Fashoda a small French detachment that had travelled from French West Africa to stake a claim. For a time it appeared that an Anglo-French clash would take place, but the French, much more concerned with Germany than the Sudan, gave way. The Fashoda incident in 1898 led to resolution of other imperial conflicts between Britain and France and contributed to the improved relations that led to the Anglo-French entente of 1904.

Southern Africa

Southern Africa produced the most difficult problems for British imperial policy. In the Cape Colony tensions existed between the two principal white populations, the British and the Boers. The situation was further complicated by a large black population, which provided labor for the farms, mines, and factories. The colony of Natal, to the east of the Cape Colony, was dominated by British planters using African or East Indian laborers. The most pressing problems of the area grew out of the relationships between the two British colonies and the Boer republics. The Orange Free State and the Transvaal maintained a frontier existence with loose central authority. Relations had been aggravated by Disraeli's annexation of the Boer republics in 1877 and Gladstone's withdrawal from the Transvaal in 1881.

The man who attempted to resolve this tense situation was Cecil Rhodes, who rose to dominance of the diamond mines in the interior and also political control of the Cape Colony. Rhodes was an imperialist who dreamed of a broad band of British territory linking southern Africa with the British possessions in East Africa, the Sudan, and Egypt. He was also a skilled propagandist, who could play effectively upon imperialist sentiments in Britain.

In 1888 Rhodes received a concession from Lobengula, king of the Matabele, to settle the territory to the north of the Boer republics, which became Rhodesia (now Zimbabwe). The next year the Salisbury government chartered the British South Africa Company to develop the area. In 1893 Lobengula led a revolt of the Matabele which was crushed, and thereafter the settlement of Rhodesia proceeded rapidly.

As a result of Rhodes' expansive policies, the Boer republics were trapped between the Cape Colony and Rhodesia. The Boers were led by the tough president of the Transvaal, Paul Kruger, who saw the Boer way of life jeopardized by the influx of outsiders (Uitlanders) who came into the Transvaal to develop the gold mines. Kruger resisted the claims of the Uitlanders for political rights and in 1895 the Uitlanders, supported by Rhodes, plotted to overthrow him. The plot was revealed prematurely when Rhodes's agent in Rhodesia, Dr. Jameson, led a party of men into the Transvaal before the Uitlanders were ready to rise. As a result of the Jameson Raid, as it was called, Rhodes was driven from office in the Cape Colony and Kruger began preparing for war, hoping to obtain German aid.

The fall of Rhodes and the prospect of German involvement in the Transvaal changed the views of the Salisbury government. The Colonial Secretary was Joseph Chamberlain, leader of the Liberal Unionists. Chamberlain was a strong imperialist but he had mistrusted Rhodes and his highly personal form of imperial expansion. As the grievances of the Uitlanders mounted the Salisbury government decided that it was necessary to overthrow Kruger to prevent extension of German influence into the region. Kruger in turn decided that the time to drive out the British was now or never.

The Boer War began in 1899 and consisted of three phases: Boer invasions of Natal and the Cape Colony, which were repulsed; a British invasion of the Orange Free State and the Transvaal, which led to the destruction of the Boer army; and a period of guerrilla warfare as British troops hunted down Boer commandos. Winston Churchill, who was covering the war as a journalist, came to public attention when he was captured by the Boers and made a daring escape. By the time the war ended in 1902 Rhodes was dead, and Kruger died shortly after.

In Britain the Boer War created a heated political controversy, especially within the Liberal Party, as patriots and imperialists supported the war while opponents depicted it as the action of a swaggering bully. The war which had been entered into so lightly produced long lists of dead and wounded, and the efforts of a professional army to put down desperate guerrillas led inevitably to atrocities. As reports reached the newspapers of British concentration camps in which large numbers of women and children had died, public opinion in Britain turned against the war. Although Britain had won the war in southern Africa, the opponents won the war of words at home.

The Boer War discredited the imperialistic policies of the previous twenty years as well as the Conservative government that had been principally responsible. Five years earlier Rudyard Kipling, the British writer who best understood the nature and problems of Britain's far-flung empire, had warned in his *Recessional* (1897) of the retribution that came to peoples whose pride was swollen by the transitory experience of dominion over others.

"Far-called, our navies melt away," he wrote, thinking of the future. "On dune and headland sinks the fire: Lo, all our pomp of yesterday/Is one with Nineveh and Tyre." He concluded with a prayer: "For frantic boast and foolish word—Thy Mercy on Thy People Lord!"

Chamberlain and Imperial Federation

During his years as Colonial Secretary, Joseph Chamberlain's major concern was to draw the English-speaking, self-governing parts of the empire together in an imperial federation. Threatened by the rise of international tensions and the declining competitiveness of the British economy, Chamberlain tried to redress the balance by steps toward greater imperial unity. The Golden Jubilee of Queen Victoria in 1887 and her Diamond Jubilee ten years later were used by Chamberlain to bring the political leaders of the self-governing colonies to London to discuss closer relationships. Chamberlain's proposals fell upon unsympathetic ears. Having gained the right to manage their own affairs, the colonial leaders were unwilling to commit themselves to closer ties.

Chamberlain also encouraged the political and economic development of the empire. The discovery of vast goldfields in Australia more than tripled the population and led to broad diversification of the economy. Handsome cities emerged from the former frontier society, and trade and industry grew rapidly. Increasing economic and social integration, and concern with German influence in the Pacific islands, led in 1901 to the federation of the six Australian colonies into the self-governing dominion of Australia. New Zealand agriculture was stimulated by the advent of refrigerated ships to carry lamb chops and dairy products to Britain. In 1907 New Zealand also received dominion status. Chamberlain worked to improve the productivity of the dependent colonies in Africa and the British West Indies through encouragement of investment, development of new crops, and the conquest of tropical diseases.

In 1903 Chamberlain, still seeking the elusive goal of imperial unity, took a bold step. He defied accepted free trade doctrines and the political attractions of "cheap food" by proposing a protective tariff with preferential rates for the colonies. Having done so, Chamberlain discovered that the colonies were unenthusiastic, and that he had unleashed a disastrous political crisis at home.

THE EDWARDIAN AGE

A New Century Dawns

When Queen Victoria died in 1901 there was a strong sense that one age had passed and another was beginning. The revered queen was succeeded by her handsome and pleasure-loving son who became King Edward VII (1901–1910). Under Edward VII the British monarchy reached its peak of splendor and magnificence, and the king set the tone for an upper-class way of life which turned away from Victorian earnestness to emphasize pleasure and show. The splendid social season in London in the winter was varied by long stays at elegant country estates in summer, trips to continental resorts or the Riviera, sometimes protracted residence in milder climates, such as Italy and the south of France, and always the long English weekend, devoted to visits, shooting, picnics, parties, horseraces, long walks and talks, reading novels, and generally pleasant leisure activities. For those fortunate enough to be born, married, or accepted into that social milieu, it was a pleasant life indeed, soon to be gravely wounded by World War I.

The new century was heralded by a galaxy of brilliant writers. H. G. Wells, product of an impoverished background, gained prominence as a writer of science fiction through *The Time Machine* and *The War of the Worlds.* Wells was fascinated by technology, which he saw as the principal means of human improvement. A political and social radical, he advocated socialism, world government, emancipation of women, and free love. His enormously popular *An Outline of History* (1920) presented historical evolution as the story of Progress.

George Bernard Shaw, who was born and raised in Dublin, early sought a literary career in London. He failed as a novelist and succeeded as a music critic, but he found his place as a playwright, criticizing Victorian social values in plays such as *Arms and the Man* (the romantic view of war) and *Mrs. Warren's Profession* (prostitution and the economic system that encouraged it). Oscar Wilde made a name for himself by spoofing conventional Victorian attitudes in *The Importance of Being Earnest.*

In philosophy and science new ideas shattered established views, from Albert Einstein's concept of the shape of the universe and the nature of matter, to the explorations of Sigmund Freud, the Viennese psychiatrist, into the depths of human personality. The automobile, airplane, and radio appeared, introducing the revolution in communications and transportation which has been such a notable feature of the twentieth century. It was clear to perceptive observers that the new century would be much different from the old.

The Liberal Revival

A year after the accession of Edward VII, Lord Salisbury, the last of the great Victorians, retired due to ill health. Leadership of the Conservative government passed to lesser lights: Salisbury's cool, intellectual nephew, Arthur Balfour, who had acted almost as deputy premier in Salisbury's later years, and the willful, impulsive Joseph Chamberlain, leader of the Liberal Unionists. Sir Henry Campbell-Bannerman, whose forthright opposition to the Boer War had appealed to many Liberals, was recognized as the spokesman for those elements in the Liberal Party who were committed to progressive ideas. In 1903 the Liberals and the Labor Representation Committee agreed to support each other's candidates against the Conservatives in the next election. A new yeastiness was entering into the body politic.

The Conservatives contributed significantly to their own downfall. In 1902 they passed an Education Act that reorganized the schools by placing them under the control of the counties and county boroughs. The act also made these authorities responsible for providing secondary and technical

*David Lloyd George and
Winston Churchill on
Budget Day, 1910.
Baldwin H. Ward/
Corbis-Bettmann.*

education. In many respects the act was a forward-looking step, but it offended many Liberals by giving financial support to voluntary (private) schools, which were operated mainly by the churches. The sale of strong drink was another issue. Although both parties agreed that some control was necessary, there were bitter differences between Conservatives and Liberals about the best way to do it. The Conservative Licensing Act of 1904, which limited the number of pubs, was seen by many Liberals as inadequate and a sellout to "Demon Rum."

In 1903 the Conservative ministry suffered a body blow when Joseph Chamberlain resigned from the Cabinet and announced his conversion to a protective tariff with imperial preference. Chamberlain's proposal attacked the twin foundations of Victorian economic policy—free trade and cheap food. Many Conservatives broke with their leaders on the issue, including a promising young M.P., Winston Churchill. In 1905 Balfour resigned. The Liberals took office and prepared to carry their case to the people in an election. The long Conservative dominance had ended.

The Liberal government that took office in 1905 was exceptionally talented. As Prime Minister, Campbell-Bannerman displayed unexpected qualities of idealism and practical political sense and was capable of recruiting and leading a cabinet of remarkable individuals. When ill health forced Campbell-Bannerman to retire in 1908, he was succeeded as Prime Minister by Herbert Asquith, previously chancellor of the Exchequer. Asquith, a successful lawyer from a middle-class family, brought to the office keen intelligence and a quick wit, and was assisted personally and financially by his second wife, Margot, the lively daughter of a wealthy businessman. In some respects the most striking member of the ministry was the fiery young Welshman, David Lloyd George, whose intense personal ambition was fuelled by sympathy for the poor and antagonism toward aristocracy and privilege.

Early in 1906 the Liberals called an election, which was one of the most decisive of modern times. In the new Parliament the Liberals held 401 seats, the Conservatives and Liberal Unionists 157, the Irish Nationalists 83, and there were 29 Labour members. There were more than 300 new members, most of them middle-class professionals prepared to have government take on new responsibilities. Although the issues were confused and the positions of the major parties far from clear, the election revealed an important shift in the mood of the electorate.

Social Legislation

The Liberals took office determined to come to grips with the main problems of industrial society while maintaining, as much as possible, their historic principles of individual liberty and responsibility and low public expenditure. Trade unions were seen as the best way for industrial workers to promote their own well being, and the Trade Disputes Act (1906), passed to overturn the Taff Vale decision, gave trade unions freedom to engage in strikes and other forms of industrial action without fear of suits for damages. The Miners Eight-Hour Day Act was justified as regulation of an abuse that could not be left to collective bargaining.

While employed workers could normally be expected to look after themselves, old age and sickness were hazards for which the worker could not be held personally responsible. The Old Age Pension Act (1908) was one of the few pieces of Liberal legislation that drew upon the Treasury. It provided modest assistance to impoverished elderly people with a pension of 5 shillings per week for persons over seventy, a modest sum but large enough to help those who had some personal or family resources to draw upon. The National Insurance Act (1911) established a system of insurance to provide medical care to workers and pay benefits to workers who were unable to work due to sickness or disability. Workers and employers contributed to a fund from which benefits would be paid. Low-income workers would get free medical care by signing up with a doctor, and doctors were paid on the basis of the number of patients on their lists.

The most drastic change in Liberal ideas concerned unemployment, which traditionally had been thought of as a matter of personal responsibility. Liberal policy was much influenced by a young journalist named William Beveridge, who published in 1909 a book entitled *Unemployment: A Problem of Industry.* Beveridge pointed out that much unemployment was the result of economic forces, including cyclical fluctuations and technological change, for which the individual could not be held responsible. Since this kind of unemployment was the result of industrial factors, Beveridge argued that the cost of coping with it should be born by industry. This principle was adopted in the National Insurance Act. Unemployment became the responsibility of industry, with benefits paid from a fund based on contributions from employers and workers. Although limited at first to a few industries, the principle was later extended to others. Provision for workers in occupations not covered by the act and for those suffering from long-term unemployment was still the responsibility of the poor relief system.

Liberal doctrines of economic individualism had always recognized the special claims of those who could not be considered free agents, such as women and children. As the Liberal ministers proceeded in their investigations of industrial problems, they became aware of two kinds of workers who needed special assistance—casual laborers and workers in "sweatshop" industries, who were paid by the piece. These workers were protected neither by the factory acts nor by trade unions, nor were they covered by the National Insurance Act. Their position in a competitive job market was weak, and they could scarcely be expected to bargain for themselves.

Winston Churchill, who joined the cabinet as President of the Board of Trade in 1908, played an important part in dealing with these problems. Advised by Beveridge, Churchill obtained legislation establishing a system of labor exchanges, which served a useful purpose in helping casual workers find employment. Churchill also responded to the needs of "sweated" workers by proposing the Trade Boards Act (1909), which was vigorously supported by the women's labor movement. Under the act boards were established to set minimum wages in piecework industries such as the making of clothing.

Another example of the readiness of the Liberal government to give assistance to those who needed it, as long as the government was not expected to pay, was the Provision of Meals Act, which permitted local school authorities to provide one meal a day for school children. Thus the Liberal government preserved the principles of public economy and individual responsibility where possible, while responding to those aspects of life in an industrial society where that premise could clearly be seen to be inoperative.

The Liberals and the Lords

As the Liberal government proceeded on its course, a major point of constitutional conflict emerged—the power of the House of Lords, in which the Conservatives were strongly entrenched. The Conservatives, who had a long tradition of concern for social problems, were not strongly opposed to Liberal measures to deal with the pressing evils of industrial society. But the Conservative majority in the House of Lords rejected Liberal measures dealing with voting, schools, licensing of pubs, and other schemes dear to the hearts of certain Liberal constituencies. It was clear that other Liberal goals which were even more controversial, such as Home Rule for Ireland or disestablishment of the Anglican Church in Wales, would encounter a fight to the death in the Lords.

But the battle was fought on the question of the budget. In 1909 Lloyd George, who had succeeded Asquith as chancellor of the Exchequer, was confronted with the need to raise more revenue, both for naval rearmament and to meet the costs of social legislation. His budget included taxation which fell principally on the wealthy: a progressive income tax, increased death duties (inheritance taxes), and new taxes on land. Stung to fury by Lloyd George's anti-aristocratic and "soak the rich" pronouncements, the House of Lords rejected the budget, thus challenging the long-established doctrine that public finance was the exclusive concern of the House of Commons.

The Liberals, with Lloyd George in the vanguard, now had a popular issue with which they hoped to defeat the Conservatives. They turned to the voters for support in an election held in January, 1910. They were disappointed. Lloyd George's attack on the House of Lords may have been of some electoral benefit, but the Liberals lost heavily and became dependent on the support of the Irish Nationalists and forty Labour members. Although the peers agreed to pass the budget, the Liberals decided to seize the nettle and proposed a Parliament Bill that would curtail the powers of the upper house.

In the midst of this controversy King Edward VII died, to be succeeded by his son, George V. The accession of a new king required an election, which was held later in 1910. This election was indecisive. When the Lords tried to amend the Parliament Bill, Asquith came forward with the promise of the king to create the number of peers needed to pass the bill. In circumstances of high excitement enough Conservative peers abstained or voted for the bill to permit it to pass.

The Parliament Act of 1911 provided that the House of Lords could delay a bill for two years, but if passed in three consecutive years by the House of Commons a bill became law without consent of the Lords. Another provision of the act reduced the maximum term for elections from seven to five years. Separate legislation provided salaries for members of Parliament.

The inevitable effect of the Parliament Act was to reduce further the political power of birth and privilege and to increase the power of political parties and party leaders. Although the delaying power of the House of Lords was still important, essentially the hereditary aristocracy had followed the monarchy into a role that was more ornamental and advisory than effective.

The Empire

The Liberals brought to their countrymen overseas their historic confidence in self-government, replacing the Conservative emphasis on authority and paternalism. Many Liberals had opposed the Boer War, and their solution to the problem of South Africa was reconciliation of British and Boers, cemented by political unity in a federation. With the death of Kruger, the Boers found leaders in Louis Botha and Jan Christian Smuts who were ready to accept these principles as the basis for a political settlement. The result was the Union of South Africa, formed in 1910, which established a federal union of the Cape Colony, Natal, the Orange Free State and the Transvaal, with Botha as its first prime minister.

The major objections in Britain to the Union came from persons concerned with the future of the black population, who saw the Union as a coalition of the whites to maintain superiority over the blacks. In South Africa many of the Boers did not share the commitment of Botha and Smuts to participation in the British Empire. Both of these problems returned to haunt the Union of South Africa at a later time.

British control of India created the conditions for its own decline. The British governed India with Indian civil servants who were educated in schools that used the English language and taught British ideas of government and law. In so doing the British brought to India their ideas of liberalism and nationalism, and gave the Indians a common language in which they could communicate these ideas to each other. The predictable result was that an Indian independence movement arose, led primarily by high-caste, educated Hindus who coveted for themselves the pomp and power held by the British Raj. In 1885 the Indian National Congress was formed to seek selfgovernment within the British Empire using constitutional means. In 1907 a more radical group came to power within the Congress, demanding Swaraj (independence) and prepared to use all means to obtain it.

One problem was India's large Moslem minority, who preferred British rule to an independent government dominated by Hindus. The Moslems had not adopted British education to the extent of the Hindu leaders, but they were an important element in the Indian Army and their views had to be taken seriously.

In India, as elsewhere, the Liberal government believed that an installment of political responsibility was the best answer to nationalist movements. The Government of India Act (1909) provided for elected Indian members of the central and provincial legislative councils. Separate representation was included for Hindus and Moslems. As a further expression of good will, King George V visited India to receive the title Emperor of India. The capital of India was moved from the seething cauldron of Calcutta to the historic capital of the Mogul Empire, New Delhi. As in South Africa, these measures gave some satisfaction at first, but in the long run they whetted the appetite of nationalist leaders for more.

Ireland

As always, the nearest and most difficult problem was Ireland. Irish discontent was political, in that Irish leaders felt that they needed power to deal with Ireland's special problems. It was also social and religious, with a dominant Protestant minority facing a Catholic majority, most of whom were poor and uneducated. With passage of the Parliament Act of 1911, the way was now clear for the Liberals and their Irish Nationalist allies to pass a Home Rule Bill. The Conservatives, who could no longer rely on the blocking power of the House of Lords, fought Home Rule by appealing to public opinion. The center of resistance to Home Rule was in Ulster (northern Ireland), which was predominantly Protestant.

The Ulster Protestants formed a paramilitary body called the Ulster Volunteers, and prepared to fight to keep from being engulfed in a self-governing Ireland dominated by Catholics. Using the slogan, "Ulster will fight and Ulster will be right!" the Ulster Protestants were supported by many prominent Conservatives, who attended mass meetings in Belfast, London, and elsewhere. Efforts by the Liberal government to stop Protestant resistance met with insubordination in the army.

The Conservatives decided to make a last-ditch stand in the House of Lords, despite the Parliament Act and the Liberal-Irish Nationalist majority in the House of Commons. The Home Rule Bill was passed by the Commons in 1912 and again in 1913. Each time it was rejected by the Lords, using the delaying powers reserved by the Parliament Act. The Bill was passed for the third time in 1914, after which it became law without consent of the Lords. By that time World War I had broken out, and it was thought prudent to suspend the operation of the act. Thus in Ireland, India, and South Africa, Liberal principles of selfgovernment achieved an uneasy peace until nationalist feelings were further aroused by World War I.

Emmeline Pankhurst,
militant suffragist leader.
Corbis-Bettman.

Domestic Unrest

The partisan conflict unleashed by the controversial Liberal program was matched by other forms of public unrest. A series of strikes by the large unions—such as the miners, railway workers, Lancashire cotton workers, and London dockers—showed that the labor movement was impatient with the slow progress of collective bargaining and determined to display its strength.

The women's suffrage movement also came to a climax. Although most of the "suffragists" sought to achieve their goals by the normal means of political persuasion, a militant group called "suffragettes," led by Mrs. Emmeline Pankhurst and her daughters, Sylvia and Christabel, adopted more extreme tactics. They heckled Liberal speakers, broke windows in main shopping streets, put acid in mailboxes, and set fire to empty houses. When imprisoned they went on hunger strikes, and their jailers resorted to forced feeding.

The Liberals believed in the rule of reason, and their reluctant and ineffectual efforts to use coercion against Ulster Protestants, strikers, or suffragettes made them look weak and foolish. It appeared as if the political system was becoming less able to resolve major issues by the established methods of persuasion and voting.

THE ROAD TO WAR

Alliances

The greatest failure of leadership was not at home. It was the failure of European diplomacy to resolve the rivalries and fears of the major European states that eventually led to war. The core problem was the power of unified Germany, which grew rapidly economically and maintained large and efficient ground forces. In 1890 Otto von Bismarck, "the Iron Chancellor" who had led in the unification of Germany, was dismissed by the Emperor William II, a grandson of Queen Victoria. A vain and impulsive man, the Emperor abandoned Bismarck's quest for stability and set out to make Germany the dominant power of Europe. His unpredictability drew France and Russia closer together, while the Germans claimed that they were "encircled" and clung more tightly to Austria-Hungary, their only reliable ally. Britain, feeling threatened in a Europe of alliances, began looking for friends. The age of "splendid isolation" was drawing to its close.

When Salisbury retired in 1902 the Conservative government, now led by Arthur Balfour, abandoned hope of good relations with Germany, turning instead to France. The result was an *entente* (understanding) with France in 1904, which was an agreement to resolve old differences and maintain friendly relations. The entente was not an alliance and was not specifically directed against Germany or any other power, but it led to Anglo-French military conversations dealing with cooperation if war should break out in Europe.

The French, who had an alliance with Russia, worked zealously to bring their two friends together. After Russia was defeated in the Russo-Japanese War (1904–1905) by Britain's ally, Japan, the Russians became more amenable to that idea. The Revolution of 1905 set that great empire in the direction of constitutional government, and that made an entente more acceptable in Britain. In 1907 Britain and Russia came to an agreement that resolved their imperial conflicts in Persia (Iran) and Afghanistan, thus forming the Triple Entente of France, Russia, and Britain. Since the German-Austrian alliance nominally included Italy, they were called the Central Powers or the Triple Alliance.

From the British perspective the greatest danger was the naval rivalry with Germany. It was a commonplace of the time that seapower was a vital factor in national power, and Germany, already the strongest land power in Europe, began building a strong navy. The British could see only one reason for such a fleet—to threaten Britain in the North Sea and the English Channel, and eventually to mount a challenge in the realms of trade and colonies.

The Liberal government responded with an ambitious naval building program, an undertaking made more necessary by changes in naval technology and design that made much of the Royal Navy obsolete. The question of seapower, which was vital to Britain but of secondary importance to Germany, did more than anything else to poison relations between the two countries and keep Britain firmly in the camp of the Triple Entente.

The British Army remained small and was composed of career soldiers. It was light and mobile, for it was stationed mainly in the colonies and had been developed to police the empire and deal with the natives. Under the Liberals the Army was thoroughly reorganized to give it firm central command, improved organization and weaponry, and better discipline. A small cluster of airplanes for reconnaisance marked the beginning of British airpower. It was clear that British ground forces could not cope with the powerful German army, but Britain did not intend to get involved in a major land war in Europe.

The Outbreak of War

World War I was preceded by a series of preliminary conflicts. In 1908 Austria-Hungary, supported by Germany, annexed the province of Bosnia, thus provoking violent protests from Serbian nationalists, who viewed Bosnia as an important part of the greater Serbia that they sought to achieve. In 1911 Britain and France stood together to protect the French position in Morocco against German threats. In 1912 and again in 1913 wars broke out in the Balkans, and finally another Balkan crisis led to the outbreak of general war.

On June, 28, 1914, the Archduke Franz Ferdinand, heir to the Austro-Hungarian monarchy, visited Sarajevo, capital of Bosnia, where he was assassinated by Serbian nationalists. The Austrians were determined to make an example of Serbia, and they issued an ultimatum that was soon followed by a declaration of war. The Serbians turned to their allies, the Russians, who decided that support of Serbia was essential to their influence among their "little Slavic brothers" in the Balkans. They began mobilizing their vast, unwieldy army.

The Germans gave full support to Austria-Hungary, which was their only reliable ally. The French felt it essential to support the Russians, thus confronting Germany and Austria with a two-front war. At this point military considerations overrode the possibility of a diplomatic resolution of the crisis. The German military strategy was to strike hard at France first, relying on the slow Russian mobilization to give them time to defeat the French before turning eastward to meet the Russians. Thus, every day given the Russians to mobilize was a day lost on the western front. When the Russians refused to stop their mobilization, the Germans attacked France through Belgium, the most feasible route. World War I had begun.

Britain and the Crisis

The Liberal government was deeply divided as it faced the mounting European crisis. The ententes with France and Russia were not alliances, and the conversations between British and French military staffs carried no formal obligations. Britain had one clear commitment—a guarantee of Belgian neutrality made in 1839.

However, as the crisis unfolded Britain had a larger concern—the possibility that the European continent might be dominated by one power, as in the days of Philip II of Spain, Louis XIV of France, or Napoleon. Germany's modern navy, which threatened the security of the island nation, aggravated the threat. Beyond these strategic considerations lay the Liberal belief in international law, which appeared to be threatened more by Germany than by any other power.

The hazards of war were great. Economically, Britain and Germany had become important trading partners, and these profitable relations were threatened. London was the world center of banking and finance, which would be totally disrupted. War might stimulate labor unrest at home and nationalist agitation in Ireland. The Liberal agenda of political and social reform would have to be suspended. The support of the empire for a land war in Europe was doubtful. Germany might be victorious, and Britain's opportunity to serve as a neutral peacemaker would be lost.

The German attack on Belgium settled the matter, for it invoked the British guarantee. At this point, Britain declared war. When Sir Edward Grey, Foreign Secretary, was called upon to explain the policy of his government he used such arguments as national honor, the sanctity of treaties, the balance of power, and international law. Although these noble words undoubtedly concealed a good deal of muddle, there is reason to believe that in his mind, and in the minds of his countrymen, those concepts were worth fighting for.

SUGGESTIONS FOR FURTHER READING

In addition to books cited in the previous chapters, good general books are Peter Stansky, *England since 1867: Continuity and Change* (1973); Keith Robbins, *The Eclipse of a Great Power: Modern Britain, 1870–1975* (1994); Martin Pugh, *State and Society: British Political and Social History, 1870–1992* (1994); and J. F. C. Harrison, *Late Victorian Britain, 1875–1901* (1990).

On foreign policy, Bernard Porter provides a broad introduction in *Britain, Europe, and the World, 1850–1986: Delusions of Grandeur* (1987). Another useful work is *British Foreign Secretaries and Foreign Policy: From the Crimean War to the First World War* (1986). Relevant books cited in chapter 13 are by Chamberlain, Hayes, Bartlett, and Bourne. See also Michael L. Dockrill, *Diplomacy and World Power: Studies in British Foreign Policy, 1890–1950* (1996). For the armed service see Kennedy, Barnett, and Farwell, cited above.

Introductions to political history are Bernard Porter, *Britannia's Burden: The Political Evolution of Modern Britain, 1851–1990* (1994); Brian H. Harrison, *The Transformation of British Politics, 1860–1995* (1996); Malcolm Pearce, *British Political History, 1867–1995* (1996); and Peter Clark, *A Question of Leadership: Gladstone to Thatcher* (1991). The growing importance of political parties is examined in T. A. Jenkins, *Party, Parliament, and Politics in Victorian Britain* (1996). Among the studies of individual parties are Chris Cook, *A Short History of the Liberal Party, 1900–1976* (1976); Michael Bentley, *The Climax of Liberal Politics: British Liberalism in Theory and Practice, 1868–1918* (1987); and G. R. Searle, *The Liberal Party: Triumph and Disintegration, 1886–1929* (1992). For the Conservative Party see Martin Pugh, *The Tories and the People, 1880–1935* (1985). Other aspects of the political process are discussed in Henry Pelling, *Popular Politics and Society in Late Victorian Britain* (1979); John Belchem, *Class, Party, and the Political System in Britain, 1867–1914* (1990); Paul Adelman, *Victorian Radicalism: The Middle-Class Experience, 1830–1944* (1984); and Andrew Adonis, *Making Aristocracy Work: The Peerage in the Political System in Britain, 1884–1914* (1993).

The standard works on British economic history in this period and after are William Ashworth, *An Economic History of England, 1870–1939* (1972) and several works by Sidney Pollard, including *Britain's Prime and Britain's Decline, The British Economy, 1870–1914* (1989). The role of labor is covered in E. H. Hunt, *British Labour History, 1815–1914* (1981) and David Kynaston, *King Labour: the British Working Class, 1850–1914* (1976). David Powell considers *British Politics and the Labour Question, 1868–1990* (1992).

On social history, books cited in chapters 13 and 14 that continue to be relevant are *The Cambridge Social History of Britain;* Perkin, *Origins;* Laybourn, *Evolution;* and Thompson, *Respectable Society.* David Cannadine, *The Decline and Fall of the British Aristocracy* (1996) is important and fresh. See also W. D. Rubinstein, *Elites and the Wealthy in Modern British History* (1987). Harold Perkin covers a major development in *The Rise of Professional Society: England Since 1880* (1989). Mark Girouard's books on life in the Victorian country house, cited in chapter 14 are delightful. Girouard has also written *The English Town: A History of Urban Life* (1990). See also Donald Olsen, *The City as a Work of Art: London, Paris, Vienna* (1986). Standish Meacham, *A Life Apart: The English Working Class, 1890–1914* (1977). Growing public concern with the problems of the working class is brought out in Herman Ausubel, *In Hard Times: Reformers among the Late Victorians* (1973).

For religious history some of the books cited in previous chapters are relevant to the late Victorian period. A major social reform movement is traced in Lilian L. Shiman, *Crusade Against Drink in Victorian England* (1988). Important intellectual changes are presented in Heyck, *The Transformation of Intellectual Life* (cited in chapter 14) and Reba Soffer, *Ethics and Society in England: The Revolution in the Social Sciences, 1870–1914* (1978). For a different, but no less important presentation of late Victorian ideas, see Hesketh Pearson, *Gilbert and Sullivan: A Biography* (1935) and Leslie Baily, *Gilbert and Sullivan and their Victorian World* (1976).

In addition to books about women cited earlier, see also Patricia Jalland, *Women, Marriage and Politics, 1860–1914* (1988); Constance Rover, *Women's Suffrage and Party Politics in Britain, 1866–1914* (1967); Patricia Hollis, *Ladies Elect: Women in English Local Government, 1865–1914* (1987); and Lilian L. Shiman, *Women and Leadership in Nineteenth-Century England* (1992). A good survey of changes in the lives of women is Jane Lewis, *Women in England, 1870–1950: Sexual Divisions and Social Change* (1985). Lewis has also edited a collection of essays entitled *Labour and Love: Women's Experience of Home and Family, 1850–1940* (1986).

Useful general histories of Scotland (cited in chapter 13) are by Ferguson and Smout. Additional works are I. G. C. Hutchison, *A Political History of Scotland, 1832–1924: Parties, Elections, and Issues* (1986), and Olive Checkland, *Industry and Ethos: Scotland, 1832–1914* (1989).

Trevor Lloyd's history of the empire (cited chapter 13) is a good place to begin. For the international perspective of "the new imperialism" see William L. Langer, *The Diplomacy of Imperialism: 1890–1902* (1950). C. C. Eldridge, *Victorian Imperialism* (1978) gives a general overview as does Max Beloff, *Imperial Sunset. Vol. I: Britain's Liberal Empire, 1897–1921* (1970). James Morris, *Pax Britannica* (1980) examines the empire at its height. A good survey is Bernard Porter, *The Lion's Share: A Short History of British Imperialism, 1850–1983* (1996). The debate over imperialism is discussed in A. P. Thornton, *The Imperial Idea and its Enemies: A Study in British Power* (1959). See also C. J. Lowe, *The Reluctant Imperialists, 1870–1902* (1969). C. C. Eldridge explores *England's Mission: The Imperial Idea in the Age of Gladstone and Disraeli, 1868–1880* (1973). Lance E. Davis and Robert Huttenback make an economic assessment of the empire in *Mammon and the Pursuit of Empire: The Political Economy of British Imperialism, 1860–1912* (1986). Differing interpretations of imperialism are reviewed in Robin Winks, *British Imperialism: God, Gold, Glory* (1963). Ronald Robinson, John Gallagher, and Alice Denny discuss Victorian ideas of empire in *Africa and the Victorians* (1961) and D. M. Schreuder examines *The Scramble for Southern Africa, 1877–1895* (1980). Byron Farwell explains *The Great Anglo-Boer War* (1976).

Biographies cited in chapter 14 that apply to this chapter are Longford and Weintraub on Queen Victoria and Stansky, *Gladstone*. A major figure of the late Victorian period is presented by Aubrey L. Kennedy in *Salisbury, 1830–1903: Portrait of a Statesman* (1971). See also Peter Marsh, *The Discipline of Popular Government: Lord Salisbury's Domestic Statecraft, 1881–1902* (1978). Salisbury's foreign policy is examined in John A. S. Grenville, *Lord Salisbury and Foreign Policy: The Close of the Nineteenth Century* (1964), and in C. H. D. Howard, *Spendid Isolation: A Study of Ideas Concerning Britain's International Position and Foreign Policy during the later Years of the Third Marquis of Salisbury* (1967). Joseph Chamberlain is examined by Peter Marsh in *Joseph Chamberlain: Entrepreneur in Politics* (1994). Good biographies of Rhodes that strip away the mythology are Brian Roberts, *Cecil Rhodes: "Flawed Colossus"* (1988) and Robert I. Rotberg, *The Founder: Cecil Rhodes and the Pursuit of Power* (1988).

Entering the twentieth century, a good guide is Alfred F. Havighurst, *Britain in Transition: The Twentieth Century* (4th ed., 1985). A general textbook is Trevor Lloyd, *Empire to Welfare State, English History, 1906–1992* (1993). The growing role of government is traced in James E. Cronin, *The Politics of State Expansion: War, State, and Society in Twentieth-Century Britain* (1991). Political leadership is featured in J. P. Mackintosh, *Prime Ministers in the Twentieth Century* (1977). The challenge to the Conservative Party is presented in Frans Coetzee, *For Party or Country: Nationalism and the Dilemmas of Popular Conservatism in Edwardian England* (1990) and Gregory D. Phillips, *The Diehards: Aristocratic Society and Politics in Edwardian England* (1979). The origins of the Labour Party can be followed in Henry Pelling and Alastair J. Reid, *Short History of the Labour Party* (1996) and Keith Laybourn, *The Rise of Labour: The British Labour Party, 1890–1979* (1988). See also Laybourn, *The Rise of Socialism in Britain, c. 1881–1951* (1997).

The foundations of "the New Liberalism" are examined in George L. Bernstein, *Liberalism and Liberal Politics in Edwardian England* (1986) and David Brooks, *The Age of Upheaval: Edwardian Politics, 1899–1914* (1995). A key feature of "the new Liberalism" is detailed in Bentley B. Gilbert, *The Evolution of National Insurance in Great Britain: The Origins of the Welfare State* (1966). Another important aspect is discussed in James Schmiechen, *Sweated Industries and Sweated Labor: The London Clothing Trades, 1860–1914* (1984). For the women's movement, see David H. J. Morgan, *Suffragists and Liberals: The Politics of Woman Suffrage in England* (1975) and Sandra S. Holton, *Feminism and Democracy: Women's Suffrage and Reform Politics in Britain, 1900–1918* (1986). Roger Fulford, *Votes for Women* (1957), is a lively account. David Powell attempts to pull things together in *The Edwardian Crisis: Britain, 1901–14* (1996). Jonathan Rose defines *The Edwardian Temperament, 1895–1919* (1986). J. B. Priestley provides an interesting overview in *The Edwardians* (1970). A stimulating but controversial work is George Dangerfield's, *The Strange Death of Liberal England* (repr. 1980). Samuel Hynes tries to identify *The Edwardian Turn of Mind* (1968).

At the turn of the century, the problem of Ireland reached one of its periodic crises. General books by Beckett, McCaffrey, and Foster (cited in chapter 13) continue to be useful. David G. Boyce discusses *The Irish Question and British Politics, 1868–1996* (1996) and *Nationalism in Ireland* (1991). Nicholas Mansergh, *The Irish Question, 1840–1921* (1975) is authoritative. See also F. S. L. Lyons, *Ireland Since the Famine* (1985), *Parnell* (1991), and *Culture and Anarchy in Ireland, 1890–1939* (1979). Other useful works are Thomas W. Heyck, *The Dimensions of British Radicalism: The Case of Ireland, 1874–95* (1974), Conor Cruise O'Brien, *Parnell and His Party, 1880–1890* (1964), and Patricia Jalland, *The Liberals and Ireland: The Ulster Question in British Politics to 1914* (1980). Britain's complex and disappointing relationship with South Africa is traced in Nicholas Mansergh, *South Africa, 1906–1961: The Price of Magnanimity* (1962).

There is a vast literature on the coming of World War I. British foreign policy relating to the war is explored in Cedric J. Lowe and M. L. Dockrill, *The Mirage of Power: British Foreign Policy, 1902–1922* (1972) and George W. Monger, *The End of Isolation: British Foreign Policy, 1900–1914* (1976). A readable brief account is Laurence Lafore, *The Long Fuse: An Interpretation of the Origins of World War I* (1992). Two books by Barbara Tuchman tell vividly the tale of the march to disaster: *The Proud Tower: A Portrait of the World before the War, 1890–1914* (1966) and *The Guns of August* (1994). See also Paul Kennedy, *The Rise of Anglo-German Antagonism, 1860–1914* (1980).

Important biographies for the early twentieth century are Philip Magnus, *King Edward the Seventh* (1964) and Keith Middlemas, *The Life and Times of Edward the Seventh* (1972); Ruddock F. MacKay, *Balfour: Intellectual Statesman* (1985); John Wilson, *CB: A Life of Sir Henry Campbell-Bannerman* (1973); Richard Jay, *Joseph Chamberlain: A Political Study* (1981); Roy Jenkins, *Asquith: Portrait of a Man and an Era* (1965); Stephen Koss, *Asquith* (1976); Keith Robbins, *Sir Edward Grey* (1971); John Grigg, *The People's Champion, 1902–1911* (1978); Bentley B. Gilbert, *David Lloyd George: A Political Life: The Architecht of Change, 1863–1912* (1987); Kenneth O. Morgan, *David Lloyd George* (1981); and *Keir Hardie: Radical and Socialist* (1975). Additional biographies of Lloyd George and Winston Churchill are cited in chapter 16.

CHAPTER SIXTEEN

An Era of World Wars
1914–1945

The First World War was a cataclysm that devoured Europe. The great empires of the East—Germany, Austria-Hungary, Russia, and the Ottoman Empire—collapsed, setting off radical and nationalist revolutions. France was deeply wounded: two decades later it had not recovered sufficiently to stand up against a resurgent Germany under Adolph Hitler. Italy, politically and economically weak, floundered during the war and shortly thereafter came under the control of the first of the fascist dictators, Benito Mussolini.

Britain created the largest army in its history and mobilized its industry to produce unprecedented quantities of military supplies. It sacrificed large numbers of ships and seamen to German submarines, and devoted extensive overseas investments to the insatiable financial demands of war in an industrial society. The war took millions of lives and intensified old problems while creating new ones. There was little pride or joy in a victory of exhaustion, and twenty years later Britain had to fight again, under much less favorable auspices.

THE FIRST WORLD WAR

A War of Attrition

When Germany attacked France through Belgium in August, 1914 the nations of Europe expected a short war: either a quick German victory over France and Russia (as the Germans planned), or an Allied check to the German advance, followed by a peace conference. Britain sent a small expeditionary force to France to bolster the French forces and ordered its fleet to bottle up the the German fleet, thus keeping the Channel and the sea lanes open.

The Germans found they had taken on more than they could handle. British and French forces stopped the German juggernaut at the Marne River and at Ypres in Belgium. In the meantime the Russians, utilizing the railroads which had been built in the previous decade, were able to mobilize more quickly than the Germans had anticipated. When Russian forces threatened the homeland of the German officer class in Prussia, the Germans were compelled to shift forces to the Eastern Front, weakening their attack sufficiently to enable the Allied lines to hold. In the West, both sides began digging trenches that eventually stretched from the Channel coast to the Swiss border. While the Germans were annihilating vast Russian forces in a war of movement in the east, stalemate set in on the Western Front.

By 1915 the leaders of the combatant states had two choices: a compromise peace or vast, desperate efforts for victory. They chose the latter. They raised mass armies and devoted the resources of industrial production to supplying them. Britain sent the Territorial Army, the equivalent of the American National Guard, into the trenches and began recruiting a large volunteer army.

Lacking room for maneuver and without the mobility of World War II, generals on both sides made desperate efforts to break through the trenches, taking frightful losses to no effect. Until the fighting ended in November, 1918, fruitless attacks came one after another—deafening artillery barrages followed by mass infantry assaults through barbed wire and minefields. Machine-guns chattered their deadly refrain and the crunch of mortar shells sounded among the troops rushing across No-Man's Land. Surviving attackers who leaped with bayonets into the trenches to grapple face-to-face with the enemy rarely accomplished much—at best the other army was pushed back a few miles into a new line of trenches. When Germany finally cracked in 1918 after four years of attrition, the battle lines had changed very little in the West, although eastern Europe and the Middle East had fallen into chaos.

The Western Front devoured a generation. The British armed forces swallowed up nearly six million men, a third of the male population between their teens and mid-forties. In 1916 the Asquith government ordered conscription of military-aged men when volunteers proved too few to satisfy the voracious appetite of the Western Front. The war cost the lives of nearly 750,000 British fighting men—more than had been killed in all Britain's previous wars combined. The empire sacrificed another 200,000 lives. Thousands more were permanently crippled by wounds, poison gas, or mental breakdown.

Politicians and diplomats, unwilling to admit the disaster into which they had led their nations, and generals determined to have victory at all costs, looked vainly for alternatives that would preserve their reputations. The British public, as in other belligerent nations, was whipped to fury by national pride and tales of enemy atrocities. Few generals on either side gained distinction as strategists, for all believed in the efficacy of the offensive when modern weapons had given the advantage to the defensive.

Sir Douglas Haig, who from 1915 commanded the British Expeditionary Force, was a cavalryman like many British generals. Hoping for a breakthrough followed by a cavalry charge, Haig kept thousands of horses behind the front, eating vast quantities of hay. Seeking an alternative to head-on offensives that got nowhere, Winston Churchill at the Admiralty organized an attack on the Turks at the Dardanelles, hoping to come to the assistance of the Russians by that route. Despite the sacrifices of thousands of Australian and New Zealand soldiers on the beaches of Gallipoli, this venture also ended in failure. Churchill was made the scapegoat and driven from office.

The only major battle between the British and German fleets, near Jutland in 1916, was indecisive. Britain retained control of the seas and the German surface fleet was no longer a factor in the war. Both sides used seapower for economic war: the British with their characteristic blockade of a European land enemy, and the Germans with a new and deadly weapon—the submarine.

New weapons changed warfare: the first extensive use of the deadly machine gun; poison gas, which was as dangerous to the user as the intended victim; the tank and the airplane, became effective only near the end of the war. Britain and France persuaded Italy to enter the war on the Allied side in 1915, a step that led to savage battles with the Austrians in the north of Italy.

The Germans incited the Irish to rebel; the British incited the Arabs to rise against the Ottoman Empire of the Turks. Even as the Russian Empire was collapsing on the Eastern Front, the United States, under President Woodrow Wilson, entered the war in the West, bringing new fighting forces and economic resources that eventually tipped the balance.

War Socialism

World War I was a conflict of industrial power as much as military power, and the home front had to be organized to manufacture and transport enormous quantities of military supplies. Slowly and reluctantly the Liberal government, with the cooperation of businessmen and the trade unions, created a kind of war socialism in which the government controlled finance, trade, industry, and labor to meet the needs of the war. Sinkings of British ships by German submarines led to shortages of food, inflated food prices, long queues of shoppers, and in 1918 loosely enforced rationing of meat and other scarce foods.

Military victory seemed more important than the peacetime principles that had guarded property rights and personal liberties. The government ac-

British troops going into the trenches in France, 1917. Corbis-Bettmann.

quired sweeping discretionary powers under the Defence of the Realm Act, personified as the meddlesome Aunt DORA. Industry was called upon to supply vast quantities of military equipment such as rifles, gas masks, and munitions. In 1914 the British army had approximately 1,300 machine guns; over the next four years it acquired an additional 240,000. Government arsenals and private contractors could produce only a fraction of the needed armaments. The government set up a special Ministry of Munitions which built large new factories employing more than a million workers. War socialism eventually brought victory. Its success helped undermine the cult of laissez-faire and inspired a new faith in centralized planning and government by experts.

Wartime Political Leadership

In 1914 the Liberals and the Conservatives had an equal number of seats in the House of Commons, but with Labour and Irish support the Liberals controlled the government. Politically, the situation was anomalous. The Liberal government was responsible for conducting the war, but the Liberal Party and its Labour and Irish allies had the most critics and doubters. The Conservative opposition was the most nationalistic and strongly supported the war. Herbert

Asquith, the Liberal prime minister, found it desirable to bring some of the Conservative leaders into his Cabinet. Lloyd George, the Cabinet's most dynamic leader, was put in charge of the Ministry of Munitions.

As the war dragged on, Asquith was increasingly criticized by the press, the public, and his own colleagues. In 1916 Lloyd George intrigued with the Conservatives and some of his Liberal colleagues to force Asquith to resign. Lloyd George then became prime minister, largely with Conservative support. The majority of the Liberals were bitter at Lloyd George's treatment of Asquith and his apparent lack of principles. The new prime minister became one of Britain's greatest war leaders. He was prepared to marshall the full human and material resources of the nation to win the war. The Conservatives who had hated Lloyd George for his domestic policies, supported the quick-witted Welshman when he identified himself with a military policy of decisive victory and abandoned his schemes of domestic reform.

Lloyd George had the self-confidence to surround himself with talented and independent-minded men and women. He had great personal charm and a genius for arousing enthusiasm. He was also a master of political and personal manipulation. He insisted on action in the stuffy and hidebound administrative departments, and he created new administrative structures where needed. He was a master of improvisation, a pragmatic solver of crises, and a man of compromises who worried little about consistency. He was also a man with a great zest for life, including an abundant love life, which he managed to keep secret despite his place at the center of public affairs.

Under the traditional system, government policy was shaped by a Cabinet comprised of approximately twenty men, nearly all of them burdened with departmental administration. Lloyd George established a type of democratic dictatorship, headed by himself and supported by a War Cabinet of five or so men, most of whom were freed from departmental duties that would distract them from high policy. In 1917 Lloyd George brought Winston Churchill, his former Liberal colleague back into office as Minister of Munitions. He also recognized the importance of Labor Party support and gave its leader, Arthur Henderson, a seat in the War Cabinet. Ramsay MacDonald, one of the founders and leading figures in the Labour Party, resigned his leadership post in 1914 in opposition to the war, but he found few supporters within his party.

Victory

By the time Lloyd George took charge, the contending armies were locked in a mighty struggle to the death. The Germans hoped that submarine warfare would knock Britain out, and even dropped a few bombs on London. Britain relied on the blockade to deprive Germany of the materials needed to wage industrialized warfare. In 1917, the British army launched a vast offensive in Belgium that failed after suffering 400,000 casualties. In the meantime, Russia was engulfed in revolution and dropped out of the war, enabling the Germans to concentrate their forces on the Western Front. Earlier that year, the United States entered the war and began building a mass army to come to the aid of the Allies.

American involvement in the war tipped the balance, as fresh young American bodies entered the trenches and American supplies poured into Britain and France. Early in 1918 the Germans launched their last great offensive and failed. The Allies counterattacked, and the German army crumbled. The Austrian and Ottoman empires collapsed, and a revolution in Berlin forced the Kaiser to abdicate. The new government sued for an armistice, and on November 11, 1918, the guns stopped firing. Mercifully, the killing was over.

SOCIAL CONSEQUENCES OF THE WAR

The Labor Shortage

The war brought about great changes in the lives of women. The growth of the labor force and the dwindling number of available men gave women opportunities to enter jobs previously closed to them. Employers who hired women paid them about half the wages earned by men who did the same work. About 800,000 additional women worked in industry, another 250,000 in farming, and 100,000 in transport. Offices and retail shops offered women jobs with greater permanence. About 200,000 women took jobs in government offices and more than twice this number worked in private offices. Hundreds of thousands became retail sales clerks.

Domestic service, which had been the most important form of employment open to women, declined greatly as women found better opportunities. The role of women in the war helped change the minds of former opponents of women's suffrage. Wartime life also gave women much more personal freedom, since they had money of their own and freer social contacts at work and elsewhere.

The scarcity of labor compelled the government to court the working class. Labour Party leaders were included in the wartime coalition governments and grievance boards were created on which union leaders served with management. Employers competed for workers, not only with higher wages but by providing amenities such as canteens that served inexpensive hot food. Strikes took place despite these gestures. Senior trade union officials usually cooperated with the government but shop stewards, who combined ordinary employment with local union responsibilities, gave disgruntled workers militant leadership. The discontent of the industrial workers was not ideological but grew out of local grievances such as high rents and a sense that the opportunity to advance their interests should not be missed.

The introduction of many new people into the labor force, including women, aroused the concern of established workers, who felt their jobs and established work rules were at stake. Trade unions threatened to strike to keep out anyone who had not performed the normal apprenticeship, which would have barred most available men and virtually all women. The government persuaded the trade unions to accept the wartime dilution of skilled workers with the unskilled by promising that the practice would be temporary. In fact, unskilled and semiskilled workers remained numerically dominant and their wages rose more than the wages of skilled craftsmen.

Wartime Morale

During the war some of the old distinctions in the class structure became blurred. Before the war only the upper and middle classes had paid income tax, but during the war the better-off workers paid too. The scarcity of domestic servants forced many middle-class families to do their own cooking and cleaning, and made it virtually impossible for the aristocracy to maintain their great stately homes and former elaborate lifestyles.

To stimulate cooperation with its war policies, the government combined propaganda with censorship. As public radio broadcasting did not exist, the mass circulation newspapers exerted the greatest influence, showing their support for democracy by debasing the fund of knowledge and reason upon which democracy depends. The newspapers depicted the Germans as a subhuman race which threatened Western Civilization—cruel Huns who executed innocent civilians, raped women, and tossed babies onto their bayonets. The royal family, which traced its ancestry to George I, patriotically changed its name to Windsor, an example followed by many others with German names. Those who opposed the war were stigmatized as traitors. As the war dragged on and the casualty lists lengthened, the initial enthusiasm for the war was replaced by a dogged determination.

A minority rejected the official propaganda. Many who supported the war disliked conscription, and sentiment in favor of a compromise peace grew in the Labour Party. To justify terrible military losses and the sacrifices of civilians the government promised great rewards after the victory was won: national security, social justice, an enduring peace, and a better world. When peace came the government lacked the will and perhaps the ability to honor its commitments. The people considered themselves cheated and there was widespread cynicism about politicians and skepticism about the war.

Underlying particular complaints were doubts about the old beliefs in the basic goodness of man and a universe ruled with justice and compassion. The intellectuals were the most openly shaken as they considered the holocaust created by nations that had counted themselves as centers of civilization, but their disillusionment spread in less visible ways into the general public.

Lloyd George and the Peace

The Lloyd George Coalition

As soon as possible after the war ended Lloyd George called an election to capitalize on the glories of victory and give him a strong political base for his role in the peace settlement. The sacrifices of war, in the trenches and at home, were rewarded by the Representation of the People Act (1918), which removed virtually all restrictions on the vote for adult males and gave the vote to women over thirty, although it was primarily younger women who had served in the factories and on the farms. Lloyd George and the Conservative leader, Andrew Bonar Law, agreed to continue their wartime cooperation by not opposing each other's candidates.

Lloyd George pulled out all the stops in using his talents for demagoguery, uttering cries of "Hang the Kaiser" and "make Germany pay." He promised to make Britain "a land fit for heroes." The Liberals split. Those who did not support Lloyd George did not receive the endorsement ("coupon") given to the candidates of the coalition government. The Labour Party left the coalition and for the first time appeared as an independent major party, adopting a socialist platform written by Sidney Webb. The election was the first in which women voted, but their votes do not seem to have affected the outcome.

The election was a landslide victory for the Lloyd George coalition government, but most of Lloyd George's supporters in the new House of Commons were Conservatives. The Labour Party came in second, even though its socialist platform was objectionable to many of its working-class supporters. The Irish Nationalists virtually disappeared, since most of the Irish M.P.s were advocates of an independent Ireland and refused to take their seats. The Liberal Party, led by Asquith, lost heavily and ceased to be a major political force. The war and Lloyd George had destroyed the great Liberal Party, with its commitment to limited government, popular democracy, personal freedom, free trade, and a humane but nonsocialist approach to social problems.

The Versailles Settlement

The Peace Conference met at Versailles, outside Paris, and here Lloyd George's talents as a problem-solver and mediator were taxed to the fullest. The American president, Woodrow Wilson, came to Versailles with idealistic visions of democracy, national self-determination, and international cooperation which he naively thought applied to a Europe fallen into chaos and drenched in blood. The French, on the other hand, were primarily concerned to prevent a revival of German military power and were determined to make Germany pay their massive cost of rebuilding. Despite his election rhetoric, Lloyd George attempted to be a mediator between the two points of view. A stable Europe and a prosperous Germany were important to the British economy, but Britain also had to make certain that the sacrifices of war were not in vain.

The Peace of Versailles left Germany intact, although France regained Alsace-Lorraine and German territory was given to Poland to provide an outlet to the sea. At the insistence of France, heavy reparations were imposed on Germany, not only to pay for the cost of rebuilding, but to drain the German economy for years to come. Germany was limited to a small army, and the German border with France could not be fortified. Britain insisted that the German navy be drastically reduced. Germany lost its colonies, including strategic islands in the Pacific, which were given to the victorious powers as mandates of the League of Nations.

The collapse of the Russian and Austro-Hungarian empires led to the establishment of quarrelsome, unstable states in eastern Europe. By this time Russia had come under the control of Lenin and the Bolsheviks, who carried out a violent revolution that shocked Europe and proclaimed itself a model for proletarian revolutions elsewhere. The fall of the Ottoman Empire set the Arab world ablaze. Britain took over the administration of Iraq, Palestine, and Jordan and continued its control of Egypt and Suez, thus accepting a role in the Middle East that led to endless trouble.

Prior to the war, a movement called Zionism had emerged that called for establishment of a Jewish state in Palestine with its capital in Jerusalem. In 1917 Britain, in order to win the support of the Zionists, issued the Balfour Declaration, which stated British approval of a Jewish national "home" in Palestine as long as the rights of the Arabs were respected. This principle was also incorporated into the peace settlement and became the legal basis for Jewish immigration into Palestine.

Woodrow Wilson salvaged something with the establishment of the League of Nations, but the U.S. Senate rejected the Versailles Treaty and refused to join the League. Public approval of the idea of the League was strong in Britain, which for the next twenty years was its strongest supporter. Not trusting the League, France wanted an alliance with Britain and the United States to provide security against a German resurgence. When the United States rejected the Triple Guarantee, Britain also refused to go along. The French, left alone and fearful, made alliances with Poland, Rumania, and Yugoslavia, to have some support against a revival of German militarism.

Concerned at Japanese imperialist designs on China, the United States insisted that Britain abandon its alliance with Japan. At the Washington Naval Conference of 1920–1921 Britain accepted naval parity with the United States, which left Australia, New Zealand, its East Asian colonies, and the Pacific Ocean to American protection. Britain still had important commercial and imperial interests throughout the world but no longer had the strength to defend them.

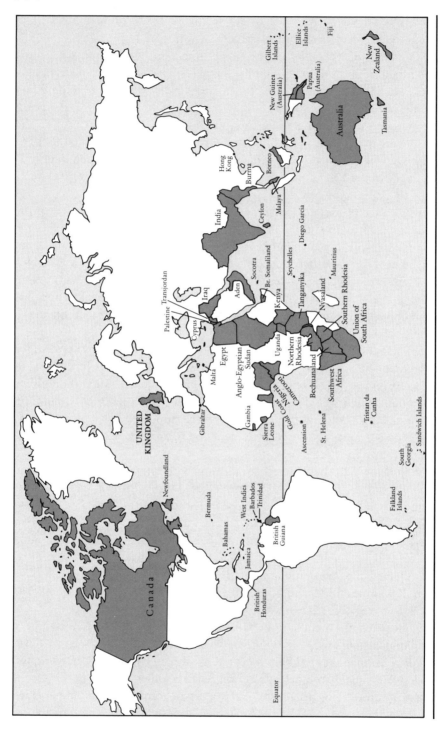

The British Empire after World War I

The Empire

The state of the British empire illustrated the contrast between the appearance of power and the reality of long-term decline. The white-dominated selfgoverning dominions—Canada, Australia, New Zealand, South Africa—had supported the mother country in the war with soldiers, money, and supplies. Some Britons hoped that wartime unity foreshadowed greater political and economic cooperation in the postwar world. Instead, the dominions emerged as fully independent nations tied to Britain only by bonds of sentiment and tradition. In 1926 an imperial conference described the United Kingdom and the dominions as "autonomous communities within the British Empire, equal in status, in no way subordinate to one another." In the Statute of Westminster (1931) Parliament renounced its legislative authority over the dominions.

A different situation existed in the parts of the empire with populations that did not have long experience in self-government. Here small educated elites sought political power for themselves by using the rhetoric of freedom and democracy. In India the Congress Party, comprised almost entirely of educated Hindus, came under the leadership of Mohandas K. Gandhi, who won the support of the Hindu peasants by his ascetic lifestyle and appeals to native traditions of selfsufficiency.

The goal of the Congress Party was independence (Swaraj), which Gandhi sought to achieve by nonviolent civil disobedience, such as boycotts of British goods, violations of the salt monopoly, refusal to pay taxes, and hunger strikes. Despite Gandhi's commitment to nonviolence, violence broke out frequently. In 1919 soldiers of the Indian army fired on demonstrators at Amritsar, which provided the Congress leaders with martyrs and a British atrocity that could be used to arouse Indian public opinion.

A major problem in India was antagonism between the Hindus and the Moslem minority, for the Moslems preferred British rule to domination by the Hindus in an independent India. The Moslems, who were numerous in the Indian army, formed the Moslem League to protect their interests. The Government of India Act (1919) sought to satisfy Indian leaders by increasing Indian participation in government, but by this time moderation and slow progress were unacceptable to the Congress Party and resistance to British rule continued.

The Irish Crisis

World War I brought to a head the long-simmering problems of Ireland, heightened by the ideals of national selfdetermination espoused by Woodrow Wilson at the Versailles Conference. The Irish sense of nationalism was strengthened by the movement that called itself Sinn Fein, which fostered interest in the

General Post Office, Dublin. Site of the Easter Rising. Private collection.

Gaelic language, Irish history and culture, and modern Irish poets and play-wrights. As always, Irish nationalism was opposed by Ulster Protestants who, like the Moslems in India, did not favor independence that would put them in a minority.

In 1916 a small group of militant Irish nationalists attempted an upris-ing that began with the seizure of the General Post Office in Dublin on Easter Monday. The rebellion did not arouse the broad public support its leaders had expected, and it was crushed by government forces. The rebels were booed by bystanders as they marched through the streets to prison, but when their lead-ers were executed they were seen as heroes and martyrs. Sinn Fein was radicalized into a party of violent revolution. To avoid antagonizing American public opinion, the British spared Eamon de Valera, the Brooklyn-born son of a Cuban father and Irish mother, who had been raised in Ireland.

In the elections for Parliament in November 1918, Sinn Fein won almost every seat outside Ulster. The Sinn Feiners refused to sit in the British Parlia-ment and convened in 1919 to declare themselves the duly elected legislature of an independent Irish republic. A new Home Rule Act, passed by the British Parliament, infuriated Sinn Fein, because it set up a separate parliament for Ulster. To fight for Irish unity and independence, Sinn Fein created a military force called the Irish Republican Army (I.R.A.). While De Valera was in America raising money for the Irish Republic, Michael Collins led the I.R.A. in a war of terrorism using ambush, kidnappings, and assassinations. Informers were viewed as traitors to Ireland and were punished by shooting off their kneecaps. Sympathetic Irish-Americans contributed money to the I.R.A. for the fight against the British.

To subdue the I.R.A, the British recruited a new police force from among demobilized soldiers. Known as "Black and Tans" because of the color of their uniforms, they lacked the discipline of the army and committed atrocities that rivaled those of the I.R.A. The climax of terror came on "Bloody Sunday" in November 1920. In the morning the I.R.A. murdered a number of British officers in their homes while their families watched. In the afternoon the Black and Tans fired at random into a crowd at a football match.

The I.R.A. were no match for the British militarily, but they had a powerful ally in the war-weariness of the British people. Lloyd George, as usual, played the role of problem solver, for the Protestants of Ulster were determined not to be part of an Irish state. Late in 1921 Lloyd George arranged negotiations in London with the leaders of the Irish insurgents. He offered to concede virtual independence to Ireland as a free state within the British empire, but with Ulster continuing as part of the United Kingdom. Most of the Sinn Fein negotiators, led by Michael Collins, accepted the terms as the best they could get. When they returned to Ireland with the Treaty, they faced strong opposition from De Valera and his supporters, who would not accept the loss of Ulster. A majority in the Irish legislature endorsed the Treaty and the voters supported the pro-Treaty party in new elections.

The adherents of the Treaty set up the Irish Free State with its capital in Dublin. Then came the ultimate tragedy as Irish patriots fought each other. De Valera and his followers rebelled against the Free State in June 1922, and Ireland was torn by civil war. Collins was charged with "selling out" the ideal of a free and united Ireland, and murdered by I.R.A. extremists. By April 1923 the government of the Irish Free State had established its authority and De Valera was again a prisoner. Remnants of the I.R.A. continued to function as an underground terrorist organization.

The Fall of Lloyd George

Lloyd George thrived in the hectic atmosphere of the years immediately after the war, devoting his political shrewdness and vast energies to peace in Europe, pacification of Ireland and India, and the problems of postwar reconstruction. Property owners, professional men, and the solid middle class relied on him to save them from socialism at home and Bolshevism abroad. Half-hearted and ineffectual military intervention against the Bolsheviks in Russia embarrassed Britain, frustrated Lloyd George's Conservative supporters, and upset working-class and radical opinion.

The demand for consumer goods from a world starved by wartime austerities produced for a short time abundant jobs, high wages, and strikes. Skillfully mediating industrial disputes, Lloyd George postponed confrontation with the trade unions until unemployment weakened them. He pacified the coal miners with the appointment of a commission to study the problems of the industry. When a majority of the commission recommended one form or another of nationalization, Lloyd George used the disagreement over specifics as an excuse not to act. To fulfill the promise of "homes fit for heroes" the government paid local authorities and private builders generous subsidies to build houses.

Then in 1921–1922 the economy collapsed, spoiling Lloyd George's strategy for killing socialism with kindness. The old export industries such as steel, coal, and textiles suffered most. During the war American, Japanese and other producers had invaded established British markets, and after the war German reparations payments and inter-governmental debts snarled international finance and trade. By mid-1921 there were more than two million out of work in Britain, and until the beginning of World War II unemployment never fell below a million. The unemployed received modest money payments ("the dole") that enabled them to survive. The government did little to provide new jobs. Economy replaced reform as the official watchword, and expenditures for housing, education, and other programs of social reconstruction were drastically cut.

As problems mounted rank-and-file Conservatives rebelled against Lloyd George, although their leaders still saw him as the popular figure who could keep them in office. Back-bench Conservatives criticized the cost of subsidies for working-class housing, complained that wartime controls restricting business and industry continued too long, and above all they resented the settlement in Ireland. They worried that Conservative leaders might accept a permanent merger of the Coalition parties. They saw Lloyd George as a corruptor of British politics, for he expanded the practice of rewarding generous contributors with titles of nobility, and he maintained a substantial political fund collected by Coalition Liberals to use as he liked.

Lloyd George sought to save his position by a diplomatic triumph. He tried to conciliate Germany at the expense of France, but instead the Germans signed an ominous treaty of friendship with Russia. Next he intervened in a war between the Turks and the Greeks, for the Turks under a bold leader named Mustapha Kemal sought to drive the Greeks out of territory along the Turkish coast granted to them in the peace settlement. Lloyd George threatened to fight when the Turks marched on their prewar capital, Constantinople, which was still occupied by the Allies. The French would not support Lloyd George against Kemal, who refused to back down in the face of his threats.

When the Turks were victorious, Conservative back-benchers decided they had had enough of Lloyd George's frenetic activity. In 1922, over the opposition of most of the Conservatives in the Cabinet, a caucus of Conservative M.P.s at the Carlton Club decided that the party should withdraw from the Coalition and return to politics as usual. The Conservative leaders yielded and Lloyd George was forced to resign. The ailing Bonar Law came out of a brief retirement to lead a purely Conservative government.

THE TWENTIES

The Politics of Mediocrity

When Lloyd George resigned in 1922 he was succeeded by the Conservative leader, Sir Andrew Bonar Law, who called an election that resulted in a three-way split between Conservatives, Liberals, and Labour, although the Liberals were further split between followers of Asquith and Lloyd George. A few months after taking office Bonar Law retired to be succeeded by Stanley Baldwin, a shrewd political operator who dominated British politics for the next fourteen years.

As prime minister, Baldwin lacked Lloyd George's energy and imagination, but he understood the Conservative Party and the ordinary voter. He practiced the politics of conciliation—supporting moderate reforms more than some Conservatives liked—and through the new medium of radio he impressed the public with his straightforwardness and honesty. Almost immediately Baldwin took an important decision when he came out in favor of a protective tariff and called an election on that issue. The Liberals, historically devoted to free trade, were reunited in opposing protectionism. When no party won a majority the Liberals allowed Ramsay MacDonald, leader of the Labour Party, to form a government with their support.

MacDonald had been a leader in forming the Labour Party prior to World War I and had gained respect for his principled opposition to Britain's involvement in the war. Despite being born the illegitimate son of a penniless maidservant, his good looks, elegant manners, and Scots accent—which bore no working-class taint—enabled him to enter the society of duchesses and millionaires. In domestic policy his socialist ideals inspired vague, eloquent speeches, but his dependence on the Liberals made socialist legislation impossible. MacDonald was most active in foreign affairs, where he extended diplomatic recognition to the Soviet Union and worked to strengthen cooperation between Britain and France.

In an effort to strengthen his hand politically, MacDonald called an election late in 1924. The election was influenced by anti-Communist hysteria, which was pressed hard by Baldwin and the Conservatives. The Labour government was accused of sympathy toward Communism and the Soviet Union. The Conservatives won the election with ease. The Liberals, whose following was whittled away from the right and the left, were the biggest losers.

Baldwin was able to put together a much stronger government in 1924– 1929 than in his first ministry. Those Conservatives who had earlier supported Lloyd George now fell in line behind Baldwin, as did ex-Liberal Winston Churchill, whose opposition to Soviet Bolshevism and domestic socialism was intense. Churchill, as chancellor of the exchequer, returned the pound to the gold standard, unfortunately at an overvalued rate that harmed British exports. The foreign secretary, Austen Chamberlain, son of the Liberal Unionist leader, Joseph Chamberlain, led in negotiating the Locarno Treaties (1925) which breathed a spirit of reconciliation by guaranteeing the borders of Germany, France, and Belgium and establishing a network of arbitration treaties to resolve future differences peaceably. Germany joined the League of Nations and Allied occupation forces were withdrawn from the Rhineland.

Baldwin wanted to reduce the class orientation of British politics by promoting legislation that would improve the lives of the urban working class. Neville Chamberlain, younger brother of Austen, led in legislation to reform local government finance and improve pensions for the elderly, widows, and orphans. Confronted with mass unemployment and poverty, the system of poor relief that went back to the Poor Law of 1834 was drastically changed. The Conservatives were also active in building housing for low-income people. The Tory Democracy of Disraeli was still alive in the Conservative Party.

The General Strike of 1926 was the most dramatic event of the second Baldwin government. The strike grew out of a dispute in the coal industry: the owners wanted to reduce wages to compete with cheap foreign coal, and the government wanted to end the subsidy that enabled them to keep wages up. The miners refused to accept any cut in pay, even when a royal commission proposed to couple a reduction with reorganization of the industry. After the coal miners called a strike, the Trades Union Congress (T.U.C.) decided to support them with a national walkout, a long-discussed move that union leaders thought would be a decisive blow.

The General Strike backfired. Despite rank-and-file solidarity in the unions, the government maintained essential services with the help of volunteers who drove trucks, soldiers who unloaded ships, and sailors who shoveled coal at power stations. After nine days Baldwin maneuvered the T.U.C. into calling off the General Strike without obtaining anything in return. The coal strike continued until hunger broke it later in the year.

In 1929 an election was due in which Baldwin and the Conservatives ran on the slogan "Safety First." Lloyd George made a last-ditch effort to restore the Liberals as the party of reform with a democratic, free-trade, non-socialist program, but its following had been steadily eroded by the Conservatives on the right and Labour on the left. Instead, the voters turned to Labour, which became the largest single party in the House of Commons.

MacDonald formed a second ministry, although he still needed Liberal support. The MacDonald government soon staggered under the assault of the Great Depression, which began with the 1929 stock market crash in the United States and in the next several years became a general breakdown of international finance and trade. Britain was more dependent on the world market than any other country, and British financial institutions and industry were hard hit. By the end of 1930 the unemployed in Britain numbered two and a half million, with no relief in sight.

The MacDonald government had difficulty in paying its bills, and it had to cut spending to obtain loans from bankers fearful of socialism. Philip Snowden, the Labour chancellor of the exchequer, believed that the revival of Britain's export industries required low taxes and expenditures and that the pound based on gold was essential to Britain's trade throughout the world. Despite pressure from his Labour Party colleagues, Snowden was unwilling to approve large expenditures for relief of the unemployed. Some of the Labour members of the Cabinet refused to abandon their working–class constituency to the demands of the bankers and economic experts. Unable to agree on a policy, the MacDonald government resigned.

Throughout the 1920s the lack of strong leadership, the absence of well-defined issues, and the existence of three political parties made the idea of coalition attractive. In 1931 another political coalition seemed the way to obtain national unity in the face of economic disaster. King George V asked MacDonald and Baldwin to form a coalition government, perhaps the last time a monarch played an important role in the political process. To the surprise of his Labour Party colleagues, MacDonald agreed and continued as prime minister, but without the support of his party. Most Liberals and a few Labor M.P.s supported the National Coalition Government, but the Conservatives were dominant, and Stanley Baldwin called the tune from behind the scenes. Lloyd George remained in political exile.

The National Government was pledged to maintain the gold standard, but as international bankers feverishly converted their sterling balances into gold, it became necessary to suspend payments. Left to float in the international money markets, the pound declined moderately, but the major influence on the British economy was the worldwide breakdown of international finance and trade.

The National Government called an election in October 1931 in which it asked the voters for a "doctor's mandate." The result was a sweeping victory over the Labour Party, shattered by MacDonald's "betrayal" and the impact of devastating unemployment. The next year Neville Chamberlain succeeded where his father had failed when the National Government abandoned Britain's historic free trade policy and introduced a protective tariff.

Life in the Twenties

In the 1920s the trend-setting elements of society reacted against the high idealism and personal sacrifices of the wartime period and placed more emphasis on personal pleasure and sensual gratification. This new attitude was seen in the "flappers," young women who defied conventions about dress and behavior and who, it was suspected, flouted the conventional prohibition of premarital sex. The flappers cultivated a boyish appearance, with breasts flattened, slender figures, bobbed hair, skirts just below the knee, flesh-colored silk stockings, high-heeled shoes, bold lipstick, rouge-tinted cheeks, bare arms, and rejection of the whale-boned corset which had confined the bodies of proper Victorian women. Slenderness became an enduring feminine ideal which condemned to diets the full-figured women considered beauties in the Edwardian era.

Despite obtaining the vote, women exercised little political influence after the war. For young middle-class women, social and economic changes mattered more. Though women failed to keep their wartime industrial jobs, many continued to work in offices and retail establishments. Their social freedom grew in relatively superficial things, such as smoking in public, and in more fundamental matters such as having smaller families. Acceptance of contraception, at least among the comfortable classes, owed much to the efforts of Dr. Marie Stopes, author of *Married Love* (1918) and founder in 1921 of Britain's first birth control clinic.

American influences were important in the development of a consumption-oriented society. Woolworth stores drove out the little shops; Hoover vacuum cleaners were so popular that vacuuming the floor was called "hoovering." Ford began manufacturing cars in Britain and Firestone manufactured tires. American influence also encouraged a more open and less-inhibited lifestyle. Jazz bands became fashionable for dancing, and the American practice of smoking cigarettes conquered the country. Hollywood films contributed to American influence in slang, dress, and manners; attending the cinema became a ritual with all classes of society, and 90 percent of all films shown came from Hollywood. Max Factor cosmetics changed dramatically the public face of women, enabling them to imitate the appearance of movie stars. Another American practice that took root in Britain was the newspaper gossip column, which tyrannized the fortunate few to titillate the many.

In contrast, radio (the "wireless") created a distinctively British institution. Radio was recognized as a powerful new cultural force, and for that reason it was established as a monopoly controlled by a semiautonomous institution, the British Broadcasting Corporation, chartered by the government. The BBC was paid for by license fees on radio sets. Though criticized as stuffy, puritanical, and paternalistic, the BBC established high standards in broadcasting, unencumbered by commercials. The BBC acted as schoolmaster to the nation by offering its audience high-quality programs introduced by announcers with impeccable upper-class accents.

THE THIRTIES

The National Government

The National Government organized in 1931 was formed to preserve the gold standard and free trade; within a year it had abandoned both. It was supposed to bring together the ablest individuals from all parties to deal in a nonpartisan way with the financial and economic crisis. In fact it was led by mediocrities: the well-meaning but muddled MacDonald, the steady but uninspiring Baldwin, and the hard-working Neville Chamberlain. The two most dynamic men in British public life, David Lloyd George and Winston Churchill were not asked to join because lesser men feared their energy, persuasiveness, and ambition.

The National Government's first priority was financial retrenchment. As a country that had flourished on the basis of trade and financial services, it was believed that the essential requirement for Britain was to reduce taxes, interest rates, public expenditures, and borrowing. The National Government balanced the budget in 1931 by cutting social programs, the pay of public employees, and unemployment benefits. The government adopted no massive program of public works to create employment, as was done in the United States under President Franklin D. Roosevelt.

In 1934 the National Government tried to persuade industrialists to locate factories in especially depressed areas, and it made small grants to subsidize training centers and other services to the unemployed. In addition, private schemes of "rationalization" were encouraged to reduce production in the most afflicted industries by closing old and inefficient plants. The Conservatives served their landed constituency by organizing agricultural marketing boards, and showed their interest in the middle class by lowering interest rates, which made it easier for house buyers to get mortgages.

The major problem of the National Government was the millions of men and women for whom the depression of the 1930s meant unemployment, poverty, frustration, and crumbling selfrespect. Even in good times working-class life was a grinding struggle to get by, often with the help of the neighborhood pawnshop and credit at the local shops. In 1932 nearly three million people lacked jobs, and even after the worst was over almost two million people remained unemployed.

Hunger marchers from Kent follow their fife and drum band into London to participate in large demonstrations against the means test, 1932. UPI/Corbis-Bettmann.

The north of England, industrial Scotland, and Northern Ireland suffered most. They depended heavily on declining industries—textiles, shipbuilding, coal—which had been losing ground to foreign competition even before the collapse of the world market. The young moved away or lived on the dole in poverty and idleness. In 1931 as part of its economy drive, the National Government reduced the number of weeks for unemployment insurance benefits, cut the dole and excluded most married women from it, and subjected the dole to the unpopular household means test which reduced payments when any member of the household received any income. Most of these cuts were restored a few years later, when the economy improved.

The thirties were a time of intense political and social controversy. The Depression and rising tensions in Europe stimulated disputes between left-wing and right-wing activists over foreign policy and economic justice. Some intellectuals became Communists and praised the Soviet Union, and a small but active Communist Party offered the Soviet model as an alternative to capitalism. Sir Oswald Mosley, an eccentric aristocrat who had once been a Labour minister, organized the British Union of Fascists in 1932 without attracting much of a following. Hunger marches from the distressed areas to London dramatized the plight of the unemployed, but they never reached a revolutionary size.

Though bitter about the events of 1931, the Labour Party remained committed to democratic, parliamentary institutions. Within the party, intellectual socialists and tough-minded union leaders coexisted in an uneasy relationship. The Labour Party was active in peace movements, and in support of the League of Nations. In 1935 a dedicated and mild-mannered moderate, Clement Attlee, was chosen leader of the Labour Party.

Revival and Renewal

The thirties were not entirely negative in British economic and social development. The economic distress inflicted by the Depression on certain areas and industries obscured a shift in the British economy away from the export-oriented heavy industries of the north to light manufacturing, retailing, and service industries in metropolitan London and nearby counties. Unemployment in those sectors of the economy which served the domestic market was lower, but most of the jobs paid low wages and trade unions were weak. The middle class grew in numbers, especially those who were salaried employees of central and local government or large business firms.

The cheapness of imported raw materials and food contributed to a modest economic revival in the mid-thirties. The prices of meat, grain, and cotton fell even more than prices for the manufactured goods which Britain sold abroad. Cheap building materials, low wages for construction workers, and low interest rates for mortgages stimulated housing. Before World War I the middle class had usually rented the houses in which they lived; in the 1930s large numbers of them became homeowners.

The industries that prospered in the 1930s produced consumer goods: automobiles, radios, household appliances, furniture, and the like. In 1930 there were about a million automobiles in Britain, and within the decade the figure doubled. Gas and electric cookers (stoves) replaced coal ranges. The electric power industry increased enormously to meet the needs of offices, shops, industry and homes. Leisure became a profitable business. By the end of the 1930s paid annual vacations became common for workingmen, which were often taken at seaside resorts such as Brighton, Bournemouth, or Blackpool. The dream world of the cinema provided relaxation and escape. After the development of talking pictures in the late twenties, a quarter of the population went to film shows twice a week.

THE COMING OF WORLD WAR II

Appeasement and the Road to War

Early in 1933 two leaders came to power who were to have a great influence on Britain: Franklin D. Roosevelt was inaugurated as President of the United States and Adolph Hitler became Chancellor of Germany. Hitler quickly established himself as a dictator and began his long-stated plans to rearm Germany, undo the Versailles settlement, and make Germany the dominant power of Europe. Ever since 1919 British leaders had regarded the Versailles treaty as needlessly harsh toward Germany, but efforts to modify the treaty had foundered on French determination to keep Germany weak and defenseless. Although the British view might have been helpful in the 1920s, when Germany was governed by a democratic republic, such an approach became suicidal when Germany came under Hitler.

Nevertheless, Britain tried to avoid war by redressing German grievances, a policy known as "appeasement." Another reason for seeking good relations with Hitler was fear of the Soviet Union and communism, sentiments especially strong among Conservatives. The situation was further complicated by Benito Mussolini, the Fascist dictator of Italy, who was at first a rival of Hitler and might become a valuable ally.

Hitler immediately began arming Germany secretly, and in 1935 he threw off the mask when he introduced national conscription. The French were in one of their frequent political crises and did nothing, while the British decided that Germany had as much right to an army as its heavily armed neighbors. Britain showed its good will by an Anglo-German naval agreement that permitted the Germans to increase the size of their navy, although Hitler did not have much interest in seapower. The British public began to feel uneasy about rising militarism in Europe, but Stanley Baldwin faced an election in 1935 and he did not wish to have the voters unduly upset. The Conservatives won the election handily and Baldwin became prime minister.

In the meantime Mussolini attacked Ethiopia to expand his empire in Africa. Britain's delegate to the League of Nations, Anthony Eden, protested strongly against this violation of international law, but behind the scenes British and French diplomats considered it wiser to yield to Mussolini in order to gain his support against Hitler. Armed with modern weapons, the Italians destroyed an Ethiopian army bearing spears and shields. The prestige of the League of Nations and the ideal of collective security had vanished. Mussolini decided to make an alliance with Hitler.

In 1936 Hitler threw down the gauntlet when he sent German troops into the Rhineland and began to fortify the German border with France. If permitted, this action would prevent the French from intervening in Germany or aiding their eastern European allies, Poland, Rumania, and Yugoslavia. Unfortunately, the French were again in the process of forming a government and unable to respond. In Britain, the Baldwin government was absorbed in domestic issues and militarily unprepared to act. Furthermore, it was argued that the Germans had not invaded anyone; as one British minister put it, they were simply entering their own back garden.

While Hitler was rearming Germany, Baldwin was distracted by events in the royal family. The death of King George V complicated the political scene in Britain, since his successor, King Edward VIII (1936), wished to marry a glamorous American divorcee, Mrs. Wallis Warfield Simpson, a prospect that was highly disturbing to the Conservative political elite. When Baldwin forced the king to choose between the throne and Mrs. Simpson, young King Edward VIII, in a dramatic broadcast, surrendered his crown "to marry the woman I love." Edward VIII was succeeded by his brother who became King George VI (1936–1952).

One of the few prominent British political figures to sound the alarm concerning German intentions was Winston Churchill, but he was at this time viewed as a discredited maverick of eccentric views, an opinion strengthened by his quixotic support of the king's desire to marry Mrs. Simpson. Churchill's warnings went unheeded. The next year Stanley Baldwin retired with the plaudits of a grateful nation. He was succeeded as prime minster by his long-time colleague, Neville Chamberlain.

By 1938 Hitler had rearmed and fortified Germany, and he turned to absorbing additional German-speaking areas into his Third Reich. In March, 1938 he moved quickly to annex his homeland, Austria. In September he insisted on annexing the German-speaking part of Czechoslovakia, known as the Sudetenland. The Czechs were ready to fight, but Chamberlain was determined to avoid war, and he had public opinion on his side. The French had just emerged from another political crisis and were unwilling to do anything. Furthermore, neither Britain nor France was militarily ready for a war to defend Czechoslovakia.

While war hysteria gripped Britain, Chamberlain held two meetings with Hitler and then met at Munich in October with Hitler, Mussolini, and the French premier. Chamberlain accepted Hitler's assurances that the Sudentenland was his only goal. Hitler was given the Sudetenland, the Czechs were told to yield, and Chamberlain returned to a cheering crowd, where he announced that he brought "peace in our time." A sense of relief swept over the nation, but the feeling remained that a showdown had only been delayed. When Hitler took over the rest of Czechoslovakia the next spring, Chamberlain made treaties with Poland and other threatened states of eastern Europe. He declared that further German aggression would mean war and accelerated the process of British rearmament, but Britain's military response to any further German aggression was unclear.

As the European crisis grew, the Labour Party had little to offer in the way of constructive criticism. Although they hated Hitler, Mussolini, and the Japanese militarists, the Left was firmly opposed to war and distrusted the Baldwin government. In principle the Labour Party favored strong action against an aggressor through the League of Nations and a collective security agreement in which Russia would take part. They opposed rearmament, for they believed that funds should be devoted to social justice instead. Some on the political Left were pacifists, holding that war was never justified.

The Left was profoundly affected by a civil war that broke out in Spain in 1936. Generalissimo Francisco Franco, the Fascist leader of conservative forces in Spanish life, led an uprising to overthrow the Spanish republic, which was controlled by democratic and socialist groups supported by communists. Hitler and Mussolini sent aid to Franco, which aroused the British Left to fury and persuaded some that a war against Fascism was justifiable and inevitable. With German and Italian support, Franco was victorious and established a fascist dictatorship, but Spain was left prostrate for a generation.

A major factor in the European scene was the Soviet Union, which was viewed by the British and French governments as a threat as dangerous as Germany. Soviet participation in the crisis over Czechoslovakia was refused. In 1939, however, Britain decided to seek Soviet support in resisting further aggression by Hitler, who made it clear that he was determined to reclaim German territories given to Poland at Versailles.

Stalin was doubtful of Britain's determination or ability to fight. While negotiations with Britain proceeded, he secretly agreed with Hitler to partition Poland. In August the German-Soviet Pact was announced, and on September 1, 1939, Hitler's forces attacked. The German army quickly defeated the Poles with a new kind of attack called "blitzkrieg" (lightning war) featuring fast-moving tanks and motorized troops supported by fighter planes and bombers. Britain and France declared war on Germany, but they were committed to a defensive posture and there was little they could do to help Poland. The Commonwealth countries joined the alliance, but Ireland remained neutral. Two weeks later Stalin invaded Poland to take his share. World War II had begun.

WORLD WAR II BEGINS

The Phony War and Norway

When Britain and France declared war they took up defensive positions and watched apprehensively as the German blitzkrieg ran rough-shod over the Poles. The French had drawn the conclusion from World War I that modern weaponry gave the advantage to the defensive. They based their military planning on vast fortifications along the Franco-German border called the Maginot Line, which ended at a hilly, wooded area called the Ardennes. The French border with Belgium was not fortified, because the French planned to enter Belgium when war was declared and fight the Germans there. The Ardennes were lightly held, because the French decided that a modern army would have difficulty moving through such rugged country. The British reluctantly accepted the

French plan, and when war was declared they sent a small Expeditionary Force to join the French along the Belgian border. Since the Belgians did not want to provide the battlefield, the Allies were not permitted to to cross the border to take up defensive positions.

In the meantime the British had been preparing for a different kind of war. They did not want to fight another massive land war on the continent, and they were confident that they could not be invaded by sea. They believed that the war would be decided by airpower. They organized a separate Royal Air Force and began building bombers, with speedy little fighter planes to protect them. It was a truism among British military planners that "the bomber will always get through." For this reason, the Chamberlain government gave priority to defense against German air raids, building bomb shelters and evacuating from London and other large cities more than a million children, mothers of small children, pregnant women, and teachers. When the bombs did not immediately fall most of the evacuees drifted back from the countryside and small towns where they had been sent.

Winston Churchill had been vindicated in his opposition to appeasement, and it was known that he was a fighter. As a result of pressure from within the Conservative Party, he was taken into the Chamberlain ministry as first lord of the

Evacuation of children from London, 1938. UPI/Corbis-Bettmann.

Admiralty, a post that he had held during World War I. Instead of a land war in Belgium, Churchill wanted to fight the Germans on the periphery of Europe, using British seapower and mobile troops to make trouble for Germany. One possibility was to cut off vital German imports of Swedish iron ore, which were shipped out of the Norwegian port of Narvik and along the Norwegian coast.

Hitler forestalled Churchill's plans by a sudden invasion of Norway and Denmark in April 1940. Britain landed forces in Norway to aid the stubborn Norwegian resistance, but in vain. Churchill's Norwegian campaign was a dismal failure that brought back memories of Gallipoli. Blame for Britain's ineffective war effort fell on Chamberlain. A vote in the House of Commons showed a serious loss of support among members of his own party, and Chamberlain resigned. Churchill, whose vigor and pugnacity could not be denied, became prime minister in May 1940, just as the Germans fell with full fury upon France and the Low Countries.

Churchill had no doubt that he was the right man to lead Britain. His bulldog-like chin, his cigar, and his fingers raised in a V-for-Victory salute made him the wartime image of John Bull. He came to symbolize his country's courage, stubbornness, and love of freedom. In the crisis year of 1940 he offered only "blood, sweat, toil, and tears." His carefully prepared speeches brought home to the British people the gravity of the dangers they faced and instilled confidence in eventual victory.

The prime minister spent most of his time on military and diplomatic affairs, with a coalition Cabinet comprised of ministers from all three major parties being responsible for domestic matters. The leader of the Labour Party, Clement Attlee, became deputy prime minister, and Ernest Bevin, leader of the Transport Union, took the lead in organizing the labor force for war as minister of labour. Their accomplishments during the war gave them prestige which stood them in good stead when the war came to an end.

BRITAIN STANDS ALONE

The Fall of France

In May 1940 the Germans unleashed the blitzkrieg against the Netherlands, Belgium, and France. As planned, the British and French forces moved into Belgium to take up defensive positions. They had walked into a trap. The German *panzers* (motorized forces) squeezed through the supposedly impassible Ardennes and dashed unobstructed across the plains of northern France, cutting off the Allied force from its base. The French Army crumbled, the politicians fled in panic from Paris to the south, and the British decided the best thing to do was retreat to the ports along the Channel.

Churchill made desperate efforts to encourage the French to renew their resistance in the south of France, for large French forces were still sitting useless in the Maginot Line, but all was in vain. Instead, a motley armada of warships, ferries, and small civilian boats evacuated about 225,000 British troops and over 100,000 Frenchmen from the Channel port of Dunkirk. Britain had suffered a staggering defeat and the army had lost most of its equipment, but the troops were safely back in their island, and their leader was full of fight.

It was vitally important to Britain to control the sea, and in this respect the French fleet was important, for it must not fall into German hands. When the French in Algeria would not sail their warships to British ports, the British navy entered the harbor of Oran and sank them, with great loss of life. It was the ultimate disaster in a bitter tragedy.

After Dunkirk, Britain's paramount concern was invasion by the triumphant German army standing poised at the Channel coast. At first Hitler hoped that Britain would accept defeat and sue for peace, but he failed to reckon with the defiant spirit of Winston Churchill and an aroused British people. When the British bombed Berlin, Hitler ordered an invasion.

As the British prepared to defend their island the key factor was air power, for without control of the air Hitler's armada could not sail. The fighter planes that had been built to protect the bombers were called upon to defend Britain itself. In July and August a desperate struggle took place over the Channel ("The Battle of Britain"), as the fighter pilots of the Royal Air Force threw back the German *Luftwaffe* (air force). In September Hitler called off invasion plans and began preparations for his main goal: to attack the Soviet Union and establish German rule of eastern Europe.

The "Blitz"

With German invasion plans checked, Air Marshall Hermann Goering assured Hitler that the resistance of the stubborn British could be broken by bombing. The British faith in "victory through airpower" would be tested by being on the receiving end. The German "blitz," as the British called it, began in September 1940 and continued through May 1941. London was the main target, although other cities were hard hit. When daylight bombing proved too costly the Germans turned to bombing at night, their bombers following the silvery Thames to the target, which was lighted by fires set by incendiary bombs.

The Germans made one Londoner out of six homeless, and the government had to organize emergency shelter, clothing, and meals. Bombs tore up gas and electric lines; air raids and false alarms disrupted industrial production. Thousands worked by day in essential war industries and spent their nights as wardens watching from the rooftops and putting out fires. Those who were easily frightened left London, which perhaps explains why morale did not break. Thousands of Londoners huddled night after night in the Underground stations, where musicians and entertainers did something to brighten the scene.

The East End slums near the docks were hit hard, but no place was safe. King George VI, Queen Elizabeth, and the two princesses remained in London throughout the war, sharing the experiences of their subjects when Buckingham Palace was hit. Other industrial towns were bombed, with surprisingly little effect on war production. Production of tanks in Coventry returned to normal within six weeks of a devastating raid. The Germans also bombed places without military importance, such as the cathedral town of Canterbury. In May 1941 Hitler gave up and turned his attention to the Soviet Union. The first attempt to win a war with airpower had failed, but the Luftwaffe did not have the big bombers that Britain and America were building. In Britain, the blitz fostered national unity and determination to resist, for all were in it together.

Britain Fights Back

As soon as Churchill knew that Britain was safe from invasion he looked for a place to fight back, which was provided by Hitler's inept ally, Benito Mussolini. After the defeat of France, Mussolini attacked Greece and his forces in Libya attacked Egypt. Churchill sent everything he could spare to Egypt, and the Italians were driven pell-mell back across the desert to where they had started. It seemed that Mussolini might lose his entire North African empire.

When Mussolini's forces were stopped by the Greeks, Churchill saw an opportunity to establish a foothold on the European continent, from which he could rally the conquered nations and harass the German empire. He rashly diverted British forces from North Africa to Greece, which brought down upon them Hitler's panzers, who for a second time drove the British into the sea. Hitler also sent General Irwin Rommel and his Afrika Corps to aid Mussolini in North Africa. In 1941 Rommel drove the weakened British forces back to Egypt in a masterful display of blitzkrieg.

American Aid

In the meantime other pressing problems were at hand. German submarines were sinking British ships faster than they could be replaced, and Britain faced starvation. In the United States President Franklin D. Roosevelt decided that Britain could not be permitted to fall, but in 1940 he was locked in a presidential campaign and opposed by powerful isolationist forces. From the time he became prime minister, Churchill had engaged in a frank correspondence with Roosevelt, making clear Britain's desperate situation. In the summer of 1940,

"We shall let them have it back," Churchill told the bombing victims as he surveyed damage done in
Bristol, 1941. UPI/Corbis Bettmann.

when German invasion loomed, Roosevelt cleared out U.S. arsenals to send
thousands of rifles to Britain. Later in the year he arranged the transfer of
fifty destroyers to aid the British navy in fighting the German submarines.

Early in 1941, after his election to a third term, Roosevelt proposed Lend-
Lease, by which the United States would send massive supplies of food, gasoline, ships, planes, and guns to Britain. It was useless to provide Lend-Lease
goods that would be sent to the bottom by submarines, so the U.S. Navy provided convoys for British merchant ships. Thus Britain was able to survive
and hope for a better day.

A WIDER WAR

American Involvement in the War

The war changed dramatically in 1941, for Hitler attacked the Soviet Union in
June, and Japan attacked the United States on December 7. No one knew what
to expect from the Soviet Union, which suffered heavy defeats before throwing back the Germans at the gates of Moscow. The next year the German
attack was stopped at Stalingrad, and at that point the Red Army began a
counterattack that eventually reached Berlin.

The Japanese attack on Pearl Harbor wreaked great destruction on the U.S. Navy, and Japanese forces quickly seized the Philippines and many strategic Pacific islands. The Japanese onslaught also affected the British empire in the loss of Hong Kong, Malaya, Burma, and the great naval base at Singapore. The security of Australia and India was threatened. The Japanese advance was stopped by American naval victories in the battle of the Coral Sea in May 1942 and the battle of Midway in June. Thereafter the Japanese dug in to hold their enormous gains.

With the United States in the war, Churchill was confident that the democracies would eventually achieve victory. Shortly after Pearl Harbor, he travelled to Washington, D.C., where the United Nations Alliance was proclaimed. British and American military staffs met and agreed to give primary attention to the war in Europe while holding the line against Japan.

The American generals wanted to build up a large force in Britain for a head-on attack across the Channel into the heart of Hitler's empire. Churchill, fearing a repetition of the stalemate and trench warfare of World War I, clung to his strategy of war on the periphery of the Nazi empire while encouraging nationalist uprisings. He urged an attack on Germany and Italy through the Mediterranean. Since the United States was not yet ready for a direct invasion of the continent, Churchill's strategy was adopted. The decision was made for a landing in North Africa. A vast bombing offensive against Germany was also set into motion.

In November 1942 an Allied army commanded by General Dwight D. Eisenhower landed in French North Africa. A month earlier the British Eighth Army in Egypt, under General Bernard Montgomery, had broken through Rommel's lines at El Alamein on the Egyptian border. Methodically, "Monty" drove across the desert to link up with the main Allied force in Algeria and Tunisia. Hitler sent large reinforcements, and when his army in North Africa surrendered in May, 1943, he suffered a serious defeat with heavy losses.

Allied Conferences

In January 1943 victory was in sight in North Africa, the Russians had trapped a German army at Stalingrad, the submarine menace was coming under control, and the United States had taken the first step on the long road back in the Pacific with a victory at Guadalcanal. Roosevelt and Churchill met at Casablanca in Morocco to plan their next moves. Roosevelt announced that the goal of the Allies was the "unconditional surrender" of the enemy. Since it was too late in the year for a cross-Channel attack on Germany through France, it was decided to continue in the Mediterranean by invading Sicily and then Italy.

Sicily was captured in July 1943; Mussolini fell from power; and the Allied forces invaded southern Italy, expecting an easy victory. Hitler, however,

General Bernard Montgomery (left), Commander of British ground forces, 1944.
UPI/Corbis-Bettmann.

sent German forces to Italy that made the Allies pay dearly for every advance. Churchill's Mediterranean strategy had cleared the Mediterranean and saved Britain's Middle Eastern possessions, but it had done little to destroy Hitler's war-making power.

In November 1943, when the Allied forces were still tied down in Italy, Roosevelt and Churchill met with Stalin at Tehran, in northern Iran. By this time the Red Army had taken the offensive and Stalin complained that the Western Allies had let the Russians do most of the fighting. Despite Churchill's reluctance, the Americans were determined to launch the cross-Channel attack. Stalin was promised that the great invasion of Hitler's Reich would come in the spring of 1944. After the conference, General Eisenhower was named Supreme Allied Commander and preparations for the invasion began in earnest.

Wartime

The overriding effect of the war on British life was the sense of a national community, united in work and sacrifice, with one goal—to win the war. When the Battle of Britain and the blitz ended, there was no doubt that Britain could

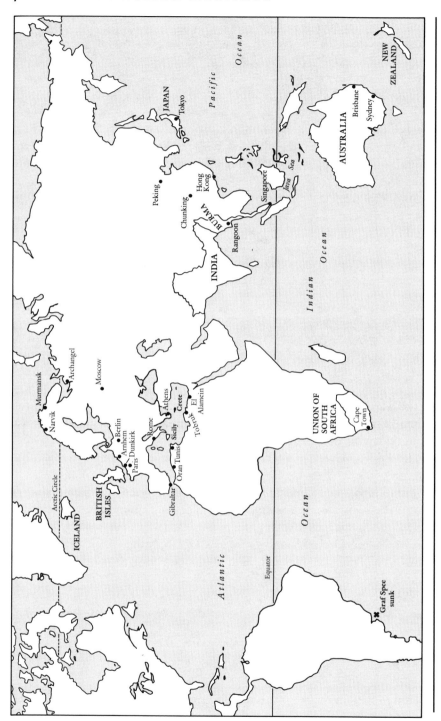

British Involvement in World War II

hold out. The main threat to Britain was submarine warfare, and Britain was able to survive that due to American aid in ships, food, gasoline, and other requirements of war. By 1943 effective anti-submarine warfare had largely negated the German submarines.

In addition to its own armed forces, which eventually included six million men and women, Britain deployed five million troops from the Commonwealth and empire. Altogether, Churchill brought into battle almost as many military personnel as the United States. With the Russians and the Americans in the war, it seemed clear that the Allies would eventually win if they could stick together and make a maximum effort.

Authority was centralized in the Churchill ministry, and Churchill became a virtual dictator. It was accepted that the government would devote the full resources of the nation to the war. Civil servants, businessmen, and labor unions worked together to accomplish miracles of production. There was a great marshalling of experts for intelligence, science, and data collection. Shortage of labor was a crucial factor: skilled workmen were kept on the job, women were conscripted for war work, and union work rules and restrictions were relaxed. High taxes and rationing prevented inflation, and U.S. Lend-Lease aid enabled the people to receive adequate allowances of food, clothing, and fuel. An Emergency Medical Service, established to serve victims of air raids, expanded its role to provide free medical and hospital care to all who suffered illness or injury attributable to the war, which included almost everything. After the war it became the basis of the National Health Service. With full employment, guaranteed rations of necessities, and free medical care, the British working class were better off than before the war.

Churchill knew the importance of civilian morale and gave much attention to it. Press coverage of the war was extensive and positive, and the BBC nightly news was noted for its accuracy. Class distinctions were minimized, as people worked together and shared the dangers and discomforts of wartime Britain. London was "blacked out" for most of the war, but people got around anyway using the Underground (subway). Hotels, restaurants, and cinemas were busy. People had to make do with homemade pleasures, but morale was high until the last year of the war, when the grim life of a protracted war became almost too much. The British had to learn to live with several million "Yanks" until that amazing day when they departed *en masse* for Normandy.

Victory

Finally the cross-Channel attack that the Americans had advocated and Churchill had feared came to pass. In the first half of 1944 vast Allied forces assembled in Britain for the invasion. On June 5 it was announced that Allied troops in Italy (including this writer) had entered Rome. The next day General Eisenhower's forces landed in Normandy, and for six weeks a bitter struggle took place in the hedgerows. The artificial harbors, or "mulberries," developed by British engineers allowed the Allies to unload huge quantities of supplies without a major seaport.

At the end of July German resistance broke and the Allied armies raced across France and into Belgium. In August American and Free French forces from Italy (including this writer) landed in southern France and swept up the Rhone Valley to join with the main Allied armies. The smell of victory was in the air. In September the attack stalled, as German resistance stiffened and supply lines lengthened. General Montgomery tried to shorten the war by dropping paratroops into the Netherlands, but his plan failed badly.

In December Hitler assembled his last resources and counterattacked through the Ardennes which, despite the lesson of 1940, were lightly defended. The German breakthrough was a momentary reverse, but "the Battle of the Bulge" provided the Allies with the opportunity to wipe out Hitler's last army. In the meantime the Russians rolled up great gains on the Eastern Front.

Another part of Allied strategy was a massive bombing attack on Germany. The British bombed by night, attacking population centers. The Americans bombed by day, seeking targets related to the German war effort but in most instances bombing the general population too. After the war a careful study of the results of bombing showed, as in Britain, that its effect on war production was modest. Despite the bombing and shortages of necessities, German morale held strong to the bitter end.

Late in 1944 and early in 1945 the Germans struck back at British civilians with the V-1, a pilotless plane or buzz-bomb. This was followed by the V-2, a rocket that could be neither seen nor heard. These "vengeance weapons" had no effect on the outcome of the war, but they killed a considerable number of people and a large number of homes were destroyed. The V-2 was the forerunner of the awesome missiles of today.

In March 1945 the Western Allies invaded Germany in overwhelming force while the Russians drove toward Berlin. Although strategic bombing had softened up the enemy, brutal ground warfare on both fronts was needed to drive the final stake into the heart of Hitler's empire. Allied victories on the ground ended the evil concentration camps and gas ovens of the Holocaust. German resistance collapsed and, facing capture by the Russians, Hitler committed suicide. A few days later the Germans surrendered unconditionally.

The war in the Pacific continued until August 1945 when two atom bombs persuaded Japan, which was already beaten and in desperate straits, to surrender. Although the atom bombs were built and dropped by the Americans, British scientists had played an important role in their development.

Churchill had led Britain through its darkest hours and to its greatest victory. In June 1945 it was time for an election, for the electoral process had been suspended during the war. Churchill wanted to preserve the coalition into the postwar world, but the British people did not see him as the man who could fulfill their aspirations for the future.

The Labour Party was led by Clement Attlee, whose service in the Cabinet during the war had gained widespread respect. Other Labour Party leaders had shown leadership and a capacity for government. The Labour Party promised a better Britain for all while Churchill campaigned poorly, railing against the dangers of socialism. The result was a landslide victory for Labour. Churchill resigned and was replaced by Clement Attlee and a Labour government.

The United States also had a new leader, for President Roosevelt, Churchill's friend and Britain's powerful ally, died in April 1945 and was succeeded by vice-president Harry Truman. By this time the wartime cooperation of the Western Allies and the Soviet Union was dissolving in quarrels and recriminations. The joy of victory was soon replaced by the bitterness of the Cold War.

SUGGESTIONS FOR FURTHER READING

Alfred T. Havighurst, *Britain in Transition: The Twentieth Century* (1985) provides a good overview and bibliography. Other general works are T. O. Lloyd, *Empire to Welfare State: English History, 1906–1992* (1993); A. J. P. Taylor, *English History, 1914–1945* (1965); W. N. Medlicott, *Contemporary England, 1914–1964* (1967); Robert Blake, *The Decline of Power, 1915–1964* (1985); Max Beloff, *Wars and Welfare: Britain, 1914–1945* (1984); Keith Robbins, *The Eclipse of a Great Power: Modern Britain, 1870–1992* (1994); Roy Douglas, *World Crisis and British Decline, 1929–1956* (1986); and Bentley B. Gilbert, *Britain, 1914–1945: The Aftermath of Power* (1996). An interesting, but idiosyncratic short history is Peter Clarke, *Hope and Glory: Britain, 1900–1990* (1996). A good general history of the interwar period is Charles L. Mowat, *Britain Between the Wars, 1918–1940* (1971). A valuable reference work is *Twentieth-Century Britain: An Encyclopedia*, F. M. Leventhal (ed., 1995).

Britain's military role in World War I must be studied in relation to other combatants. Cyril Falls, *The Great War, 1914–1918* (1959) is a good introduction to the conflict. Keith Robbins, *The First World War* (1993) is a competent brief summary. See also J. M. Bourne, *Britain and the Great War, 1914–1918* (1989) and David Woodward, *Lloyd George and the Generals* (1983). The war on the battlefield is portrayed in Timothy Travers, *The Killing Ground: The British Army, the Western Front, and the Emergence of Modern Warfare, 1900–1918* (1987). Alan Moorehead offers a vivid account of *Gallipoli* (1956). For the soldiers themselves, see Ian F. W. Beckett and Keith Simpson (eds.), *A Nation in Arms: A Social Study of the British Army in the First World War* (1985) and Denis Winter, *Death's Men: Soldiers of the Great War* (1978). The social influences of World War I are discussed in Arthur Marwick, *The Deluge: British Society and the First World War* (1991) and *Women at War, 1914–1918* (1977). See also J. M. Winter, *The Great War and the British People* (1986) and *The Experience of World War I* (1995). Trevor Wilson, *The Myriad Faces of War: Britain and the Great War, 1914–1918* (1988) and Paul Fussell, *The Great*

War and Modern Memory (1975) study cultural influences. Robert Graves, *Goodbye to all That: An Autobiography* (repr. 1995) is a vivid, first-hand account of life and death in the trenches by a major writer.

Many books cited in chapter 15 also apply to this chapter. Keith Middlemas examines economic factors in *Politics in Industrial Society: The Experience of the British System since 1911* (1979). See also Keith Laybourn, *Britain on the Breadline: A Social and Political History of Britain between the Wars* (1990). The fortunes of the the the Conservative Party can be followed in John Ramsden, *The Age of Balfour and Baldwin, 1902–1940* (1978) and Stuart Ball, *Baldwin and the Conservative Party: The Crisis of 1929–31* (1988). *Conservative Century: The Conservative Party Since 1900* (1994), Anthony Seldon and Stuart Ball (eds.), offers a long perspective. David Marquand examines *The Progressive Dilemma: From Lloyd George to Kinnock* (1991) and Trevor Wilson recounts the sad story of *The Downfall of the Liberal Party: 1914–1935* (1966).

Britain's postwar foreign policy can be followed in W. N. Medlicott, *British Foreign Policy Since Versailles, 1919–1963* (1968); Bernard Porter, *Britain, Europe, and the World, 1850–1982: Delusions of Grandeur* (1987); C. J. Bartlett, *British Foreign Policy in the Twentieth Century* (1989); David Reynolds, *Britannia Overruled: British Policy and World Power in the Twentieth Century* (1991); F. S. Northedge, *The Troubled Giant: Britain Among the Great Powers, 1916–1939* (1967); and Anthony Clayton, *The British Empire as a Superpower, 1919–39* (1986). Paul Kennedy considers military power in *Strategy and Diplomacy, 1870–1945* (1983) and *Realities Behind Diplomacy: Background Influences on British External Policy, 1865–1980* (1983). See also British Foreign Secretaries, cited in earlier chapters.

Studies that deal with key aspects of British policy prior to World War II are Arnold Wolfers, *Britain and France Betweeen Two Wars Conflicting Strategies of Peace from Versailles to World War II* (1968) and Martin Gilbert, *Britain and Germany Between the Wars* (1964). *Britain and the Spanish Civil War* (1997) by Tom Buchanan can be supplemented by K. W. Watkins, *Britain Divided: The Effect of the Spanish Civil War on British Political Opinion* (1976). Elizabeth Monroe, *Britain's Moment in the Middle East, 1914–1971* (1981) and Peter Lowe, *Britain in the Far East: A Survey from 1819 to the Present* (1981) deals with Britain's commitments in that area.

For British policy toward Hitler see Keith Eubank, *The Origins of World War II* (1990); W. N. Medlicott, *Britain and Germany: The Search for Agreement, 1930–1937* (1969); Martin Gilbert, *The Roots of Appeasement* (1967); William R. Rock, *British Appeasement in the 1930s* (1977); Keith Middlemas, *Diplomacy of Illusion: The British Government and Germany, 1937–39* (1991); Robert A. C. Parker, *Chamberlain and Appeasement: British Policy and the Coming of the Second World War* (1993); and J. Q. Adams, *British Politics and Foreign Policy in the Age of Appeasement, 1935–39* (1993). Donald Lammers examines the appeasers in *Explaining Munich: The Search for Motive in British Policy* (1996). A stimulating view is offered in A. J. P. Taylor, *The Origins of the Second World War* (repr. 1996).

On the economy, William Ashworth, *An Economic History of England, 1870–1939* (1972) continues to be authoritative. It can be supplemented by Sidney Pollard, *The Development of the British Economy, 1914–1990* (1992) and Derek H. Aldcroft, *The British Economy Between the Wars* (1983). For organized labor see previously cited books by Pelling and Laybourn. A stimulating thesis is offered by Martin J. Wiener in *English Culture and the Decline of the Industrial Spirit, 1850–1980* (1981).

Good surveys of social history are Asa Briggs, *A Social History of England: From the Ice Age to the Channel Tunnel* (1994); John Stevenson, *British Society, 1914–1945* (1984); A. H. Halsey, *Change in British Society* (1995); and Arthur Marwick, *Britain in the Century of Total*

War (1968). See also Sean Glynn and John Oxborrow, *Interwar Britain: A Social and Economic History* (1976). Robert Graves and Alan Hodges, *The Long Weekend: A Social History of Great Britain, 1918–1939* (repr. 1994) is entertaining. The continuing influence of social class is shown in Ross McKibben, *Classes and Cultures: England, 1918–1951* (1998). J. B. Priestley's *English Journey* (1934) describes the emergence of twentieth-century society, and George Orwell's *The Road to Wigan Pier* (repr. 1986) is a classic account of the lives of the working class during the 1930s. Walter Greenwood, *Love on the Dole* (1933) is a sensitive novel about the despair of the unemployed.

For the development of the welfare state see previously cited books by Laybourn and Midwinter. Bentley B. Gilbert explains *British Social Policy, 1914–1939* (1970).

Important studies of the mass media are Stephen Koss, *The Rise and Fall of the Political Press in Britain, Vol. II* (1984) and Asa Briggs, *The History of Broadcasting in the United Kingdom* (5 vols., 1995). Briggs's *The BBC: The First Fifty Years* (1985) is a summary account. An assessment is offered by D. L. LeMahieu in *A Culture for Democracy: Mass Communication and the Cultivated Mind in Britain between the Wars* (1988). See also Ernest Betts, *The Film Business: A History of British Cinema, 1896–1972* (1973).

E. R. Norman, *Church and Society in England, 1770–1970: A Historical Study* (1976) covers the declining influence of the Church of England, and Alan D. Gilbert examines *The Making of Post-Christian Britain* (1980).

Many previously cited books on the history of women are also relevant to this chapter. The role of women in wartime is examined by Arthur Marwick (book cited above) and Gail Braybon, *Out of the Cage: Women's Experiences in Two World Wars* (1987) and *Women Workers in the First World War: The British Experience* (1981).

World War II spawned an enormous body of military history and personal memoirs, the first of which was the splendid work by Winston Churchill entitled *History of the Second World War* (6 vols., 1948–54), especially *The Gathering Storm*. A stimulating introduction to the war is A. J. P. Taylor, *The War Lords* (1977). Peter Calvocoressi and Guy Wint present a broad account from a British point of view in *Total War: The Causes and Courses of the Second World War* (1972). See also *The Struggle for Survival: The History of the Second World War* (1989) by R. A. C. Parker. A thoughtful work by one of Britain's best military historians is J. F. C. Fuller, *The Second World War, 1939–1945: A Strategical and Tactical History* (1962). Good general books are Henry Pelling, *Britain and the Second World War* (1970), Angus Calder, *The People's War, 1939–1945* (1969), and Arthur Marwick, *The Home Front: The British and the Second World War* (1976). See also *Overpaid, Oversexed, & Over Here: The American GI in World War II Britain* (1992). Special studies of the war are Stephen W. Roskill, *The Navy at War, 1939–1945* (1960); Corelli Barnett, *Engage the Enemy More Closely* (1991) and *Churchill and the Admirals* (1978); and Geoffrey Bennett, *Dunkirk: The Great Escape* (1977).

Good general histories of Scotland and Ireland cited earlier are Smout on Scotland and Foster on Ireland. A good history of modern Wales is Kenneth O. Morgan, *Rebirth of a Nation: Wales, 1880–1980* (1981). The political conflict in Ireland is examined in David G. Boyce, *The Irish Question and British Politics, 1868–1996* (1996) and Lawrence McCaffrey, *The Irish Question: Two Centuries of Conflict* (1995). Edgar Holt covers the Easter uprising in *Protest in Arms* (1961). The British province in Northern Ireland is examined by Paul Bew in *The State in Northern Ireland: Political Forces and Social Classes* (1996).

Trevor Lloyd follows the empire through to its end in *The British Empire, 1558–1983* (1984). The final years are outlined in Bernard Porter, *The Lion's Share: A Short History of British Imperialism, 1850–1995* (1996); Colin Cross, *The Fall of the British Empire, 1918–1968*

(1969); and Raymond Callahan, *Churchill: Retreat from Empire* (1984). Michael Edwardes, *The Last Years of British India* (1963) and Judith M. Brown, *Modern India: The Origins of an Asian Democracy* (1994) complete the story of British rule there.

Good biographies of members of the royal family are Harold Nicolson, *King George the Fifth: His Life and Reign* (1952); Frances Donaldson, *Edward VIII* (1974); John W. Wheeler-Bennett, *King George the Sixth: His Life and Reign* (1958). For the life of Lloyd George see Bentley B. Gilbert, *David Lloyd George: A Political Life: The Organizer of Victory* (1992), and Chris Wrigley, *Lloyd George* (1992). David Dutton, *Austen Chamberlain: Gentleman in Politics* (1987) explains much of Britain's foreign policy after World War I. The three leading politicians of the interwar period are presented in Keith Middlemass, *Baldwin* (1969); David Marquand, *Ramsay MacDonald* (1977); and Keith Feiling, *The Life of Neville Chamberlain* (1947). The remarkable career of Winston Churchill spans the period. The official biography is by Randolph Churchill, continued by Martin Gilbert. Henry Pelling's *Winston Churchill* (1974) is a useful one-volume overview, as are Piers Brendon, *Winston Churchill: A Biography* (1984); Robert Blake, *Churchill* (1993); and Keith Robbins, *Churchill* (1992). Peter Stansky edited essays entitled *Churchill: A Profile* (1973). For "Monty" see Arthur G. Chalfont, *Montgomery of Alamein* (1976).

CHAPTER SEVENTEEN

Recovery and Crises
1945–1979

World War II transformed Britain more completely than any event since the Norman Conquest. Two superpowers, the United States and the Soviet Union, dominated the world. Britain was now a second-rank power, diplomatically and economically, and could no longer hold its empire. Its political institutions had again proven their worth, but the people had changed. They were concerned less with Britain's place in the world and more with making a good life for all in their island home. Perhaps the sacrifices of two World Wars had taught them an important lesson.

THE LABOUR GOVERNMENT, 1945–1951

Austerity

The Labour government led by Clement Attlee came to office with a group of strong leaders who had gained experience as part of the Churchill coalition government. The party was an uneasy combination of well-educated, middle-class socialists committed to governmental management of the economy, and trade unionists concerned with advancing the interests of the workers through collective bargaining. At first the two elements worked well together, but eventually their differences weakened the Labour government and party.

The task of reconstruction was enormous, especially since American assistance was no longer available. Britain's factories had been inefficient and run-down before the war, and rebuilding or repairing them had been impos-

*Ernest Bevin (left) and
Clement Atlee.
UPI/Corbis-Bettmann.*

sible under wartime conditions of all-out production. German bombs had destroyed or damaged hundreds of thousands of homes and during the war ordinary construction and repair had been suspended. Britain had lost many of its prewar markets to competitors and other former customers had no way of paying. Only the United States could supply much of the manufactured goods, raw materials, and food which Britain needed, and these imports required dollars which Britain did not have.

The Cold War convinced the American public that it was necessary to support the nations of western Europe. To forestall Communist revolutions and possible Soviet involvement, in 1947 the American Secretary of State, General George Marshall, proposed that aid be given to rebuild the economies of the democratic European states. In 1948 the Marshall Plan began to pump billions of dollars of assistance into Britain and other war-ravaged countries.

In November 1947 Sir Stafford Cripps became chancellor of the exchequer. This intense, austere man preached self-denial with religious fervor. He continued the wartime rationing, and to curtail consumption further, he let prices rise. Bread and potatoes were briefly rationed, which had never happened during the war when American Lend-Lease had provided many of Britain's needs. Meat was rationed until the mid-1950s. In 1947 declining productivity in the mines, a shortage of railroad cars to move the coal, and an exceptionally severe winter combined to create a desperate fuel shortage. Reluctant to confront the Coal Board and the miners with the looming crisis, the government failed to intervene in a timely and vigorous manner. Factories had to be closed for lack of fuel, idling millions of workers and undercutting the effort to export goods overseas. Households were deprived of electricity, widely used for home heating, for five hours each day. Probably more than anything else, the fuel crisis of 1947 led to a loss of public confidence in the Labour government.

As a world center of financial services, the strength and reliability of the pound sterling had always been a major consideration of British governments. With a high level of public spending and personal consumption, inflation became a major problem. In 1949 Cripps devalued the pound by about 30 percent, which made exports cheaper and imports more expensive. Although this step was damaging to the City (the financial district of London), it was beneficial to manufacturing and the economy began to revive.

Nationalization and Welfare

The Labour government came to office pledged to a planned economy directed by the government. People knew that strong leadership and mobilization of resources had enabled Britain to carry out a remarkable war effort. They remembered the breakdown of capitalism and free enterprise in the 1930s, resulting in mass unemployment. It seemed that only government could provide the leadership, direction, and capital needed for Britain to survive in the chaotic postwar world.

Labour's plan for Britain included five main elements: economic planning, socialism, trade union power, full employment, and the welfare state. Economic planning meant that the government, rather than market forces, would establish priorities and give direction to the economy. Despite the powers given to government, economic policy was dominated by the Treasury, which was concerned with Britain's acute fiscal and monetary problems, and broad economic planning never was implemented. By socialism was meant public ownership (nationalization) of selected basic industries. The process of nationalization seemed inevitable, for most British industries were in desperate condition and required massive investment that only the government could provide.

The Bank of England, which had long served as a quasi–public institution, was nationalized, giving the government full control of the supply of money and credit. Public ownership of the coal industry raised the hope that its productivity and labor-management relations might improve. Electricity, gas, railroads, scheduled airlines, overseas cables, buses, and most long distance trucking also were brought under national ownership. The old owners were compensated. Some of them, such as the gas companies, had been municipal authorities. After the nationalizations, 80 percent of the British economy still remained under private enterprise.

Despite the change in ownership, there was little change in the operation of the nationalized firms. Semi-autonomous public boards, largely recruited from the former managers, ran the nationalized industries; workers and consumers had little influence. In general the Conservatives had little complaint about the industries that the Labour Government nationalized. These industries were old and inefficient. The major controversy over nationalization arose when the Labour government nationalized the iron and steel industry, which was efficient and could stand on its own feet.

The Labour Party was based on the trade unions. The Labour government promised to maintain full employment, and in return the unions were expected to cooperate in the creation of an economy that was efficient and fair. With an enormous amount of rebuilding to be done, full employment was maintained. For the first few years cooperation between the government and the unions was good, but eventually the prewar conflict between labour and management revived, backed up by strikes, which remained legal. Worker effort and morale did not improve and the problem of absenteeism continued. Plans for modernization of British industry fell by the wayside. The workers wanted steady employment doing what they had been doing, not modernization that might eliminate jobs and change their cherished and inefficient work rules.

The principal objective of the Labour Government was to establish the welfare state, by which they meant a combination of compulsory insurance and free services to meet the basic needs of the people "from the cradle to the grave." The social welfare legislation that the Labour Party enacted affected the lives of ordinary people more than did the nationalization of a few industries. Improved insurance schemes offered benefits for maternity, retirement, death, widows, the unemployed, the sick, and the victims of industrial accidents. The benefits were low, on the assumption that full employment would enable people to save, while free medical care and education plus low-cost transportation and other public services would enable people to live inexpensively. For those inadequately served by the insurance system there was a catch-all program of national assistance. With full employment, the cost of these welfare services was reasonable compared to the cost of unemployment and other social problems during the 1930s.

Related to the welfare state was the commitment of the Labour government to provide more and better housing. Before the war, the working class had been poorly housed, and much of the destruction of bombing had taken place in working-class neighborhoods. Funds were committed to local councils to clear bombed-out areas and build millions of houses that were rented at low cost. The age of high rises had not yet arrived, and most of these houses are still being used.

The creation of a free National Health Service was the most popular of the new institutions and programs of the welfare state. The National Insurance Act of 1911 had led the way, and by 1945 almost two-thirds of doctors and half the population had signed up for medical care under the act. Led by Aneurin Bevan, a fiery Welshman, in 1948 the Labour government completed the development of universal health care by establishing the National Health Service. British residents became entitled to free medical, dental, and hospital care as well as free drugs, eye glasses, and dentures. The system adopted was for individuals to sign up with family doctors for their basic medical care, who would refer them to specialists as needed. Doctors were permitted to engage in private practice in addition to the work they did for the National Health Service.

The great change was to nationalize the community hospitals, many of which were old and ill-suited to the needs of doctors and patients. Even worse were the huge Victorian mental asylums, where abuse of patients was endemic. Not until the 1960s did economic conditions permit an extensive program of hospital building.

In its early years the National Health Service was overwhelmed, as people received treatment for health problems that had previously been ignored. Unquestionably, abuses occurred, but the system proved to be workable, and it provided far better medical care than the British people had received under private medicine.

The Labour government gave less attention to education. Many in the Labour Party opposed the selective system of British schools, where the brightest children (after age eleven) went to grammar schools that led to higher education, and most children went to schools that prepared them to enter the work force. Some Labour leaders, who had attended grammar school defended the existing system, but most preferred comprehensive schools, where children of all abilities and social classes would be educated together. Differences between the major parties concerning "selection" versus "comprehension" hampered establishment of a consensus on schools.

Labour's Foreign Policy

With the end of World War II Britain's foreign policy situation was totally changed, for the United States and the Soviet Union dominated world affairs, and Europe was divided and devastated. The Soviet Union established control over eastern Europe (including East Germany) and encouraged Communist parties in western Europe to foment revolution and support the foreign policy of the Kremlin. In 1946 Winston Churchill declared that "an iron curtain" had divided Europe. The Cold War had begun.

The British foreign secretary, Ernest Bevin, was determined that Britain could continue to be a major European and imperial power. He was a tough-minded union leader who had fought Communists for years in the labor movement. Prompted by Churchill and Bevin, the United States assumed responsibility for the defense of western Europe through the North Atlantic Treaty Organization (NATO). Under an American commander, NATO maintained heavily armored ground troops along the Iron Curtain, backed up by powerful naval, air, and nuclear forces. Britain was a a prominent member of NATO, contributing ground and naval forces that it could ill afford. As Socialists, many members of the Labour Party were opposed to militarism and tended to sympathize with the Soviet Union. George Orwell's *Animal Farm* (1946) and *Nineteen Eighty-Four* (1948) were written to refute this point of view.

The Marshall Plan and the Cold War contributed to a movement toward economic union in western Europe. In 1951 France, Germany, the Netherlands, Belgium, Luxembourg, and Italy founded the European Coal and Steel Community. Britain refused to join: its global role took precedence over Europe, and the Labour Party's paramount concern was to establish a socialist economy at home.

The Commonwealth was still important to Britain, for trade within the empire was conducted in sterling instead of scarce dollars, and the Commonwealth countries were still good markets for British goods and important sources of raw materials. In many Commonwealth countries British influence had crumbled. Canada, Australia, and New Zealand had established close economic and military relationships with the United States. The Union of South Africa came under the control of Afrikaner (Boer) nationalists who rejected dependence upon Britain. They also controlled the transportation and communications of British colonies to the north.

In the Middle East, the United States took over Britain's role in the defense of Greece and Turkey from Soviet threats. Britain's major base was the Suez Canal Zone, which it held on a lease from Egypt until 1956. British forces were also stationed in the Persian Gulf, to protect British oil interests there.

Palestine was Bevin's bitter failure. He followed Britain's traditional pro-Arab policy despite the Jewish sympathies of the American government and many members of the Labour Party. Concerned for the rights of the Arabs, Bevin attempted to restrict postwar Jewish immigration to the British-controlled territory. Attempting to maintain peace between the Arabs and the Jews in Palestine cost Britain money and lives. Seeing that no peaceful settlement was possible, Britain withdrew in 1948. In the war that followed, the Jewish settlers defeated the Arabs and established the state of Israel. The Arabs blamed their defeat on Britain, while Britain gained no credit with the Israelis.

In India the Labour government conceded the claims of Indian nationalists to independence, although the cost in Indian lives and social disruption was enormous. From early in the century, successive British governments had given way to the demands of the Indian educated elite for self-government, gradually extending Indian participation at the central and local levels. The crucial problem was the lack of unity in India, which was divided into countless castes, regions, nationalities, languages, and religions. Divisions were especially acute between the Moslems and the predominantly Hindu Indian National Congress, which made it difficult for the British to withdraw without condemning the subcontinent to civil war. Although the Hindus were much more numerous, the Moslems were more warlike and provided most of the soldiers for the Indian army.

Unwilling to abandon the Moslem minority to rule by the Hindu majority, in 1947 Lord Louis Mountbatten, the last viceroy of India, used the threat of unilateral withdrawal to persuade the Congress and the Moslem League to agree to a partition. Under the plan, the main Moslem areas in northeastern and northwestern India would form the new state of Pakistan, while the Congress took control of the largest part of India. As a result, full-scale religious warfare was avoided, but hundreds of thousands died in local riots, and millions more died or suffered great hardships as they fled to the part of the subcontinent assigned to their religion. When the dust had settled, India and Pakistan existed as separate states and native leaders held the political power formerly exercised by the British, but the people of India had paid a high price for this change of rulers.

The Fall of Labour

The Labour Party won another election victory in 1950. The margin of victory was narrow, and a weary, divided ministry found it difficult to proceed. Cripps died, and Ernest Bevin retired. Bitter disputes broke out within the Labour Party in 1950 when Britain joined in the Korean War and supported the decision of NATO to rearm West Germany as an ally against the Russians. To help finance these moves, the Labour government imposed small charges on eyeglasses and dentures. Aneurin Bevan, devoted to his beloved National Health Service, resigned in protest at a government which placed the Cold War ahead of the well-being of its own people.

The Labour Government called an election in 1951 in an effort to get a clear mandate to rule, but instead it lost a close election to the Conservatives, still led by Churchill. The fall of the Labour government in 1951 marked the end of the immediate postwar era. Labour had taken Britain through the difficult postwar years and had imposed lasting changes on British government and society. As a symbol of Britain's recovery and hopes for a better future, the Labour government organized a national celebration called the Festival of Britain. Modernistic buildings arose on the site of a bombed-out district along the Thames to house plays, concerts, and art exhibits. London's streets were still pockmarked with bomb craters, and the sausages had little meat in them, but the road to prosperity and a better life for all seemed open.

RETURN TO CONSERVATISM

Establishment of a Consensus

In the 1950s the problems spawned by World War II and its aftermath began to disappear. The emergence of new leaders contributed to the sense of change. In 1952 King George VI died, to be succeeded by his daughter, Queen Elizabeth II (1952–present). As prime minister, Winston Churchill represented the views and glories of the past, but his vitality had declined and the burdens of government passed to younger men. In 1955 Churchill, who had been born in the age of Gladstone and Disraeli, retired from politics. He was succeeded as prime minister by the foreign secretary, handsome, dapper Anthony Eden. Clement Attlee, a veteran of Labour politics since the days of King Edward VII, retired to the House of Lords, a body he had long wished to abolish.

The Conservative government formed by Churchill in 1951 preserved most of the changes of the Attlee government, both in the nationalized industries and the welfare state. Churchill, remembering the splendid contributions of British labor during World War II, was eager to maintain good relations with the trade unions. Of the nationalized industries only iron and steel and long distance trucking were sold back to private enterprise. Though the Conservatives established small fees for dentistry and prescriptions, they accepted the comprehensive National Health Service financed by general taxation. They kept many wartime restrictions (meat rationing continued until 1954) and retained rent control of most working-class housing. They continued to build council houses, but increased the proportion of homes built for owner-occupiers. Thus continuity was maintained while the Conservatives reaped the benefit of an improving economy. A consensus concerning the role of government had been achieved.

Suez and the Illusion of World Power

The Conservatives, who traditionally presented themselves as the "patriotic" party, were in tune with most public opinion when they sought to maintain Britain's role as a great power. Britain continued to be active in the United Nations, NATO, and other international organizations. A symbol of great power status was the first British atomic bomb, detonated in 1952. In March 1953

Josef Stalin died, and the Soviet Union came under the control of weak leaders. In the same year, Gen. Dwight D. Eisenhower, with whom Churchill had worked closely during World War II, became president of the United States and ended the Korean War. Churchill sensed an opportunity to resolve Cold War tensions, but his proposals for a summit meeting of major leaders foundered when he suffered a stroke. The opportunity passed, and the dangerous, costly Cold War continued for another thirty-six years.

Britain's influence in the Middle East was damaged in 1952 when King Farouk of Egypt, in most matters a British puppet, was overthrown by Colonel Gamal Abdul Nasser, who sought to make himself the leader of a Pan-Arab movement. Under pressure from Nasser the British left Egypt in 1954, in return for Nasser's guarantee of free navigation of the Suez Canal. In 1956, when the lease ran out, Nasser nationalized the canal and looked to the Soviet Union for support.

Anthony Eden, who had succeeded Churchill as prime minister, was determined to maintain Britain's waning influence in the Middle East. In collusion with Britain and France, Israel went to war with Egypt and won a stunning victory. The British and French sent troops into the Canal Zone, but their tardiness gave Nasser time to block the canal with sunken ships. The United Nations, supported by the United States, denounced the Suez intervention and imposed economic sanctions. Faced with global condemnation, the British withdrew and the French had no choice but to follow. Eden had a nervous breakdown, resigning as prime minister in 1957. His Conservative followers were aghast at the humiliation that he had brought upon Britain and the Conservative government.

Harold Macmillan and the Restoration of Confidence

Eden's successor, Harold Macmillan, restored Conservative morale and public confidence. Born into a distinguished family of publishers, socially and educationally Macmillan came out of Britain's top drawer. He had distinguished himself in the 1930s as one of a progressive group of young Conservatives and an opponent of appeasement. In World War II he had served as Churchill's representative in the Mediterranean theater. In the 1950s he emerged as a poised, shrewd political leader who always seemed in control of the situation. A newspaper cartoonist pictured Macmillan as Supermac, a kind of Superman with moustache and drooping eyelids.

Under Macmillan's leadership the Conservative Party again presented itself as the natural ruling party, led by practical men uncomfortable with the kind of ideological disputes that characterized Labour. The consensus established under Churchill held: the planned economy, full employment, nationalized industries, trade union power, and the welfare state. In the general election of 1959 Macmillan campaigned on Britain's growing prosperity, telling the voters that they "never had it so good." The Labour Party was badly beaten, and for the third successive election the Conservatives had increased their majority. Little attention was given to the election of an energetic young woman, Margaret Thatcher, for a constituency in the north of London.

Although the Conservative Party was historically the advocate of imperialism, Macmillan presided urbanely over the dissolution of most of what remained of the British empire. In 1960 he warned white South Africans that "The wind of change is blowing through this continent, and, whether we like it or not, this growth of national consciousness is a political fact." After Ghana became independent in 1957 Britain took steps to grant independence to Nigeria, Kenya, and other African colonies, Jamaica and other Caribbean possessions, Singapore, and Malaysia. The Central African Federation broke into its constituent parts, Zambia (Northern Rhodesia), Malawi (Nyasaland), and Rhodesia (now Zimbabwe), where a white government remained in control. The white regime in the Union of South Africa found the new Commonwealth uncongenial and left it.

White-ruled Rhodesia became a source of intense controversy in Britain and throughout the world. In 1965 the white settlers in the colony declared their independence to prevent Britain from imposing a government that would give control to the black majority. Despite many bitter words and an economic boycott, the white Rhodesians led by Ian Smith and supported by the Union of South Africa maintained their power until 1980, when a constitutional conference finally established the black-dominated state of Zimbabwe with special concessions to the white inhabitants.

In military affairs old views were swept away by recognition of new realities. Britain drastically reduced the number of men in uniform, ended conscription, and closed overseas bases. There were painful rows when historic regiments were amalgamated. The most divisive issue was Britain's development of nuclear weapons, an issue intensified in 1957 when Britain exploded a hydrogen bomb. An articulate and influential segment of British public opinion rejected nuclear weapons as immoral and demanded that Britain set an example by renouncing them. Thousands of men and women from all walks of life and representing a wide range of political opinions joined in the protest marches of the Campaign for Nuclear Disarmament.

The European Economic Community

Despite the relative prosperity of the Macmillan years, the British economy failed to grow as rapidly as those of its neighbors. The standard of living was improving, but in other countries it grew faster. The European Coal and Steel Community had become the European Economic Community (known as the

Common Market), which combined the West European nations into a single economic system and had enjoyed strong economic growth. Britain had refused to join the Common Market when it was formed in 1957, citing its "special relationships" with the United States and its Commonwealth.

By 1960, however, those relationships were wearing thin and the Macmillan government applied for membership. Despite the economic advantages, many in both political parties were reluctant to accept the infringement of sovereignty that membership entailed. Macmillan's application was vetoed in 1962 by President Charles DeGaulle of France, who was convinced (perhaps rightly) that the British did not share the European outlook and were too tied to the United States and other "Anglo-Saxon" countries.

The Fall of the Conservatives

For Macmillan 1963 was the year of reckoning. His political magic was losing its potency, and in the preceding year he had earned the nickname "Mac the Knife" by purging one-third of his colleagues from the Cabinet. In 1963 a scandal broke out concerning an affair between John Profumo, the debonair Secretary of State for War and Christine Keeler, a young model who was also involved with a Russian naval officer. Profumo at first told the House of Commons that the charges were false, then admitted them and resigned. Investigations revealed that Profumo was part of an unsavory world of call girls, drugs, and violence. Although Macmillan was not personally involved, the episode communicated an image of decadence and incompetence in high places.

Later in the year a serious medical operation convinced Macmillan that he must resign as prime minister and leader of the Conservative Party. He announced his retirement from his hospital bed. The Conservatives had no procedure for electing a leader, who traditionally had emerged out of a consensus of prominent party members. Macmillan and other party leaders turned to the foreign secretary, the Earl of Home (pronounced Hume), a member of the House of Lords. Lord Home renounced his title, and as Sir Alec Douglas-Home he was elected to the House of Commons and became prime minister. The selection of Lord Home by a group of insiders led the Conservatives to establish the rule that the leader would be elected by the Conservative members of Parliament in a secret ballot.

Macmillan was the last prime minister born in the reign of Queen Victoria. His successor was a competent man, but as a former peer he made the Conservative Party appear out-of-date and out-of-touch. In the election called the next year (1964), Labour, now led by forty-eight-year-old Harold Wilson, appeared as the party with younger leaders and new ideas and won a narrow victory. Margaret Thatcher was reelected for her north London constituency.

Recovery and Social Change

The Standard of Living

Despite Britain's underlying economic problems, since the 1950s the British people have enjoyed a rising standard of material comfort and a wide range of personal and social freedoms. At moments of crisis newspaper headlines screamed about economic disaster, and sometimes government policies intended to strengthen the national economy pinched the average person, but ordinarily the problems of the economy troubled only the experts.

In the 1950s Britain began moving into an age of economic well-being for the majority of its people, who also benefited from the the comprehensive services and subsidies of the welfare state. Virtually full employment and improved wages brought to an end the prewar culture of poverty. By the middle 1950s a third of all the pawnshops that had flourished a generation earlier had closed for lack of customers.

British businessmen courted the increasingly prosperous mass market with advertising and hire-purchase plans (installment buying) for cars, television sets, refrigerators, and washing machines. Multiple-branch retail chains such as the Marks and Spencer clothing stores offered standardized quality at a high level while keeping prices down. Self-service supermarkets replaced the numerous small shops that had made shopping a social occasion but far from efficient economically. New technologies created frozen foods, synthetic fabrics, and cheap plastics.

The new products and the new stores eased the household burdens of women. Prepared foods attractively packaged simplified cooking. The automatic washer, the laundromat, detergents, and permanent press greatly reduced the chores of washing and ironing. Popular women's magazines reflected and reinforced the forces for change. In early 1950s one of them, *Woman,* added a million sales with a how-to-do-it format including careers, cookery, child rearing, cosmetics, and sex.

Leisure changed greatly: there was more of it, more money was spent on it, and more of it was enjoyed at home or in cars that were extensions of home. The television set quickly changed from a luxury to a necessity for all classes of the population. Television viewing took people out of the pubs, as the increase in the sale of bottled beer showed. At first the state-owned British Broadcasting Corporation, financed by license fees, enjoyed a monopoly. Beginning in 1955, the Independent Television Authority offered an alternative financed by advertising. ITV attracted many working-class and lower-middle-class households away from the BBC with a schedule of light entertainment and American adventure and crime programs. Competition from television forced many cinemas to close, and the diversion of advertising revenues reduced the number of newspapers.

A Changing Society

Some people criticized the changes that were transforming British society. They complained that Britain was becoming Americanized and losing its national character. In the late 1950s and the early 1960s church attendance declined dramatically. The special English vice of gambling grew more conspicuous after 1960 when Parliament legalized gambling casinos and off-track betting. In 1956 Bill Haley's *Rock Around the Clock*, followed by the recordings of Chuck Berry and Elvis Presley, thrilled British youth and transformed popular music. In the 1960s, a young group of musicians and singers, the Beatles, expressed the youth culture's rejection of traditional values. Beginning in 1964, their attractive music and Liverpool accents sold millions of records on both sides of the Atlantic. In 1965 the Queen honored the Beatles for their contribution to exports by granting them membership in the Order of the British Empire.

The triumph of the Beatles swept away the older music and introduced the age of rock. The young, who had the most time and discretionary income to devote to leisure, developed a subculture in which recorded rock music played a prominent part. Helped by improved record players and inexpensive discs, the record industry sold four times as many records as before the war. Swinging London replaced the staid image of the British as old-fashioned and stuffy.

Shopping center in Croydon, Surrey, 1975. Private collection.

Gaudy boutiques on Carnaby Street and King's Road, unisex clothing, long-haired males and mini-skirted girls provided outward signs of a new cult of revolt and material gratification in which the young acted as trend-setters.

Pornographic books, magazines, and films, and live sex shows became commonplace. Though street solicitation was prohibited in 1956, prostitution itself was legal and many brothels thinly disguised as saunas advertised in the newspapers. It became common for young couples to live together without marriage or the prospect of marriage, and by the mid-1960s two out of three children born to mothers under twenty had been conceived out of wedlock. Before the decade ended homosexual acts and abortion were legalized, and capital punishment was abolished. Respect for law and order declined. In 1965 only seventy-nine policemen were victims of assault in Britain, but ten years later the number had grown to 2,835.

Other social changes that developed more quietly had greater significance than pop singers and short skirts. In 1911 only 14 percent of women

The Beatles. Michael Ochs Archive.

who worked were married; in 1966, 55 percent. Between 1911 and 1966 the number of blue collar workers remained comparatively stable, despite an increase in population, while white collar workers increased by 176 percent. In 1948 there were fewer than two million private cars; in 1968, nearly eleven million. Though the proliferation of the automobile gave a new mobility to individual drivers it led to a reduction in railroad service and changed the countryside. In 1970 eighteen-year-olds received the right to vote, and another statute required employers, beginning in 1975, to pay women equal pay for the same work.

Education changed dramatically to meet the needs of a technological age and a decidedly different younger generation. By the standards of virtually every other industrial country, British education remained highly stratified by social class. Some boys from well-off families attended prestigious private schools such as Eton and Harrow, misleadingly called "public schools." Students in the state system were sorted out, on the basis of an examination taken at age eleven, between university-oriented grammar schools and schools that prepared students for entry into the workforce. To break down class differences, the Labour Party favored comprehensive schools that offered both grammar school and other secondary school curricula, and this became the dominant trend in the 1960s.

An important new development was the growth in racial tensions. One of the legacies of empire was the immigration into Britain of hundreds of thousands of black people from the West Indies and Asians from India and Pakistan. In the late 1950s there were racial riots in the Notting Hill section of London and elsewhere. In 1963 Parliament passed the first of a series of immigration bills that made it difficult for immigrants to enter Britain from the nonwhite parts of the Commonwealth but allowed people from the white Commonwealth countries to immigrate with relative ease. These bills were accompanied by legislation to protect the rights of Commonwealth immigrants of all races already in Britain. The immigrants made a valuable contribution to the British economy. They were willing to keep their shops open late; they were indispensable to the operations of London Transport; and they added new foods, music, and styles to British life.

A NEW GENERATION IN POLITICS

Harold Wilson

The triumph of Labour in the election of 1964, and the ministry of Harold Wilson, brought a new direction to the Labour Party. Unlike Attlee and nearly all the Conservative leaders, who were part of the old elite of public school boys, Wilson had been educated in a grammar school, a state-supported sec-

West Indian immigrants prepare to disembark at Southhampton before the Commonwealth Immigration Act is enforced, 1963. UPI/Corbis-Bettmann.

ondary school. The son of a Yorkshire pharmacist, Wilson studied at Oxford, taught economics there, spent the war as a civil servant, and was elected to Parliament in the Labour landslide of 1945. A few years later he became the youngest member of Attlee's cabinet, and in 1950 he was one of the left-wing ministers who followed Aneurin Bevan out of office. In 1966 Wilson called an election to strengthen his support in Parliament and was rewarded with a comfortable majority.

Harold Wilson was a political juggler who had to deal with a variety of contradictions as Britain moved into a different kind of world. He had to manage a national economy, the paramount goal of the Labour Party, when Britain was increasingly involved in the world economy. To satisfy left-wing members of his party, he renationalized iron and steel, but his main concern was to develop new high-tech industries. He had to win the support of the growing salaried class of white-collar workers while holding his political base in the wage-earning workers of the declining manufacturing industries. The welfare state was an established fact and one of Labour's most cherished achievements, but the nation was increasingly unable to pay for it. British industry had become unimaginative and sluggish, and militant trade union leaders stubbornly maintained inefficient work rules, backing up their demands with wildcat (unofficial) strikes on the shop floor.

Wilson advocated a new approach to managing the economy, using control of money, credit, and interest rates instead of Labour's traditional emphasis on public ownership. In 1967 he was forced to devalue the pound, an admission that the British economy was still weak and inefficient in comparison with other industrial nations. To fight inflation the Wilson government cut capital investment in the nationalized industries and doggedly resisted wage demands. Drastic reductions of train service were made, despite the complaints of the unions and the public. Wilson proposed legislation to decrease the number of strikes by encouraging mediation and restricting wildcat strikes. Predictably the trade unions, which were still the backbone of the Labour Party, were opposed and forced the government to abandon this idea.

Wilson's emphasis on advanced knowledge and technology, led to a rapid growth of British higher education. Oxford, Cambridge, and the Victorian "red brick" universities were expanded, and new universities with handsome buildings and innovative curricula were established. Wilson was especially proud of the polytechnics, which offered career-oriented programs. The Open University had no campus, and enabled students to obtain a degree through televised lectures and correspondence.

Students admitted to universities received grants from the government to cover their tuition, and local governments provided grants for their living expenses, which led to a doubling of the number of full-time students in higher education from 1963–1970. Despite financial aid, few working-class children continued their schooling beyond their mid-teens.

In 1970 Wilson called an election that he expected to win. The new Conservative leader, Edward Heath, resembled Wilson in that he too was educated in a local grammar school. Son of a modest builder of houses, Heath attended Oxford on a scholarship. During the war he raised his status by attaining the rank of colonel. He was handsome and earnest, but at times his sincerity made him dull.

By 1970 the consensus established after World War II was beginning to break down as the British economy floundered. Heath promised a change of direction, with steps to strengthen the free market economy, restrict the powers of the unions, and reform the welfare state. While Wilson concentrated on looking prime ministerial, Heath waged a vigorous campaign and won an upset victory. Although Harold Wilson later returned to office, the Labour Party, with its socialist policies and trade union domination, was increasingly seen by the British public as obsolete.

Edward Heath and the Politics of Growth

Heath's proudest accomplishment was the successful negotiation of Britain's entry into the European Economic Community, effective on New Year's Day, 1973. It was made possible by the retirement of President DeGaulle several years earlier. Entry into the Common Market was a controversial decision. Some Conservatives did not want to weaken national sovereignty, or abandon long-established relationships with the United States and the Commonwealth. Left-wingers in the Labour Party objected to the loss of a managed national economy; trade unionists feared a partnership with nations that were less sympathetic to unions. Underlying the sense of unease was recognition that Britain was no longer master of its own destiny. The island people who had held out against Philip II, Louis XIV, Napoleon, and Hitler now found it necessary to capitulate to friendly but highly competitive rivals.

Heath took office committed to the view that Britain would have to modernize its economy to make it competitive within the Common Market and in the world. While opening up the economy to free enterprise and market forces, he saw the need to present the Conservative Party as the guardian of the social programs upon which so many people depended. His prescription for Britain's problems was economic growth, which would develop new industries and jobs while making it possible to maintain high levels of consumption and the welfare state.

Instead, Heath discovered that his policies created great disruptions in the national life. The government allowed the money supply to increase to encourage investment and consumer demand; the result was not constructive investment but a binge of speculation, consumer spending, rapidly rising house prices, and inflation. Heath reacted by abandoning his free-market principles ("the U-Turn") and imposing wage and price controls. In 1972 the Organization of Petroleum Exporting Countries (OPEC), a new factor in the world economy, achieved a dramatic increase in oil prices. As a result, the Heath government was forced to let the pound float downward to its international value, which added to price inflation and brought great disruption to Britain's financial sector. The boom collapsed, with widespread unemployment.

It was widely believed that economic growth was choked by the restrictions imposed by organized labor and especially by wildcat strikes. Heath tried to resolve these problems by an Industrial Relations Act, which organized labor resisted with crippling strikes on the railroads, at the electric power stations, and in the coal mines. An energy crisis arose in 1973 when defeat in the Arab-Israeli war led OPEC, dominated by the Arabs, to impose an embargo on shipments of oil. Taking advantage of the situation, the coal miners demanded wage increases well beyond the guidelines. Heath responded by ordering business and industry to go on a three-day week to save energy. Street lights were turned off and television broadcasting was reduced. When the miners went on strike Heath, driven to desperation, called for an election to determine "who governs Britain."

By 1974, the British public had seen enough of the headstrong Heath. They wanted to continue the consensus politics of the past. Harold Wilson and Labour won a slim victory, and later in the year Wilson called another election that strengthened his majority. Heath's Conservative Party was outraged by his rashness in provoking a showdown with the miners in the middle of an energy crisis and his decision to call an election in the midst of an emergency. After two electoral defeats in 1974, the Conservatives began looking for a new leader.

The Emergence of Margaret Thatcher

Resentment of Heath among Conservative backbenchers (members of Parliament who did not expect to hold office) provided an opportunity for Margaret Thatcher, who had been minister of education and science under Heath. Mrs. Thatcher had come to public attention when the Heath ministry, seeking to reduce the role and cost of government, cut the budget for her department. She had to choose between reducing expenditures for educational purposes or no longer providing free milk to students who could afford to pay. When she chose the latter, she aroused an angry hullabaloo and was known thereafter as "Thatcher, the milk snatcher."

Mrs. Thatcher challenged Heath's leadership in the annual leadership ballot of the Conservative members of the House of Commons. Although others had stronger claims to the leadership than she did, she won with the support of the backbenchers. Like Harold Wilson and Sir Edward Heath, Mrs. Thatcher was a representative of the middle-class "grammar school" graduates who were providing the new leadership of Britain. Her father was a small-town grocer and local councillor, and she received from her family an ethic of work and thrift that she sought to apply to government and the economy. She was educated at the local grammar school and took a degree in chemistry at Oxford with the support of scholarships. After graduation she was employed as a chemist, but her true interest was politics.

As a student, Margaret Thatcher had been active in Conservative Party organizations. As soon as she was established in her career as a chemist she gained political experience by running for Parliament in a Labour-dominated constituency where she was expected to lose, and did. There she met her husband, a wealthy businessman who provided her with a supportive companion and the financial means to pursue a political career. She abandoned politics for a few years to raise twins and develop a new career as a lawyer, but in 1959 she was elected to the House of Commons in the Macmillan victory of that year.

As a Cabinet officer under Heath, Mrs. Thatcher had developed her own ideas about leadership and the principles that the Conservative Party should adopt. She was not a consensus politician. She charged that previous Conservative governments had done little more than ratify what Labour had done, or had attempted to go Labour one better in extending the role and responsibilities of government. She brought to Conservatism an ideology of limited government, fiscal restraint, private enterprise in a market economy, and individual responsibility.

T H E   C E L T I C   F R I N G E

Devolution

The United Kingdom includes four main nationalities: the English, Welsh, Scots, and the Irish of Northern Ireland. In the 1970s disunifying tendencies threatened to unravel the proud Union Jack, as nationalist movements arose seeking greater self-government or "devolution." Devolution was weak in Wales, but Scotland already had separate administrative, legal, and religious institutions and a distinct national culture. The movement for devolution was especially threatening to the Labour Party, which had much of its strength in Scotland and Wales.

Unwilling to alienate potential supporters, both parties reluctantly agreed to submit the issue to the decision of the people concerned. In 1979 referenda were held in Scotland and Wales. In Scotland a majority of persons voting approved devolution, but the referendum required approval by 40 percent of eligible voters, and the turnout was too low. In Wales, Labour's support for the proposal was challenged by Neil Kinnock, a charismatic speaker, who played a leading role in the resounding defeat of the measure. By that time the economic crisis in Britain seemed more important than establishing more units of government.

Northern Ireland

One of the most serious problems to face Britain during the difficult seventies was the wave of terrorism and violence that wracked Northern Ireland. When Ireland became a separate state after World War I, the six northern counties (Ulster) remained part of the United Kingdom. The Protestant majority of Ulster looked to the union as a guarantee that they would not become subject to an Ireland dominated by Catholics and powerfully influenced by the Roman Catholic Church. Northern Ireland had its own ministry, civil service, police, and parliament, and also elected M.P.s to the Parliament in Westminster. Its people participated fully in the benefits of the British welfare state. Irish nationalists, however, insisted that they would never be satisfied until all of the island was united under the government in Dublin.

Influenced by struggles for civil rights in the United States, in the late 1960s a civil rights movement sprang up among the Catholics of Northern Ireland, who experienced discrimination in jobs, housing, and political power. Bernadette Devlin, a student, became a prominent leader of marches and demonstrations demanding equality, which provoked violent clashes with the police. The civil rights movement was concerned with changes in Ulster, but its efforts were complicated by the activities of a revived Irish Republican Army (the I.R.A.), which advocated political unity of the entire island.

The shootings and bombings of the I.R.A. and the unpopularity of the Ulster police led the British government to send troops into Ulster to preserve order until a political resolution of the conflict could be achieved. The Ulster Protestants viewed the army as sent to support the status quo, while the Catholics resented this new assertion of British power. Neither side was much interested in reconciliation or compromise. As was likely in such a volatile situation, violence increased, capped by Bloody Sunday in 1972, when British paratroopers trying to control a mob killed thirteen Catholics. Heath, who did not shrink from confrontations, suspended the Protestant-controlled government of Ulster and announced direct rule from London, a policy that outraged both Protestants and Catholics. Angry at the failure of the authorities to suppress the I.R.A., Protestant paramilitary organizations began a counterterror.

Wearily the British government searched for a way in which the peoples of Ulster could live together. In 1974 Britain introduced a new provincial government in which the two religious communities would share power. Leaders of the Protestant majority did not wish to share power, and working-class Protestants organized a wide-spread strike that forced the collapse of this experiment. A convention was elected in 1975 to draw up a new constitution, but it could agree on nothing.

Meanwhile sectarian murders struck down hundreds on crowded Belfast streets and lonely rural roads, in homes darkened for sleep and in noisy bars. When beatings and bombings in Northern Ireland did not achieve the goal, the I.R.A. extended the terror into Britain. Seven died and 120 were injured when two Birmingham pubs were bombed in 1974. Late that year the I.R.A. called a holiday truce which was extended in return for the gradual release of interned suspects. The truce slowed but did not stop terrorism. In 1975 London was struck by a series of bombings at the Tower of London, Harrod's department store, the Hilton Hotel, and several underground stations. There were dozens of frightening hoaxes as well. The British government, press, and people roundly criticized Americans, primarily of Irish extraction, who sent weapons and financial aid to the I.R.A. Britain found that a policy of direct rule and martial law did not accomplish its purpose and only brought the problems of Ulster closer to home.

THE DOWNFALL OF LABOUR

Wilson Again

Harold Wilson's two victories in the elections of 1974 put him back in No. 10 Downing Street, but they did not provide him with policies that would enable Britain to meet the dramatically changed world economy of the 1970s. The miners received a pay increase and Heath's Industrial Relations Act was repealed, but the fundamental flaws in the British economy remained. Inflation, inefficiency, and wildcat strikes continued while unemployment rose. Wilson made a "social contract" with the unions to fight inflation if they would hold down wage increases and strikes. The major accomplishments of Wilson's brief second ministry were steps to benefit women: legislation requiring equal pay for equal work, maternity leave for women workers, and special benefits to mothers, including single mothers. The elderly were aided by improved pensions.

Wilson's political agility was again demonstrated on the issue of British membership in the European Economic Community. British membership was opposed in the Labour Party by left wing socialists, and in the Conservative Party by right-wing nationalists. Nimbly Wilson avoided taking a stand by proposing a referendum on the issue, a device previously unknown in the British constitution. The voters gave overwhelming approval to continuance in the Common Market, and that question was settled.

In 1976 Harold Wilson announced his decision to resign. Wilson had prolonged the role of the Labour Party as a major political party, but at the same time his political legerdemain had concealed the fact that its prescriptions for the country had either been discredited (socialism) or accomplished (the welfare state). The new ideas in the Labour Party came from the radical left and were too extreme to have credibility with the voters.

Wilson's successor as prime minister was James Callaghan, a likeable veteran of Labour Party politics. Callaghan continued Wilson's economic policies, trying to sustain Britain's socialist economy, welfare state, and extended foreign policy commitments. It was an impossible task. Britain was grossly overstretched because it was not generating the economic growth needed to support its expectations. For a time the growing wealth of the western world, in which Britain shared, had disguised the fact that the British system was not functioning well. Likeable and well-meaning as he was, James Callaghan was not the person to make fundamental changes, and the Labour Party was determined to preserve the system on which its power was based and its hopes were pinned.

Callaghan's main problem was to hold his party together while beginning financial reforms to deal with inflation and industrial breakdown. The problems of Britain were complicated by a severe world recession that combined inflation and stagnation ("stagflation"). Vast sums of money, much of it derived from high oil prices, flitted through global markets, making it difficult for any national government to manage its economy. Inflation in Britain was higher than in most industrial countries. Unemployment exceeded the worst figures since World War II. The International Monetary Fund gave Britain a credit of almost four billion dollars in exchange for humiliating controls on public spending and unpopular restraints on consumption.

Callaghan knew that the inflationary environment of the 1970s had invalidated the old economic nostrums. In 1976 he said to the Labour Party's annual conference:

> "We used to think you could spend your way out of a recession by
> cutting taxes and boosting spending. I tell you in all candour that this
> option no longer exists and that in so far as it ever did exist, it only
> worked by injecting a bigger dose of inflation into the system."

With the exception of the strong German mark, the other members of the European Economic Community had similar problems. To fight inflation, they established the Exchange Rate Mechanism (ERM) to keep their currencies in a close relationship with the mark and each other. The Callaghan government, devoted to Labour's concept of a socialist, managed economy, refused to join. Instead, Labour's left-wingers insisted upon another dose of socialism. British Leyland, Britain's bankrupt auto industry was nationalized, and proposals were made to nationalize the floundering shipbuilding and aerospace industries. Labour's "social contract" collapsed, as workers demanded wage increases to keep up with inflation.

Margaret Thatcher, leader of the Conservative opposition, attacked socialism and called for restrictions on the trade unions. A nationalistic, racist organization called the National Front emerged, demanding withdrawal from the European Economic Community, advocating capital punishment and a crackdown on crime, and opposing further nonwhite immigration. The Scottish Nationalist Party was furious at the failure of devolution, which it attributed to opposition from the Labour Party in Scotland.

The British economy almost ground to a halt in the winter of 1978–1979—"the winter of our discontent," it was called. A strike of road haulers had a devastating effect until it was settled with a wage increase in defiance of the Callaghan ministry's guidelines. Workers in the public services also went on strike: ambulance drivers, water and sewer workers, and garbagemen, leaving heaps of trash littering city streets. In Liverpool unburied corpses were stored in a vacant factory; a strike of school janitors kept hundreds of thou-

Top: Barbican public housing towers, London, built in the 1950s and 1960s.
Bottom: Noonday business at Barbican, 1975. Private Collection.

sands of children home from school. National Health service hospitals would take only emergency cases; other ill people were left untended. The National Front conducted confrontational marches, engaging in street clashes with left-wingers. There was a sense that Britain had come to the end of the road.

In March 1979 the Labour government was defeated in the House of Commons, 311-310 on a vote of No Confidence in which the Conservatives were joined by Liberals, Ulster Unionists, and Scottish Nationalists. The five-year period for parliamentary elections was drawing to a close, and Callaghan had no choice but to call an election under disastrous circumstances. As leader of the Conservative Party, Margaret Thatcher campaigned aggressively on the need for Britain to develop a competitive, free enterprise economy and blamed the trade unions for many of Britain's problems. She criticized those who abused the welfare state to live in a culture of dependence. She emphasized the importance of values such as strong families, home ownership, personal savings, educational opportunities, and law and order. She neutralized the National Front by supporting restrictions on immigration.

Despite the great advances made since World War II, by 1979 Britain was living on borrowed time and money. The consensus of the past had broken down, and Mrs. Thatcher promised drastic change. Uncertain what to expect, the British people decided to give her a chance. In the election of May 1979 Margaret Thatcher and the Conservatives won a majority of seats in the House of Commons with 44 percent of the votes. Labour polled 37 percent.

Mrs. Thatcher's victory was not a matter of personal popularity. She was not well known, and her reputation was that of a strident extremist. Thatcher and the Conservative Party were the beneficiaries of a backlash arising from Britain's desperate condition. The British people, including many of the skilled workers, had turned against the Labour Party, socialism, and trade union power.

The day after the election Callaghan resigned, and Mrs. Thatcher and her husband drove to Buckingham Palace to receive the reins of government from the Queen. Margaret Thatcher had become the first woman leader of a major industrial state.

SUGGESTIONS FOR FURTHER READING

Many of the books cited for chapter 16 continue to be useful for the postwar period. Good general introductions are C. J. Bartlett, *A History of Postwar Britain, 1945-74* (1977), Alan Sked and Chris Cook, *Post-War Britain: A Political History* (1993); Kenneth O. Morgan, *The People's Peace: British History, 1945-1989* (1990); and Peter Clarke, *Hope and Glory: Britain, 1900-1990* (1996). An assessment is offered by David Childs in *Britain since 1939: Progress and Decline* (1995).

British politics are surveyed in David Dutton, *British Politics since 1945: The Rise and Fall of Consensus* (1997). Dennis Kavanagh pursues the same theme in *Consensus Politics from Attlee to Major* (1994). Good introductions to the postwar Labour governments are offered by Kenneth O. Morgan, *Labour in Power, 1945-1951* (1985) and Henry Pelling, *The Labour Governments, 1945-51* (1984). A more recent study of the same topic is Robert D. Pearce, *Attlee's Labour Governments, 1945-51* (1994). Alex J. Robertson tells a dramatic story in *The Bleak Midwinter 1947* (1987). The ministries of Harold Wilson are covered in Robert R. James, *Ambi-*

tions and Realities: British Politics, 1964–70 (1972). Kevin Jeffreys examines the change in Labour Party views in *Retreat from New Jerusalem, 1951–64* (1997). *The Heath Government, 1970-1974: A Reappraisal* (1996), Stuart Ball and Anthony Seldon (eds.), offers an assessment.

The change in Britain's world role resulting from World War II is discussed in Joseph Frankel, *British Foreign Policy, 1945–1973* (1975) and F. S. Northedge, *Descent from Power: British Foreign Policy, 1945–1973* (1974). One of the most important changes in Britain's external policies is examined in C. J. Bartlett, *"The Special Relationship": A Political History of Anglo-American Relations since 1945* (1992) and *The Special Relationship: Anglo-American Relations since 1945* (1986), a useful collection of essays edited by William R. Louis and Hedley Bull. Louis also covers *The British Empire in the Middle East, 1945–1951* (1984).

Martin Chick analyzes the planning behind the nationalization of industry in *Industrial Policy in Britain, 1945–1951* (1998) and Norman Chester covers *The Nationalization of British Industry, 1945–1951* (1975). B. W. E. Alford assesses *British Economic Performance, 1945–1995* (1995). James E. Cronin, *Industrial Conflict in Modern Britain* (1979) deals with one of Britain's most persistent and damaging problems.

Pauline Gregg covers *The Welfare State: An Economic and Social History of Great Britain from 1945 to the Present Day* (1969). The problems of the welfare state are discussed in William Breckinridge and Stephen Clark, *Economics and Politics: Poverty and Social Security in Britain since 1961* (1982). Charles Webster tells a fascinating story in *The National Health Service: A Political History* (1998). George A. N. Lowndes surveys *The Silent Social Revolution: An Account of the Expansion of Public Education in England and Wales, 1895–1965* (1969). Ian R. G. Spencer covers *British Immigration Policy since 1939: The Making of a Multi-Racial Britain* (1997), and Catherine Jones reviews *Immigration and Social Policy in Britain* (1977).

Arthur Marwick offers a good introduction to *British Society since 1945* (1996) and *Culture in Britain since 1945* (1991). See also Judith Ryder and Harold Silver, *Modern English Society* (1985). Bernard Levin examines *The Pendulum Years: Britain and the Sixties* (1970), and Norman Shrapnel is highly critical of *The Seventies: Britain's Inward March* (1980). John Colville, *The New Elizabethans, 1959–1977* (1977) reviews broad changes in British life. Anthony Sampson, *The Changing Anatomy of England* (1982) and other books gives much attention to movers and shakers. Philip Norman, *Shout! The Beatles in their Generation* (1977) deals with a phenomenon that extended Britain's influence in an unexpected way. Jane E. Lewis discusses *Women in Britain since 1945* (1992).

On the Celtic fringe, Kenneth O. Morgan deals with *Modern Wales: Politics, Places, and People* (1995). For Ireland, books by Boyce and McCaffrey cited earlier are relevant. Paul Bew reviews *The British State and the Ulster Crisis: From Wilson to Thatcher* (1985).

For the last years of the British Empire see books cited in chapter 16. See also Muriel E. Chamberlain, *Decolonization* (1985) and John Darwin, *Britain and Decolonisation: The Retreat from Empire in the Post-War World* (1988).

Memoirs and biographies are especially important for recent history. Good biographies are Trevor Burridge, *Clement Attlee: A Political Biography* (1995); Robert D. Pearce, *Attlee* (1997); Alan Bullock, *The Life and Times of Ernest Bevin* (1960); Ben Pimlott, *Hugh Dalton* (1985); F. M. Leventhal, *Arthur Henderson* (1989); Michael Foot, *Aneurin Bevan: A Biography* (1963); David Dutton, *Anthony Eden: A Life and Reputation* (1997); Philip M. Williams, *Hugh Gaitskell: A Political Biography* (1979); Nigel Fisher, *Harold Macmillan: A Biography* (1982); Alistair Horne, *Harold Macmillan* (1991); and John Campbell, *Edward Heath: A Biography* (1993). The memoirs of Harold Macmillan, published from 1966–1973, are of exceptional interest. Kenneth O. Morgan has written *Callaghan: A Life* (1997) and a biographical history of the Labour Party in *Labour People: Leaders and Lieutenants, Hardie to Kinnock* (1987).

CHAPTER EIGHTEEN

The Thatcher Revolution
1979–1997

Margaret Thatcher began a process of institutional change that transformed British government and the British economy. In part, these changes were dictated by the breakdown of the economic system established by the Labour Party from 1945–1951, the intransigeance of the trade unions, and the collapse of Labour party unity when confronted with these problems. The rise of a global economy was a contributing factor. But the direction taken by Britain was a consequence of the leadership and ideas of Margaret Thatcher. Her reforms were completed by her Conservative successor, John Major. Tony Blair, leader of "New Labour," accepted the Thatcherite changes and won a landslide electoral victory in 1997. Under Blair, Thatcherism became the basis for a new era of change as Britain prepared for the twenty-first century.

MARGARET THATCHER AND "THATCHERISM"

The Prime Minister

Margaret Thatcher came to office determined to change Britain in the direction that she had identified while in opposition. She was a strong advocate of reducing the role of government in the national life, budgetary and monetary restraint to stabilize prices and interest rates, and free enterprise in a competitive market economy. She undertook extensive reform of the central government, and struggled to reduce the cost of local governments. She was determined to limit the powers of the trade unions and to begin dismantling social-

*Margaret Thatcher. Reuters/
Corbis-Bettmann.*

ism by selling off the nationalized industries. She was convinced that the open-ended commitments of the welfare state made it impossible to control public expenditure and contributed to a dependency culture among those who relied upon it.

In her first three years Margaret Thatcher was one of Britain's most unpopular prime ministers. In the Conservative Party, some of the former party leaders resented the way she had pushed aside Sir Edward Heath, who remained her implacable opponent. Her tough-minded approach to the economy and the welfare state violated the long-held tradition of Tory Democracy in her own party and the humane instincts characteristic of the British people. The Labour Party saw her attack on socialism and trade union power as rejection of the principles that had shaped Britain since World War II. And she was a victim of the world recession and the immediate effects of her own policies.

The most pressing challenge facing the Thatcher ministry was to cope with industrial breakdown and mounting unemployment. Mrs. Thatcher believed that the root cause of the recession was inflation, which in 1980 reached 18 percent. High inflation discouraged business investment, led to short-term speculation and profiteering, and penalized saving. She introduced unpopular tax increases and budget cuts, and by 1982 inflation had fallen to 4 percent.

The measures taken to attack inflation initially led to increased unemployment, which rose from 4.3 percent of the labor force in 1979 to 9.8 percent in 1982. Many of Britain's languishing industries in the Midlands and the North never did recover, and thousands who lost their jobs in the shakeout never regained employment. As inflation declined the British economy began to revive, but a high price had been paid.

The Thatcher government was also beset with a rash of strikes, as workers were wracked by inflation and job losses. Mrs. Thatcher was determined to limit the power of the trade unions. Supported by a public driven to desperation by "the winter of discontent," she struck back with the Employment Act of 1982, which sharply restricted the power of trade union leaders to call strikes and engage in picketing.

Mrs. Thatcher also had a bone to pick with the European Community. She recognized the importance of access to Europe for British trade, but she abrasively stated her determination to reduce Britain's financial contribution, which she regarded as excessive. Eventually she succeeded, but the disputes of "the Iron Lady," as she was called, did not end there. When the European Community began preparations for closer political and monetary union, she stated emphatically her determination to preserve British sovereignty.

In a speech at Bruges, Belgium, Mrs. Thatcher stated that the European Community should be one of distinct nationalities: "France as France, Spain as Spain, Britain as Britain, each with its own customs, traditions, and identities." She criticized the complex regulations of the Community, adding: "We have not successfully rolled back the frontiers of the state in Britain only to see them reimposed at the European level." She urged the Community to turn its attention to expansion into eastern Europe, a step that would require reconsideration of its costly system of agricultural and regional subsidies.

Defeat in the election of 1979 brought a dramatic change in the Labour Party. Bitter differences broke out between moderates and left wingers. James Callaghan retired from the party leadership and Michael Foot, a mild-mannered, scholarly man became the new leader. The left wing of the party became dominant, and party meetings were filled with discord. In March 1981 four prominent Labour politicians left the Labour Party to found the Social Democratic Party, a party with a strong commitment to the welfare state but not committed to socialism or dependent on the trade unions. In June they allied with the Liberal Party to form a nonsocialist alternative to the Labour Party.

The Falklands War

In April 1982 Mrs. Thatcher was challenged by General Leopoldo Galtieri, leader of Argentina, whose troops invaded the Falkland Islands, a British possession in the South Atlantic. Britain and Argentina had conflicting claims to the islands, which were inhabited by eighteen hundred British citizens. Mrs. Thatcher reacted vigorously to this overt aggression and sent a force of ships, planes, and troops to the rescue. The Queen's second son, Prince Andrew, was a helicopter pilot on one of the aircraft carriers.

Britain's willingness to wage war came as somewhat of a surprise to the international community. The members of the European Community and the Commonwealth imposed crippling economic sanctions on Argentina, and the Security Council of the United Nations condemned the invasion. At first the United States tried to achieve a peaceful resolution, but eventually America provided logistical support that was of great value to the British forces. While a fierce air war raged at sea, British troops landed on the Falklands and were rapidly reinforced. The Argentine forces surrendered, the Galtieri regime collapsed, and Mrs. Thatcher had won a military victory that harked back to the days of Drake and Nelson.

The Election of 1983

Mrs. Thatcher's prestige had leaped with the victory in the Falklands, and the economy was beginning to recover. To take advantage of her new popularity, Mrs. Thatcher called an election in June 1983. Michael Foot, leader of the Labour Party, was constantly embarrassed by the leftwingers in his party, who wanted to abandon NATO and the nuclear deterrent, and restore socialism and trade union power. Labour's platform was unlikely to appeal to an electorate that mistrusted the Soviet Union and remembered the collapse of the British economy in the winter of 1978–1979. The Social Democratic/Liberal Alliance was gaining stature as a party of the moderate left. The divisions of the opposition made it possible for Mrs. Thatcher to win a strong majority of seats in the House of Commons with 42 percent of the popular vote. Labour obtained only 28 percent of the vote, and the Alliance, with 25 percent, showed the possibility of becoming the main opposition party.

THE THATCHER AGENDA

Privatization

Buoyed by her election victory, Mrs. Thatcher moved boldly to carry out her restructuring of the British economy. In her first ministry she had begun by selling off some of the smaller nationalized industries (privatization), which had gone well. Her first major privatization came in 1984 with British Telecom, the nationalized telephone company. After an aggressive advertising campaign aimed at small purchasers, more than a million people applied for shares. Mrs. Thatcher boasted that she had established a new policy of "people's capitalism." After privatization, British Telecom's equipment and service improved dramatically, and instead of being a laggard it became a world leader in communications.

In 1986 British Gas, with its vast network of gas pipes reaching every home and business, was privatized in an even bigger deal. The largest privatization of all was the sale of the government's shares in British Petroleum. Additional privatizations were the sale of British Airways, Rolls Royce aircraft engines, and the British Airports Authority, which operated most British airports. Later the water and electricity companies were sold to private investors. One of the most successful privatizations was selling off public housing units to the tenants. In 1980 a Housing Bill was introduced that gave tenants of council houses the right to purchase their houses at low prices. Home ownership brought a profound change to working-class life, and also eroded the base of the Labour Party.

The Trade Unions

In her second ministry, Mrs. Thatcher was ready for a showdown with organized labor. As coal was replaced by oil, natural gas, and nuclear power, the nationalized coal industry fell into steep decline, and the Coal Board decided to close money-losing pits. Mrs. Thatcher knew that the miners' union would strike, and she was determined to avoid another defeat like the debacle that

Houses of Parliament. Private collection.

had destroyed Sir Edward Heath's ministry in 1974. When Arthur Scargill, the combative leader of the miners' union called for a strike, he received luke-warm support from the labor movement. The miners in the more productive pits, fearful of losing their jobs, continued working. In violation of the rules of his union, Scargill did not call a strike vote, knowing that he would lose. In-stead, he used militant pickets from the threatened mines to intimidate those miners who opposed the strike. Leaders of the transport workers and railwaymen expressed support, but their members continued working and moving coal.

The Coal Board knew that it was essential to maintain electric power, and they made elaborate preparations to keep the generators working. Gener-ating plants were hastily converted from coal to oil or gas. Nuclear plants were operated at maximum capacity. When Scargill's pickets tried to block the mines that were operating, the Employment Act of 1982 was used to bring in hun-dreds of police to restrain the pickets. The Coal Board offered bonuses to strikers who returned to their jobs, and by March 1985 the strike had ended in defeat for Scargill and the miners. Margaret Thatcher had won the battle that Sir Edward Heath had lost ten years earlier. Unions continued to be important in British industry, but their main weapon—the strike—had been blunted, and they could no longer dominate the economy.

Northern Ireland

In Northern Ireland the Thatcher ministry fought a battle that it could not win. Mrs. Thatcher was determined to preserve Northern Ireland as part of the United Kingdom and fight I.R.A. terrorism, but she was also willing to work with the Republic of Ireland and the Catholics of Northern Ireland to resolve grievances. Violence continued in Northern Ireland, and in 1981 the I.R.A. took its campaign of terrorism to the mainland, setting off bombs in London and elsewhere. In 1984, when the Conservative Party's annual confer-ence was being held, an I.R.A. bomb was set off in the hotel where Mrs. Thatcher and other Conservative leaders were staying. Mrs. Thatcher escaped unhurt, although six people were killed and many others were injured.

The next year Britain and the Republic of Ireland agreed to work together against terrorism and to cooperate in dealing with nationalist (Catholic) complaints. The unionists (Protestants) were unhappy with this arrangement, which they thought would lead eventually to a takeover of Northern Ireland by the Republic. The I.R.A. and gangs of Protestant militants continued their violence, and resolu-tion of the discontents of Northern Ireland seemed as far off as ever.

The Election of 1987

By June 1987 the economy was doing well, and Mrs. Thatcher called another election. She was respected for her leadership, but she was not personally popular, due to her assertive manner, continuing high unemployment, and cuts in popular social programs. Labour was led by Neil Kinnock, a dynamic Welsh-man handicapped by the outmoded policies of his party. The Social Demo-cratic-Liberal Alliance, which had done so well in 1983, was in disarray. Once again, the Conservatives won a majority of seats with only 42 percent of the votes. After the election, the Alliance parties fused to create the Liberal Demo-cratic Party, led by Paddy Ashdown. Kinnock, assisted by Tony Blair, a rising star, began rebuilding the structure and policies of the Labour Party.

The Welfare State

Margaret Thatcher believed that the structure of the British state was ineffi-cient, and she was determined to reform it from top to bottom. Her general principle was to concentrate decision-making at the top and decentralize the delivery of services. She undertook extensive reform of the civil service based on a core of top civil servants to advise ministers on matters of policy and decentralized agencies to conduct routine administration of programs. Tough controls were imposed on spending by local governments, many of which were controlled by Labour. Agencies and local governments were required to "con-tract out" many services to private enterprises through competitive bidding.

Through the National Health Service (NHS), Britain provided free medi-cal care to all its people. With improved medicine and greater longevity, the overburdened NHS floundered and a chorus of complaints arose. Despite its problems, the NHS was popular with the British public, and Mrs. Thatcher knew that something had to be done about it. The Thatcher ministry trans-formed the NHS by decentralizing its operations and introducing the prin-ciple of "the internal market." At the top, the NHS doled out the money to doctors and hospitals and maintained general supervision. Doctors were given block grants (fundholding) which they used to purchase services from special-ists and hospitals, who presumably competed for their business.

As Minister for Education and Science under Heath, Mrs. Thatcher had developed strong ideas about schools. She believed that the curriculum did not include enough basic subjects, and that teachers were more concerned with the personal development of students than substantive learning. She was also a bitter opponent of the National Union of Teachers (NUT), one of the most articulate and militant unions in the Labour Party.

The Thatcher school reform had two main objectives. One was to raise standards by establishing a national curriculum giving more attention to En-glish, mathematics and science. The National Curriculum would be backed up by national tests at ages seven, eleven, fourteen, and sixteen. The test re-sults of each school would be published, thus putting schools and teachers on the spot. Mrs. Thatcher also wanted to end control of schools by local educa-tion authorities, which often were dominated by Labour and the NUT. Schools were authorized to "opt out" from local control and receive grants directly from the Treasury. It was thought that these "grant-maintained" schools would maintain higher standards and serve as benchmarks for the local-authority schools. A program of grants was established to assist students from low-income families in attending private schools.

Margaret Thatcher was highly critical of the universities, which she felt were inordinately expensive and offered many courses that were irrelevant to the modern world. To cut costs, she stopped university expansion and proposed that students pay tuition fees. This proposal aroused a mass of complaints from the middle class, the core of the Conservative Party, and had to be withdrawn. Students also received grants from their local governments for living costs. The Thatcher squeeze on local government expenditure meant that these did not keep pace with inflation. The Thatcher ministry favored the polytechnics, which had career-oriented programs and lower costs. They continue to grow, and their enrollments eventually exceeded the universities'.

BRITAIN AND THE WORLD

The Cold War

Mrs. Thatcher had grown up during World War II, when Britain and the United States had stood together against the evil Nazi empire of Adolf Hitler. When that war had ended a new threat had emerged: the Soviet Union, victorious and powerful under Joseph Stalin, had extended its power over Eastern Europe and threatened Western Europe with military conquest or Communist revolutions. Once again Britain and the United States had joined to oppose a threatening dictatorship and the Cold War had been born.

Mrs. Thatcher held strong views on British foreign policy. She was concerned about Britain's declining role in world affairs, which she believed was due not only to diminished resources but also to a failure of national will. Although much had changed by 1979, Mrs. Thatcher clung to the vision of a "special relationship" with the United States, in which the two countries, linked by a common language and heritage, stood together for their own security and for the democratic principles fundamental to both. When Ronald Reagan was inaugurated president of the United States in January, 1981, Mrs. Thatcher had an ally who had built his career as an avid Cold Warrior, and who shared her views about government and the free-market economy.

The rise of Mikhail Gorbachev to power in the Soviet Union offered a possible resolution of the Cold War, and Mrs. Thatcher reacted quickly. Gorbachev visited London in December 1984 and Mrs. Thatcher declared: "I like Mr. Gorbachev; we can do business together." She urged President Reagan to seek an accord with Gorbachev on control of nuclear weapons, and other steps were taken to relax superpower tensions.

By 1989 the Soviet economy was falling apart, and the satellite states of Eastern Europe began throwing off Soviet domination. In November, 1989 the Berlin Wall fell and the next year the formerly Communist East German state joined with West Germany to restore a united German nation. The Russian people blamed Gorbachev for their political and economic breakdown, and Boris Yeltsin began his rise to power. In 1991 the Soviet Union collapsed, and Russia became an independent state headed by Yeltsin. By that time Mrs. Thatcher was out of power, but her role as middleman between the United States and the Soviet Union had been helpful in keeping a dangerous transition from becoming a conflagration.

China

Another major foreign policy issue was China, which was entering a period of economic growth that would eventually make it a major force in the world. Britain's immediate concern was the future of Hong Kong, for Communist China was determined to take over the colony when the British lease expired in 1997. Although the people of Hong Kong wanted to keep their unique position as a center of finance and trade, the Chinese were determined to obtain sovereignty, and Britain had no choice but to attempt to get the best deal possible for the colony. Britain agreed to cede Hong Kong to China in 1997, and the Chinese, in turn, agreed to give Hong Kong special status for fifty years. Nevertheless, many residents began moving their wealth and families to places that offered better long-term security.

THE DECLINE AND FALL
OF MARGARET THATCHER

The Community Charge (Poll Tax)

From the beginning of her ministry Mrs. Thatcher had struggled to reform local government in the interest of efficiency and economy. One step was to abolish the Labour-controlled Greater London Council, which coordinated the governments of the broad metropolitan area. Mrs. Thatcher's main concern was to control the cost of local government. The central government provided 60 percent of the money for local government, the rates (the real estate tax) providing the remainder. Business and homeowners, who were mainly Conservatives, paid most of the rates, while Labour-controlled governments in major industrial cities spent the money for public services that mainly benefited renters.

Anti-poll tax demonstration,
March 31, 1990.
Corbis/Reuters.

Mrs. Thatcher was determined that everyone should pay part of the cost of local government, which would make the people a force for economy. Legislation was passed to replace the rates with a community charge (poll tax) on every person over eighteen. Local governments would determine the level of the poll tax, and presumably they would feel the public's indignation if the tax was too high.

The poll tax aroused a storm of protest. Taxing the rich and the poor equally seemed so unfair that the general public was incredulous. Homeowners found that their poll taxes were higher than their rates had been. A widely circulated photograph showed a wealthy nobleman speaking to a poor woman who rented space on his estate to park her tiny mobile home: both paid the same poll tax! Many renters could not pay or flatly refused to pay, and riots broke out in London and elsewhere. People blamed Margaret Thatcher for their poll taxes, not their local government, as she had intended. Conservatives were appalled at the public outcry, and the Labour Party saw a winning issue. The poll tax boomeranged, but Margaret Thatcher insisted on seeing it through.

The Gulf War

While Mrs. Thatcher's problems at home were growing, she was distracted by another foreign crisis. In August 1990 Saddam Hussein, the militaristic dictator of Iraq, suddenly invaded his oil-rich neighbor, Kuwait. Mrs. Thatcher, victor of the Falklands War, urged President George Bush to organize an international alliance against Saddam. Led by the United States, a massive allied force was assembled to restore the independence of Kuwait. In a stunning victory viewed on television throughout the world, the Iraqui forces were defeated, but Saddam remained in power and the core of his army escaped. Britain contributed more than 50,000 troops to the victory.

The End (November, 1990)

As the buildup for the Gulf War took place, Mrs. Thatcher was driven from office by members of her own party, many of whom had been restless under her constant drive for reform. The poll tax was the last straw. In November 1990, when the annual leadership election took place, she was challenged by Michael Heseltine, a man of leadership ability who resented her dominating ways. Although Mrs. Thatcher won a majority, she had fallen short of the required number of votes, and a second ballot would be needed. Members of her Cabinet told her that her support in the party was crumbling and that she could not win.

Accepting the inevitable, Margaret Thatcher resigned, a victim of the same procedure that she had used to take over from Heath. She insisted that the Conservatives choose a rising young politician, John Major, instead of her archrival, Heseltine. After serving eleven remarkable years and winning three elections, the reign of Margaret Thatcher had ended, but the principles of Thatcherism continued to shape the government, economy, and social institutions of the United Kingdom and exert an influence throughout the world.

JOHN MAJOR AND THATCHERISM

The Successor

John Major was a politician of a new generation. He was too young to remember World War II, and, unlike his predecessors, he had not attended a university. He grew up in modest circumstances in Brixton, a low-income, racially mixed part of London. He left school at age 16 and got a job in a bank to help support his family. Major was personable and articulate, and was elected to the House of Commons in 1979. He had risen to prominence under Margaret

Thatcher, but he got along well with all elements of the Conservative Party. His low-keyed manner was welcomed by the public after eleven years of Margaret Thatcher. One of his first steps was to get rid of the poll tax. A variation called the council tax was implemented, which combined some characteristics of the rates with a modified tax on individuals.

John Major was prime minister when the Gulf War took place, and his popularity soared as a result of the victory. Like President George Bush, his high ratings in the polls began to fall as another period of inflation and economic stagnation began. Overexpansion during the Thatcher boom years had led to high interest rates, followed inevitably by bankruptcies, foreclosures of mortgages, and rising unemployment. Major's efforts to keep the pound in step with other European currencies through the Exchange Rate Mechanism (ERM) aggravated the situation. The south of England, which had been spared the worst of the Thatcher recession, was especially hard hit.

An election was due in 1992, and John Major and the Conservative Party had to go before the voters in the depths of a recession. Major's main assets were his pleasant personality, evident honesty and openness, and ability to communicate with ordinary people. On several occasions he talked to the voters from a soapbox.

Having lost three elections to Margaret Thatcher, it was evident that the Labour Party would have to change. Neil Kinnock, assisted by Tony Blair, a rising young Labour M.P., undertook to transform Labour into a party of the moderate left that could appeal to the growing middle class and to white-collar workers. The Liberal Democrats, led by Paddy Ashdown, hoped that a close contest would increase their negotiating power. Margaret Thatcher did not seek reelection. She received a peerage and entered the House of Lords, where she continued to speak out on major issues.

In a surprise victory, John Major and the Conservatives received 42 percent of the votes and a margin of 21 seats in Parliament. Labour rose to 35 percent of the popular vote, but clearly had not made itself electable. Kinnock resigned as leader of the Labour Party and was succeeded by John Smith, a Scot, who died suddenly two years later.

Smith was succeeded by Tony Blair, who projected youth and vitality. Blair realized that a party based on socialism and the trade unions could not win. He accepted the Thatcher reforms and promised to move forward from there. He proposed to create a new Labour Party that would recognize the importance of capitalist enterprise and the workings of the market, but would be humane in its concern for the welfare of individuals and the larger community. He declared that his policy toward the unions would be "fairness, not favours." He promised to deal vigorously with social concerns such as education, crime, and the breakdown of the family.

The Maastricht Treaty

John Major hoped to establish better relations between Britain and the other members of the European Community, but he was hampered by the strong antagonism felt toward Europe by many members of the Conservative Party. These feelings were enhanced by proposals from other countries for a federal union, a prospect that aroused alarm within the Conservative Party and large segments of the British public. In December 1991 the European Council of Ministers met at Maastricht in the Netherlands to sign a treaty creating the European Union, which was intended to lead to a federal Europe. Major insisted that Britain could accept the treaty only if it could "opt out" of the proposed European money (the euro) and the labor regulations (the Social Chapter) of the European Union. He got his "opt-outs" and returned to Britain, convinced that he had satisfied the reservations of the "Euro-Skeptics," Conservatives opposed to closer European integration.

The parliamentary debates on the Maastricht Treaty were bitter and prolonged. Both parties had members who were opposed to the treaty, but the differences were most intense among the Conservatives. John Major pleaded for unity in support of the treaty and his "opt-outs." He emphasized the need to strengthen Britain's economic interests in Europe while preserving British sovereignty in monetary policy and labor regulations. The debates had to go through many stages, and eventually John Major had to make the treaty a vote of confidence to get it through the House of Commons.

After the election of 1992, the popularity of John Major and the Conservative Party began to decline. The recession continued and interest rates remained high to maintain the value of the pound in the Exchange Rate Mechanism (ERM). In September 1992 ("Black Wednesday"), after vast expenditures to support the price of the pound on the international markets, John Major was forced to abandon the ERM and let the pound sink to its market level. Unpopular tax increases were necessary to cope with the ERM debacle and the problems of a depressed economy. Embarrassing examples of sleaze and mismanagement occurred. Most damaging to John Major was his inability to unify his party on relations with the European Union.

THE COMPLETION OF THE THATCHER AGENDA

The Thatcher Inheritance

John Major's main accomplishment was to carry through to completion the Thatcher agenda of reform. Unlike Mrs. Thatcher, John Major realized the importance of the welfare state to ordinary people and tried to make it work better. He introduced *The Citizen's Charter*, which required all government offices to post a statement of the services that they would perform and provide compensation for avoidable mistakes or delays. The decentralization of departments into agencies continued, as did the process of "contracting out" public services.

The Major ministry completed the the privatizations of the nationalized industries, as the sales of the electricity and water companies were finalized and the privatization of the coal industry and British Rail began. Plans were made to sell off the Post Office, but these had to be abandoned because the public feared that convenient small post offices would be closed. Proposals to privatize London Underground (the subway system) met similar objections. The minimum wage was abolished. Trade unions continued as facilitators of management-labor relations, but their role as independent factors in the economy was gone.

The Thatcher ministry's plans to reform education had developed slowly, and implementation of Thatcherite principles was left largely to the Major ministry. Additional grant-maintained schools were established, although most places preferred to keep their schools under control of the local education authorities. After long wrangles with the teachers, the National Curriculum and testing program went into effect. The universities prepared to charge tuition fees, and the government established a student loan program to help students meet their living costs.

The Major ministry was also responsible for implementing the Thatcher reform of the National Health Service, including fund-holding doctors and a competitive market for the services of hospitals and specialists. The problems of welfare dependency were also addressed with "tough love" policies intended to get the long-term unemployed back to work. After a specified period of time, the unemployed would be removed from the welfare rolls and given a "job-seeker's allowance," to be used only while job-hunting or receiving training that would lead to employment.

Northern Ireland

Like Mrs. Thatcher before him, John Major was determined to preserve the unity of the United Kingdom, but within that framework he would do all he could to bring peace to Northern Ireland. In December 1993, Major and the prime minister of the Republic of Ireland issued a joint declaration that called for an end to terrorism and violence in the north. They stated that political talks with all parties concerned (which would include Sinn Fein, the political wing of the I.R.A.) could begin after a cease fire was firmly in place. John Major promised the anxious unionists (Protestants) of Northern Ireland that no changes would be made without a referendum. The I.R.A. continued its bombing campaign in Britain, but finally a cease fire was declared in August 1994. Unionist paramilitary groups also agreed to peace. The British public was relieved that an end to terrorism seemed to be in sight.

The remaining obstacle was the refusal of the I.R.A. to give up its weapons. John Major and the unionists refused to negotiate with a loaded gun under the table, and once again the peace process stalled. In 1996 the I.R.A. returned to violence, setting off huge bombs in London and Manchester. It seemed that John Major's effort to bring peace to Northern Ireland had failed.

BRITISH SOCIETY IN THE 'NINETIES

The People

Britain is an urban country, with most of the population concentrated in large metropolitan areas or towns of considerable size. That leaves large areas of farmland or wasteland, so that the country has a great deal of open space. Once away from the large cities and thickly populated southeast, Britain does not seem at all crowded.

The total population of the United Kingdom is slightly under 60 million, with 52.4 million living in England. The population has increased by 10 percent since 1961, partially due to longer lifespans and partially due to a modest increase in births. Immigration has contributed to a growing population, although in recent years it has declined. At present 5.5 percent of the population identify themselves as belonging to some ethnic minority, and the number is expected to double in the next 40 years before stabilizing at about 10 percent of the population. The largest minority groups come from India, Pakistan, Bangladesh, the British West Indies, West Africa, or Chinese living outside the People's Republic of China. These populations are concentrated in London and the industrial towns of the Midlands and the North.

Britain today is a far cry from the country that brought Mrs. Thatcher and the Conservatives into power. In 1992 two-thirds of the people owned their own homes, as opposed to one-half that number in 1979. In 1992 98 percent of households had a television set and 87 percent had a telephone. Twenty-two percent of adults owned shares in companies (mainly the privatized companies) compared to less than half that number in 1979. By 1992 the working population in manufacturing and mining (19 percent) had been cut in half. Financial services and other service occupations, including tourism (a major industry) had become the basis of the British economy.

One of the consequences of Thatcherism was to increase significantly the disparity between the wealthiest and the poor. A study by the Rowntree Foundation showed that between 1979 and 1992 the real income of the richest

10 percent had risen by 55 percent, while the real incomes of the poorest 10 percent have stayed the same. In the United Kingdom the top 1 percent of the population owns 18 percent of the wealth, and the top 10 percent owns 49 percent. For many of the top 10 percent their assets are concentrated in their homes and private pension plans. The bottom 50 percent of the population own only 8 percent of the wealth. For these people, their job or pension is almost all they have, and when unemployed they have nothing to fall back upon but the benefits of the welfare state.

In November 1996 the *Economist* reported the results of the 1996 British Social Attitudes Survey, which showed that family ties are strong. In a medium-sized country, two out of three adults live within an hour's trip of their mother, and one out of two adults see their mother at least once a week. Only 19 percent of parents report that they see their children less than once a month. Only 3 percent with a living mother never see her. A third of children have provided their parents with regular care or help because of illness or some other problem over the past five years. Many younger adults would turn first to their parents if they had to borrow a large sum of money.

The study concluded: "For the bulk of the people, their family continues to be a central and enduring part of their lives—as secure as can reasonably be expected against the supposed threats from social, cultural, and even occupational pressures."

A phenomenal, if short-lived, British sensation—The Spice Girls. Corbis

Nevertheless, the two-parent nuclear family is becoming the exception rather than the rule in Britain. Four out of ten families include a married couple with children. Another three out of ten couples choose not to have children at all. The remaining thirty percent of families consist of single parents. Today, one-third of all children are born out of wedlock and most of them will grow up in a one-parent family. Britain has 1,000,000 single mothers and only 41 percent of them are employed.

The British people are considerably better off than they were in the 1970s. On average, disposable income in real terms per household rose by 45 percent from 1971–1990, and households now are considerably smaller. The increase in well-being can be seen in the large numbers who take holidays abroad, Spain being the most popular destination and France a close second. Ownership of a color television is almost universal. Since the BBC does not have commercials, it is funded by an annual license fee for owners of television and radio sets. The annual license fee for a color television has been £89 and rising, which is virtually a poll tax, since almost everyone has one. There are also profit-making television and radio stations that earn income by showing commercials. Britain is a major contributor to popular culture through films, television programs, rock groups, and entertainers such as Rowan Atkinson ("Mr. Bean") and the Spice Girls.

THE RISE OF TONY BLAIR AND "NEW LABOUR"

"New Labour"

With the prestige of the Major ministry and the Conservative Party declining, Tony Blair knew that he still had to prove the fitness of himself and the Labour Party for government. He reorganized the party in a way that strengthened his control of the central machinery and democratized the constituency organizations. He accepted the Thatcher reforms of government and the economy, and worked hard to assure business that the changes of the 1980s in business and industrial relations would not be reversed. He realized that Labour had to improve its standing among women, where the Conservatives had a big advantage. Glenda Jackson, a distinguished actress with two Oscars, who was also a Labour M.P., toured the country bringing Labour's message to women and young people. Labour also placed ads in women's magazines, the first political party to do so.

Labour also proposed extensive constitutional reforms to bring government closer to the people. The most important proposal was devolution (limited self government) for Scotland, which had failed in 1979 but now had strong public support. Devolution for Wales was also proposed, as was a strong government for the London metropolitan area, including an elected mayor. Proposals were launched for a bill of rights, a freedom of information act, reform of the House of Lords, and some form of proportional representation. John Major, supported from the House of Lords by Lady Thatcher, took a strong stand on preserving the unity of the United Kingdom and the integrity of its historic constitution, but the tide clearly was running the other way. People felt that their government was not working very well and needed a shake-up.

The Labour Landslide of 1997

By spring, 1997 the five-year limit had been reached, and it became necessary for John Major (like Callaghan in 1979) to call an election under unfavorable circumstances. Polls indicated a strong Labour lead, and Tony Blair's main concern was to avoid making a mistake that would upset his favorable prospects. His managers had studied carefully the Bill Clinton campaigns in 1992 and 1996, and brought American-style campaigning to Britain. The great difference was that, in Britain, candidates and parties cannot buy television or radio time, which raised the intellectual level of campaigns and reduced the need for fundraising.

The Conservative campaign fell apart, as differences within the party broke wide open and candidates began running as individuals, not party members. John Major was left dangling as the leader who could not lead, although he remained personally popular. His efforts to appeal to the public from his soapbox fell flat. The voters had decided that it was time for a change, and they liked the ideas and style of Tony Blair.

The election on May 1, 1997, was a landslide for Tony Blair and "New Labour." Although Labour had only 44 percent of the vote, that translated into a huge majority of seats in the House of Commons. The Tory vote collapsed in the large cities, Scotland, and Wales, leaving them the party of the small towns and rural England. The Liberal Democrats benefited as some Conservatives voted for them.

The next day John Major went to Buckingham Palace and resigned; later in the day the Queen called upon Tony Blair, age forty-three, to form a new government. Tony Blair, his wife Cherie (a successful lawyer), and their three children moved into No. 10 Downing Street; Cabinet appointments were announced over the weekend; and by Monday morning "New Labour" was in business. Unlike the United States, there was no elaborate inauguration or celebration. The Conservative era introduced by Margaret Thatcher had lasted for eighteen years, but Thatcherism, as adopted and modified by Tony Blair, lived on

"NEW LABOUR" IN OFFICE

Political Leaders and Parties

Tony Blair and "New Labour" came into power in May 1997, with a mandate from the country to carry out the ambitious agenda of reform stated in their election manifesto. After eighteen years in opposition, the British Labour Party, transformed by Tony Blair, would now have a chance to show that it could fulfill its election pledge to "make Britain better.".

Like Margaret Thatcher, Blair was a man of the northeast of England. He was born in Edinburgh in 1953 of English parents. His father was a successful barrister with political ambitions. The family lived for a time in Glasgow, and then in Australia. Eventually they settled in Durham. Blair's father was a staunch Conservative who was a candidate for Parliament when he suffered a stroke that destroyed his career and ended his political ambitions. Tony Blair later said that his father's stroke was "one of the formative events" of his life.

Blair attended a prestigious school in Edinburgh (Fettes) and enrolled at Oxford, where he adopted a hippie appearance and played guitar in a rock band while cautiously staying out of trouble. A pious Christian, he joined the Labour Party and identified himself as "a Christian socialist." While studying law in London, he met another student, Cherie Booth; they were married in 1980 and have three children. In 1983 he was elected to Parliament as member for Sedgefield, a declining mining constituency near Durham. As an M.P., he became active in efforts to change the Labour Party from its commitments to socialism and the trade unions to a liberal party of the left. He became leader of the party in 1994.

The principles of Tony Blair have been described as "Thatcherism with a smiling face." He stated that his goal was to "modernize" Britain: develop a flexible and technologically advanced economy that would be competitive in the global marketplace, manage fiscal and monetary policy to achieve long-term economic growth with low inflation, fight chronic unemployment by strengthening the work ethic and providing training in marketable skills, create an efficient and up-to-date welfare state with positive incentives toward personal responsibility ("compassion with a hard edge"), encourage people to rely more on non-governmental institutions, reform the constitution of the United Kingdom to bring government closer to the people, establish a clear sense of national identity, and identify a role for Britain in Europe and the world. With the exception of constitutional change, where Mrs. Thatcher was a strong unionist, his agenda led some to identify him as "son of Thatcher."

William Hague

After the debacle of May 1997, the Conservative Party had no choice but to make a fresh start. As their leader, the Tories chose William Hague, age thirty-six. Hague was obviously talented, but he was inexperienced, and it would take time for him to develop a following in the party and the country. The party had been defeated mainly due to public dislike of its members, not its policies, most of which Blair had adopted. Even worse was the disaster in the constituency organizations, and Hague realized that the party had to be rebuilt from top to bottom. Hague worked hard to restore the strong support that Margaret Thatcher had enjoyed in smalltown and rural England, in the suburbs, and among skilled workers.

Hague also had to develop new policies, for Tony Blair had deprived the Tories of the issues by which they had been identified for the previous eighteen years. The one clearcut issue that remained for the Conservative Party was relations with the European Union. Preservation of the pound sterling and keeping Brussels at arms length were themes that resonated with the public and could lead to a revival of the Conservatives as the "patriotic" party. Hague announced that in the next election the Conservatives would oppose adoption of the European single currency (the euro). As constitutional change gave greater self-government to Scotland, Wales, and Northern Ireland, Hague could also present the Tories as the party of England, where most of the population and wealth of the United Kingdom were located.

The Liberal Democrats, led by Paddy Ashdown, shared most of Tony Blair's policies. Ashdown's problem was to establish enough distance from Labour to give the Liberal Democrats some reason for their separate existence. One reason was local government, where the Liberal Democrats often competed successfully against the Conservatives or Labour. Blair indicated that his goal was to merge Labour and the Liberal Democrats into a single party of liberal reform, but this idea was resisted by many in his own party and also by many Liberal Democrats, who had no desire to join with Labour, "new" or not.

The Policies of "New Labour"

At the beginning of his ministry, Tony Blair made two crucial decisions. One was that Britain would not join the single currency for the duration of the existing Parliament, approximately five years. The British economy was flourishing, and Blair feared that the euro countries might drag Britain down. Furthermore, the euro was the only issue that might revive the Conservatives. Blair had a large agenda of domestic reform, and he did not want it disrupted by heated debates about Europe, of the kind that had destroyed John Major.

The second major decision was to continue the Conservative tax increases and spending plan for another two years. The purpose was to assure world markets that "New Labour" would be fiscally responsible and would keep inflation low. Blair and his chancellor of the Exchequer, Gordon Brown, were determined that there would be no return to "boom and bust." Many Labour members were unhappy about that, because they had spending proposals for worthy projects that had to be delayed. The flourishing state of Britain's economy increased the revenue and gave Blair a little leeway. Gordon Brown presented a moderate budget that did not pinch anyone very much and contained something for almost everyone.

Tony Blair poses with his wife and children at No. 10 Downing Street. Agence France Press/Corbis-Bettmann.

A surprising feature of the Blair ministry was the extent of constitutional change, which took on a momentum of its own. Devolution for Scotland and Wales passed quickly. A settlement was reached in Northern Ireland to establish a government and assembly based on power-sharing between the Protestant and Catholic communities. The leaders of the moderate Protestant and Catholic parties formed a coalition that would squeeze out the extremists on both wings. Sinn Fein, the political wing of the I.R.A., was not included in the new government, because an extremist faction in the I.R.A. refused to give up ("decommission") their vast arsenal of weapons and explosives.

These changes have led to demands for similar institutions for England, or for the English regions, which have their own special needs. Proposals have been made to establish elected mayors on the American model for major cities. A Greater London Authority with a popularly elected mayor and council was approved for the London metropolitan area. The consequences of these decentralized power centers for the government of the United Kingdom are quite unpredictable.

When institutional reform begins, it is hard to stop. The House of Lords will be reformed, including removing the voting powers of the hereditary peers. Dramatic changes are taking place in the voting system, as proportional representation is adopted in Scotland, Wales, and Northern Ireland. A commission on electoral reform recommended proportional representation for the British House of Commons, a paramount goal of the Liberal Democrats, but the proposal has met strong resistance within the Labour Party. The Blair ministry seems to have stumbled into a flurry of constitutional reform that may make it more difficult to achieve the substantive issues to which it is committed.

One of Blair's major goals was to reduce unemployment, which remained high in the old industrial areas, especially among young males. His approach was to provide inducements to the unemployed to seek work rather than living on the dole. His "New Deal" required unemployed young adults to undergo education and training or lose their unemployment benefits. Blair was willing to invest large sums in programs to prepare young people for the rapidly changing economy of the late twentieth century. These reforms were not just a matter of improving the labor force. There was in Tony Blair a strong moral conviction that people should work, save, and take responsibility for themselves and their families.

Proposals were also advanced to reform Britain's tangle of welfare benefits, emphasizing need rather than rights. An example was child benefit, which went to all mothers, wealthy or poor. Welfare reform encountered strong resistance within the Labour Party, especially from women, who had become a major factor in "New Labour." Blair also proposed reform of pensions to encourage personal saving for retirement, and again he encountered resistance from his own party. Tony Blair found that welfare and pension reform were projects that created serious political problems while achieving only modest financial and administrative gains.

The Blair government continued the Thatcherite effort to improve student performance through the National Curriculum and national testing. The main difference was to return more power to local education authorities and reduce Mrs. Thatcher's benefits to private schools. The ministry also returned to the "Old Labour" goal of abolishing grammar schools and selective admissions, replacing them with comprehensive schools. In the National Health Service, Mrs. Thatcher's division between purchasers of health care (doctors) and providers (specialists, hospitals) continued, but not on the basis of market competition.

Foreign Policy

In foreign policy, Tony Blair made clear his determination to stick closely to President Bill Clinton and the United States. In defense policy, Britain decided to increase the mobility of its forces, to enable Britain to cooperate more effectively with the United States, other nations, and the United Nations in world trouble spots. Blair offered full support to Clinton when controversy arose concerning Iraq's refusal to permit unrestricted U.N. inspections of weapons sites. The continued floundering of democracy and capitalism in Russia was an important concern, but the major world problem was a financial crisis in East Asia. In most of these problems, there was little that Britain could do except cooperate with international organizations, and in these efforts the Blair ministry contributed its share.

The European Union

The electoral victory of Tony Blair was widely cheered on the continent. Blair's youth and enthusiasm were personally attractive, and he represented a breath of fresh air to a continent dominated by elderly conservative politicians. Blair hoped (naively as it turned out) that he could exercise some leadership within the European Union to promote reforms similar to the ideas of "New Labour." The Blair influence may have contributed to the electoral victories of center-left parties in France, Germany, and Italy, but it soon became clear that these governments resembled "Old Labour" rather than the "New Labour" commitment to the market economy, labor flexibility, and individual responsibility.

Furthermore, the new Social Democratic government of Germany demanded that Germany's contribution to the cost of the European Union be reduced, which would require reduction of subsidies that were important to France, Italy, and poorer countries. The reduction of Britain's financial contribution obtained by Margaret Thatcher in 1984 was threatened. Proposals were made to harmonize taxes, labor regulations, and welfare benefits, which would threaten the free economy that was working well for Britain. Most important was the introduction of the common currency (the euro), which Britain did not adopt. Structural reform of the European Union would be dominated by Germany and France and British influence would be negligible. Many in Britain liked it that way.

The Royal Family

For several years party politics had frequently been upstaged by the personal problems of the royal family. Most sensational was the breakdown of the marriage of the Prince of Wales and his wife, the Princess Diana. In December, 1993 the Prince and the Princess announced their separation. They had two children: Prince William (then ten) and Prince Harry (then eight). Earlier the Duke of York and his uninhibited commoner Duchess (Sarah Ferguson) had decided to end their marriage after months of lurid coverage in the tabloid newspapers.

The troubles of the royal family were intensified in 1994 by two astonishing television interviews in which Prince Charles and Princess Diana publicly revealed details of their unhappy marriage. By the end of 1995 the Queen had had enough and declared her desire for a divorce. Agreement was reached in the summer of 1996, and the divorce became final in August.

Princess Diana gave up any claim to become Queen or be called "Her Royal Highness," but she continued to be called Princess of Wales. As mother of the two princes, she was formally still part of the royal family. Charles and Diana were given equal custody of their two sons, who were in boarding school. Princess Diana found a new focus for her life in supporting good causes such as AIDS research and the prohibition of land mines. However, she still enjoyed the self-indulgent life of the elite of money and celebrity, and she took up with Dodi El Fayed, a Hollywood movie producer, who was the son of a wealthy Egyptian property tycoon.

In August 1997, Princess Diana and Dodi were killed in a horrible automobile accident in Paris. An astonishing outburst of public emotion followed her death, as thousands of people flocked to Kensington Palace, her residence, to sign books of condolence and leave flowers. People saw the princess as emblematic of youth, beauty, and goodness in contrast to the stuffy royal family and stale institutions of Britain. The Queen, then vacationing in Scotland, was criticized for failing to respond promptly to this outburst of public grief. Tony Blair stepped in quickly to arrange a funeral that was televised throughout the world. At the funeral, Elton John sang his song, *Candle in the Wind*,

Princess Diana with her sons, Prince William and Prince Henry, visiting Niagara Falls, 1991.
Reuters/Corbis-Bettmann.

dedicated to the princess. During the next three months 35 million records were sold, with the proceeds dedicated to the princess' charities. The Queen designated Kensington Palace as a memorial to Princess Diana. The palace would become a "people's museum" where Diana's apartments and mementos would be on view and parts of the royal art collection would be displayed.

Settling Down

In the election campaign of 1997, Tony Blair had promised: "What we have said we will do, we will do." In December 1998, the *Times* poll confirmed that his sky-high personal popularity continued. The poll showed that 64 percent of voters liked him; only 24 percent did not. More people who identified themselves as Conservatives liked Tony Blair (49 percent) than their own party leader, William Hague (41 percent). People believed that Blair would keep his election promises, but also they were satisfied that he would do nothing drastic. The economy was doing reasonably well. The Conservative Party under William Hague was making little progress; and the Liberal Democrats were too much like Labour to increase their modest following.

Blair's major problem was the fissure that began to emerge between those who were still devoted to "Old Labour" and those who shared his "New Labour" views. Tony Blair was determined to avoid the squabbling that had discredited the Labour Party in the 1980s. He maintained strong personal control of the ministry, its policies, and its media relations, which led to resentment among some of his followers and charges that he was "a control freak." The low tax, tight money policies of Gordon Brown were accepted as necessary within the global economy, but other aspects of the Thatcher-Major legacy became bones of contention within the Labour Party. Blair's support of President Bill Clinton's sporadic involvements in global hotspots ran counter to Labour's anti-military instincts. Britain's uneasy relationship with the European Union, and especially the unpredictable consequences of the single currency, created anxiety. Reform of Parliament and the electoral system touched the large body of new Labour M.P.s in their most sensitive spot—their chances for reelection.

By 1999 the high hopes and grandiloquent rhetoric of Tony Blair had been toned down considerably. He was learning the art of government: leading the country, but also recognizing and responding to the variety of people, possibilities, and interests that required his attention. Capable ministers had established themselves in the major departments, and some unsuccessful ministers had been removed. The prime minister's popularity remained high. It seemed clear that "New Labour" would not introduce another period of radical reform, but would give Britain steady, competent government for its full five years. Most of the British people were willing to settle for that.

Suggestions for Further Reading

Earl A. Reitan provides general coverage of the period in *Tory Radicalism: Margaret Thatcher, John Major, and the Transformation of Modern Britain, 1979–1997* (1997). The book has a selective "Bibliographical Note." Valuable reference works are *Twentieth-Century Britain: An Encyclopedia* (cited chapter 16) and *British Political Facts, 1900 to 1994* (7th ed., 1994), ed. by David and Gareth Butler. Some of the useful books published on recent British history by the Institute of Contemporary History are listed in Reitan, *Tory Radicalism.*

The *Boundaries of the State in Modern Britain*, S. J. D. Green and R. C. Whiting (eds.) (1996) deals with the different levels and many activities of government. Dennis Kavanagh and Bill Jones are authors of *British Politics Today* (5th ed., 1994). Margaret Thatcher's memoirs, entitled *The Downing Street Years* (1993) and *The Path to Power* (1995) present Lady Thatcher's retrospective interpretation of her political career, but also are packed with information and provided with valuable appendices. Penny Junor has written *John Major: From Brixton to Downing Street* (1996), but for a fuller assessment of his political importance see Reitan, *Tory Radicalism.* There are many assessments of Thatcherism, including Andrew Gamble, *The Free Economy and the Strong State: The Politics of Thatcherism* (1994); Shirley Letwin, *The Anatomy of Thatcherism* (1992); and Peter Riddell, *The Thatcher Era and its Legacy* (1991).

On the welfare state, including the impact of Thatcherism, Laybourn, *The Evolution of British Social Policy,* cited in previous chapters, remains a good place to begin. Anthony Sampson, author of a series of anatomies of Britain, concludes with *The Essential Anatomy of Britain: Democracy in Crisis* (1992). Stephen Edgell makes a similar effort in *A Measure of Thatcherism: A Sociology of Britain* (1991). A. H. Halsey reviews social institutions in *Change in British Society* (4th ed, 1995). For contemporary Britain, a good introduction is *British Civilization* (3rd ed., 1995) by John Oakland.

APPENDIX

KINGS AND QUEENS OF ENGLAND

Bretwaldas

ca. 560–591	Caelwin, king of the West Saxons
560–616	Ethelbert, king of Kent
ca. 600–616	Raedwald, king of East Anglia
616–632	Edwin, king of Northumbria
633–641	Oswald, king of Northumbria
654–670	Oswiu, king of Northumbria

King of Mercia

757–796	Offa

Kings of the West Saxons

802–839	Egbert
866–871	Ethelred
871–899	Alfred
899–924	Edward the Elder

Rulers of England

959–975	Edgar the Peaceful
978–1016	Ethelred the Unready
1016–1035	Canute

1042–1066   Edward the Confessor
1066   Harold Godwinson

Normans

1066–1087   William I
1087–1100   William II
1100–1135   Henry I
1135–1154   Stephen

Angevins-Plantagenets

1154–1189   Henry II
1189–1199   Richard I
1199–1216   John
1216–1272   Henry III
1272–1307   Edward I
1307–1327   Edward II
1327–1377   Edward III
1377–1399   Richard II

Lancastrians

1399–1413   Henry IV
1413–1422   Henry V
1422–1461   Henry VI

Yorkists

1461–1483   Edward IV
1483   Edward V
1483–1485   Richard III

Tudors

1485–1509   Henry VII
1509–1547   Henry VIII
1547–1553   Edward VI
1553–1558   Mary I
1558–1603   Elizabeth I

Stuarts

1603–1625	James I
1625–1649	Charles I
1649–1660	Commonwealth and Protectorate
1660–1685	Charles II
1685–1688	James II
1689–1702	William III and Mary II
1702–1714	Anne

Hanoverians

1714–1727	George I
1727–1760	George II
1760–1820	George III
1820–1830	George IV
1830–1837	William IV
1837–1901	Victoria
1901–1910	Edward VII
1910–1936	George V (House of Windsor)
1936	Edward VIII
1936–1952	George VI
1952–	Elizabeth II

PRIME MINISTERS OF ENGLAND

1721–1742	Sir Robert Walpole
1742–1744	John Carteret
1744–1754	Henry Pelham
1754–1756	Duke of Newcastle
1756–1757	William Pitt, the Elder
1757–1761	Pitt the Elder and the Duke of Newcastle
1761–1762	Duke of Newcastle and Lord Bute
1762–1763	Lord Bute
1763–1765	George Grenville
1765–1766	Lord Rockingham
1766–1768	William Pitt, Lord Chatham
1768–1770	Duke of Grafton
1770–1782	Lord North
1782	Lord Rockingham
1782–1783	Lord Shelburne

1783	Charles James Fox and Lord North	
1783–1801	William Pitt, the Younger	
1801–1804	Henry Addington	
1804–1806	William Pitt, the Younger	
1806–1807	Lord Grenville	
1807–1809	Duke of Portland	
1809–1812	Spencer Perceval	
1812–1827	Lord Liverpool	Tory
1827	George Canning	Tory
1827	Lord Goderich	Tory
1828–1830	Duke of Wellington	Tory
1830–1834	Earl Grey	Whig
1834	Lord Melbourne	Whig
1834–1835	Sir Robert Peel	Tory
1835–1841	Lord Melbourne	Whig
1841–1846	Sir Robert Peel	Tory
1846–1852	Lord John Russell	Whig
1852	Lord Derby and Benjamin Disraeli	Tory
1852–1855	Lord Aberdeen	Coalition
1855–1858	Lord Palmerston	Liberal
1858–1859	Lord Derby and Benjamin Disraeli	Conservative
1859–1865	Lord Palmerston	Liberal
1865–1866	Lord John Russell	Liberal
1866–1868	Lord Derby and Benjamin Disraeli	Conservative
1868–1874	William E. Gladstone	Liberal
1874–1880	Benjamin Disraeli	Conservative
1880–1885	William Gladstone	Liberal
1885–1886	Lord Salisbury	Conservative
1886	William Gladstone	Liberal
1886–1892	Lord Salisbury	Conservative
1892–1894	William Gladstone	Liberal
1894–1895	Lord Rosebery	Liberal
1895–1902	Lord Salisbury	Conservative
1902–1905	Arthur Balfour	Conservative
1905–1908	Sir Henry Campbell-Bannerman	Liberal
1908–1916	Herbert H. Asquith	Liberal
1916–1922	David Lloyd George	Coalition

1922–1923	Andrew Bonar Law	Conservative
1923–1924	Stanley Baldwin	Conservative
1924	J. Ramsay MacDonald	Labour
1924–1929	Stanley Baldwin	Conservative
1929–1931	Ramsay MacDonald	Labour
1931–1935	Ramsay MacDonald	National Government
1935–1937	Stanley Baldwin	Conservative
1937–1940	Neville Chamberlain	Conservative
1940–1945	Winston Churchill	Conservative
1945–1951	Clement Attlee	Labour
1951–1955	Winston Churchill	Conservative
1955–1957	Sir Anthony Eden	Conservative
1957–1963	Sir Harold Macmillan	Conservative
1963–1964	Sir Alec Douglas-Home	Conservative
1964–1970	Harold Wilson	Labour
1970–1974	Edward Heath	Conservative
1974–1976	Harold Wilson	Labour
1976–1979	James Callaghan	Labour
1979–1990	Margaret Thatcher	Conservative
1990–1997	John Major	Conservative
1997–	Tony Blair	Labour

INDEX

Combined index for Volumes I and II.
Volume II begins on page 171.